French Fascism

French Fascism: The Second Wave 1933–1939

ROBERT SOUCY

YALE UNIVERSITY PRESS
NEW HAVEN & LONDON

Photographs are from Roger-Viollet. Grateful acknowledgment is made to the following for permission to quote: University of Chicago Press for William D. Irvine, "Fascism in France and the Strange Case of the Croix de Feu," *The Journal of Modern History* 63 (June 1991), copyright © 1991 University of Chicago Press; Yale University Press for Paul Jankowski, *Communism and Collaboration: Simon Sabiani and Politics in Marseille, 1919–1944*, copyright © 1989 Yale University Press; Sam Goodfellow for Sam Goodfellow, "Fascism in Alsace, 1918–1945," Ph.D. diss., Indiana University, September 1991; for id., "Fascist or Conservative? The Croix de Feu/PSF in Alsace," French Historical Studies conference paper, October 15, 1993; and for id., "The French Radical Right in Alsace, 1924–45," French Historical Studies conference paper, March 30, 1990; Kevin Passmore for Kevin Passmore, "The Right and the Extreme Right in the Department of the Rhône, 1928–1939," Ph.D. diss., Warwick, England, 1992; Journal of Contemporary History for Robert Soucy, "French Fascism and the Croix de Feu: A Dissenting Interpretation," *Journal of Contemporary History* 26, no. 1 (January 1991); and Cambden House for Robert Soucy, "Brasillach and Drieu on the Spanish Civil War and French Fascism," in Luis Costa, ed., *German and International Perspectives on the Spanish Civil War*, copyright © 1992 Cambden House.

Set in Trump Medieval type by The Composing Room of Michigan, Inc. Printed in the United States of America by BookCrafters, Inc., Chelsea, Michigan.

Library of Congress Cataloging-in-Publication Data
Soucy, Robert, 1933–
French fascism : the second wave, 1933–1939 / Robert Soucy.
    p.   cm.
Includes bibliographical references and index.
Companion vol. to the author's French fascism: the first wave, 1924–1933.
ISBN 0-300-05996-5 (alk. paper)
1. France—Politics and government—1914–1940. 2. Fascism—France—History.
I. Title.
DC396.S66   1995
320.5'33'0944—dc20   94-30025
                                       CIP

A catalogue record for this book is available from the British Library.

The paper in this book meets the guidelines for permanence and durability of the Committee on Production Guidelines for Book Longevity of the Council on Library Resources.

10 9 8 7 6 5 4 3 2 1

For Sharon

Contents

Acknowledgments

I wish to thank the American Council of Learned Societies, the National Endowment for the Humanities, the American Philosophical Society, and the Committee for Research and Development of Oberlin College for grants to pursue this work. Clayton Koppes and Steven Volk offered valuable advice on parts of the manuscript. Richard Millmann helped me refine the chapter on the Solidarité Français. I am particularly grateful to William Irvine and Sam Goodfellow for their critical reading of the whole manuscript and for their generosity in sharing with me their expert knowledge on the Croix de Feu. Irvine, a supportive colleague for many years, has enlivened me on more than one occasion with his vigorous mind, scholarly integrity, and gallows humor. I owe a special debt to Barbara Soucy, who during the early stages of research for this book was of enormous help. Charles Grench and Otto Bohlmann were fine editors to work with, and the manuscript editing of Lawrence Kenney of Yale University Press has been superb. All remaining shortcomings in the text are, of course, mine.

Although much of this book is based on my own research into primary sources, it owes a great deal to the previous archival work of other scholars—including those whose interpretations, but not whose facts, I disagree with in places. Without the writings of Eugen Weber, Philippe Bourdrel, Dieter Wolf,

Jean-Paul Brunet, Philippe Burrin, Philippe Machefer, William Irvine, Paul Jankowski, Sam Goodfellow, Kevin Passmore, Richard Millmann, Paul Mazgaj, and other researchers, this book could not have been written.

Finally, thanks to Sharon Soucy, a life enhancer whose example constantly reminds me of what a fascist is not.

NOTE TO THE READER

With the exception of quotations from Yves Simon's *Road to Vichy* and Simone de Beauvoir's *Prime of Life*, all translations are mine. The reader should also be aware that in order to reduce the length of this book, I have sometimes consolidated three references or more in a single note, usually at the end of the paragraph in question. Thus if a source is not immediately cited, it will be cited shortly thereafter in a note including more than one source, each source listed in the order of the material it refers to in the text. Sometimes, too, page numbers referring to a previously noted single source will be placed in parentheses in the text.

Abbreviations

AF — Action Française (French action). Charles Maurras's royalist fascist party.

CF — Croix de Feu (Cross of fire). Colonel de la Rocque's fascist party.

CF/PSF — Croix de Feu/Parti Social Français (Cross of fire/French social party). Refers to continuities between the two movements after 1936.

CFTC — Confédération des Travailleurs Chrétiens (General confederation of Christian workers)—Catholic trades union organization in Lyon.

CGT — Confédération Générale du Travail (General confederation of labor). Communist trades union organization.

CGTU — Confédération Générale du Travail Unitaire (General confederation of unified labor). Socialist trades union organization.

EVP — Equipes volantes de propagande (Mobile propaganda teams). The PSF's equivalent to the paramilitary shock troops of the CF.

FARAC — Fédération des Associations Régimentaires et Anciens Combattants (Federation of regimental and veterans' associations).

FR — Fédération Républicaine (Republican federation). Louis Marin's Catholic conservative parliamentary party.

JP — Jeunesses Patriotes (Patriotic youth). Pierre Taittinger's fascist party.

MSF   Mouvement Social Français (French social movement). The charity and recreational organization of the PSF.

NSDAP   Nationalsozialistische Deutsche Arbeiterpartei (German national socialist workers party). Hitler's party.

PCF   Parti Communist Français (French communist party).

PPF   Parti Populaire Français (French popular party). Jacques Doriot's fascist party.

PSF   Parti Social Français (French social party). After 1936, the purportedly more democratic version of CF.

RNP   Rassemblement National Populaire (National popular reassembly). Marcel Déat's fascist party.

RPF   Rassemblement du Peuple Français (Reassembly of the French people). Gaullist party.

RF   Redressement Français (French recovery).

SF   Solidarité Française (French solidarity). François Coty's and Jean Renaud's fascist party.

SFIO   Section Française de l'Internationale Ouvrière (French section of the Workers' International). French socialist party.

SPF   Syndicat Professionel Français (French professional union). Trades union of the PSF.

UNC   Union Nationale des Combattants (National union of war veterans). Right-wing veterans' association.

UPR   Union Populaire Républicaine (Popular republican union). The FR's major affiliate in Alsace.

VN   Volontaires Nationaux (National volunteers). Youth movement of the CF.

French Fascism

Introduction

THE DEBATE OVER FASCISM

Did fascism have a significant following in France in the 1930s? Did its supporters come predominantly from the political right or the political left? Were
its social, economic, and cultural goals essentially revolutionary or conservative? These and other questions remain highly controversial in France, both in
popular and scholarly discourse. Fueling the debate have been memories of
Vichy's collaboration with Nazi Germany during the Second World War and the
emergence of Jean-Marie Le Pen's neofascist National Front in more recent
years.

As Jacques Julliard has observed, in France the word *fascist* has become "an
all-purpose insult" used by political opponents to discredit one another, and
historians have sometimes contributed to the battle with their various interpretations of fascism. According to Julliard, there is nothing surprising about
this scholarly dimension of the debate, since "the genealogy of fascism is a
formidable polemical theme where each camp strives to throw upon the other
its part of the responsibility for this political teratology."[1]

There is also, of course, a good deal of scholarly agreement about fascism. Few
historians would object to Zeev Sternhell's view that among the major charac-

teristics of fascist ideology during the interwar period, in France and elsewhere, were an attack on liberal democracy, a belief in Social Darwinism, a reversion to tribal nationalism, a revolt against decadence, and an appeal to irrationalism. Hardly anyone would dispute Michel Winock's observation that "the style of war is the style of fascism" or Henry Turner's comment that fascism benefited from "a deep cluster of values based on martial valor." Most specialists in the field would also agree with Serge Berstein that before fascism came to power it received much of its public support from members of the lower middle classes who, threatened by the Depression, opposed to Bolshevism, and fearful of downward social mobility, were attracted to a movement that offered to "revalorize" authority through recourse to violence.[2]

Most scholars also find it important to distinguish between the liberal (or conservative) right and the fascist (or radical) right, thus condemning the tendency of some American yippies and French *gauchistes* in the 1960s to indiscriminately lump conservatives and fascists together irrespective of their differences. To call de Gaulle a fascist, for example, simply because he was anti-Communist (so was Hitler) is simplemindedness indeed. Not only, as Charles Maier has warned, does such thinking "minimize distinctions at the cost of what is similar," but it is deeply unfair to democratic conservatives who opposed fascism during the 1930s. Arno J. Mayer has underlined the differences that exist among conservatives, reactionaries, and counterrevolutionaries (fascists, for Mayer, being in the last category), pointing out that whereas the first two groups often find mass politics and violent methods distasteful the last thrives on them.[3]

Historians part company, however, on other issues. Among the most highly contested are whether fascism during the 1920s and 1930s was more left than right, more socialist than capitalist, more revolutionary than conservative, more populist than elitist, more plebeian than bourgeois, and more traditionalist than modernist. Were important sections of the traditional right in Europe, even in long-standing democracies like France and England, complicit with fascism during the interwar period or were they immune to its appeal? Did conservatives and reactionaries share many of fascism's basic values and goals or, as Paul Sérant has claimed for France, is it true that "to pretend to establish a kinship between fascism and traditional [conservative] doctrines would be in vain"?[4]

Since the Second World War, the leading historians of German, Italian, and French fascism have differed widely in their responses to such questions. Although it would be a gross simplification to portray these scholars as falling into two analytically monolithic or rigidly opposed camps (since within each camp there is considerable interpretive heterogeneity and across both there are a number of shared conclusions), it is nevertheless clear that where the left and right elements in fascism are concerned two generally conflicting schools of thought have emerged.

The first school includes such distinguished historians and political scientists as J. R. Talmon, Renzo de Felice, Eugen Weber, Ernst Nolte, René Rémond, Philippe Machefer, Zeev Sternhell, Pierre Milza, Jean-Paul Brunet, Philippe Burrin, Serge Berstein, and Paul Mazgaj. The second school is represented by such equally impressive scholars as William Sheridan Allen, Denis Mack Smith, S. William Halperin, Arno J. Mayer, Michael Kater, Charles Meier, John Weiss, William Irvine, Reinhard Kuhnl, Otto Bauer, and Jacques Julliard. There are also major historians—Edward Tannenbaum, George Mosse, David Schoenbaum, and Michel Winock, for example—who bridge the two schools in important ways, depending on the specific issues involved.

Typical of the first school is Renzo de Felice, who has argued that fascism's intellectual origins lie in the terror phase of the French Revolution and continue "as an element of European left-wing radicalism." According to Felice, the traditional Italian right tended to be antifascist, since it distrusted the masses and sought their political demobilization.[5] René Rémond and a number of French scholars have underscored the revolutionary, populist, and plebeian elements in fascism, characterizing it as basically anticonservative, antiestablishmentarian, and antibourgeois. Thus for these scholars such socially conservative paramilitary movements as the Jeunesses Patriotes (JP, Patriotic youth) and the Croix de Feu (CF, Cross of fire) were not fascist.[6] Eugen Weber has portrayed French fascism as more neosocialist than conservative in inspiration, describing as fascist Georges Valois's Faisceau ("Communists came to join them") and Marcel Bucard's Francistes (which "drew both its elements and its spirit from the left") but not the Action Française (AF, French action) (which was too right wing) or the CF (its members "simply do not qualify as anything more than patriotic conservatives"). According to Weber, to identify fascism with reaction is "wide of the mark," while Zeev Sternhell has contended that "in many respects, one can write the history of fascism as that of an incessant attempt to revise Marxism, of a permanent effort toward neo-socialism."[7]

Members of the second school, by contrast, hold that conservative ideology was not only compatible with fascism on a number of issues but that sections of the European right (including, for William Irvine, some important sections of the right in France) voluntarily entered into complicity with fascism when they believed that their social and economic interests were seriously threatened by the left. Although these scholars acknowledge that some former leftists went over to fascism during the interwar period, they view them as small in number and renegades from socialism. Historians of the second school see much more collusion between conservatives and fascists than those of the first school. Alan Cassels, Edward Tannenbaum, Denis Mack Smith, and Charles Maier have all written of the political support that Mussolini received from upper-class Italian liberals, the contemporary term for parliamentary conservatives.[8]

According to Maier, many large landowners and industrialists in Italy chose to support fascism after 1920 because they felt threatened by peasant ferment in the countryside and worker militancy in the cities and because they became convinced that "they must look outside of government for guarantees of order." "The counterrevolutionaries of the towns went to the aid of beleaguered elites in the countryside," while in Parliament many liberals allied with Mussolini to defend rural and urban property rights. The result was a "joint liberal-Fascist assault" on the postwar strength of the mass parties of the left and left-center. Indeed, until the Matteotti crisis of 1924 (brought on when a Socialist member of Parliament was murdered by Fascist thugs), "many influential liberals viewed fascism merely as a regrettably cruder but muscular wing of liberalism." "Unprepared to acquiesce in political democratization," Maier continues, "and to share power over their local government, factory, or fields, men of influence accepted and even patronized Fascist violence."[9]

William Sheridan Allen, Otto Bauer, Arno J. Mayer, Michael Kater, and John Weiss have also portrayed Nazism in Germany as fundamentally antileftist. Allen defines fascism in both Italy and Germany as "essentially an attempt by the middle classes to suppress the political aspirations of their working classes." Bauer maintains that German conservatives deliberately exaggerated the Marxist threat to achieve this end: "The capitalists and large landowners did not entrust the fascist hordes with the power of the State so as to protect themselves against a threatening proletarian revolution, but so as to depress the wages, to destroy the social gains of the working class, to eradicate the trade unions and the positions of power gained by the working class."[10]

Arno J. Mayer has dwelled on the points of convergence between conservatives and fascists in times of crisis, maintaining that without the complicity of upper-class conservatives fascists are never able to succeed. For Mayer, this does not mean that conservatives opt for fascism in all crisis situations, since they have a considerable range of counterrevolutionary alternatives from which to choose and since they are usually uncomfortable with fascist violence. Normally, they seek equilibrium and stability through pluralism and compromise. In times of acute economic crisis, however, they sometimes form a "cartel of anxiety" with fascist counterrevolutionaries against the political left. In Germany in the 1930s, "fascist leaders offered their shock troops as auxiliary forces of order to a panic-stricken ruling power elite." Fascists became useful demagogues who played upon the mutual antagonisms of upper and lower bourgeois toward Marxism while projecting a "populist, reformist and emancipatory image of their purposes." Fascism's revolutionary rhetoric was a smokescreen for counterrevolutionary goals.[11]

Some scholars, including Felice and Sternell, have described fascism as being much more revolutionary before it came to power than after. Felice has shown the ease with which radical fascists had their influence reduced by conservative fascists after 1922, and Sternhell has acknowledged Mussolini's support of big business during the same period. Wolfgang Sauer has written, "A look at the fascist regimes in operation . . . would show that, whatever the revolutionary potential of the movements, the revolutionary results are meager." Edward Tannenbaum has also remarked on the "frequent difference between ideology and practice."

George Mosse and David Schoenbaum have described Nazism as being more subjectively than objectively revolutionary, noting that for some Germans the Third Reich *felt* more democratic than the Weimar Republic. John Weiss, on the other hand, has insisted that "fascism cannot be understood if it is viewed as a revolution. It was a counterrevolution. Its purpose was to prevent the liberalization and the radicalization of Italy and Germany. Property and income distribution and the traditional class structure remained roughly the same under fascist rule. What changes there were favored the old elites or certain segments of the party leadership." In 1971 Arno J. Mayer thought that the "excessive preoccupation" of scholars with the revolutionary aspects of fascism had led to a relative neglect of its counterrevolutionary aspects. Indeed, Mayer suggested that this preoccupation was part of a Cold War mentality.[12]

This book on the second wave of fascism in France between 1933 and 1939, like the volume that preceded it on the first wave between 1924 and 1933, supports the second school of interpretation more than it does the first and finds French fascist ideology deeply counterrevolutionary even before it came to power, at least where the largest French fascist movements of the period were concerned: the JP, the Solidarité Française (SF, French solidarity), the CF, and the Parti Populaire Français (PPF, French popular party). In doing so, it disputes the view held by many French scholars that fascism was never a serious political force in France during the interwar period and that the fascism that did exist sprang more from the left than from the right. William Irvine has called this second interpretation the consensus view of French fascism, inasmuch as it has dominated most French scholarship on the subject since the Second World War.[13] It has been the orthodoxy of many American and English historians as well.

THE CONSENSUS SCHOOL OF FRENCH HISTORIOGRAPHY

Consensus historians have bolstered their position by defining fascism a priori as socially and economically radical, thus excluding from consideration some of the most significant right-wing authoritarian movements in France during the 1920s and 1930s. They apply this formula especially to Colonel de La Rocque's CF, the largest and fastest growing party on the French right between 1936 and 1939. By characterizing fascism as being sharply at odds with conservatism, including the CF's social and economic conservatism, they rule out the CF as fascist. Thus consensus historians have been able to present fascism as being weak in France, since movements that fit their definition of fascism were indeed quite small during the interwar period. By defining fascism in a way that removes the CF from consideration, they have been able to argue, in a circular fashion, that fascism had little mass support in France.

According to the consensus definition, one adopted by many scholars trained at the École des Sciences Politiques in Paris, French fascism was not only politically and culturally but also socially and economically radical. Fascists were more "uprooted" than traditional conservatives. They were social radicals opposed to established hierarchies, "déclassés, parvenus [and] adventurers who had nothing in common with the notables" and who dreamed "only of overthrow" on behalf of national socialism. Georges Valois, an ex-syndicalist, and Jacques Doriot, an ex-Communist, were therefore fascists, but Pierre Taittinger and Colonel de La Rocque, whose views had always been socially conservative, were not.[14]

Yet, as Irvine has pointed out, if all the components of the consensus definition of fascism were applied consistently, it would prevent not only Taittinger and La Rocque from being labeled fascist but Hitler and Mussolini as well! For Irvine, there is something odd about portraying fascism and conservatism during the interwar period in such mutually exclusive terms: "The notion that fascists cannot consort with 'liberals' or 'conservatives' is surely a fiction unique to France. No one, for example, ever suggested that the presence of liberal politicians such as Vittorio Orlando and Antonio Salandra . . . on the 1924 fascist electoral ticket renders Mussolini's movement less fascist."[15]

Irvine also takes issue with Philippe Burrin's contention that Colonel de La Rocque simply did not fit the typical fascist profile. According to Burrin, "Nothing about La Rocque, his past as an officer, his social origins, the circles in which he moved, resembled that of a fascist leader of déclassé, marginal, or modest origins and expert in the agitation and manipulation of crowds."[16] Irvine responds: "The assumptions here are more than a little problematic. La Rocque is very different from Mussolini and Hitler, although social origins may be the least important of the differences. But Hitler and Mussolini were also very different from one another. Moreover, it is not clear to what degree the fascist qualities of a movement can be derived from its leader. Certainly it would be quite wrong to suggest that ex–army officers with social contacts among the *bonne bourgeoisie* are refractory to fascism. Such elements were notoriously present in National Socialism and, above all, in Italian fascism."[17]

Irvine also disputes Pierre Milza's contention that because the CF had little working-class support it was "less plebeian and more bourgeois" than fascist organizations. Irvine asks,

> But which fascist organizations? Over-representation of the middle and upper middle classes and under-representation of the factory laborer were surely characteristic of the social composition of both Italian fascism and Nazism. Moreover, as Milza admits, by 1937 [La Rocque's party had] made significant breakthroughs in 'the working class milieu': it claimed 19 percent of its membership was drawn from industrial workers, 16 percent from peasants, 24 percent from white-collar workers, 15 percent from small businessmen and 26 percent from the liberal professions. Milza is at some pains to insist that 'this does not mean that it was fascistized.' All it means is that the Croix de Feu had become a 'large modern interclass force' that prefigured Gaullisme. What distinguishes a 'large modern interclass force' from a 'fascist' one? Milza never explains his use of terminology. Stressing the (incontestable) lineages between the Croix de Feu and post-war Gaullisme would seem to undermine the movement's fascist credentials. (273–74)

Why, Irvine wonders, have Milza and other scholars been so invested in denying that the CF was fascist? Irvine's answer: "If the Croix de Feu can be shown to have been fascist, then two principal tenets of the French historiography of fascism collapse. It would no longer be possible to argue, in the tradition established by René Rémond forty years ago, that French fascism was the work of an isolated minority. Nor would it be possible to maintain . . . as Zeev Sternhell has done, that fascism was omni-present in France but only among dissident members of the Left seeking to revise Marxism. A serious scholarly examination of the Croix de Feu might reveal that French fascism was both widespread and clearly on the political right" (294).

THE STERNHELL CONTROVERSY

Although French consensus historians are in accord with Sternhell in emphasiz-ing the left-wing aspects of fascism, they have been highly critical of him for asserting that fascist ideas have had a long history in France and that these ideas continue to be deeply imbedded in French political discourse—to the point, Sternhell writes, that they have "permitted a large number of intellectuals to be fascist without knowing it."[18] In some respects, the scholarly reception given Sternhell's books in France is reminiscent of some of the critical responses originally given to Robert Paxton's *Vichy France: Old Guard and New Order, 1940–44* (1972), a study which suggested that during the German occupation France had been more a nation of collaborators than a nation of resisters.[19]

In 1984 Serge Berstein, reviewing Sternhell's *Neither Right nor Left: Fascist Ideology in France,* seconded René Rémond's conclusion that fascist ideas (which had been "imported" from abroad) had never received much support in France since, to cite Rémond, old democratic habits had created efficacious barriers to "irrational" movements like fascism. Berstein himself describes France as largely "allergic" and "impermeable" to fascism, even during the Depression years, when followers of fascism, he says, were never more than a marginal minority. According to Berstein, if some intellectuals ("less numerous than Sternhell believes") were attracted to fascism, their success was ephem-eral, and they were unable to obliterate "the profundity of democratic culture in France." "We are forced to acknowledge," he continues, "that those countries which escaped fascism are the old democracies where that form of government had been implanted for a long time and was profoundly rooted in their political culture, whereas those nations which knew fascism were those where democ-racy was only a recently constructed edifice." Thus, argues Berstein, even during the Depression, both England, which had as many unemployed as Italy, and the United States, which had thirteen million unemployed (compared to Germany's six million), rejected fascism. Similarly in France, "no [fascist] leader imposed himself, no fascist party was able to take root."

Berstein concedes that Jacques Doriot's sizeable PPF, with its "symmetrical rejection of capitalism and bolshevism," its "totalitarian practices," and its "exacerbated cult of the leader," had been "incontestably fascist." It was also fascist, according to Berstein, because its followers were a mixture of "workers, syndicalists, intellectuals, and technicians." Nevertheless, the general appeal of fascism remained weak in France, as indicated by the fact that by 1939 the PPF was in decline and was revived during the occupation only with German help. Jean-Paul Brunet therefore is correct to write, "If the PPF was fascist, France was not."

Berstein acknowledges that Colonel de La Rocque's movement had had a "real success" between 1936 and 1938, but he maintains that rather than having been fascist it had been a party of "the modern right whose nationalist dimension was essential." Indeed, Berstein argues that because La Rocque proposed nothing that was "incompatible with [French] national traditions" his movement was not fascist. For Berstein, "René Rémond [has] demonstrated in a definitive manner that there was practically nothing in common, except for a paramilitary style and a contentious language, between the French [antiparliamentary] leagues, largely conservative, and the fascist current."[20] In Berstein's mind, then, Sternhell is mistaken to argue that France had a significant fascist tradition.

Jacques Julliard and Michel Winock, by contrast, have commended Sternhell for having performed an important service for French scholarship. According to Julliard, Sternhell has played "the glass-breaking role formerly held by Robert Paxton regarding Vichy." "French historiography," writes Julliard, "often approaches subjects of contemporary history with so much caution and timidity that the intervention of foreign historians is necessary so that problems considered taboo will be openly discussed." Winock adds that, until Sternhell, French historians had written only of "our national allergy to fascism" and had even practiced an "autocensorship" on the subject.[21]

Sternhell himself has commented on the storm of criticism aroused by his writings. Agreeing with one interviewer that he had particularly shocked the French public with his claim that prior to the First World War France had been the birthplace of fascist ideology and that during the 1930s fascist ideas had been quite widespread in France, he said,

> It has been truly a very rough affair. But the reticencies, the resistance, and the criticisms stem from two essential causes. First, there is a certain effort at repression; there is a problem of the collective unconscious, a refusal to cope with the disagreeable side of history. France is the France of the French Revolution of 89, it is the liberal and democratic republic, the open society. People refuse to admit that France had also secreted a political culture antipodal to the

revolutionary and rationalistic tradition of the eighteenth century. People refuse to admit that there has been another side to the nation's history. The most striking thing is the refusal to conceive of Vichy as something other than an accident, a parenthesis, or a regime imposed by the occupier.[22]

I agree with Sternhell that there has been an indigenous fascist tradition in France that predates the First World War and that the appeal of fascist ideas in France has been much stronger, especially in the 1930s, than heretofore acknowledged by many French scholars. I differ with him, however, in that I do not find French fascism, at least in its major manifestations, to be essentially leftist in either its intellectual origins or mass politics. In my view, Sternhell takes too narrow an approach to the subject in focusing more on intellectuals (not always the most representative) than on mass movements and in taking too much of fascism's rhetoric about national "socialism" at face value, thereby ignoring many of the rationalizations and mystifications perpetrated by such propaganda.

Sternhell characterizes fascism as a "revision of Marxism" that launched "an assault upon capitalism" and aimed at "a socialism for all." He writes that "in France, real authentic fascism was always born on the left, never on the right," that in Italy fascism was "an unprecedented war machine against the bourgeois order," and that this is why "so many" men of the left "slid toward fascism" during the interwar period.[23] Much of the evidence in this book contradicts this view of fascism.

I agree with Michel Winock, Jacques Julliard, and other French scholars who fault Sternhell for neglecting the social history of fascism. Winock describes Sternhell's *Neither Right nor Left* as "a pure history of ideas," "without direct relation to events." Winock comments, "In search of the platonic idea of fascism, [Sternhell] fails to analyze the conditions of its eventual rise in France."[24] Julliard criticizes Sternhell for asserting that in France fascist ideology came closest to "the ideal type, to the 'idea' of fascism in the platonic sense of the term" precisely because it "never passed the stage of theory and never suffered the inevitable compromises" that it did in Italy and Germany.

Julliard considers this approach a form of historical idealism that leads Sternhell to describe a kind of transcendental fascism divorced from social reality. Julliard believes that "all the proceedings of recent historiography tend, by contrast, to privilege the study of practice in relation to that of discourse, at the very least to not take the latter for ready cash." Consequently, Julliard believes that Sternhell has "artificially separated fascist ideology from fascism itself."[25]

Winock and Julliard point out that Sternhell largely ignores both the major

French fascist movements and the major French fascist intellectuals of the 1930s in favor of less sizeable movements and less influential intellectuals whose origins were on the left. Thus, writes Winock, Sternhell "quickly passes over vulgar fascism," that of the paramilitary nationalist leagues, of Doriot's PPF, of the cagoulards, of the writers of *Je suis Partout*, "not to mention the scarecrows of the Croix de Feu," in order to focus on the ideas of the Belgian socialist Henri de Man, the French socialist Marcel Déat, and the writings of others who proposed "a socialism without a proletariat." Julliard concludes that Sternhell not only shows no interest in the mass organizations of the extreme right but also "totally pass[es] over in silence" such leading fascist intellectuals of the period as Pierre Drieu La Rochelle and Robert Brasillach, preferring to dwell instead on certain articles of the left-wing Catholic review *Esprit* and on writings of the young Pierre Mendès-France.[26]

In this book I concentrate on the largest, not the smallest, fascist movements in France between 1933 and 1939. I deal at length with the social history of French fascism in the 1930s, especially the relation between fascist ideology and its major financial backers and political constituencies. My research has shown that police reports from the thirties to the French Ministry of Interior often tell us more about the underlying dynamics of French fascism than do French fascist speeches, newspapers, and books. Certainly French fascists themselves were not inclined during this period to identify publicly their financial backers or publicize their internal feuds and other delicate matters. The police reports often do.

These reports, *if used prudently*, are an invaluable means of penetrating the facade of French fascism and revealing some of its most important inner workings—which is why they have been mined with rich results by historians of both the consensus and nonconsensus schools (Eugen Weber, Paul Mazgaj, Jean-Paul Brunet, Philippe Burrin, Alan Douglas, Stewart Doty, Paul Jankowski, William Irvine, Sam Goodfellow). By contrast, to take everything in the writings of French fascists at face value would be naive indeed. Fascists writing propaganda had far more reason to distort the truth than did informants reporting to the police or police reporting to their superiors, especially to a succession of ideologically varied ministers of interior.[27]

Although chapter 6 deals with four of the most prominent French fascist intellectuals of the 1930s—Bertrand de Jouvenel, Pierre Drieu La Rochelle, Robert Brasillach, and Louis-Ferdinand Céline—there is no attempt in this book to write a general history of the hundreds of French writers and journalists who propagated similar ideas both before and after 1933. To do so, would require another volume and would be highly repetitive. I am primarily concerned with the major social, political, cultural, and emotional interests that fascist ideas served for the thousands of French men and women who adopted them, particularly with the way they were used to rationalize class interest, political domination, and patriarchal rule. This is one reason for the recurring analyses in this book of the social implications of various French fascist ideas, for the repeated decoding of French fascist propaganda, and for the exposure of various conservative elements in French fascist discourse.

HISTORICAL FASCISM IN ITALY AND GERMANY

The view of French fascism presented here is based on the way mass fascisms elsewhere, especially in Italy and Germany, operated in practice both before and after they came to power. It acknowledges, however, that a variety of fascisms existed in Europe in the 1930s (as Eugen Weber has pointed out) and that these differed from one another in important respects while at the same time having a good deal in common. It is a mistake, for example, to equate all fascism, especially Italian fascism, with German Nazism. Italian fascism was not only much less racist than German Nazism, but also less totalitarian. Too many historians, especially French consensus historians intent on denying that fascism had any mass appeal in their country during the interwar period, have compared the CF to the German variety of fascism only, to Nazism, thereby rejecting the notion that Colonel de La Rocque was fascist on the grounds that he was both antiracist and anti-German (a characterization that itself, as we shall see, is simplistic).

To distinguish the CF from German Nazism because the CF was less racist does not distinguish it from Italian fascism, which was also less racist. As Robert Paxton and Michael Marrus have noted, Mussolini was no Hitler in his attitude toward Jews, at least before 1937, and even as late as 1943 fascist Italy remained a haven for Jews escaping Vichy France:

> Unlike German nazism, Italian fascism had never put anti-Semitism at the center of its program. Until Mussolini decided to throw in his lot with Hitler in 1937, the Italian regime did not persecute Jews. Indeed, it welcomed them into its ranks. Mussolini himself spoke from every possible point on the compass about Jews: he praised them warmly on some occasions, wrote slanderous articles about them on others, and negotiated genially with Zionist leaders. In the fall of 1933, a group of American Jewish publications named Mussolini among twelve Christians who had been 'most outstanding in their opposition to anti-Semitism.' . . .

Once the Duce's European and imperial ambitions pointed toward a German alliance, however, his policy toward the Jews hardened. In October 1938, Fascist Italy issued its own racial laws and gave further momentum to an official anti-Jewish campaign.

Even after this crucial shift, anti-Semitism did not strike deep roots in Italy. . . . Many sections of Italian society looked upon racism as a ridiculous notion, cooked up by the Germans in their insufferable campaign of domination.[28]

After fascist Italy invaded eight French departments in 1940, it refused, as late as 1942, to allow anti-Jewish measures to be applied to its occupation zone, defending "foreign Jews as well as Italian nationals, not only in their own country but also in France." German authorities in France found this attitude "particularly revolting."[29]

Although there were major differences between Italian fascism and German Nazism where racism was concerned, the two fascisms shared an anti-Marxism that led them, once they came to power, to crush not only left-wing trade unions but also liberal fellow travelers who supported civil liberties for all. Like Hitler's regime, Mussolini's was far more totalitarian toward the left than toward the right, depriving the labor movement of all independence and giving management more. As Charles Maier has pointed out, "In the initial months of Fascist administration, the government dissolved about twenty provincial administrations where the left was entrenched and, in the first year of power, 547 communal governments, 90 percent of which had been under Socialist or Popolari [political democrats] control. Left-wing newspapers were sequestered, and social cooperatives turned over to Fascist administration."[30]

Until the Duce instituted a war economy in the mid-1930s, he allowed industry to run its affairs with a minimum of government interference. Despite his previous anticapitalist rhetoric, he cut taxes on business and did nothing to impede the rapid growth of economic cartels. In 1926 he rescinded the eight-hour-day law for Italian workers and decreed a general wage reduction. Between 1928 and 1932, real wages in Italy dropped by almost half. Between 1926 and 1934, the purchasing power of Italian farmworkers declined by 50 to 70 percent, partly as a result of a government policy that restricted migration to the cities and thus allowed landowners to keep farm wages low. In 1930 Mussolini acknowledged that under his regime the general standard of living had fallen, but he stated that "fortunately, the Italian people were not accustomed to eating much and therefore felt the privation less acutely than others."[31]

Hitler's brand of alleged national socialism was not prolabor either. William

L. Shirer, an American journalist who covered Germany in the 1930s, has described the Nazi double-talk that accompanied Hitler's designating May Day 1933 a national holiday, "The Day of National Labor":

> Though Hitler had just destroyed the Communist and Socialist parties and now secretly planned to destroy the unions, he promised the latter that the first May Day under National Socialism would be celebrated as never before. Actually it was. But not in the manner expected by the lulled union leaders. They were flown to Berlin from all parts of Germany, along with big delegations of workers. And out at Tempelhof Field thousands of banners were unfurled acclaiming the Nazi regime's solidarity with the worker.
>
> Before the massive rally, Hitler received the workers' delegates in the ornate hall of the Chancellery in the Wilhelmstrasse.
>
> 'You will see how untrue and unjust,' he said, 'is the statement that the [Nazi] revolution is directed against the German workers.' . . .
>
> The next morning, May 2, the trade-union offices throughout the country were occupied by the police, the SS and the SA. All union funds were confiscated, the unions dissolved and the leaders arrested, beaten, and carted off to concentration camps. . . .
>
> Within three weeks the hollowness of such promises was exposed. Hitler decreed a law bringing an end to collective bargaining and outlawing strikes. [Robert Ley, the Nazi minister of labor] explained the decree to the country. It promised, he said, 'to restore absolute leadership to the natural leader of the factory—that is, the employer.' Henceforth, he added, the employer was to be 'the master of the house.'[32]

Although Hitler was notoriously disdainful of commercial considerations and sought to establish the primacy of politics over economics, he did little to alienate big business after his ascension to power in 1933. On the contrary, as T. W. Mason has shown, he did a good deal to benefit it. He not only crushed the German left and its trade unions, but also gave German businessmen a free hand to run their enterprises without government interference and allowed certain industrialists to reap huge profits from his rearmament program. This was one reason many Germany conservatives accepted Nazism so readily even though Hitler deprived them of the political power they had enjoyed under the Weimar Republic. If some German workers originally benefited from the rearmament boom, before long—as Ian Kershaw has shown—they were worse off than they had been under the Weimar Republic because of longer working hours, wage freezes, and brutal conditions.[33]

According to George Mosse, Hitler's revolution was largely a cultural revolution, one that acknowledged class grievances without threatening the class structure. Although its socialism was supposed to mean "the absence of privi-

leged individuals in a community where only the battle for the Volk has meaning" and was supposed to produce an "end to class differences on behalf of the
unity of the Volk," in practice class differences and class privileges remained
largely untouched. As one Nazi writer described the ideal National Socialist
youth, "He knows that it makes no difference how much the fathers of the boys
earn, or whether they live in a one-room or an eight-room apartment. . . . To
maintain comradeship is equivalent to active socialism." Theodore Abel has
also noted that Nazi talk of the *Volkgemeinschaft* [People's community] was
misleading. During his rise to power Hitler often inferred, in conveniently vague
terms, that the aim of the Volkgemeinschaft was to abolish class privilege, and
Abel notes that some gullible Germans believed him. Once in power, however,
Hitler used national unity as an excuse for destroying those organizations most
committed to democratizing the class structure. In practice, the Volkgemeinschaft brought not more economic egalitarianism but less.[34]

In *The Nazi Party: A Social Profile of Its Members and Leaders, 1919–1945*
(1983), Michael Kater has charted the relative support that Hitler's party received from various social and professional groups within the German population before and after the Nationalsozialistische Deutsche Arbeiterpartei
(NSDAP, German national socialist workers party) came to power. Using Nazi
membership records, electoral statistics, and other sources, Kater has shown
how in the three years before Hitler was named chancellor, the following groups
were overrepresented in the NSDAP in the sense of comprising a higher percentage in the party than in German society at large: (1) the lower middle classes,
which included small merchants and small and intermediate businessmen,
small farmers, craftsmen, white-collar workers, elementary school teachers and
low civil servants; and (2) members of the elite, which included big businessmen, big landowners, high school teachers, university professors, university
students, and high civil servants. By contrast, blue-collar workers and the lower
classes in general were strikingly underrepresented in the Nazi party. Kater
found that the overwhelming majority of German workers remained loyal to
either the German Socialist or Communist parties.

Neither, according to Kater, did "marginal men of plebeian origin" receive
many leadership positions within the NSDAP. Most of the leadership came from
the lower middle classes, with members of German elite groups being overrepresented in the top positions. Kater finds it "grossly misleading" for some historians to speak of the plebeian connections between the Nazi leadership and the
populace "in view of the very low proportion of blue-collar workers in any of the
Nazi cadres." He writes, "While the elite was consistently overrepresented in

the rank and file of the party, this situation was more evident in the cadres: the higher the cadre, the greater the degree of overrepresentation. The converse applied to the working class: always underrepresented in both formations, this class was far less in evidence in the cadres, and its representation there declined with increasing rank."[35]

Kater notes that representatives of big industrial and agrarian interests played a decisive role in convincing President Paul von Hindenburg to appoint Hitler chancellor in 1933. It is ironic, writes Kater, that "the Nazi Party, which had taken its name from the working class and had attained national prominence as a mass formation supported by the lower middle class, was finally elevated to the seat of power by the German elite" (71). Although most of Hitler's financial support came from small and intermediate businesses, not from big capitalism, "influential lobbies representing heavy industry" did contribute some of their political funds to the Nazis just as they did to other conservative parties of the period. In this way, they curried favor with whomever won.

But, Kater emphasizes, it was the German elite in the larger sense, much more than heavy industry alone, that provided Hitler with the political edge he needed to be finally appointed chancellor:

> Between 1929 and Hitler's assumption of power in January 1933, the attrac-ion of the NSDAP as a political alternative to other bourgeois parties in-creased considerably for the upper middle class and former aristocracy. . . . There is little doubt that the September elections of 1930, in which the right-of-center bourgeois parties lost significantly to the Nazis, solidified business executive and entrepreneurial interest in the NSDAP. . . . By 1933 Hitler had succeeded in maintaining and even in strengthening the ties between his party and important representatives of the still vastly influential social elite. (62–63, 70)

Moreover, according to Kater, the Nazis did not create a counterelite after they came to power or carry out the social revolution they had once promised. Although Hitler and some of his followers may have intended to replace the old elite with a new one after Germany had won the war, they were unable to do so before 1945—partly because so many members of the old elite had joined the party. In Kater's words,

> The Nazi functionary corps was not a counterelite composed of 'marginal men' on the fringe, from largely plebeian origins, as Daniel Lerner and others have stated. . . .
> To classify as a counterelite, the leaders would have had to bring about the completion of the National Socialist revolution, but this they were not able to do. And, coming after and aping in various respects their austere Prussian

precursors, they retained far too many epigonal characteristics to be considered a new species. After the changeover from one elite to the other, the new leadership was unable to take up a truly contrary posture and thus to function as a counterelite. There were too many elements of accommodation, of fusion, of absorption. In social composition alone, the pattern of mutual interactions and interlockings between the two groups was nearer to collusion than to collision. . . . Often the lines were so blurred that no one could tell who the turncoats were. (232–33)

Two other studies of the social bases of German Nazism—those of Thomas Childers and Detlef Muhlberger—generally agree with Kater; Renzo de Felice and Jill Lewis have pointed out that workers were underrepresented in Italian and Austrian fascism as well.[36] In keeping with these conclusions, my book defines certain predominantly middle-class political movements in France during the 1930s as fascist, including those, like the SF, the CF, and the PPF, that rejected the label *fascism* even as they propagated its ideas. In this respect, too, the book disagrees with the consensus view of French fascism.

DEFINING FASCISM

Acting on William Irvine's observation that "dissenters from the established consensus of French fascism are traditionally challenged to give their own definition," I propose the following: Fascism was primarily a new variety of authoritarian conservatism and right-wing nationalism that sought to defeat the Marxist threat and the political liberalism that allowed it to exist in the first place. Most fascism therefore shared with the traditional right a fundamental social and economic conservatism that was strongly opposed to Marxism.

Although this view of fascism does not deny that a small minority of fascists in the 1930s had left-wing aspirations, it objects to devaluating the predominantly conservative socioeconomic goals of mainstream fascism in Italy, Germany, and France. At the same time, it underscores the willingness of fascists to use more authoritarian means than democratic rightists. It also encompasses the cultural authoritarianism that characterized fascist ideology and acknowledges the role it played in buttressing political and social authoritarianism. Under fascism, hierarchy was to govern all human relationships, whether between bosses and workers, parents and children, or men and women. Fascism was more paternalistic than egalitarian.

In its response to poverty, mainstream fascism in the 1930s relied not on pressure from the bottom up but on charity from the top down—with the emphasis on *private* charity, not government assistance. In Italy and Germany, fascism's proposed solution to the Depression was not more mass purchasing power at home but more imperialism abroad, not higher wages but trickle-down plunder. During the 1930s, French fascists not only supported French imperialism in North Africa and Indochina but also German expansionism eastward at the expense of Soviet communism. They also defended property rights, the profit motive, lower taxes, less government spending, and union busting.

This book does not neglect the antibourgeois rhetoric employed by most fascist propagandists, including their claims that they were national socialists who were neither right nor left. It exposes, however, the probourgeois reality that they regularly defended, a reality constantly mystified by an appeal to antirationalist and antiutilitarian values. This does not mean that fascists failed to take the so-called spiritual side of fascism seriously; on the contrary, it provided a moral justification for their acts of intolerance and brutality. It means only that this spirituality was hardly anticonservative where upper-class social and economic interests were concerned. Fascism's commitment to a militarized spirituality did play an important role in distinguishing its followers from more liberal, hedonistic, and humane conservatives.

Fascism was therefore more than interest politics, but it was also interest politics. Certainly, fascist intellectuals saw themselves as engaged in much more than a defense of capitalism and class privilege, insisting that their spiritual revolution transcended crass materialism; but when it came to social and economic issues they repeatedly supported a capitalist economy, managerial authority, and social hierarchy. Subjectively, fascists were obsessed with spiritual issues, but objectively they supported conservative economic interests. Their criticisms of bourgeois decadence paled before their hatred of Marxist decadence.

Nonfascist conservatism distinguished itself from fascist conservatism by its support, albeit sometimes wavering and indecisive, for electoral democracy and civil liberties—at least as long as the Marxist threat could be contained by parliamentary means. As we shall see, this contrast was blurred by the fact that fascists sometimes engaged in electoral politics before they came to power and even professed, when it was useful to do so, to be committed to certain republican principles. This was only one of the shifting gray areas between the fascist and traditional rights of the era.

Fascism generally surpassed traditional conservatism during the interwar period by developing new propaganda and organizational techniques, all part of an effort to mobilize the masses for right-wing ends. Although fascism's innovations differentiated it from many previous conservative movements, it also attracted many conservatives, especially younger rightists, to its cause. After 1936, France's major conservative electoral party in the early 1930s, the Fédération Républicaine (FR, Republican federation), lost many of its most militant members to Colonel de La Rocque's CF. Unlike the parties of the traditional right, which relied on sedate party congresses to bring the faithful together, the CF staged a number of public rallies and huge nationalistic parades featuring immense columns of disciplined supporters whom La Rocque, a former colonial officer, reviewed like a military commander (albeit in civilian clothes). In addition, the CF excelled at grass roots organizing, creating a network of local headquarters, social clubs, vacation resorts, and charity centers throughout France. Doriot's PPF sought to enhance its appeal with fascist symbols and liturgy, some borrowed from Germany but given an obligatory French twist.

Stylistically, fascisms in Europe during the interwar period differed from country to country and in France from movement to movement. All, however, tried to portray themselves as more dynamic than their conservative rivals, *dynamic* often meaning more paramilitary or more authoritarian. In France, between 1924 and 1939, the Legion, the Faisceau, the JP, the Francistes, and the SF all had their blueshirts (thinly veiled French versions of Mussolini's blackshirts and Hitler's brownshirts). The CF eschewed blueshirts as too foreign for its taste, but this did not prevent it from having its own paramilitary followers hold repeated mobilization exercises in preparation for a political H hour and D day.

Paramilitary troops, new organizing techniques, and stirring ceremonies were not by themselves, of course, enough to ensure fascist political success, as Sir Oswald Mosley in England and Marcel Bucard in France were to demonstrate. Indeed, in England and France, too close an imitation of German or Italian liturgies could be counterproductive if they were perceived by the public to be antinationalist in nature, which is one reason fascist leaders in France repeatedly emphasized how French their movements were. Even in Germany, Hitler's propaganda techniques were unsuccessful when political circumstances were not ripe. In 1928, the Nazis polled less than 3 percent of the vote.

In order to prosper, fascism needed to cater to right-wing social, economic, and cultural interests within a favorable political context. In France, this context varied according to how seriously conservatives felt menaced by the Marxist threat and by the electoral democracy that allowed it to exist. For some conservatives, therefore, the most appealing aspect of fascism was its political authoritarianism, especially its promise to deal firmly with Communists and Socialists.

If fascism was more politically innovative than traditional conservatism, it could be just as backward-looking in cultural matters. European fascism was not always as modernistic as some scholars have suggested. Under the Third Reich, Joseph Goebbels subsidized an exhibit of modern art not to honor its glory but to expose its "decadence." Although in Italy and Belgium writers like Filippo Marinetti and Paul de Man defended fascism as an expression of futurism, most fascist writers, notably those in Germany and France, went to great lengths to defend cultural rootedness and traditional values.[37]

As Shelly Baranowski has shown, in 1933 and 1934 church periodicals in Germany praised Hitler for cracking down on prostitution, pornography, and abortion and for protecting the Christian family against the threat of secularism. The Protestant theologian Martin Niemoller, who was eventually imprisoned at Dachau for opposing Nazism, originally supported Hitler in the hope that he would contribute to a religious reawakening in Germany that would defeat atheistic communism.[38] On February 14, 1933, the French Catholic newspaper *La Croix* declared, "If Hitler rises against Communism and manifests an intention to suppress it, or at least to vigorously fight it, such a project can only meet with general approval."

Like fascists in Germany, fascists in France repeatedly defended cultural traditionalism and repeatedly castigated modern mores, including those that encouraged feminism. There were exceptions (Pierre Drieu La Rochelle admired Van Gogh and was once attracted to surrealism, Marinetti did advocate a fascist futurism, and so on), but on the whole mainstream fascism throughout Europe extolled the values of what Maurice Barrès had called "the earth and the dead."

In sum, fascism in Europe shared a good many attitudes with the traditional right, not only in its social and economic but also in its cultural ideology. It is not surprising, therefore, that there were repeated crossovers between conservatism and fascism during the interwar period—as Charles Maier has shown for Italy and Michael Kater for Germany. In France, as Irvine has discovered, in 1934 "a large number (probably a majority) of the senators and deputies of the Jeunesses Patriotes also belonged to the Republican Federation," and in 1935 "a number of deputies of the Republican Federation belonged simultaneously to the Croix de Feu."[39] Indeed, for many rightists, fascism was simply a more dynamic form of conservatism.

CONTEXTUALIZING FASCISM

Even the best definition of fascism can be misleading if it reduces fascism to a static, unhistorical phenomenon. Fascists operated in various national contexts, the French context being different from the Italian and German in crucial respects, and fascists responded opportunistically to these contexts in diverse ways. Historians have often emphasized the differences between the pagan national socialism of Hitler and the Catholic reactionary authoritarianism of Francisco Franco, Engelbert Dollfuss, and Antonio Salazar. Although these differences were important, so too were Hitler's and Mussolini's attempts to appeal to Christians before they came to power. Before 1933, and even as late as 1936, Hitler often sounded more like Salazar than the tyrant he became. Indeed, in 1935 many Germans regarded Hitler as a moderate on the Jewish Question, since in propagating the Nuremberg Laws he seemed to have rejected more extreme alternatives.

In some circumstances, fascists trimmed their authoritarianism or at least its public expression and even posed as defenders of freedom of speech and assembly, especially when *their* freedom of speech and assembly was threatened. In other circumstances, most notably when they came to power and were able to command the loyalty of the army and the police, they abandoned this pretense. In 1932 Hitler was still an electoral politician; in 1934 he was not.

Before Hitler came to power he promised to protect conservative, Catholic, and Protestant Germans from Marxists, atheists, and Jews—only to subdue the former as well after he had repressed the latter. Hitler ran for the presidency not as a totalitarian but as someone who would crush the left while sparing the right; otherwise, Hindenburg would never have appointed him chancellor. (Symbolic of this deception was the civilian cutaway that Hitler wore when he was inaugurated as chancellor in January 1933.) The Reichstag fire and Hitler's emergency decrees came later, and his most authoritarian measures came even later still.

Before 1933, members of the conservative establishment in Germany mistakenly thought they would be able to control Hitler, and the former corporal was careful at first not to disabuse them of this illusion. During his first few months in power, Hitler avoided cracking down on all segments of the population at once. Employing his famous "salami slicing" technique, he first attacked Marxists and Jews, and only when they were sufficiently crushed did he risk moving against dissident Catholics, Protestants, and conservatives, until eventually the whole salami was sliced.

Few historians today would regard Hitler's alleged moderation in 1935 as proof that he was not a fascist, a standard that has not always been applied to the expediency of Colonel de La Rocque and other French fascists during the interwar period. In *Mein Kampf* (1925), Hitler wrote that even the leader of the Nazi party was to be elected and that "members of the movement [were] free to call him to account before the forum of a new election, to divest him of his office in so far as he has infringed on the principles of the movement or served its interests badly." Hitler's talk of "Germanic democracy" was combined, to be sure, with stronger stuff. Once elected, the leader was to have "unconditional authority," for Nazism "rejected the principle of majority rule in which the leader is degraded to the level of a mere executant of other people's will and opinion." In 1925 Hitler did not bother to hide his opportunism in choosing to pursue the electoral path to power: "[Our] movement is anti-parliamentarian, and even its participation in a parliamentary institution can only imply activity for its destruction, for eliminating an institution in which we must see one of the gravest symptoms of mankind's decay."[40] A similar dualism, as we shall see, was also present in the moderation that French fascists claimed in the 1930s.

Mussolini did not present himself as a totalitarian before he came to power. As Maier has observed, "Before the Fascist take-over, Mussolini reaffirmed to the business community . . . that fascism meant an end to the 'statism' they detested."[41] In 1922 Mussolini presented himself as a man who could work within the parliamentary system—and was even tempted to do so, except, as Maier writes, "his constituency reminded him and forced him to brandish anew the violent tactics that were the real currency of his movement." Maier adds that the liberal politician Giovanni Giolitti was "right about Mussolini's willingness to enter the parliamentary bargaining system; and the liberals who supported Mussolini were correct about his willingness to preserve their social hegemony" (324).

Even when Mussolini proposed a new electoral law in 1923 that favored fascist representation in parliament and that laid the basis for his eventual dictatorship, he was careful to announce, according to Maier, that "he did not wish to undercut parliament but to strengthen it and overcome the discredit into which it had fallen." Equally conciliatory in 1923 was Mussolini's claim that he was disbanding his squads of blackshirts as part of an effort to heal the breach between parliament and the Italian people (347, 348). In short, it would be a mistake to view fascism in Italy and Nazism in Germany as publicly defending totalitarianism before they came to power, at least if totalitarianism is taken to mean the crushing of the right as much as of the left.

French fascists were equally opportunistic. With the exception of the members of the royalist AF, they labeled themselves republican, that is, nonroyalist and nominally democratic. Because, unlike their Italian and German counterparts, they never came to power during the interwar period, they always denied (during this period) that they had any totalitarian intentions. This was particularly true in 1934, when Hitler's crackdown on right-wing dissidents in Germany greatly disturbed many French conservatives. Anxious not to alienate these conservatives, French fascists emphasized their opposition to "statism" (government intervention in the economy), at least to left-wing statism, and called for more decentralized government and regional liberties. At the same time, they placed these demands within a corporatist framework that would have enabled factory managers and local notables to exert more power over the lower classes.

Although the French conservative press had either praised or condoned Hitler's repression of the German left in early 1933, it objected when some German rightists, including a number of Catholics, began to suffer a similar fate a few months later. In March 1933 *La Croix* criticized the elections in Germany for taking place under a "reign of terror" and called upon the German Catholic Center party to vote against Hitler. In January 1934 the right-wing newspaper *L'Echo de Paris* also denounced the terror that was taking place in Germany, especially when the Nazi regime forced the bishops of Bavaria and Württemberg to submit.

Unlike German conservatives, who underestimated the extent of Hitler's ruthlessness before he came to power, French conservatives had the benefit of hindsight. They had little desire for a French Hitler to repress *them*. On the other hand, many French rightists continued to view Mussolini much more favorably than they did Hitler, regarding him as a dictator who had faithfully protected Italian conservatives and was less barbaric.

The French right was particularly shocked by Hitler's blood purge of June 1934, the infamous Night of the Long Knives. This purge claimed the lives not only of allegedly leftist members of the SA but also of General Kurt von Schleicher and his wife, who were murdered in their home by Nazi brownshirts. It also placed another prominent rightist, Franz von Papen, under house arrest. The lesson was clear: even the most respectable members of German society (both von Schleicher and von Papen were Junker aristocrats who had served as chancellors of Germany) were no longer safe under Nazism. Not surprisingly, after June 1934 fascist leaders in France took pains to distance themselves from this aspect of Hitler's rule.

Indeed, after 1934 all of these leaders, with the exception of Marcel Bucard, who had little public support, refused to label themselves fascist. Although they continued to display more sympathy for Italian fascism than for German Nazism, they were careful to emphasize their own nationalism and to insist that they were not the lackies of any foreign power, especially not of France's hereditary enemy, Germany.

Consensus historians have too often ignored the fact that before 1941, and even afterward, there was no contradiction in supporting French fascism and being anti-German. On May 24, 1940, with the Germans invading France, the French fascist newspaper *Je suis Partout* praised the government for appointing the well-known Germanophobe Georges Mandel minister of interior, and that same month Jacques Doriot, the head of the fascist PPF, fought bravely as a sergeant in the French army against the Germans (he was later awarded several decorations for holding up the advance of a German column). As we shall see, a number of French fascists even joined the Resistance.

Between 1936 and 1939, Colonel de La Rocque, the most important French fascist leader of the period, repeatedly disavowed any connection between his movement and Hitler's. Only later, in 1941, would he call for "continental collaboration" with the Germans. Like other fascist leaders of the 1930s, La Rocque was adept at tailoring his politics to circumstances. In 1936, after the Popular Front came to power and his movement was banned as a paramilitary organization, he transformed the CF into an electoral party. Prior to 1936 and after 1940, he sang a less democratic tune.

In sum, no static conception of fascism, no ahistorical definition, can do justice to the various doctrinal fluctuations that fascism underwent in France, Italy, and Germany during the interwar period. This is no reason, however, to sink into pure nominalism. For all the slippery aspects of fascism, both in action and thought, certain common denominators characterized mainstream fascism throughout Europe during this period—and in France also characterized the CF, the PPF, the SF, the JP, the Francistes, and the AF. Differences existed between these movements, of course, but this did not negate their important similarities. There were differences of leadership, of style, and of foreign policy. Certainly nationalistic fascists in one country were opposed to submitting to nationalistic fascists in another country, at least as long as they had a choice.[42] But with the exception of German fascism's racial doctrines, on most of the central political, social, economic, and cultural issues of the era, the ideological kinship between the major fascist movements of the period was all too evident.

COMMON DENOMINATORS OF EUROPEAN FASCISM

Among the major common denominators of the most successful European fascist movements of the interwar period was first of all, and most fundamentally, a strong distaste for democracy—for social and economic as well as political democracy. It was only in cultural matters, in their pandering to some of the most parochial, authoritarian, and vicious aspects of popular culture, that fascists were, in a sense, democratic. Fascism's strong distaste for political, social, and economic democracy was accompanied by a rejection of class conflict on behalf of class collaboration; a desire to eliminate left-wing trade unions and replace them with corporatist or company unions; a passionate right-wing nationalism that denounced Marxist and liberal internationalism in foreign affairs and Marxist and liberal divisiveness in domestic affairs; preachments that spiritual goals were higher than material ones, which allowed fascist theoreticians to treat left-wing demands for more economic justice as metaphysically shallow; a tendency to define spiritual regeneration in military terms; a hatred of cultural decadence; and a taste for violent solutions to political conflicts, which included the notion that it was virile to crush one's opponents with physical force.

Although it is important to categorize mainstream fascism as accurately as possible, it is even more important to understand why it came about in the first place. Why did it attract so much public support in France after 1936? What conditions, forces, interests, ideas, and emotions contributed to its rise? Why was it authoritarian, callous, and cruel? What, for example, led Colonel de La Rocque in 1941 to praise the "ardent vitality of Hitlerian and fascist regimes" and to call upon the Vichy regime to carry out the "extirpation of contaminated elements" in France?[43] What led Pierre Drieu La Rochelle, a supporter of Doriot's PPF, to describe pity for the victims of Franco's firing squads in Spain as sentimentalism, and Bertrand de Jouvenel, another PPF writer, to extol the "brutal barons" of the Middle Ages as precursors of fascism's "new man"? Why in the late 1930s were thousands of French men and women, in spite of the many terrible consequences that fascism had already produced in Italy and Germany, attracted to fascist ideas? These are some of the questions I explore in this book. But first of all it is imperative to take into account the immediate historical context in which the second wave of fascism emerged in France between 1933 and 1939 and to acknowledge the role that this context, a changing one, played in both aiding and limiting the rise of French fascism.

1 · Social and Political Context

THE DEPRESSION AND ITS POLITICAL CONSEQUENCES

The resurgence of fascism in France in the early 1930s and its eventual decline in the late 1930s cannot be understood in the absence of some account of the larger historical context in which it operated, particularly the political consequences of the Depression in France. Although France suffered less from the Depression than did Germany, the effects were still grim. As one contemporary later recalled, "Part-time unemployment prevented the statistics of total unemployment from assuming at once alarming proportions. Widespread anxiety developed slowly; a more and more painful misery settled gradually among the masses. . . . For fear of being thrown into the hell of unemployment, the workers consented almost in silence to incredibly low salaries."[1] The historian Gordon Wright has noted that the Depression in France developed into the longest and most severe economic crisis France had known for a century and that when the recovery did set in it was slower than in most countries.

Adding to the crisis was the flood of immigrants that began pouring into France in the late thirties, including Jews fleeing from Nazi Germany. As Paula Hyman, David Weinberg, Robert Paxton, and Michael Marrus have shown, anti-immigration feelings were widespread in France in the 1930s, even in some

Jewish and liberal circles. Immigration also became a major issue for fascists, who, while denying that they were racists, protested the arrival of left-wing Jews.

Politically, mass economic hardship led to a resurgence of the left in France, as the extreme left, the Communists, entertained hopes of an impending revolution and the center left, the Socialists and Radical-Socialists, called for more social legislation to alleviate the suffering. The elections of 1932 brought a new Cartel des Gauches (left-center coalition) to power in parliament, and four years later another national election produced an even more left-wing government, the Popular Front, an alliance of Socialists, Communists, and left-wing liberals under the leadership of Léon Blum. The result was that many French conservatives, including many democratic conservatives who called themselves moderates, felt beleaguered. William Irvine tells of the reaction of France's major *modéré* electoral party of the 1930s, the Republican Federation:

> The mobilization of left-wing forces into the Popular Front, the substantial electoral victories of the Socialists and especially the Communists, and the dramatic growth of organized labor and its increased militancy seemed to presage major changes in French society. Although in retrospect the crisis of the 1930s seems less severe, to contemporary observers it augured a dramatic, and perhaps revolutionary transformation of France. These real, if myopic, anxieties of French conservatives were magnified by the international crises. The *modérés* believed, not without some justice, that the French social order could not survive both the current domestic upheaval and the shock of war. Many came to believe that events both inside and outside France were conspiring to destroy the traditional social fabric and push France into revolution.[3]

Since 1875 most French conservatives, supporting the Third Republic rather than an Orleanist or Bonapartist restoration, had relied on political democracy to defend their interests. However, when major threats from the political left and left-center developed in the 1920s and 1930s, some conservatives turned to more authoritarian alternatives. The first wave of organized fascism in France emerged in 1925, following the election of the first Cartel des Gauches in 1924. It receded two years later when a right-center coalition led by Raymond Poincaré stole its thunder by defeating the cartel.[4] With the onset of the Depression in France in 1931 and the election of a new cartel majority in parliament in 1932, a second wave of fascism emerged in France. Not only did the AF and the JP gain new support, but three new fascist movements were launched: the CF (founded earlier but greatly politicized by Colonel de La Rocque after 1931), the SF in 1933, and the Francistes in 1933. In 1936, following the election of the Popular Front, the PPF was also founded.

All of these movements sought to capitalize on public discontent with a parliamentary system that was ineffectual in dealing with the Depression. Between 1932 and 1934, France underwent six successive governments, none able to garner a working parliamentary majority. One cabinet after another was toppled as even Socialists and Radical-Socialists split on whether to raise income taxes and increase government spending, the Socialist solution, or keep taxes low and reduce government spending, the Radical-Socialist solution. One result was a rising public outcry, largely but not solely from the political right, for a revision of the Constitution that would break the stalemate by strengthening the power of the executive and reducing that of the legislature. For conservative revisionists like André Tardieu and François Coty, constitutional revision was meant to favor a conservative executive who would use his additional powers to keep the working classes and their disempowered legislators under control. The positive reaction of the French right-wing press to Hitler's actions against Communist and Socialist organizations in Germany in 1933 was indicative of this spirit.[5]

Some French fascist movements of the period damned parliamentarianism altogether (the royalist AF called the Third Republic the Sow), but most insisted that they were still committed to a republican form of government, albeit to a stronger form of republicanism than that provided by the Third Republic. They advocated constitutional revisions that would not only increase the power of the executive but also create corporatist representative bodies (representing occupational groups rather than regions), which would further reduce the power of the Chamber of Deputies.

By 1936 the JP and the CF, France's two largest right-wing paramilitary leagues, were on cozy terms with the Fédération Républicaine (FR), the social and economic programs of all three being virtually identical. Three vice-presidents of the FR were also leaders of the JP, and a number of the FR's parliamentary deputies were members of the CF, including some who had also served as vice-presidents of the FR. Writes Irvine,

> The pre-1936 leagues had a special appeal for an elite party like the Republican Federation because they could attract a mass membership, which conservatives did not command. They provided invaluable allies for the Federation, both as electoral auxiliaries and as counterrevolutionary shock troops. Despite its formal republican and democratic scruples, the Federation did not look too closely at the political coloration of its prospective allies. In any case, programatically, the leagues borrowed most of their ideas from the *modérés*. Although more skeptical of parliament than most *modérés* and more authoritarian in outlook, the leagues were close enough to the traditional

conservatives to permit a substantial overlapping of membership. . . . The possibility of a fascist seizure of power worried the Federation far less than either a Communist or even a radically reformist victory.[6]

By late 1936, even some members of the French Radical party, that traditional bastion of French political liberalism, flirted with fascism. One of the most shocking moments in the history of French radicalism occurred in October at Biarritz, at the party's annual congress, when at the opening session delegates opposed to the Popular Front, the sit-down strikes, and French intervention in the Spanish Civil War stood and sang the "Marseillaise" with their arms outstretched in a modified version of the fascist salute, while left-wing Radicals responded with the "Internationale" and the Marxist clenched-fist salute.

According to reporters, the fascist-saluting delegates vastly outnumbered the Marxist-saluting delegates and easily drowned out the "Internationale" with the "Marseillaise." Edouard Daladier, who had risen to speak on behalf of the Popular Front, had difficulty making himself heard above the hooting and jeering from the floor, a demonstration that continued for a quarter of an hour. As one of the leaders of the right-wing protesters declared afterward, "I am here to tell the government, in the name of a considerable number of Radicals, that we have had enough, and that we do not want to surrender to the orders of Moscow."[7]

It was a sad day for French radicalism, however much a journalist from *Le Temps* tried to minimize the demonstration by concluding in a follow-up article on October 24 that "between the party of revolution and [the party of] fascism, there is the great party of the 'Marseillaise.'" The next morning, rightist Radicals sought to smooth things over by replacing their fascist-looking salute with one that put both hands above their heads. This failed to erase the fact, however, that, if only for a moment and if only symbolically, the majority of the delegates at the congress of Biarritz had allowed their anticommunism to submerge their antifascism, to the point of visually associating themselves with fascism.

A movement with a greater connection to fascism, at least in 1934, was the Union Nationale des Combattants (UNC, National union of war veterans), one of France's largest veterans' organizations with a membership of nearly one million. On February 6, 1934, some ten thousand of its members joined with members of France's fascist leagues to hold a mass demonstration in Paris against the "Socialist threat" and the "rotten" politicians of the Third Republic. On February 4, the UNC's newspaper, *Le Petit Bleu*, published a cartoon on its front page picturing the Chamber of Deputies in flames and some of the deputies hanging by their necks from lampposts on the Concorde bridge. The president of

NC at the time was Georges Lebecq and the vice-president Jean Goy.
q was a Paris municipal councilman who, along with fifteen other conservative municipal councilmen, signed a proclamation on the eve of February 6 calling for the demonstration. Goy was a right-wing member of the Chamber of Deputies in 1934 who in 1942 would collaborate with the Nazis. Most of the rank and file of the UNC, however, were much less fascist than their leadership and more concerned on February 6 with resisting cuts in veterans' benefits than with toppling the Third Republic.

THE RIOTS OF FEBRUARY 6, 1934

A year after Hitler came to power in Germany, Paris witnessed a violent assault on the French Chamber of Deputies that had fascist overtones. The driving force behind the so-called fascist riots of February 6, 1934, was not the UNC but the nationalist leagues: the AF, the JP, the SF, the CF, and the Francistes. Their demonstration was treated sympathetically by most of the right-wing press in France both before and after the riots occurred.

The riots of February 6 were part of a conservative backlash to a shift to the left in the French government. The liberal politician Edouard Daladier, in order to gain Socialist support for his new cabinet, agreed to fire Paris's reactionary prefect of police, Jean Chiappe, and appoint a Socialist, Eugen Front, as minister of interior. Many conservatives were outraged by this "sellout" to the Socialists and feared that without Chiappe, who had a reputation for treating left-wing demonstrations ruthlessly and right-wing demonstrations benignly, their persons as well as their property might be endangered.

Conservatives also exploited the Stavisky affair to arouse public anger against Daladier. When in January 1934 it was discovered that a confidence man, Alexander Stavisky, had defrauded hundreds of investors in municipal bonds in Bayonne and that he had benefited for years from the protection of friendly politicians, the scandal became a political football. Authoritarian conservatives seized the occasion not only to condemn individual politicians but to blame such corruption on parliamentary democracy itself. The fact that Stavisky was Jewish was used by the AF to give the affair an anti-Semitic cast as well. Conservatives in the Chamber of Deputies used the affair as a pretext for defeating the new cabinet Daladier had proposed, a cabinet that they feared might raise taxes and make other compromises with the Socialists.

The right-wing press campaign that followed was led by the AF, whose newspaper blared, "DOWN WITH THE THIEVES!" and condemned parliament for not balancing the budget and for failing to "reduce the burden of taxation."[8]

The firing of Chiappe was the last straw. The AF called for a mass prot. demonstration on February 6. French newspapers from the extreme right to the center-right denounced the firing of Chiappe and protested the opening to the left. On February 4, *L'Echo de Paris* decried Chiappe's having been "delivered to the hatred of the Socialists and the Communists" and portrayed the fired prefect of police as "the man who for so many years had assured order in Paris [and] who had broken, one after another, all attempts at revolutionary insurrection." *Le Temps* condemned Daladier for caving in to the Socialists and declared that "the worn decor of our electoral and parliamentary theatre risks being thrown out overnight by a national uprising." On February 5, *Le Figaro* protested the "dictatorship of the revolutionary parties" and ran a proclamation of thirteen Paris municipal councilmen denouncing this "tyranny of sectarianism and immorality." On the morning of February 6, *L'Ami du Peuple* declared, "The country is in danger! Daladier is leading you like sheep to be butchered by Léon Blum." That same day *La Croix* noted that the Socialists had always been opposed to Chiappe because he had "severely bridled" their "revolutionary actions."

On February 5, Colonel de La Rocque announced that the CF would participate in the demonstration, claiming that "a government at the service of the red flag is attempting to reduce us to slavery." He added that the CF would "impose a government of decent Frenchmen free of any abject political combinations." La Rocque telegraphed CF paramilitary units throughout France: "The goal we pursue is to put an end to the dictatorship of the Socialist influence and to call to power a clean government *free of politicians of whatever kind*" (italics added).[9]

Such rhetoric notwithstanding, there was no fascist plot to overthrow the Third Republic on February 6. Charles Maurras, La Rocque, Pierre Taittinger, and the other league leaders were caught by surprise when the demonstration escalated into a massive riot that nearly stormed the Chamber of Deputies. Although the goal of these leaders was undemocratic in that they sought to prevent an elected parliament from expressing the will of the voters at large (on the evening of February 6 the chamber was slated to vote for or against the installation of Daladier's new cabinet), they had no intention of attempting a coup d'état. The organizers of the demonstration had not armed their followers in advance.

Furthermore, not all of the demonstrators involved were members of the fascist leagues. The large contingent of UNC members who participated were primarily concerned about veterans' benefits. Not to be outdone, the Communists also sent a group of ex-servicemen to defend these benefits. Members of the French League of Taxpayers who joined the demonstration, although extremely right-wing, also had limited aims. The AF, the SF, the JP, the CF, and the Francistes had broader goals, but they assumed that a counterrevolutionary coup was well beyond their reach in February 1934.

On the evening of February 6, some 40,000 demonstrators, divided into different columns and meeting at various rendezvous points, sought to increase pressure on the Chamber of Deputies through street action. At the Place de la Concorde, separated from the Chamber of Deputies by the Seine River, some 10,000 demonstrators clashed with the police defending the bridge. It was here that the bloodiest fighting took place, although there were other battles at other approaches to the Chamber of Deputies as well. Casualties on both sides were heavy. William L. Shirer, who witnessed the riots, later summarized the police statistics: "Among the estimated 40,000 rioters, fourteen were killed by bullets and two died later from their wounds; some 655 were injured, of whom 236 were hospitalized and the rest treated at first-aid stations. The police and the guards lost one killed and 1,664 injured, of whom 884 were able to resume service after their wounds were dressed. The guardians fired 527 revolver bullets; the number of shots fired by the rioters was never ascertained. It was the bloodiest encounter in the streets of Paris since the Commune of 1871."[10]

The same evening some 3,000 members of the CF also tried to intimidate parliament from the left bank of the Seine, one of their columns approaching the Chamber of Deputies from the rear by way of the rue de Bourgogne. In contrast to the spontaneous violence of AF, SF, and other demonstrators at the Place de la Concorde, the CF column was well disciplined. La Rocque was not with these troops, choosing to direct their movements and those of another CF column from a secret headquarters, using messengers to transmit his orders. The column on the rue de Bourgogne turned back when it ran into a barrier manned by Republican Guards.

The other CF column, approaching from the nearby rue Saint-Dominique, was also stopped by police forces, but about a hundred marchers broke through and made it to the rear gates of the Chamber of Deputies, where they were met by police reserves who beat them back with clubs. When at 9:00 P.M. La Rocque learned that the Chamber of Deputies had adjourned and that the parliamentarians were leaving the building, he telephoned both columns to encircle the chamber but to desist from further assaults. The next day he boasted, erroneously, that "the Croix de Feu had surrounded the Chamber and forced the deputies to flee."[11]

On February 7 Daladier chose to resign rather than risk further bloodshed, especially between police and war veterans, and he was succeeded by the conservative Gaston Doumergue. La Rocque described the Doumergue government as a "palliative without a future," a "temporary bandage for gangrene," and he called upon his supporters to "remain disposed to clean out the gangrene which will not be long in advancing further."[12] But most of the conservative press, though praising the "justifiable" outrage of the rioters, called for an end to social disorder, fearing that it could lead to civil war. That fear was exacerbated on February 9, when the Communists organized a counterdemonstration, which the police suppressed brutally, killing six workers. On February 12, the Confédération Générale du Travail (CGT, General confederation of labor) called a general strike in which more than four million workers participated throughout France. In Paris, for the first time in years, Socialist and Communist workers marched side by side in a mass procession to the Cour de Vincennes.

Most of the French conservative press welcomed the truce proposed by Doumergue. At the same time, these newspapers, instead of blaming the violence of February 6 on the demonstrators who perpetrated it, excoriated Daladier for having allowed the French police who were defending the Chamber of Deputies to fire upon the demonstrators. Still, the French right was generally contented with the outcome. The cartel had been defeated, and one of Doumergue's first acts in office was to appoint Chiappe to be the new minister of interior. Now the police forces of all of France, not just those of Paris, were under his direction. The appointment of Marshal Henri-Philippe Pétain as minister of war meant that the army was also firmly in conservative hands. There was no need for a fascist coup.

After June 1934, French conservatives had further reason to turn away from fascism. As previously noted, Hitler's Night of the Long Knives, which cost the lives of General von Schleicher and his wife (their photos were prominently displayed in the French press), did not set well with the French right. Neither did Hitler's subsequent repression of German Catholics and conservatives who challenged him. To murder and imprison leftists was one thing; to do the same to rightists was another. The French conservative press protested.[13]

In 1936, however, when the Popular Front came to power, conservative fears of fascism were increasingly outweighed by conservative fears of Marxism. As a result, a large section of the French right, though not a majority, began to look more sympathetically on domestic fascism.

THE POPULAR FRONT

In May 1936 French conservatives were faced with a far more serious threat from the left than they had been in February 1934, the election of the Popular Front.

The Popular Front coalition of Socialists, Communists, and liberals had come together to resist the fascist threat and pass a number of social reforms. In spite of its pledge (including that of the Communists) not to attempt to overthrow capitalism, the Popular Front was viewed by some French rightists as a prelude to Marxist revolution and civil war. Even less hysterical conservatives regarded much of the social legislation passed by the Popular Front during its first weeks in power, however modest by Marxist standards, as anathema.

Particularly galling to many French rightists were the sit-down strikes that immediately followed the election of the Popular Front in May. By June some two million workers were on strike in the Paris region alone, preventing employers from replacing them by occupying the factories in which they worked. As Gordon Wright has written, "France had known no social upheaval of such proportions since 1848."[14] Another historian, Henry Ehrmann, has underscored the personal humiliation that many French employers felt as a result of the sit-down strikes:

> In France, as elsewhere, ordinary strikes had become an accepted, though still resented, form of social anger; but the sit-down strike, then a completely novel form of labor conflict in France, added considerably to the humiliation of the employers. A factory emptied by a strike is still controlled by the boss; in a plant filled with strikers the employer has lost his place. His very position is disputed, which is more than the momentary divesting of profits. . . . When the boss of a struck plant wanted to leave the premises, he had to wait in line with his employees in order to obtain a pass from the minutely organized strike committee. The workers, while seldom lacking the customary politeness, enjoyed thoroughly and visibly the symbolic collapse of the hierarchy in the shop. . . . [As Simone Weil recalled,] "For the youth of the bourgeoisie, the shock of 1936 penetrated to irreparable depths. Nobody had done them harm. But they had been afraid, they had been humiliated by those they regarded as their inferiors, in their eyes an unpardonable crime."[15]

Blum ended the strikes by bringing together representatives of management and labor who concluded the famous Matignon accords. On June 17, workers won wage increases averaging 12 percent, the right to collective bargaining, and guarantees against reprisals for strike and other union activities. That same month, the Popular Front passed legislation in parliament providing for a forty-hour workweek and annual two-week vacations with pay for workers. The head of the CGT, Léon Jouhaux, described the outcome of the strikes as the greatest victory in the history of French labor. CGT membership quintupled to more than five million.

A host of additional measures poured forth from the Popular Front. On June

18, the fascist leagues were banned, at least in their paramilitary forms (they changed their names, transformed themselves into electoral parties, and continued to operate). The armaments industry and the Bank of France were nationalized, and special railroad fares were established to make it possible for workers to travel cheaply to vacation resorts. Attempts were made to democratize the transmission of high culture to the masses. The historian Julian Jackson has portrayed the explosion of cultural energies and street celebrations that took place during the first few months of the Popular Front. As one contemporary recalled, "In 1936 . . . we were twenty years old. But everyone was twenty years old in 1936."

Not everyone. Many businessmen and lower-middle-class conservatives remained hostile to the Popular Front. Jackson has described how the "language of hope" in 1936 was paralleled by the "language of fear," as many rightists met the Popular Front's "outstretched hand" and desire for reconciliation with the "revenge of management" and fierce opposition.[16]

Intensifying political emotions on both the right and the left after July 1936 was the outbreak of civil war in Spain, a country whose own democratically elected Popular Front government was now threatened by a military revolt led by General Francisco Franco. For much of the French public, the parallels were troubling. The bulk of the French right in 1936 preferred a parliamentary solution to France's social conflicts, although, as we shall see, a growing number of conservatives were attracted to the fascist temptation.

In *Revenge of the Bosses: Management before the Popular Front* (1986), Ingo Kolbloom recounts the bloodless counteroffensive that French industrialists carried out against the Popular Front in the months that followed.[17] Exploiting middle-class discontent with the sit-down strikes and the Matignon accords, these industrialists strengthened the right wing of the Radical party with their subsidies. In April 1937 the Radical party broke with the Popular Front, at first temporarily and a year later conclusively. Without the continuing support of the Radicals, Blum could not remain in power democratically. In April 1938, after a brief return to the premiership, he resigned for the final time. With the defeat of the Popular Front, the second wave of fascism in France receded.

During the year that the Popular Front was in power, the appeal of fascism was at its peak in France. The conservative backlash to the sit-down strikes of 1936 and to the left-wing legislation passed by the Popular Front brought French fascism a host of new supporters. The high point of French fascism during the interwar period was not in February 1934 at the time of the Stavisky affair but rather between May 1936 and April 1937, when the Popular Front was most threatening to conservative interests. The onset of the Depression in France in 1931 and the electoral victory of a new Cartel des Gauches in 1932 led to the emergence of the second wave of French fascism, and after 1936 middle-class hostility to the Popular Front caused it to swell.

Although the second wave of French fascism consisted of several rival fascist movements, some much smaller than others, its combined strength was considerable. When Hitler came to power in Germany in 1933 the total membership of the NSDAP was about 850,000 (if one includes Hitler Youth, 950,000), that is, about 1.5 percent of a national population of sixty million. In 1937 the CF alone had nearly a million members in a population of forty million. France was not as allergic to fascism as some scholars have claimed.

2 · Minor and Declining Fascisms, Newspaper Allies, and the Greenshirts

SMALL AND LARGE FASCISMS

In 1933 the extreme right in France consisted of a number of organizations and journals, ranging from insignificant fringe groups like Jean Hennessy's Parti Social National and Gustave Hervé's weekly newspaper *La Victoire* to the much larger SF movement and François Coty's mass circulation daily, *L'Ami du Peuple.* During the 1920s, the three major fascist movements in France had been the AF, the JP, and the Faisceau.[1] By 1933 only the first two survived, the Faisceau having sunk into oblivion when it lost its major financial backers in 1926. Although the JP and the AF continued to exist after 1933, their strength declined as newly founded fascist movements surpassed them.

In 1934, according to French police authorities, the largest fascist movement in France was the SF with approximately 180,000 party members (80,000 in Paris), followed by the CF with 100,000 (21,000 in Paris), the JP with 90,000 (6,400 in Paris), the AF with 60,000 (8,300 in Paris), and the Francistes with 1,500 (300 in Paris).[2] A few weeks after the riots of February 6, the SF collapsed when its major financial backer, François Coty, owing to personal business difficulties, could no longer subsidize the movement. Soon after the riots, the CF began its spectacular rise, eventually outdistancing all other French fascist movements by a wide margin.

By 1938 La Rocque's movement, renamed the Parti Social Français (PSF, French social party), had grown, according to the estimate of Philippe Machefer, to between 700,000 and 1.2 million party members, that is, to seven to ten times the size of its closest rival on the extreme right, Doriot's PPF, which had been founded in 1936. (Historians have estimated that in 1938 the PPF had between 50,000 and 100,000 members and 250,000 and 300,000 sympathizers.) Even if the minimum figure for La Rocque's movement (700,000) is taken as the most accurate, it was still larger than the total party memberships of the French Communist party and the French Socialist party *combined* in 1938 (600,000).[3]

After 1936, the history of French fascism was predominantly the history of the PSF and the PPF, these two movements having achieved the greatest mass support. Henri Dorgères's Peasant Front also attracted a large number of supporters after 1936, possibly as many as a quarter of a million, but because it was strictly a farmer's movement it remained more of an auxiliary to French fascism than a prime mover.

Ideologically, the PSF and the PPF owed a great deal to their supplanted rivals and to a fascist intellectual tradition that dated back to the 1880s. Just as this tradition had been tapped by the first wave of French fascism between 1924 and 1926, so it was by the second wave between 1933 and 1938. The party programs of the PSF and the PPF in 1936, as well as many of the spiritual justifications that accompanied them, were remarkably similar to those advanced by previous French fascist movements, including those of the SF.[4]

Yet consensus historians who agree that the ephemeral SF was fascist refuse to place the CF (which welcomed many of the SF's troops when the SF collapsed) in the same category. Of course, differences existed between these movements, but they have often been exaggerated by historians who insist that fascism never had a significant following in France.

THE FRANCISTES

One fascist movement that did not have a large following in France—and that consensus historians have willingly called fascist—was Francisme. Ideologically, the Francistes had a great deal in common with both the CF and the PPF. Founded in September 1933 by Marcel Bucard, a former member of the AF, the Faisceau, and the CF, the Francistes adopted many of the trappings of Italian fascism, including blue shirts and blue berets for its shock troops and the Roman salute for its public meetings.

Although the Francistes claimed to be committed to a national socialist revolution, their socioeconomic program was highly conservative. Bucard fundamentally agreed with La Rocque and Doriot on most of the major social, economic, political, and cultural issues of the day. What distinguished Bucard from La Rocque and Doriot was not Bucard's alleged socialism but his willingness to publicly label himself a fascist, his repeated praise of Mussolini's Italy, the vulgarity of his personality, his cruder appeals for violence, and, after 1936, his intense anti-Semitism.

Like La Rocque and Doriot, Bucard professed to support a republican form of government even as he described parliamentary democracy as decadent and "disastrous." Like them, too, he paid lip service to popular rule while calling for its demise; claimed to be devoted to political liberty ("Liberty or death!" he cried), while advocating more discipline and authority in French society; portrayed left-wing authoritarianism as a threat to freedom and right-wing authoritarianism as its safeguard; rejected anti-Semitism at first only to adopt it after 1936; decried bureaucratic centralization in government, particularly when it was Socialist centralization; called for a decentralized and regional approach to economic affairs, while demanding more unity and cohesion in political affairs; detested Marxism, class struggle, and secular humanism and extolled corporatism, class collaboration, and right-wing Catholicism; despised the French Socialist and Communist parties and demanded their "radical destruction"; and was appalled by the victory of the Popular Front in 1936.

Like spokesmen for the CF and the PPF, Bucard denounced decadent bourgeois but honored virile bourgeois. Like them, he damned Marxist materialism and promised a spiritual revolution based on the military values of the First World War. Like them, he defended private property as "the fruit of one's labor and savings" and said that he was no leftist if *left* meant "sharing property and allowing the State to interfere in private affairs." Like them, he opposed a "King-State" that would nationalize the basic means of production. Like them, he rejected Socialist egalitarianism: "Whether one likes it or not, inequality is the law of nature. . . . [The strong] are born to command, [the weak] born to obey. Society must . . . be based on a logically and solidly established hierarchy."[5] Like them, he called for a national revolution, but for one that would protect capitalism, not overthrow it. On social and economic issues, Bucard was no more leftist than La Rocque or Doriot and no less fascist for it.

Unlike La Rocque and Doriot, however, Bucard failed to attract mass support for his movement. In 1934 the Francistes had only fifteen hundred members throughout France, and in 1935 its four-page weekly newspaper, *Le Franciste*, published only fifteen thousand copies a week. Bucard lacked the necessary financial backing to create a strong movement. The one million francs in subsidies that he received from fascist Italy between 1934 and 1936 was a relatively small amount compared to the funds that the CF and the PPF took in.

According to the historian Alain Deniel, the sums that Bucard garnered from French sources were quite modest compared to those of other political organizations in France. Although Bucard sometimes portrayed himself as an antibourgeois national socialist who was on the side of the people, his major financial backers were upper middle class and socially conservative. They included two industrialists from Tours and one from Paris, two shipowners, the co-owner of a perfume company, and the president of an anti-Marxist institute for peasants and independents.[6]

THE JEUNESSES PATRIOTES

A much more important French fascist movement of the 1930s, a holdover from the 1920s, was the Jeunesses Patriotes (JP) (Patriotic youth), a movement whose ideology and previous history have been described in the first volume of this study. As late as 1935, the JP was a significant force on the French right with some eighty thousand party members, including at least seventy-six parliamentary deputies and a number of municipal councilors. It helped organize the February 6 demonstration, and its blueshirts were among those who battled the police in the Place de la Concorde. The JP's leader was Pierre Taittinger, a wealthy businessman with extensive champagne and real estate holdings. He was also a Paris municipal councilman and a member of the Chamber of Deputies.

Throughout the 1920s Taittinger's allegiance to political democracy had fluctuated widely, depending on the circumstances. In 1925 his blueshirts had given the fascist salute at JP meetings and shouted "Dictatorship! Dictatorship!"[7] Following the defeat of the first Cartel des Gauches in 1926, however, Taittinger had adopted a more democratic posture, extending his support to conservative politicians like Poincaré and professing his loyalty to the republic.

In 1933, however, taking advantage of the growing antiparliamentarianism of the period, he returned to a more authoritarian stance. Although he said he rejected a dictatorship of the old-fashioned kind, he declared himself in favor of one that would "renovate" France's economy. He declared, "This is why, like people in Italy and Germany, we will follow a Leader who will take us along new paths."[8] William Irvine has summarized the alternative that Taittinger presented to French conservatives:

> The Jeunesses Patriotes proposed an authoritarian leadership in the form of a powerful chief-of-state elected by the various *notables* and *corps* of French society. The power of parliament would be correspondingly reduced, ministers would no longer be chosen from its midst, deputies would lose all initiative in financial matters, and parliament would be limited to controlling public expenses and voting laws proposed by the chief-of-state and his ministers. The program of the Jeunesses Patriotes called for the end of the [King Parliament] and the restoration of discipline and authority to French government. Spiritually, the Jeunesses Patriotes harked back to the plebiscitarian dictatorship of the Second Empire, but in the 1930s certain elements of the Jeunesses Patriotes also seemed akin to more contemporary dictatorships. The blue windbreakers and basque berets worn by the Jeunesses Patriotes reminded contemporary observers of the Italian Blackshirts. In the Rhone, *Alerte* (the local journal of the Jeunesses Patriotes) lauded the youth who had purged Germany, Spain, and Italy of Marxism and signaled out for praise the Squadristi, the cadets of the Alcazar, and such German patriotes as Horst Wessel.[9]

None of this prevented the JP from developing close ties with the *modérés* of the FR. Not only were three vice-presidents of the FR members of the JP in 1933 (including Taittinger himself), but according to Irvine, "Many of the municipal councilors of Paris also belonged to the two organizations. At the local level the same individuals often headed the branches of both the party and the league."[10]

In 1930 relations between the JP and the FR were temporarily strained when Taittinger decided to form an electoral party of his own, the Parti Républicain National et Social (National and social republican party). The attempt fizzled, however, when Taittinger failed to attract sufficient financial support. After 1932 the JP remained subservient to the FR, causing many of Taittinger's more militant supporters eventually to go over to CF. The JP's decline was paralleled by the CF's ascent.

THE ACTION FRANÇAISE

Another established French fascist movement in 1933 that would be outdistanced by both La Rocque's CF and Doriot's PPF was the Action Française (AF), headed by Charles Maurras. I have described in the preceding volume some of the fascist characteristics of this movement, including its repeated praise for many of Mussolini's domestic policies after 1922. The reader is also referred to

Eugen Weber's classic study of the AF for a more detailed account of its activities in the 1930s.[11]

Throughout the interwar period, the AF was severely limited in its mass appeal by its defense of royalism, which was rejected by an overwhelming majority of the French population. Nevertheless, the AF had considerable influence in right-wing intellectual circles, where its highly literate and highly vicious criticisms of political, social, and cultural democracy were often echoed by non-royalist authoritarian conservatives. Yves Simon, a Catholic liberal, would later blame the AF for weakening the resistance of many French intellectuals, especially Catholic intellectuals, to fascism in the 1930s:

> Powerful among all the intelligentsia, the *Action Française* exercised . . . an almost complete dictatorship over Catholic intellectual circles. Whoever came out as a democrat in these circles was doomed to be the object of an ironic and scornful pity; he was looked down upon as a person behind the times, a survivor of another age. In order to appear up to date and to succeed in your career, you had to denounce liberal errors with an air of self-satisfied superiority, scoff at liberty, equality and fraternity, joke about progress, look skeptical when human dignity and the rights of conscience were spoken of, affirm authoritatively that every plan for international order was a bloody dream, and sneer at the League of Nations. All this went on in an atmosphere of impudent arrogance.

Simon also describes the special attraction that the AF's newspaper had for many French intellectuals of the period:

> The lover of belles-lettres, provided he was not too particular about truth and justice, was assured an hour of bliss every morning provided he subscribed to *L'Action Française*. There was a daily article by Léon Daudet, racy, violent, joyous, full of witty sayings which provoked laughter, and were easily remembered; there was the daily article of Charles Maurras, sententious, grave, doctrinal, and coldly ruthless; and there was the daily article of Jacques Bainville, who wrote as well as Voltaire. . . . Each issue of the paper, or nearly each, comprised an exposition of the [AF's ideological] system, cleverly summed up in a small number of clichés, always the same, which the reader knew by heart at the end of a month, and repeated with as much pleasure as though he had devised them himself. An habitual reader of *L'Action Française* had an answer for everything, and it never occurred to him to question the validity of what he was taught with such dogmatic assurance and literary talent.[12]

NEWSPAPER ALLIES

Along with *Action Française* (which had a circulation of 100,000), three other journals of the extreme right—*Gringoire, Candide,* and *Je suis Partout*—

influenced French intellectual circles. At the beginning of 1936, *Gringoire* had the largest circulation (640,000), followed by *Candide* (349,000), and *Je suis Partout* (40,000). The editor of *Gringoire* was Horace de Carbuccia, the son-in-law of Jean Chiappe, Paris's reactionary prefect of police in 1934. All three journals appealed to well-educated, conservative readers. Political commentary was supplemented by literary criticism and writings by leading authors of the day. Among the contributors to *Gringoire*, for example, were François Mauriac, Georges Bernanos, Colette, George Simenon, P. G. Wodehouse, and Somerset Maugham. Carbuccia said that his journal found its audience "among the big and petty bourgeoisie, among white-collar workers, in the army, on all the warships, among the students. So many friends in the Latin Quarter!"[13] By the end of 1936, *Gringoire*'s circulation had risen to 965,000.

Carbuccia noted that as an enemy of the Popular Front *Gringoire* replied to the insults of the Communists and the vulgarities of the Socialists with flippant ridicule and biting satire. According to Carbuccia, this explained why its circulation was so much greater than that of comparable journals on the left, whose earnestness was deadly boring (172–74, 177). *Je suis Partout* also had a taste for satire. Its young editor, Robert Brasillach, who touted the youthful qualities of fascism, set a flippant tone that was much closer to that of an Ivy League campus newspaper in the United States than to a serious journal of opinion in France.

Gringoire, Je suis Partout, and *Candide* were also antidemocratic and anti-Semitic. None of these journals, however, founded political organizations, although all three had ties with the AF; they were content to restrict their role to opinion making. One of the advantages of remaining independent of political parties, especially of electoral parties in need of public support, was that writers like Carbuccia and Brasillach could afford to be more openly contemptuous of the masses than could politicians like La Rocque and Doriot. But it was La Rocque and Doriot, leaders intent on achieving direct political power through mass political action, who were the greatest threats to French democracy.

THE GREENSHIRTS

An important offshoot of the AF that was politically organized was Dorgères's Peasant Front, better known as the Greenshirts, founded in 1934. Although the Peasant Front had an extensive rural following, it had no pretensions, as did the major French fascist organizations of the period, of eventually taking control of the state. Unlike the SF, CF, or PPF, it eschewed the multiclass appeal that such an aim would have required. Although Dorgères's Greenshirts sometimes supported other fascist movements (in 1938 Doriot noted they had "lent a hand" to the PPF at Rennes "as we have aided them elsewhere"), they chose to remain organizationally independent and primarily concerned with farm issues.

Because many of Dorgères's political views were the same as those of the SF, CF, and PPF, however, these organizations went to some lengths to court the front's favor. The primary appeal of the Greenshirts was to right-wing, proper-tied farmers, not to left-wing, unpropertied farmworkers. Indeed, one of the major goals of the movement was to protect the landed from the landless.

Dorgères, whose real name was Henri d'Halluin, had been a member of the AF before founding his own organization. The editor of a newspaper for farmers, *Le Cri du Sol* (Cry of the soil), he specialized in defending rural interests in earthy language. In 1937, after a Greenshirt meeting had been banned by the prefect of the Var, he responded with an article in *Le Cri du Sol* entitled "Messieurs Prefects, Hide your Asses!"[14]

In 1934 Dorgères was sentenced to three months in prison for leading a demonstration blocking the foreclosure of a farm. This made him a hero to many farmers, especially to a growing number of supporters in Algeria. In September 1935, the Paris police intercepted a telegram sent to AF headquarters which read, "The movement for agrarian defense is taking on considerable proportions in Algeria. . . . This movement, which is arousing support in the departments of Algers and Oran at a record rate, indicates the general discontent of our Algerian colons who, faced with the failures of the government, have decided to take action under the wise organization of the Peasant Front and the banner of Dorgères, whose imprisonment has aroused the desire to rebel in all the country areas of the colony."[15]

In 1934 and 1935, Dorgères's Peasant Front held numerous political rallies throughout France and Algeria, meetings that often led to brawls between Dorgères's Greenshirts and left-wing adversaries. In 1935 Dorgères called for a tax strike against the government. As a result, he was condemned to eight months in prison by a court in Rouen, a judgment that increased his popularity in rural areas. In his book *Raise the Pitchforks* (1935), he called for lower taxes, higher prices for farm goods, and higher tariffs against foreign competition. He also, despite his demand for lower taxes, urged the government to build more railroad lines in the countryside and to expand rural electrification.

Dorgères accused the politicians of the Third Republic of sacrificing the peasant to the city dweller. Although he insisted that he himself was a republi-can dedicated to liberty of conscience ("I wish to leave to each person the most complete liberty to express his philosophical and religious opinions"), he railed against the "nefarious struggle between political parties" and advocated expanding the authority of the state. A strong state, he said, would "make domestic order reign, render justice, ensure that public education was founded on a patriotic basis, and make all its servants obey it."[16] This "defense of the republican regime" was accompanied by a demand for a corporatist assembly based on occupational categories.

Although Dorgères was opposed to war (the last war, he said, had left too many peasant boys on the field of battle), he was not opposed to violence per se, especially if it was directed at France's parliamentary politicians. Whereas the CF implied that France's war veterans were best suited for this task, Dorgères believed that peasants would do just as well. In 1935 he wrote, "The pitchfork for the peasant is a work instrument, but it is also a fighting instrument which he grabs to chase off the tramps who try to steal from his farm. [It is] the weapon which will chase away the politicians who are responsible for the ruin and the dishonor of his country" (201, 202).

Dorgères also attacked the "feudal barons of finance" and the "big trusts" of the cities for exploiting France's peasants as well as urban life itself for corrupting those who had left the farm. Whereas a rural dweller lived a healthy and wise life, the proletarian of the city was "out of sorts, uprooted, bitter, the victim of [city] newspapers, cinemas, dance halls, and sordid music halls." One of the evils of military conscription was that a few months in a barracks brought the young peasant into contact with the false pleasures of the wicked city. Moreover, the exodus from the countryside had led to the "nefarious 'proletarianization' of the French people," a trend that could be reversed only by reviving artisanal production in France's villages. Urban individualism was also nefarious: "The true cell of society is the family, not the individual" (95, 103, 106, 110).

When a split developed within the Peasant Front in 1936, Dorgères founded another movement, the Committees of Peasant Defense. This organization established some sixty political federations throughout France, with a dozen of them boasting more than ten thousand members each. Six provincial newspapers carried Dorgères's message to the countryside. Although Dorgères refused to allow his movement to be absorbed by other French fascisms, he was on good terms with several of their supporters, including Jacques Lemaigre-Dubreuil, an oil baron who helped finance the Cagoule, a right-wing terrorist organization.[17]

In 1936, when the Popular Front came to power, Dorgères accused the new government of being a lackey of international communism. His previous demand for a government with more authority did not apply to Blum's government. Dorgères insisted in February 1937 that "syndicalist liberties" not be superseded by "state intervention." It was in this context, that is, with the French government having shifted to the left, that a writer for *Le Cri du Sol* wrote that although Dorgères's movement was both "profoundly national and profoundly social" it was opposed to both "Asiatic" and "fascist" dictatorships: "Certain political men of the right prefer the Mussolini of Italy or the Germany of Hitler to our country. Certain men of the extreme left have had themselves elected by French workers in order to defend, in France, the interests of the bloody fascist dictatorship of Russia and to betray their own country. Such men no longer belong to the 'soul of the country.' The peasants are nationalists, since they are all Frenchmen—with the exception of some immigrant workers and farmers. They will defend, if it is threatened, the liberty of their country, the liberty of their conscience, their own liberty."[18] As we shall see, this mixture of libertarian rhetoric with authoritarian sentiments was typical of other French fascist movements of the period as well.

Dorgères joined the Vichy government in 1941 and publicly supported Pétain as late as 1943, despite the marshal's decision to collaborate with the Germans. In 1941 Dorgères declared that "the regime of liberty [the Third Republic] was finished" but said that this regime had led only to the liberty to starve. He blamed France's defeat in 1940 partly on "the peasants themselves," who had been too prone to political divisiveness before the war (that is, some had supported the left). Under Pétain, Dorgères wrote, there would "no longer be any political dissent, no longer any battles between unions of the right and left." Pétain was not only the savior of France but the country's "boss": "It is he who is in charge, who decides, and it is he whom we obey. . . . Our duty is to follow him as we would follow a father."[19]

After the Second World War, Dorgères continued to appeal to a section of the peasantry while clinging to his fascist sentiments. In 1956 he was elected from a rural district to the Chamber of Deputies of the Fifth Republic. In 1957 he supported the tax revolt led by Pierre Poujade, and in 1965 he backed the neofascist Jean-Louis Tixier-Vignancour in his unsuccessful bid for the presidency of the Fifth Republic.

THE CAGOULE

Much smaller than Dorgères's Peasant Front was France's most notorious terrorist organization of the 1930s, the Comité secret d'action révolutionnaire

(Secret committee of revolutionary action), nicknamed the Cagoule (Hooded cloak). The Cagoule captured headlines in the French press in 1937 when its clandestine activities were finally exposed. Founded by former members of the CF and the AF shortly after the Popular Front came to power in 1936, the Cagoule was dedicated to barring the route to communism by any means necessary, including bombings and assassinations. Its leader, Eugène Deloncle, feared that the sit-down strikes of 1936 were a prelude to a Marxist revolution in France. Viewing the Third Republic as too soft on communism and drawing a parallel between the Popular Front in France and the Popular Front in Spain, Deloncle wanted for France what Franco had undertaken for Spain, a military insurrection against a legal but leftist government.[20]

Hoping that the French army would accept its services in a civil war against the reds and willing to engage in violence even prior to such an eventuality, the Cagoule created a number of armed, underground, "self-defense" groups. There were secret Cagoulard units in the provinces as well as in Paris, including Joseph Darnand's Knights of the Sword in Nice, which was one of the most active. The Cagoule even had an Arab regiment, led by an Algerian, El Maadi, who had some 300 men under his command. (In 1940 El Maadi and his men became members of the so-called French Gestapo that conducted numerous operations against the Resistance.) Although Deloncle later boasted that in 1937 he could have called upon some 12,000 men in the Paris region and 120,000 throughout France to fight against the Communists if need be, the size of the Cagoule was probably much smaller. (A standard practice of most French fascist leaders during the interwar period was to exaggerate their membership figures in order to attract financial support.) In 1937 and 1938 a police roundup of suspected Cagoulards netted only 71 persons.

It is not clear how successful the Cagoule was in its attempts to establish ties with the High Command of the French army. Deloncle told his followers that they could "always rely on the army" to help them defeat a Communist revolution. At his trial in 1948, one former Cagoulard, Gabriel Jeantet, claimed that Cagoule units throughout France would have "acted in harmony with Paris Army Headquarters in an ensemble directed by the military." Another ex-Cagoulard testified, "We were given instructions for street combat. . . . If there was [a revolutionary threat from the left], I was to go to the Place de Vincennes and put myself at the disposition of Colonel Reynaud. I did not want to do anything without the participation of the army."[21]

A leading member of the French High Command in 1936 was Marshal Pétain, who later appointed a number of Cagoulards to important government posts under Vichy. However, in 1945 both Léon Blum and Edouard Daladier denied that Pétain had cooperated with the Cagoule in 1936. In 1948, testifying at a trial of former Cagoulards, Daladier insisted that "neither any general officer nor any officer of the General Staff of the Army had ever had contact with the Cagoule"; he added that had a Communist revolution occurred in 1936 the army would have been quite capable of "handling things within a few hours" without any outside help.[22]

At the same trial, however, Major Georges Loustaunau-Lacau told how, as a member of Pétain's staff in 1936, he had created the Corvignolles, a secret organization to combat Communist activities in the army, and how he had been sent by Marshal Franchet d'Esperey (who donated 1.5 million francs to the Corvignolles) to see the retired general Edmond Duseigneur, one of the top leaders of the Cagoule. According to the historian Paul-Marie de la Gorce, "Regular reports on the activities of the Corvignolles network were addressed to Marshal Pétain and Marshal Franchet d'Esperey, to General Georges, who was then Chief of Staff of the Army, to several members of the Army Council, and to several commanders of military districts."[23] At his trial in 1948, Loustaunau-Lacan denied that any permanent liaison between the Corvignolles and the Cagoule had been established, despite their common goal. The former military governor of Paris, General Prételat, testified that he had received an offer of paramilitary support from Deloncle and some of his associates in 1936 in the event of a Communist uprising. Prételat recalled, "I had the impression that these people were good Frenchmen who wanted to help us. Unfortunately, we could not accept their services. They wanted the army to permit them to fight in civilian clothes in its ranks."[24]

In 1936 the Cagoule set about establishing a number of secret arms caches throughout France and offered target practice for its members at Montrouge, Saint-Denis, and Arpajon. In October 1937 the police raided a basement in Paris where the Cagoule stored some of its weapons. They found two tons of munitions, four hundred grenades, four hundred explosives, five thousand rounds of ammunition, twelve rifles, and sixteen submachine guns. The room also had a cell for prisoners. In the days that followed, the police discovered other arms caches and prisoner cells at other locations as well as records of secret operational plans that designated the cells for government ministers and other political enemies whom the Cagoule planned to arrest in the event of a Communist revolution. The French minister of interior in 1937, the Socialist Marx Dormoy, told a press conference, "Messieurs, it is a veritable plot against republican institutions that we have discovered. The documents that have been seized reveal that those guilty had given themselves the goal of substituting [for the republic] a dictatorial regime meant to precede the restoration of the monarchy."25

The police found a list of addresses in one of its raids and arrested a number of Cagoule members, including Deloncle and General Duseigneur, who had served as military adviser to the minister of air following the First World War. Deloncle and Duseigneur had visited both Franco and Mussolini in 1936 and had established close contacts with the Italian espionage service. Following their arrest in 1937, they were given prison sentences but were released by the Vichy government in 1940. Deloncle was given an important post in Vichy's Ministry of Armaments, the authorities apparently appreciating not only his politics but his experience as a former arms trafficker. In 1941 some ex-Cagoulards assassinated Dormoy by detonating a bomb under his bed.

The Cagoule's history of violence started in 1936. In October a member of the Cagoule who had revealed the existence of the organization to a nonmember was taken to a forest outside Paris, given thirty minutes to make his peace with God, stabbed to death, and buried on the spot. One of the most infamous acts of the Cagoule was its assassination of the Rosselli brothers in Normandy in June 1937. Carlo and Sabatino Rosselli were two Italian antifascists who had continued to criticize Mussolini after he came to power. Although the Duce finally had them arrested, they escaped from prison and found refuge in France, where they launched an antifascist Italian journal, *Justice and Liberty*. In 1936 the Rosselli brothers began calling for Italian volunteers to fight against Franco in Spain. Rome ordered the assassination of the Rosselli brothers and, having previously supplied the Cagoule with money and arms, asked it to do the deed.

Six Cagoulards, including Jean-Marie Bouvier, the son of a Parisian industrialist, carried out the task. At his trial in 1948, one of the killers, Ferdinand Jacubiez, recalled that the leader of the band, Jean Filliol, had distributed daggers to everyone before the murders and that after Filliol had shot the Rosselli brothers with an automatic pistol Jacubiez himself had stabbed Sabatino Rosselli, whose body was later found with twenty-one dagger wounds. "I thought at the time that I was acting for France," Jacubiez testified. He remembered that in the car ride home "everyone was quite gay."26

Three months later, on September 11, 1937, Jacubiez and other Cagoulards set a bomb that destroyed the Paris headquarters of the Confédération générale du Patronat français (General confederation of French management), one of France's leading business associations, located on the rue de Presbourg within a short distance of the Arc de Triomphe. The bomb was so powerful that four stories of the building collapsed. Two police officers were killed. Also blown up on September 11 were the offices of the Union des Industries métallurgiques (Union of metallurgical industries). The following day several French newspapers blamed the bombings on Communists, anarchists, and other leftists who were accused of employing the same tactics in France that their counterparts had employed in Spain. Some Spanish refugees were even arrested in Toulouse in reaction to the bombings, the police overlooking the fact that a bomb of exactly the same type had been placed two weeks before in a hangar at Toussus-le-Noble in an attempt to destroy airplanes destined for Republican Spain.

As Philippe Bourdrel, a journalist who has written extensively on the Cagoule, has pointed out, the main purpose of the rue de Presbourg bombing was to spark a red scare that would work to the benefit of the Cagoule: "These attacks, blamed on the Communists, [were meant to] arouse public opinion against them, increase the anxieties of moderates, create a climate of civil war, and prepare the way for the intervention of the true 'forces of order,' those of the Cagoule."[27]

Who joined the Cagoule? Its founder, Eugène Deloncle, was a naval engineer and graduate of the prestigious Ecole Polytechnique. A decorated war veteran and an experienced administrator, he had become the president of several maritime associations. In 1934 he had joined the AF to oppose communism. As a member of the *camelots du roi*, the combat group of the AF, he had belonged to a unit commanded by Jean Filliol. In 1936, when he decided to form the Cagoule, Deloncle was joined not only by Filliol and General Duseigneur but also by the former vice-president of the CF, Pozzo di Borgo. Di Borgo had broken with La Rocque that year when La Rocque, faced with a government decree banning his movement as a paramilitary organization, had chosen to turn the CF into an electoral party, the PSF, rather than resort to counterrevolutionary violence against the Popular Front.

When di Borgo, Deloncle, and several other Cagoulards were arrested in November 1937, *Paris-Soir* commented, "It appears that all the conspirators had belonged to the dissolved paramilitary leagues, which they had left even before the dissolution decree because they found [the leagues] too 'lukewarm.'" Typical of why these former members of the AF and the CF joined the Cagoule was the remark of René Locuty, the Cagoulard who set the bomb at the rue de Presbourg: "I acted in good faith. I wanted to defend my country against Communism." Gabriel Jeantet, the leading theoretician of the Cagoule, recalled his fears in 1936 of an imminent Marxist insurrection. "The civil war in Spain and the strike movement in France troubled us," he said. "And several banks and industrialists had opened their purses to us."[28]

At his trial in 1948, Jeantet testified that the 1.5 million francs that had been given to the Cagoule by Franchet d'Espery, a retired field marshal, was "the product of a 'collection' taken among some industrialists and businessmen who had decided to fight Communism." Jeantet and other defendants said that Jacques Lemaigre-Dubreuil, the owner of the Lesieur oil company and president of the League of Taxpayers, and André Michelin, the tire manufacturer, had given a million francs each and that Louis Renault, of Renault automobiles, had also contributed. Jeantet added that some engineers and managers at the Michelin plant at Clermont-Ferrand had formed a group, Children of the Auvergne, to combat the strike movement in 1936 and to restore discipline in its factory.[29] According to Bourdrel,

> The outstretched hand of the Cagoule brought in millions in 1936; money poured into its treasury from direct [and] indirect channels. . . . The great companies of the automobile and tire industries contributed; aperitif and toothpaste companies, just as well known, along with several banks and insurance companies, donated large sums. A later Cagoule defendant stated that Eugène Deloncle had received a million francs from Lemaigre-Dubreuil, the director of the Lesieur oil company. By all appearances, Lemaigre-Dubreuil himself belonged to the Cagoule. [Deloncle] was equally supported by Marshal Franchet d'Esperey who proclaimed his patriotism to the industrial associations and banking groups that he solicited.[30]

In spite of the conservative nature of this financing, Jeantet and Deloncle later claimed that they were socialists. In 1942, as a supporter of the Vichy regime, Jeantet defended a "national and socialist revolution" whose program was "as far removed from that of the [conservative] Bloc National as from that of the Popular Front." In a typical piece of fascist double-talk, Jentet both condemned capitalism and upheld it. Distinguishing between immoral, capitalist "sharks" who sought to bilk the public and responsible industrialists and businessmen who were dedicated to the common good, Jeantet agreed with Marshal Pétain that the profit motive should remain "the powerful motive" of production. He was both for the nationalization of the trusts and opposed to statism.[31]

The same kind of double-talk characterized Deloncle's article "Why I am a Socialist," published in 1941. Deloncle appealed to nationalists who were "profoundly socialist" and to socialists who were "profoundly nationalist" to forget their former animosities and work together on behalf of social justice. Together they would punish both the profiteers and the lazy, respecting the value of "private initiative" while making the common good their aim. "Never again should money become a means of political domination," he wrote. "Never again should the existence of trusts be tolerated." Although private property would "continue" and the owner of a firm would control its funds, class collaboration would lead to increased production, and profit sharing would lead to increased benefits for workers.

Like Jeantet, Deloncle ruled out traditional trade unions and greater plant democracy in favor of corporatist unions that would include both management and labor. Although such corporatism would no doubt have represented management far more than labor, Deloncle saw no problem: "Worker, white collar, and managerial corporatism must put an end to the enemy unions of former times. The worker therein must have larger access to social gains, while leaving all the responsibilities for the operations of the enterprise to management."[32]

In 1941 Deloncle attacked the "execrable" types who opposed collaboration with the Germans ("Jews, Freemasons, supporters of the ex-Popular Front, courtiers and creatures of England") and linked his own collaboration to the reasons that had led him to found the Cagoule in 1936:

> In March 1936, the tragic situation of France seemed crystal clear to me. On the domestic scene, the Popular Front was organizing. The Communists, the most active wing of the Popular Front, did not mask their desire to achieve revolution through force.
>
> Combat troops, forming a red guard, were being trained and prepared for action. Attempts were being made within the army, navy, and police to create Communist cells. . . .
>
> One must remember the strained atmosphere, charged with electricity, surrounding our political and social battles. France was a boiling cauldron, the neighbor of a partly exploded cauldron . . . , Spain.
>
> Blum and his team were attempting to triumph. They had suspended legality in fact, without daring, however, to do it in principle. The Code which protected the liberty of citizens and their private wealth was not abolished, but the police had been ordered not to respond to the complaints of persons whose property had been molested, sequestered, or seized.[33]

By 1942, however, Deloncle had had his fill of the Germans and resigned from the Vichy government. In 1943 he was arrested and interrogated by the Germans on suspicion of having supported the Allied invasion of North Africa. Following his release, he traveled to Spain, where he met with friends to plot the assassination of Hitler. In 1944 he was in France when two French Gestapo agents were sent to arrest him. When the agents, fearing armed resistance, opened fire with their submachine guns, Deloncle shot back with a revolver and was killed by their return fire.

Deloncle was not the only ex-Cagoulard to turn against the Germans. As early as 1940, one of Deloncle's former supporters, François Duclos, crossed the

Channel to join de Gaulle in London. In August, Duclos parachuted into Normandy and founded the famous Saint-Jacques branch of the French Resistance. During the war, he blew up railroad tracks and other military targets in France and later fought beside the Allies in Normandy and Belgium. When, after the war, he stood trial for his role in the Cagoule, he wore his Cross of the Liberation, Croix de Guerre, Medal of the Resistance, and Military Cross. As Philippe Bourdrel points out, he was "naturally acquitted."[34] Gabriel Jeantet also entered the Resistance, after 1942. Jacques Corrèze, a member of the Cagoule's central committee in 1936, fought with the Germans on the Russian front in 1941 as a member of the French Volunteer Legion against Bolshevism, only to go over to the Resistance in 1943.

Joseph Darnand, on the other hand, collaborated with the Germans to the very end, serving under Vichy as the head of the Milice, an organization that waged armed combat against the Resistance and aided the Germans in their police operations. Darnand's final words before being executed in 1945 by a Liberation firing squad were "Long live France!"

THE FASCIST LEFT: DÉAT AND BERGERY

Not all talk of fascist socialism in the 1930s was double-talk. Although the largest French fascist movements of the period were fundamentally conservative in their social and economic goals—and thus the socialism they espoused spurious—some fascist movements in France during this period were genuinely left wing, at least at their inception. Some French Communists, Socialists, and Radical-Socialists in the 1930s were drawn toward what Philippe Burrin has called the "fascist drift."[35] The most prominent were Marcel Déat, Gaston Bergery, and Jacques Doriot—although by 1937 Doriot's PPF had become clearly a part of the fascist right (and will be discussed later under this category). Déat and Bergery continued to be dedicated to left-wing goals throughout the 1930s. Neither of these leaders attracted a significant mass following, their movements being much smaller than the major French fascist movements of the period.

Both Déat and Bergery sought to increase middle-class support for socialism by incorporating certain fascist themes into their propaganda, including appeals to nationalism, authoritarianism, irrationalism, and spirituality. In doing so, they came into conflict with the vast majority of members of the French Socialist party (SFIO), who remained committed to more internationalist, democratic, rationalistic, and humanitarian principles.[36] Déat and Bergery were also at odds with the French Communist party (PCF), not because of its authoritarianism and ruthlessness, but because of its doctrines of proletarian class struggle and Marxist internationalism, doctrines that conflicted with their emphasis on class conciliation and French nationalism. In the 1930s Déat and Bergery presented their approach as a way of defeating fascism, not supporting it, as a way of subtracting middle-class support from fascism and adding it to the left. In 1940, however, their revisionism having increasingly distanced them from both the Socialist and Communist lefts in France, they chose to collaborate with right-wing fascism rather than resist it.

During the 1930s, fascist leftists in France had little success, either among French industrial workers or among progressive sections of the middle classes, the bulk of these groups remaining loyal to either the French Communist, Socialist, or Radical parties. Partly because the Communists and Socialists could point to the repression of labor unions in fascist Italy and Nazi Germany, attempts by Déat and Bergery to move Marxism in a fascist direction were rejected by most French workers. Leftists who sought to employ fascist means for socialist ends were primarily intellectuals or dissident Socialist or Radical politicians who had little mass support. As Burrin has written, the movements they launched were never of more than marginal importance.[37]

Both Déat and Bergery were influenced by the writings of the Belgian Socialist Henri de Man, especially his *Beyond Socialism* (1928). De Man argued that Marxism was being outdone by fascism in Europe because fascism had found more effective ways of mobilizing the masses, especially large sectors of the petite bourgeoisie. Marxist doctrines of class struggle alienated both bourgeois and bourgeosified workers and ignored the appeal of political and cultural nationalism. In 1933 de Man, who had witnessed Nazism's defeat of the Socialists in Germany, wrote that the left could triumph over fascism only by resorting to some of the same irrational appeals. In 1936 he added, "It is a fact that the masses have a desire to believe in authoritarian and responsible leaders and especially to love them. They get disgusted with parliamentary democracy because it tends to prevent the formation of personages of heroic stature. . . . We [Socialists] should give them joy. We should appeal to their sensibility. . . . However low their standard of living may be, men experience the greatest joys more through the pride that is inculcated in them than through the [economic] advantages that are promised them."[38]

In 1933 Déat, then still a leading member of the SFIO, called for a revision of Marxism that he labeled Neo-Socialism. He maintained that the SFIO could defeat fascism only by forging a class alliance of workers, bourgeois, and peasants against big capitalism. To win middle-class and peasant support it had to abandon all talk of collectivizing property, at least for the time being. Like de Man, Déat argued that to compete with fascism, the SFIO had to appeal to both nationalist and authoritarian sentiments. At the SFIO's annual party congress in July 1933, a Déat supporter, Adrien Marquet, recommended that the party's new slogan be "Order, Authority, Nation." When Léon Blum protested that what Déat and Marquet were defending was "almost fascism," Déat replied that he, too, wanted to "bar the route to fascism" and that he was just as Marxist as Blum, only less tied to the "shibboleths of the Jewish tradition."

Déat urged the congress not only to seek an alliance with the middle classes but to abandon the SFIO's commitment to political democracy and Marxist internationalism. Parliamentary democracy would never bring about socialism, he said, only a dictatorship could. But first, as the German experience had shown, the masses "had to be conquered," and this included the middle classes as well as the workers. For this to be achieved, sentimental notions of liberty and justice had to be scrapped for more potent appeals. Blum replied that he was horrified by what he was hearing.[39]

The majority of SFIO delegates supported Blum, viewing the slogan "Order, Authority, Nation" as an affront to their ideals of liberty, justice, and internationalism. They also objected in 1933 to Déat's abandonment of the Marxist doctrine of class struggle.[40] Despite Déat's insistence that he was still a Socialist, he was expelled from the SFIO in November 1933. Twenty-eight deputies and seven senators left with him to found their own movement, the Socialist Party of France. In 1936 Déat supported the Popular Front even though the Communists refused to support him in a runoff election, and he lost his seat in parliament.

Déat's attempts to attract middle-class support against a background of civil war in Spain, rising social tensions in France, and the threat of war with Germany led him to stress not only class conciliation but nationalistic pacifism, both at the expense of working-class solidarity. Rather than back a foreign policy that would support leftists in Germany, Italy, and Spain, who were being crushed by fascism, he supported nonresistance to Hitler, Mussolini, and Franco on behalf of the French middle classes, who, he said, wanted peace. Indeed, as early as 1934 Déat began calling for an entente with Germany and Italy despite their ruthless anti-Marxist domestic policies. During the Munich crisis in 1938, he published "Why Die for Dantzig?" a clarion call for appeasement. In 1939 he was elected to the Chamber of Deputies on a ticket that called itself the Anti-Communist Rally.

In 1940 Déat chose to support the Vichy regime, allying himself with the very socioeconomic conservatives whom he had previously opposed. In 1941 he founded the Rassemblement National Populaire (RNP, national popular reassembly), a movement that he hoped would make France even more authoritarian than it was by creating a single party for all Frenchmen. He called for even greater collaboration with Germany, criticizing Vichy's prime minister, Pierre Laval, for not being fascist enough. This hardly placed him, however, to the left of Laval. On the central committee of the RNP was Jean Goy, the former president of the UNC, the conservative veterans' organization that had participated in the riots of February 6, and Eugène Deloncle, the former head of the equally conservative Cagoule.

Rejected by both the French Socialist and Communist parties from 1933 onward, Déat had increasingly abandoned dialectical materialism for a more spiritual approach to existence, one that favored a corporatist solution to labor-management relations (including the abolition of the CGT) and urged the proletariat to realize that far more important than material rewards was the sense of contributing to a larger totality.

Déat wrote in 1942 that fascist socialism was not the enemy of the bourgeoisie but its savior: "The necessary rescue of our middle classes will be one of the happiest effects, one of the most essential objectives of the National Revolution. And that is what socialism should mean for them. Thus we are far removed from any Marxist nonsense about the automatic concentration of large enterprises and about the fatal elimination of small producers, rejected to become wage earners." Déat made it clear how far he had come from Marxist socialism (which called for the nationalization of the basic means of production) when he declared that under fascist socialism all property would be "legitimate" and there would be no "brutal transfer of property." Fascism would end class struggle and inaugurate class cooperation. "Totalitarianism," he wrote, "is a conciliation, a reconciliation."[41]

Déat criticized Vichy not for its anti-Marxism but for refusing to crush the enemies of the National Revolution even more forcefully. He called for the creation of a new kind of man in France, a "total man" who would exhibit the "virtues of the warrior." This total man would defend an "active and vigorous Aryanism" and oppose the infiltrations of Jewish "parasites" into European culture. He would know that "the purity of the race is the first condition of any demographic revival." Déat suggested even that the "precautions" taken by cattle breeders could be usefully applied to the breeding of French children.[42]

Although Déat's career is a fascinating example of the evolution of a politician from left fascism to right fascism, his impact on French politics in the 1930s was minor. Between 1933 and 1940, Déat and his fellow Neo-Socialists were unable to mount a serious challenge to the SFIO, and even under the Vichy regime, as the historian Stanley Grossmann has pointed out, the RNP was of "little importance—certainly far from the 500,000 members it claimed." The German historian Reinhold Brender reports that the RNP had only 2,638 party members during the war, of whom only 12.8 percent were industrial workers (58.8 percent being middle class).[43]

An even less influential fascist leftist of the 1930s was Gaston Bergery. In 1933 Bergery resigned from the French Radical party and founded the Front Commun (Common front). Its program was highly socialist, calling for land redistribution and the nationalization of the basic means of production—and of banks, department stores, and foreign trade as well. Small industry, small business, agriculture, and the liberal professions were to remain in the private sector. The parliamentary regime of the Third Republic was to be replaced with a syndicalist system that would allow urban and rural workers to exert direct political power through their own unions and cooperatives—the key difference between this system and right-wing corporatism being the nonmerger of management and labor. Bergery also called for an alliance among the middle classes, the working classes, and the peasantry to defeat fascism.

Bergery advocated using fascist propaganda techniques to achieve these goals. As Burrin has written, "[Bergery] was undoubtedly the first in France to resort to forms of propaganda characteristic of totalitarian regimes, mixing Bolshevik-inspired chants and recitations with nazi-inspired lighting, emblems, and flags."[44] When some of Bergery's admirers in the SFIO declared that the political left, having been put on the defensive by fascism, should itself appeal to antiparliamentarianism, nationalism, and irrationalism, Salomon Grumbach expressed the view of most SFIO members: "What we must beware of as the devil is fascism of the left, the deadly illusion that we can fight authentic fascism with its own weapons. That would enable us to have some passing successes, [but] it would kill our souls."[45]

Rejected by the Socialists and the Communists, Bergery began to look more to non-Marxists for allies. In the autumn of 1934, the Front Commun merged with Georges Izard's Third Force, which claimed to be devoted to a third way between capitalism and Marxism. In return for his support, Izard demanded "the abandonment of working class baggage, the renunciation of all anti-religious propaganda, and independence vis-à-vis both [Marxist] internationals." Although Izard brought fewer than three hundred supporters with him, Bergery agreed.

Bergery's anticommunism in domestic affairs strengthened his pacifism in foreign affairs, especially his opposition to a military alliance with the Soviet Union. Like Déat, he supported an appeasement policy toward Hitler between 1935 and 1938. In 1935 he also appealed to "brave souls" of the AF and the CF who were "neither right nor left" to join the Front Commun, a pronouncement that led some former Communists who had previously supported Bergery to abandon him.

In 1936 Bergery supported the candidates of the left in the national elections, contributing to the victory of the Popular Front. But his support for the Popular Front was short-lived. With the outbreak of the civil war in Spain and the news of the Moscow purge trials, he increasingly denounced the French Communist party and faulted the SFIO for remaining allied with it. He also criticized Blum for his "excess of parliamentarianism" and called for a "single party of the people" to replace the Popular Front.

Burrin has described Bergery's attitude toward fascism between 1937 and 1939 as ambiguous. In 1937 Bergery returned from a visit to fascist Italy praising Mussolini for having dealt a number of blows to capitalism (?), yet denying that his own movement represented a "fascism of the left." In 1938 Bergery added xenophobia and anti-Semitism to his political repertoire.

Nevertheless, the great majority of those who joined the Front Commun or read its newspaper, *La Flèche*, remained socialist in their economic goals. Bergery's supporters were largely nonconformist leftists who were opposed to Communist participation in the Popular Front. (One such leftist, a member of the Club of Friends of *La Flèche*, was André Gide.)[46]

The Front Commun achieved scant support. Contemporaries estimated party membership in 1934–35 to be between 1,500 and 8,000, the great majority consisting of students, intellectuals, and white-collar workers. There were few proletarians. In December 1938, police reported that the front had only 555 members in the provinces and 403 in Paris. In May 1939 these numbers dropped to 372 and 231, respectively. As the historian Dieter Wolf has said of Bergery's movement, it "had no influence on the masses."[47] In 1940, having cut his ties with both the Communists and the Socialists, Bergery turned to the political right. He agreed to serve on Pétain's brain trust, Vichy's National Council. In 1941 he was appointed France's ambassador to Moscow, and between 1942 and 1944, as the Vichy government continued to engage in active collaboration with Nazism, he was France's ambassador to Turkey.

Jeunesses Patriotes honor guard escorting the funeral hearse of a party member killed during the February 6, 1934, riots.

Solidarité Française members leaving Notre Dame cathedral on February 6, 1935.

Fascist demonstration at the Place de l'Etoile, 1936.

A confrontation between fascists and anti-fascists at the Place de la Bourse, 1937.

Members of the Croix de Feu parading past Colonel de La Rocque on Joan of Arc's Day.

Croix de Feu parade on Joan of Arc's Day.

Croix de Feu parade, Place de l'Etoile and Champs-Elysées.

Jacques Doriot speaking at a meeting of the Parti Populaire Français soon after its founding in 1936.

Audience listening to Jacques Doriot at a meeting of the Parti Populaire Français soon after its founding in 1936.

Jacques Doriot speaking in Saint-Denis.

Congress of the Parti Populaire Français at the Elysée Montmartre.

French fascist youth at a Congress of the Parti Populaire Français in Saint-Denis in 1939.

(*left*) François Coty. Founder of the Solidarité Française and previous financial supporter of other French fascist movements.

Léon Blum (center, with coat unbuttoned) speaking to striking workers at the Cours de Vincennes during a protest demonstration on February 12, 1934, against the February 6 riots.

(*left*) Communist demonstration on February 9, 1934, against the February 6 riots.

3 · The Solidarité Française

LEADERSHIP, FINANCING, AND MEMBERSHIP

Much larger than the fascist left in France in the 1930s was the fascist right, especially the Solidarité Française (SF), the CF, and the PPF. Although the SF survived for barely a year after its founding, during that period it was, according to French police authorities, the largest fascist movement in France. Many of its supporters went over to La Rocque or Doriot after the movement's collapse.

The SF was launched in June 1933 by François Coty, an anti-Communist, anti-Semitic millionaire (he had made a fortune from his perfume and newspaper enterprises) who had previously helped subsidize the AF, the Faisceau, the JP, and the CF.[1] When La Rocque and Coty had a falling out in 1932, Coty decided to launch a fascist movement of his own. An important advantage that Coty had over his rivals at this time was his ownership of the newspaper L'Ami du Peuple (Friend of the people), a low-priced mass circulation daily.

Coty selected the central committee of the SF from the editorial staff of L'Ami du Peuple, assigning a former army officer who had served in Indochina, Jean Renaud, to lead the movement. In 1935 Renaud was described by a reporter from Le Temps as a public speaker whose populist style had a powerful effect on audiences. Renaud himself preferred to describe his speaking style in military terms, as rough, direct, and infused with "the character of combat."[2]

Renaud's second-in-command, Jacques Fromentin, was also a former military man. Badly wounded in the First World War, Fromentin had written a column on veterans' affairs for Coty's newspaper before becoming the SF's treasurer. The head of the SF's youth movement, which comprised many of the SF's shock troops, was the Count de Gueydon, a previous member of AF who went by the pseudonym Vinceguide. The count was the son of a former French governor-general of Algeria and the cousin of Charles des Isnards, a conservative Paris municipal councilman.

The first public rally of the SF in 1933 was announced not only in *L'Ami du Peuple* but also in such major conservative newspapers as *L'Echo de Paris*, *Le Matin*, and *Le Figaro*, all of which approved of the SF's goal of "barring the route to internationalism." According to *L'Ami du Peuple*, the SF was engaged in a "struggle against inflation and Marxism." By collaborating with such movements as the JP, the League of Taxpayers, and the Agrarian party, the SF hoped to form a National Front against the new Cartel des Gauches and eventually bring down the Third Republic itself, a republic it condemned for allowing Marxism to exist in the first place. Combining conservative economic goals with moralistic rhetoric, the SF promised to put "the politicians and profiteers out of action."[3]

A few weeks after Coty launched his movement, the police were impressed by the fact that he had hired someone to head the SF's information service at a salary of 120,000 francs a year. "Such a sum," declared a report to the minister of interior, "suggests that the size of the expenses assumed by Monsieur Coty to ensure the success of his political enterprise is quite large." According to police, not all of the money was Coty's, since by July 1933 the movement was receiving outside contributions at the rate of 3,000 francs a day. Some of the funding came from two business firms, the Potin and Damoy companies. Following the riots of February 6, Georges Vautier, a member of the RF business lobby and himself the director of fifteen hydroelectric and gas companies, provided the SF with one of its largest subsidies, 2 million francs.[4]

Police also reported that in March 1934 the SF solicited funds from Jean Hennessy, the cognac producer and publisher of the newspaper *Le Quotidien*, but they did not say whether the SF succeeded or not. Marshal Lyautey, regarded by many as a friend of the extreme right, was also approached, but again there is no record of the outcome. Police noted in April 1934 that there had been rumors at SF headquarters that Lyautey, along with Coty, had offered to help finance the creation of a weekly party newspaper, to be called *La Solidarité Française*, on the understanding that if it were a success more funds would be forthcoming. Shortly afterward, the new weekly was launched with a first issue of 50,000 copies.[5]

In July 1933, a month after it was founded, the SF announced that it had recruited some 30,000 men into its combat units of blue berets, and in December 1933 it said that it had a total membership of 315,000. No doubt both claims were exaggerated. Still, as one biographer of Coty, Alfred Kupferman, has written, the initial success of the SF "seems incontestable." Following the riots of February 6, French police authorities reported to the minister of interior that the SF had some 180,000 members in France, with 80,000 centered in Paris. This figure was five times greater than that for the French Communist party at the time (35,000). William L. Shirer was told by some police officers he talked to that the strength of the SF was "probably less than a fifth" of the 180,000 figure.[6]

Some scholars have described the SF as being even smaller. Zeev Sternhell has estimated that the SF had no more than 20,000 members in 1934, with only 3,000 shock troops in Paris. Jean-Paul Brunet has described the SF as a *groupuscle* with no more than 1,500 members in all of France. A scholar who has done extensive research on the SF, Richard Millmann, accepts the official police estimate of 180,000 (the number given to the parliamentary commission that investigated the February 6 riots in 1934) but concludes that SF activists were far less numerous, with fewer than 2,000 participating in the riots. Millman also states, "If, in Paris, the league carried a weight comparable to that of the other leagues of that time, its influence seems more modest in the provinces."[7]

Millman's distinction between activists and other members of the SF applies, of course, to all of the major fascist movements of the era, from La Rocque's CF and Doriot's PPF to Mussolini's Fascio and Hitler's NSDAP. That only a minority of SF members were youthful shock troops made the SF no less a mass movement. It does appear that the number of SF members willing to engage in street fighting in 1934 was relatively small. Serge Berstein estimates that only 1,500 SF blueshirts participated in the clashes with the police at the Place de la Concorde on February 6, although they were in the forefront.[8]

The SF began its recruiting efforts in 1933 by creating local party headquarters in both Paris and the provinces. By October 1933 it had *sections* (local units) in Metz, Rouen, Tours, Bar-le-Duc, and Nice. Most of those who joined came from politically conservative backgrounds, often from the extreme right. According to police, in Bar-le-Duc many of the 100 "rightist militants" who entered the SF had previously belonged to either the Ligue des Patriotes or the Faisceau.

The president of the SF section in Bar-le-Duc was a former member of the JP, and the local SF secretary was described by the town's police as a reactionary activist. The secretary was also a member of the Christian Union of Bank Employees, a right-wing union. The vice-president of the SF in Bar-le-Duc was a Monsieur Roynette, the district manager of the Compagnie des Chemins de Fer de l'Est (Eastern railroad company) and a member of the local Union of Catholic Railroad Workers, where his influence was hardly likely to oppose management. Indeed, Roynette was such a passionate conservative that in the wake of the February 6 riots he tried to prevent a train that was carrying police reinforcements to Paris from passing through Bar-le-Duc. Shouting at the station master not to let the train depart, he was reported to have said to some of the police on board, "Aren't you ashamed of going there to fire upon your brothers . . . on war veterans . . . on fathers of families. They have had enough of you!"

At Epernay, of the approximately 250 persons who joined the SF by December 1933 many were former members of the AF, the JP, and the League of Taxpayers. At Nantes, of the 35 who joined by March 1934 most were previous supporters of the AF, the JP, and the Cercle Cathelineau, all of which were committed, like the SF, to uniting the parties of the right against the new Cartel des Gauches.[9]

Police reports indicate that most SF members in the provinces came from the lower middle classes, with individuals from the upper middle classes often holding the highest leadership positions. According to the police in Paris who collated reports from various prefectures throughout France, SF members were "for the most part merchants, artisans, and diverse white collar workers, with the exclusion of foreign or Jewish elements."[10] On the local central committees of various SF sections, it was not uncommon to find an important businessman or retired military officer as president or vice-president and a white-collar worker as treasurer. At Châlons-sur-Marne, for example, the president was a reserve military governor and the treasurer a bank clerk. Their colleagues included a reserve battalion commander, a retired adjutant, and two white-collar workers. One of the white-collar workers was an employee of the Eastern Railroad Company and the other an employee of the Mutual Insurance Company of the Marne.

At Bar-le-Duc the SF central committee consisted of a district manager of a railroad company (who served as the local vice-president of the SF), a lumber merchant, a bank clerk, and an office clerk. At Douai, the president and vice-president were insurance agents and the secretary-treasurer an entrepreneur. At Metz, the leadership included the manager of a Bon Marché department store, the manager of an insurance company, a former army officer, an insurance agent, a city hall clerk, and two traveling salesmen. At Epernay, the two principal organizers of the SF were the manager of a printing plant and a wholesale tire dealer.[11] The recurrence of men associated with the railroad, banking, and insurance industries may partly explain the SF's animosity toward statism, since these industries were among the left's main targets for nationalization in 1933.

The predominantly petty bourgeois nature of the SF's rank and file was consistent with the pronouncements of the SF's national leadership on economic matters. Like Hitler and Mussolini before they came to power, Renaud posed as a defender of the lower middle classes against the upper. Expressing sympathy for small businessmen threatened with bankruptcy during the Depression (but without specifying how he would protect them from their larger competitors), Renaud called for less government spending and lower taxes. He decried government bureaucrats who pursued a "masonic program of socialization." At the same time, he tried to attract *some* bureaucrats to his cause by pitting them against one another: "There are a million bureaucrats when there should be fewer who are better paid."[12]

The SF made a concerted attempt to win peasants to its banner. When in July 1933 it launched an extensive recruiting campaign throughout France, it targeted rural areas for special attention.[13] In his book *French Solidarity Attacks* (1935), Renaud called for a moral alliance between Dorgères's Greenshirts and his own blueshirts. Marching "elbow to elbow," they would throw the rascals out. Renaud claimed that French Communists wanted to abolish peasant property rights just as their Spanish counterparts had tried to do in the Asturies. He depicted the Socialists as urban snobs who scorned the peasantry as a "backward and broken-down race" and Léon Blum as surrounded by "the lace and silverware of a precious and ridiculous grand bourgeois" (119–25).

Renaud called for higher tariffs against agricultural imports as a way of raising farm prices in France and insisted on a complete ban on wheat and meat from abroad. He also advocated greater government restrictions on French electricity companies, agricultural cooperatives, and the "wheat trust," accusing all three of making "scandalous profits" at the expense of the small farmer (121–23, 128–29).

If Renaud's rhetoric sometimes sounded revolutionary—at one point he referred sympathetically to the peasant jacqueries of 1789 and to the storming of the Bastille—the goals he defended were largely those of a conservative peasantry devoted to private property, lower taxes, and higher farm prices (120, 130). On the other hand, his attacks on electricity companies and the wheat trust injected a left-wing element into SF ideology that was largely missing from the economic programs of other French fascist movements of the period. How genuine this element was is another matter, inasmuch as among the financial backers of the SF was Georges Vautier, a representative of several electricity companies, and inasmuch as the corporatist state that Renaud advocated would have given these companies (as we shall see) more power, not less.

The SF's attempts to win the peasantry to its cause were largely unsuccessful, partly because Dorgères and other right-wing peasant leaders maintained their autonomy and partly because French centrist governments of the period, including the left-centrist Popular Front, outdid the SF not only by passing protectionist agricultural legislation but also by funding rural electrification projects and providing government-subsidized farm credits.

In 1935 Renaud declared that no political movement could succeed in France without the support of the petite bourgeoisie, the peasantry, young intellectuals, and workers. By workers, however, he meant not factory workers so much as small-shop artisans who viewed themselves as more skilled than proletarians and who resented the intrusion of mass production techniques into modern life. Renaud's repeated denunciations of "the machine" and his defense of "industries of quality" were directed at this type of worker (156, 213).

The SF did seek to entice factory workers away from left-wing unions into company unions, called yellow unions in France. In 1933 Renaud gave five thousand francs to a group called the Association of French Workers to help finance its journal, *France Ouvrière* (Working France). This organization was already subsidized at the time by the royalist AF. When Charles Maurras, the head of the AF, learned that the SF was trying to encroach on his territory, he threatened to remove all AF members from the ranks of this so-called workers' organization and to have several of its directors, many of whom were also members of the AF, resign. Renaud withdrew from contention.

In 1935 a reporter from *Le Temps* observed that the public rallies of the SF often had a populist (*populaire*) flavor, many of those attending coming from "modest conditions."[14] If "the people" in this case were mainly artisans and petty bourgeois rather than industrial workers, they had their own reasons for political anger, an anger fueled by their fear of being reduced themselves to a proletarian condition. SF speakers attempted to direct this anger toward Jewish, Marxist, and liberal scapegoats. The reporter from *Le Temps* described an SF audience at the Salle Wagram in Paris as "a compact, agitated, turbulent crowd which applauded the violent language from the podium." But what these speakers proposed to such audiences was not class conflict or Marxist internationalism but class collaboration and French nationalism.

The Salle Wagram audience was also described as being "comprised of workers, white-collar employees, [and] even African workers with bronzed skins." What were African workers doing in such a ferociously nationalistic movement, one whose favorite slogan was "France for the French"? Indeed, four years earlier, L'Ami du Peuple had characterized North Africans in Paris as "uprooted" souls "without any hygiene" who were "hereditary-syphilitics." As Millmann has pointed out, "If Coty [was] hostile to Jews, to a certain degree he applied the same pejorative tone to numerous other minority groups living in France."[15] Yet after 1933 the SF actively recruited North African Arabs into its ranks. The reason was more practical than ideological: the SF wanted them to supplement its shock troops.

As for why Arabs in Paris would join a movement committed to French nationalism, the answer, according to the police, was simple: they received money and other favors for doing so. Their "indemnity" ranged from fifty to three hundred francs a month, "depending on how much time they could consecrate to the different missions to which they were assigned."[16] In May 1934, the Communist newspaper L'Humanité declared, "In order to win the support of Algerians, almost all of whom are unemployed workers in the greatest distress, [the SF] offers them blue shirts, army boots, packs of cigarettes, and even money." L'Humanité also claimed that the SF appealed to anti-Semitism in recruiting Arabs: "[The SF arouses Arab] anger against Jews and foreigners by assuring them that without [Jews and foreigners] there would be no unemployment in France."[17]

According to a memorandum of June 1934 from the minister of interior to the minister of foreign affairs, both the SF and the JP were offering various benefits to Arabs in Paris to attract them to their movements. (The JP had even established a North African Center to aid indigent workers who found themselves "in a difficult situation" in Paris.) At an SF meeting in Paris in April 1934, 120 North Africans were promised jobs and other support by Vinceguide if they joined the SF. By June 1934 the SF had some 50 unemployed Arab workers in its North African Brigade under the command of a former French colonial officer. The JP also had some 150 such troops.[18]

The SF's North African Brigade regularly clashed with leftist groups in Paris and its suburbs. According to police, North Africans were often among those arrested during these brawls. Several North Africans fought alongside members of the SF outside the Chamber of Deputies on the night of February 6, and one of them, Gali Meziane, was mortally wounded (150 North Africans attended his funeral). On April 22, 1934, 30 North Africans defended vendors of the SF's party newspaper at Courbevois when a group of Communists attacked them, the Arabs having been trucked in from Paris for that purpose. Following the clash, 8 North Africans were among those arrested by the police. At their trial, a sympathetic judge objected to these "partisans" being called mercenaries. On April 8, several North Africans were among 100 SF and JP blueshirts who started a fight with 50 members of the International League against Antisemitism who were selling their journal, *The Right to Live*.[19]

Just as later, during the Spanish Civil War, Colonel Franco did not let his alleged nationalism prevent him from ordering Moroccan, Italian, and German troops to kill his fellow countrymen when they sided with the political left, so Renaud and Taittinger were willing to employ foreigners against Frenchmen on behalf of their right-wing goals.

However, the role that unemployed North African workers played in the SF as a whole should not be exaggerated. The great majority of SF members were native Frenchmen, not Arab immigrants; Catholics, not Moslems; and petty bourgeois, not lumpenproletarians.

RISE AND FALL

SF membership peaked in December 1933, six months after the movement was founded. By June 1934, the SF was in shambles, financial disaster and internal dissension having reduced the movement to a fringe group. On February 6, 1934, however, the SF was still the largest fascist movement in France, and its blueshirts played a prominent role in the fighting that took place at the Place de la Concorde. According to one eyewitness, the mob that almost broke through the police barricade guarding the bridge across from the Chamber of Deputies was composed mostly of SF members. Also, on the evenings leading up to February 6, SF gangs, dressed in blue shirts, black berets, and jackboots, roamed the streets of Paris shouting, "France for the French."[20]

In the aftermath of the February 6 riots and the Communist and Socialist counterdemonstrations of February 7 and 12, the SF sought to turn the informal cooperation that had existed between the nationalist leagues on February 6 into a more permanent alliance called the National Front. According to Vinceguide, the National Front was opposed to a "red front" of 130,000 Socialists and 40,000 Communists. The AF and the JP agreed to join with the SF in this coalition even though the first two had previously been bitter rivals. In May 1934 an SF section leader praised the leaders of the JP and AF for "having made an abstraction of their political differences in order to focus on their common reason for rapprochement." In June 1935 the National Front held a public meeting presided over by General Partouneaux of the AF. On the speakers' platform were members of the AF, the JP, and the SF. According to police, "Each [speaker], without abdicating any of his personal or doctrinal differences with the others, underlined the necessity . . . of . . . achieving a union of all Frenchmen. All three praised the establishment of the National Front that had issued from February 6 and declared themselves in agreement with a formula based on the principles "Order, Authority, the Leader, France!"[21]

Soon after the riots of February 6, however, the SF began to decline, primarily because of financial problems. In late 1933, Coty lost a large part of his fortune in a disastrous business deal and had to sell Le Figaro. Six months later he had to sell L'Ami du Peuple as well. According to one police informant, by February 20, 1934, the new editors of L'Ami du Peuple had begun to burn their bridges with the SF. In April, the SF leadership had to move out of the offices at L'Ami du Peuple that Coty had previously granted them. When the SF held a major rally in Montreuil in March, the newspaper gave it only minimal coverage.[22]

Renaud responded by launching a public appeal for funds. Thanks to a two-million-franc subsidy from Georges Vautier and the hydroelectric industry in March 1934, the SF managed to stay afloat a few months longer. But without Coty's financial support, its days were numbered. Between April and August 1934, the circulation of the party newspaper, La Solidarité Française, fell from fifty thousand to fifteen thousand. Coty's death in July 1934 was the final blow. According to police, by October 1934 the SF had only fifteen to twenty thousand sympathizers, and of these scarcely five thousand were activists.[23]

Within the ranks of the SF the vaunted solidarity of the movement gave way to mutual recriminations. Vinceguide, the head of the SF's youth movement, accused Renaud and Fromentin of stealing party funds and of being too cowardly when it came to taking action, that is, of refusing to launch a repeat of February 6. Vinceguide maintained that he wanted to move the SF more to the left.

By left, however, Vinceguide did not mean the Marxist left. Not only did he continue to denounce both the Communists and the Socialists, but later, after his departure from the SF, he returned to the reactionary AF from which he had originally come. While still a member of the SF, he did make the standard fascist pitch to Communist workers, urging them to abandon the PCF for the SF, but the alternative he offered was right-wing corporatism, not revolutionary Marxism.

Replying to Vinceguide's call for action, Renaud and Fromentin declared that they would rather resign from the SF than follow Vinceguide into an adventure whereby they had everything to lose.[24] They noted that the Chamber of Deputies was already investigating the nationalist leagues for their role in the February 6 riots and was in no mood to tolerate further assaults upon its existence. Action could lead to the SF's being banned and its leaders arrested.

This was not the first time a French fascist movement had been torn by dissension, as the history of the AF, the Ligues des Patriotes, the JP, and the Faisceau had shown.[25] The youth auxiliaries of these movements had also grown restive at the lack of attempts to overthrow the republic, and some had rebelled against their parent organizations for being so cautious. In the spring of 1934, the same dynamic was present in the SF, the recent success of the riots having aroused its more militant members.

The potential for division was increased when Renaud, deprived of Coty's largesse, had to slash the funding of the SF's youth movement, the Jeunesses de la Solidarité. Just as Georges Valois in 1926 had faced rising complaints within the Faisceau when money began to run low, so too did Renaud in 1934 within the SF.[26] Like the Faisceau, which had also touted the spiritual above the material, the SF declined rapidly—and bitterly—when the material was less forthcoming.

Renaud and Fromentin fought back by attempting to discredit Vinceguide with character assassination of their own. In March 1934, they attended a meeting of the Jeunesses de la Solidarité, at which they sought to portray Vinceguide as a Communist sympathizer. When Fromentin rose to speak (Renaud having been physically prevented from reaching the speakers' platform), he was drowned out by Vinceguide's supporters, who charged Fromentin and Renaud with embezzling propaganda funds from the SF. When Fromentin replied that Vinceguide had contacts with the Soviet embassy, the remark was met with such hostility that Fromentin reversed himself and blamed two other SF members instead. When this did not work, he left the hall. The next day Fromentin concluded that, given the catastrophe of the previous evening, it was better to cut all ties with the SF's youth movement than lose control of the SF altogether.[27]

The hemorrhaging continued, however. On April 3 police reported that at a Dunkerque meeting of the SF there was no longer any confidence in Renaud as secretary-general of the party, a sentiment police found prevalent among other SF sections as well. Thus, only two months after Renaud had successfully engaged his troops in the demonstration of February 6 he was in danger of being ousted as the SF's leader. Throughout April, Renand and Fromentin complained

league, it reconstituted itself as a supposedly democratic organization, the Amis de la Solidarité Française (Friends of French solidarity). Its heyday, however, which had lasted less than a year, was clearly over.

WAS THE SOLIDARITÉ FRANÇAISE FASCIST?

During its peak, the SF—in spite of its flaunting of fascist shock troops, fascist uniforms, and fascist salutes—*denied* that it was fascist. At an SF meeting in May 1934, at which some 450 members of the audience dressed in paramilitary uniforms stood and gave the fascist salute, Vinceguide insisted that the SF was the opposite of fascist. "People treat us as fascists," he said. "We are anti-fascists. [We are] nationalists."[33] A few days earlier, another SF speaker had declared to some 200 members in uniform: "The youth [of the SF] have no other goal but to defend what is national and to return France to the French. If they have adopted a uniform, it is not to plagiarize Hitler but only to openly acknowledge their sentiments."[34] If this was a mixed message (we are not fascists, but we wish to display our fascist sentiments), there were good reasons for it.

Like other French fascist movements of the interwar period, the SF was worried that the public might link it too closely with Italy and Germany and therefore reject it on patriotic grounds. Consequently, the SF emphasized that it was no lackey of Hitler or Mussolini, that it was French above all. It was not until 1940 that some French fascists (by no means all) chose to collaborate with the Germans. Until then, all French fascists opposed a German invasion of France, insisting that a more authoritarian France was needed in order to better *resist* the Nazis.

At the same time, the SF did not deny its affinity with foreign fascisms on a number of domestic issues, especially regarding the success of these fascisms in crushing Marxism. Hence the SF's message was mixed. Decoded, it meant that the SF was not fascist where betraying French nationalism was concerned but it was fascist where eliminating Marxism was concerned.

The SF was also typical of other French fascist movements of the era in seeking to disassociate itself from Hitler's repression of dissident German conservatives after 1934, an identification that would have lost it right-wing supporters in France. While the SF praised Hitler for dealing forcefully with German leftists, it criticized the same authoritarianism when it was employed against German rightists. Thus, the SF employed a double standard, one that rejected totalitarianism, that is, the repression of both the left and the right, but not the repression of the left alone.

In January 1935 Renaud saw no contradiction in the response he gave to a reporter from *Le Temps* about his views on dictatorship. When asked whether the SF's goal of taking power meant installing a dictator, he replied, "No." Yet when later asked in the same interview whether he supported dictatorship, he said: "Yes, if one means by dictatorship an honest, strong government governed by the essential principles of authority, stability and responsibility."[35] In effect, he was reassuring French conservatives that he had no intention of establishing a bad dictatorship, one that would repress them, but that he did favor a good dictatorship, one that would repress their enemies. The SF would make France safe for conservatism, not threaten it. In *French Solidarity Attacks*, Renaud also sought to reassure French conservatives by specifying that the type of "president" he envisioned was Salazar of Portugal, not Hitler of Germany. Renaud continued to praise Mussolini, however, which was consistent with his opposition to totalitarianism. Salazar and Mussolini were both dictators who crushed the left but not the right.

In 1935 Renaud declared that although the SF was an enemy of parliamentarianism it would, "if it had time," employ all legal means to achieve its goals, including the election of as many of its representatives to the Chamber of Deputies as possible. Renaud left no doubt, however, that the SF's goals were more fascistic than democratic: "The day the National Front has a block of fifty deputies in the Chamber, elected under conditions imposed by a rigorous discipline . . . , it will be the end of the influence of Blum, Herriot, Boncour, Daladier, Frot [and other Socialists and Radicals]. Mussolini once said: 'To enter parliament is a way of leaving it.' That is the truth of our moment."[36] Renaud's allusion to the Italian dictator referred to the fact that Mussolini's takeover in 1922 had occurred when only thirty-five of his followers had been elected to an Italian parliament of more than five hundred members.

Renaud's willingness to exploit legal means for authoritarian ends did not mean that he believed in democracy, especially if democracy meant accepting the outcome of elections that brought the left to power. In 1935 Renaud told a reporter that if the Popular Front continued to flourish and if its politicians chose to provoke him, his followers would "descend into the streets with cries of 'France for the French,'" that it was "not a matter of patience, but of the moment, of the occasion." When the reporter pressed him on the question of means, Renaud replied, "There are two kinds: legal and illegal. Experience has shown us the inefficacy, the absurdity of legal means. We are against civil war, but we are no less obliged to make a choice between these two means. Ours is made."[37]

This was sheer bluster, of course, given the SF's political impotence in 1935, but it was a bluster that further undermined the SF's claim that it was not fascist. So, too, did an article in the SF's party newspaper on July 14, 1934, praising a book written by an Italian fascist that lauded Coty for "defending the mission of Rome in the world."

The SF was, in fact, highly fascist in a number of ways, including stylistically. Like Mussolini's blackshirts and Hitler's brownshirts, Renaud's blueshirts expressed some of their deepest beliefs and ideological affinities in outward symbols and public rituals. Although René Rémond has dismissed such displays as "trappings" that alone are no proof of fascism,[38] there seems little doubt that such symbols sent a definite message to contemporaries. The red-shirted Marxist who raised his arm with a clenched fist was no friend of the blue-shirted fascist who saluted in the Roman style. Indeed, if the fascist gesture meant anything at all, it meant an intense hatred of Marxism.

A standard practice at SF meetings, both in Paris and the provinces, was the fascist salute.[39] In 1935 a journalist visiting the SF's party headquarters in Paris asked about a sign on the wall which declared that the fascist salute was de rigueur. It was explained to him that the salute symbolized the movement's belief in strict discipline: "The guillotine functions without quarter, and the indignant are not exempt."[40] In 1934, four days before the riots of February 6, the SF held a rally at which the audience stood and sang the "Marseillaise" while giving the fascist salute. Two months later a heckler was roughly ejected from an SF meeting held in Montreuil (a Communist stronghold) when he objected to Renaud's being saluted by his troops "in the Roman manner." At a meeting in a Paris cinema in May 1934, SF blueshirts formed a double line welcoming the public as they entered and gave the fascist salute to members of the movement. At the end of the meeting, the whole audience stood and gave the fascist salute.[41]

Most of the audience at the meeting in May 1934 wore the party's official uniform. According to police, this consisted of a blue shirt, dark trousers, black leather shoulder belt ("in the Nazi manner"), blue armband on which there were white shields displaying the Cock of the Gauls and the inscription Solidarité Française, dark beret, military boots, and sometimes a necktie of royal blue. The prevalence of blue was meant to underscore the Frenchness of the SF's fascism, to distinguish it from Hitlerian brown and Mussolinian black.

To further enhance the military image of the movement, members of the SF's motorcycle squads were told in March 1934 to wear leather pants, vests, and caps. Three months later, it was suggested that military leggings might also be worn. All these items, available for purchase at SF headquarters, expressed a fascist preference for martial over civilian values. Since this preference was shared by other French fascist movements as well, it was not always easy to tell them apart on sartorial grounds. In April 1934, for example, the Francistes asked the SF to modify its uniform, which was quite similar to theirs, because it might "lead to confusion in the public mind."[42]

Precisely because these uniforms did stand for something in the public mind, it made those who wore them potential targets for physical assaults by their political enemies. In January 1933, when vendors of the SF's newspaper began to appear on the streets in party uniforms, they were attacked by Communist toughs. Such incidents may have dampened the paramilitary "virility" of some SF members. According to police, in November 1933 when the SF held a public ceremony in front of the statue of General Charles-Marie-Emmanuel Mangin in Paris, only a few of the participants were dressed in party uniforms. In September 1934 an annoyed Renaud insisted in a letter to one SF section that all its members order the proper attire. They refused. At their next meeting, none of the forty members who attended even bothered to wear a blue shirt.

Some SF members, however, were more militant. According to police, as late as September 1934 Renaud could count on 180 "assault troops" to do his bidding. These men had been "recruited with care" and placed under the command of a Colonel Sallerin. As "an elite destined to deliver hard blows," they were prepared to fight on short notice.[43]

Fascist shock troops, uniforms, and salutes were not the only characteristics of the SF that made its denials of fascism problematic. SF ideology was also highly fascist, preaching a combination of anti-Marxism and antiliberalism that fascists in Italy and Germany could appreciate. The SF also praised Mussolini and Hitler for their "proven energy and strong wills," called for a triple alliance between Italy, Germany, and France, defended "national socialism," advocated a more authoritarian form of government, glorified right-wing nationalism, exploited the veterans' mystique, and portrayed Jews as a menace to society. Indeed, where anti-Semitism was concerned, the SF between 1933 and 1936 was closer to German Nazism than to Italian fascism—although here too there was a certain amount of double-talk.

ANTI-SEMITISM

In 1935, Renaud insisted that the SF was neither racist nor fascist: "One must soon discard the fascist label, which has no meaning in France just as one must abandon the Hitlerian [label], since the Solidarité Française speaks in the name of a culture which is sharply and unequivocally opposed to the racial theories and concepts of the State which Hitler [uses] as a threat and a lever."[44] Yet even as Renaud criticized racial anti-Semitism, he defended cultural anti-Semitism and praised Hitler's actions against the Jews in Germany.

According to Renaud, France was not the product of one race but of several, including a Gallo-Latin fusion that made it impossible to base French character on a notion of racial purity. The SF, he said, was not interested in trying to explain the French soul by "returning to Cro-Magnon man or interrogating bones that end up crumbling under glass in museums": "Racially speaking, there is everything in us, from . . . an Iberian to a German, to a Scandinavian, to a Latin, to a Greek, indeed to a Saracen" (76). This racial mixture did not prevent a Normand peasant from having "very pure blood," but this blood was inherited not from some "hypothetical" source but from twenty centuries of ancestors living in the same country and fighting to defend it from invaders. Hitler claimed that the spirit of a race came from its blood. Renaud wrote, "No, responds the Solidarité Française. It comes from its culture." And French culture, which was deeply rooted in Latin civilization, preferred Mediterranean humanism to German racism (85, 86).

By humanism, however, Renaud did not mean humanitarianism. There should be no tolerance, he said, for invading Jews from abroad or for left-wing Jews at home who threatened to poison French culture and politics. There were Jews in France who were "masters of intrigue." They were called "Isaac, Jacob, Ezekiel, and Léon Blum," and they came from the "scum of the ghettos" of Europe. They threatened the purity of French culture with their disgusting pornography, obscene postcards, rotten literature, corrupt movies, and revolutionary politics. To better "have" a country, they attacked her soul: "They reign over the press, literature, the cinema. . . . One encounters them in the Chamber [of Deputies], in the ministries, in aviation, everywhere. . . . They control everything, buy everything, and are found behind the worst kinds of propaganda against our nation, [a nation] which has offered them its hospitability and which submits to their assaults in [the Socialist] *Le Populaire* and [the Communist] *L'Humanité*, sheets which are financed by them and which [reflect] their hatred and [their belief in] class struggle" (99).

The distinction Renaud drew between racial and cultural anti-Semitism did not prevent him from praising the Nazis for the way they had "broken the back" of the Jewish threat in Germany (76–78). The same threat, he said, existed in France. The Nazi persecution of Jews in Germany in 1935 was justified, for "who then, as the Germans have energetically shown, do not consider [Jews] the enemies of the Nation and the brothers of those who delivered Europe to the fury of war and Russia to the cruelty of their sadism?" (99).

Like Hitler, Renaud repeatedly associated Jews with communism. So, too, did François Coty. Indeed, according to Richard Millmann, Coty's anti-Semitism "seems to have been motivated, above all, by his anti-Communist obsession."[45] Renaud practiced the same kind of hyphenated reasoning, lumping Communists with Jews—and both groups with the Freemasons.

According to Renaud, the Freemasons, with their anticlerical liberalism, were undermining the moral fiber of France—and therefore they had to be connected with the Jews. "Who would not unite [the Jews] with the Freemasons, the latter being the servants of the former, . . . in the same reprobation and the same desire to rid our country of them?" France, Renaud wrote, was threatened by a "judeo-masonic-bolshevik" conspiracy.[46]

Renaud's solution to the Jewish Question was also hyphenated. It demanded not only greater restrictions on Jewish immigration but also the deportation of political leftists and antireligious souls who corrupted French society. In opposing a system of naturalization that allowed the "worst rabble of the ghettos" to "degrade and poison" the nation, Renaud singled out for immediate expulsion not only recently arrived Jews but also "all foreigners, agitators, ringleaders, and members of no matter what league or movement associated with the revolutionary International." He also called for the suppression of L'Humanité, rigorous control over Le Populaire, and the expulsion of Freemasonry (104).

Renaud maintained that the French left, financed by foreign money, was preparing to take to the barricades and that it was primarily revolutionaries and German Jews who were behind this threat. In calling upon French patriots to resist, he made no secret of his admiration for Hitler's conduct in similar circumstances, declaring in 1934 that France faced exactly the same situation that Germany had faced before the "great sweep of the Hitlerian broom."[47]

Yet in French Solidarity Attacks, Renaud insisted that the SF was neither fascist nor anti-Semitic. It was not anti-Semitic, he said, because it respected all religions, including the Jewish. What it could not tolerate, however, were Jewish activities that sought to destroy French culture by aiding the Communists: "[The SF] respects . . . the Jewish religion in the same way that it respects the Buddhist religion or the Moslem religion. But in the name of Humanism, . . . [the SF] is against the domination of the . . . nation by the Jew who is found behind all the levers of power . . . and without whom Freemasonry would be nothing. Everywhere, . . . from pornographic literature, to financial scandals, to revolutionary meetings, there is at least one Jew."[48]

Nevertheless, there were moments when Renaud implied that he was talking not about all Jews but only about atheistic, foreign, or left-wing Jews. He specifically denied that he was opposed to naturalized Jews who had fought for France in the First World War: "It is not they who are in question," he wrote (98–99). It was the refugee threat, "the invasion of prolific races," that concerned him, not Jews who had lived for generations in France and who had been assimilated into French culture. Yet in the same book in which he wrote these words, he said that the new immigrants were types who were "immutably alike." (99).

Renaud demanded that all foreigners who sought residence in France be rigorously screened and that all undesirables be denied entry "without pity." The undesirables were to include all foreigners without guaranteed jobs in France and all social revolutionaries who would make France "not a refuge for the oppressed but a depository for trash." Renaud also called for strict quotas on foreign doctors, lawyers, engineers, pharmacists, and dentists, claiming that unless such people were restricted their competition would reduce their counterparts in France to misery. He added that all foreign workers presently in France, with the exception of those who were incontestably needed in such industries as mining, should be sent home (96, 104).

At best, Renaud presented a confusing message, propagating anti-Semitism while disclaiming it, both rejecting and affirming the role of "blood," implying at times that assimilated Jews were acceptable (if they were right wing) while repeatedly using the term *Jew* in a generic and pejorative way. Just as he denied that he was fascist while in the same breath praising "the great sweep of the Hitlerian broom" in Germany, he denied that he was anti-Semitic while accusing both foreign and French Jews of undermining French culture and fomenting revolution. Such double-talk had its uses in that it enabled Renaud to appeal to both those who resented all Jews and those who resented only some Jews, to those who hated even assimilated, conservative, patriotic Jews and those who refused to reject Jewish war veterans who had fought for France. Renaud's patron, François Coty, was also a selective anti-Semite: he permitted at least two Jewish writers, André Maurois and Gustave Cohen, to publish articles in his newspaper, *Le Figaro*.[49]

In 1934 an article in *La Solidarité Française* by Ervin Reifenrath stated, "We are neither racists nor fascists." The SF, Reifenrath said, was opposed only to immigrants whose activities were "in contradiction to us," that is, to foreigners who deprived Frenchmen of jobs or wielded a nefarious political influence. The implication, once again, was that well-established French Jews and Jewish immigrants who were politically conservative were acceptable to the SF. Reifenrath had no sympathy, however, for Jews who failed to meet these requirements: "Let us crush the vermin who gnaw at the body of the State."[50]

Louis Mouilliseaux was another SF writer who took the high ground before descending to the low:

> Let us say immediately that we are not anti-Semites and that we hold liberty of conscience as one of the principal conquests of 1789. All religious beliefs deserve respect. We know that there are Jews in France who are good Frenchmen. Some fought well in the war. Honoring courage, we respect these Jews. Each is one of us to the degree that his sacrifice demonstrates his assimilation. But we also intend to remain masters of our own country, and we are opposed, from wherever it comes, to any attempt to abolish in France the ancient spiritual traditions of our fathers. Liberty of conscience . . . must not lead France to become Semitized in thought or in practice. The French spirit cannot be obliged to sink into some oriental mystique.[51]

Like Renaud and Coty, Mouilliseaux linked Jews with Marxism. Not only, he wrote, had Karl Marx been Jewish, but his doctrines of class struggle sought to divide Frenchmen so that they would fall prey to Jewish domination. These doctrines were rooted in *Jewish* race hatred: "It was here that came into play the hatred of one race for all other races. It was here that the destiny of Israel intervened" (111). According to Mouilliseaux, it was the Jews who had taken over the Russian revolution in 1917. The Bolsheviks, by creating antagonisms among non-Jews, had made it possible for Jews to dominate. The essence of Marxism was Jewish hostility toward gentiles, which Léon Blum had illustrated when he shouted at his non-Jewish adversaries in the Chamber of Deputies, "I hate you" (117).

Mouilliseaux apparently regarded his own hatred as more virtuous or at least as a justifiable response to the Jews "who started it." By accusing Jews of the very failings that fascists were so often accused of—racial hatred, cruelty, and a desire for totalitarian domination—he sought not only to turn the victim into the victimizer but to deprive the victim of any claim to moral superiority. By this reasoning, harsh measures against Jews could be engaged in with a clear conscience.

Mouilliseaux also sought to reduce moral qualms about anti-Semitism by contending that in a dog-eat-dog world one must be either the victim or the victimizer. To be humanitarian was to be the victim, since Jews were ruthless predators, especially in economic matters: "The Jews conquer constantly. The place makes little difference to them. [They form] a race of prodigious intelligence, admirable faith, and enormous vitality. They possess a formidable appetite for gold and power. . . . Everywhere where there is ruin, one sees Jews getting rich" (116).

Despite Mouilliseaux's alleged respect for assimilated Jews, he claimed that "the" Jews remained the most uniform race in the world. Even though they had been dispersed beyond Israel for centuries, they could be recognized by "the same classic type of body and soul, the same means of action, the same conceptions, the same activities, . . . the same characters." Not only were they ungrateful for the hospitality offered to them by their host countries, but they profited from their international connections to gratify their "instinctive tendency" to use money to enslave others.

Mouilliseaux also backtracked on his defense of Jews who had fought for France in the First World War. Although he said that such Jews should be honored for their sacrifice, he maintained that their role in the war had been greatly exaggerated, and he questioned the bravery of those who had survived. He said that of the 5 million Frenchmen who had been mobilized during the war only 45,000 were Jews and that 1,700,000 Frenchmen, one out of three, had died at the front, whereas only 1,100 Jews, one out of forty-three, had lost their lives in battle. "In light of this," he wrote, "to hell with those who remind us of Jewish losses" (116, 117, 122).

Moreover, Mouilliseaux wrote, the Jewish exploitation of Frenchmen that had taken place since 1918 far outweighed any contribution individual Jews had made to the war effort. Estimating France's total national wealth at one thousand billion francs, Mouilliseaux asserted that Jews owned half that amount. Thus, he wrote, "a simple calculation allows us to evaluate the number of Frenchmen who died defending a patrimony which previously they had been dispossessed of by the Jews (122). In 1934 another SF writer sounded the same theme. French soldiers, he wrote, had returned from the war only to realize that they had to fight again if they were to ensure their victory, only this time, on February 6, they had fought not against the Germans but against the "judeo-masonic-mafia" that governed France.[52]

Following the February 6 riots, various SF propagandists described the Stavisky affair as another example of "judeo-masonic tyranny." At an SF rally in April, Jacques Ditte denounced Stavisky as a Jewish swindler who had destroyed the savings of thousands of Frenchmen, adding that if all the Jews and Freemasons involved in the affair were subtracted from parliament there would be no one left in the Chamber of Deputies. At the same rally, Jacques Fromentin said that the government would not have to cut war veterans' pensions by 3 percent if it stopped paying millions to the unemployed and sent home all the Jews and foreigners who were depriving Frenchmen of jobs. The next speaker, Vinceguide, after making the standard disclaimer that he was not attacking the Jewish religion, warned that the Jews were "spreading their control over our country." He singled out "banking Judaism" as particularly pernicious and concluded that all Jews were Freemasons. Two weeks earlier at another SF meeting, Renaud had called for the formation of a national front against "the yids, the métèques [resident foreigners], and their allies, the Freemasons," whom he described as "all Communists or Socialists in league against France." Another speaker simply blamed France's woes on the Jews coming from Germany.[53]

None of these speakers mentioned a clash that had taken place that same month near the Arc de Triomphe between SF blueshirts and a Jewish "defense group" who were members of the International League against Antisemitism. The Jewish fighters had gotten the best of their SF opponents, wounding at least thirty of them before the police intervened.[54]

PRAISING MUSSOLINI AND HITLER AND CALLING FOR A FRANCO-ITALIAN-GERMAN ALLIANCE

The SF's praise of Mussolini and Hitler and its call in 1935 for a triple alliance of Italy, Germany, and France made its denials of fascism even more dubious. If Renaud's reaction to Hitler's persecution of Jews in Germany in 1935 was at least theoretically limited by his objections to Nazi racial doctrines, his approval of Hitler's repression of German Communists, Socialists, and liberals was unqualified. In *French Solidarity Attacks*, Renaud advocated a similar cleansing of France, declaring that just as Hitler had rid Germany of the Communists and Mussolini had saved Italy from the Freemasons the SF would clean up France's own "Augean stables." Germany and Italy had benefited from responsible leaders, and France, too, needed to be governed by new men with strong wills rather than by incompetent politicians.[55]

Renaud said that the SF had learned much from the way fascists in Italy and Germany had employed their shock troops. "Following the example of what has been done abroad, in Hitler's country and Mussolini's, . . . [the SF] is organizing its own defense. It is creating its own troops for protection, its own assault squads, its own blue shirts" (67).

Renaud objected to people who ridiculed Hitler as illiterate and uncultured.

Hitler, he stated, was a man of "audacity and action" and an enormously talented public speaker, a "charmer of crowds." Renaud argued even that these qualities stemmed from Hitler's southern background, from the fact that his character was more Latin than German:

> People do not want to understand that Hitler's seductiveness stems from his eyes, which are in turn caressing and cruel, from his supple and harmonious use of language, which he employs with a strong southern accent, from his expressive and attractive mimickry, which is a gift of the Latin race or the result of Latin influence.
>
> It is, in effect, by looking into his ancestry that the answer to the mystery is discovered. [It is because of] his direct descendence from a German father and an Austrian mother that he submitted . . . to Italian influence.
>
> This immediately explains why Hitler is so supple and fascinating, so eloquent and agile, among Teutons [who are] so cold, heavy, doctrinaire, and slow. (88)

Maintaining that France should never bow to German rule, Renaud contended that the best way to ensure this was to make France as strong and as "stable" as Nazi Germany. What France needed was "a government sure of itself, conscious of its power, capable of responding to the German dictator with equal ripostes, ready to throw on the floor a steel gauntlet of the same [strength] as that of the Chancellor of the swastika." At the same time, it was a mistake to believe that France and Germany would always be enemies, for they had important interests in common, especially when it came to their "implacable, pitiless struggle against the USSR" and their "battle against Freemasons and undesirable Jews" (93–94).

In 1935 Renaud called for a triple alliance of France, Italy, and Germany against England and Russia. Although Russia, he said, had not always been one of France's enemies, the fact that Russia was now governed by Communists ("the assassins of Moscow") made an anti-Russian alliance imperative. England was an enemy of a different kind, an impediment to French imperialism. Renaud recalled how he had once spoken with one of his heroes, General Mangin, about the possibilities of expanding France's colonial empire and how the general had said that if France ever allied herself with Germany it would make them "the masters of the world" (95). Renaud reiterated that such an alliance must never be at the expense of France's independence or be allowed to "degenerate first into a merger and then into domination." France was too "chauvinist" for that, and rightly so.

According to Renaud, France was rooted in Latin civilization and thus had strong spiritual ties with Italy. Such ties, he conceded, were missing with Germany, but here it was necessary for humanism to give way to realism. Although Hitler had often expressed hatred for France, he would forgo this hatred in order to benefit his people economically, which was a more solid basis for an alliance than friendly sentiments. France's leaders should be equally realistic. Despite the cultural differences that separated France from Germany, these leaders should "chat" with Hitler, "equal to equal," on behalf of the material interests they had in common (92–93).

Renaud wrote these words in 1935, not 1940, that is, five years before Hitler's invasion of France and therefore at a time when it was still possible to favor collaboration with the Germans and be a loyal French nationalist at the same time, something which, as John Sweets has shown, was far more difficult to carry off after 1940.[56] To defend an alliance with Germany and Italy and to advocate fascist policies for France itself in 1935 was, strictly speaking, still not unpatriotic.

It *was*, however, both highly undemocratic and morally callous. By 1935 some of the ruthless features of fascist rule in Italy and Germany had been well publicized in France, including Matteotti's murder by Mussolini's hirelings in 1924 and Hitler's Night of the Long Knives of June 1934. To be sure, the Holocaust had not yet begun, but plenty of other Nazi brutalities were public knowledge, including the creation of concentration camps for political prisoners. For Renaud to claim, as he did in 1935, that the new ideas coming out of Italy and Germany were not only hardy but humane indicates the extent of his fascism.

Renaud's call for a Franco-German alliance in 1935 represented a departure from the SF's original position. In 1933 François Coty was still an ardent Germanophobe. In 1932 L'Ami du Peuple had called Hitler a "demagogic agitator," and in January 1933, the day after Hitler became chancellor, the newspaper took note of his "implacable hatred for France."[57] In 1933 SF spokesmen were still focused on memories of the First World War and the renewed threat that Germany posed to French national security. At an SF rally in June, the SF's Lucien Souchon damned the Germans for violating the disarmament provisions of the Treaty of Versailles and criticized France's foreign minister, Aristide Briand, for making too many concessions to the Germans at Locarno and Geneva. Souchon derided the notion that Hitler was a "nice little boy" whose speeches in the Reichstag "were not as wicked as one liked to think," a remark that was greeted by laughter and applause from the audience.

Rather than dwell on Hitler and the Germans, however, Souchon chose to focus the blame on Briand and the parliamentary politicians of the Third Republic. Hitler would never have come to power in the first place, Souchon argued, if France had been more firm with Germany and men like Briand had not "betrayed" their country. The Germans had only done their duty as Germans, while the French had not done theirs as Frenchmen. Ultimately, it was political democracy, not Adolf Hitler, that was the greatest danger: "Our worst enemy is not abroad but at home. [Loud applause.] It is the regime of the politicians which constantly displays an attitude contrary to the interests of France." Jacques Fromentin offered a typically fascist solution, the same one proposed in the 1920s by the blueshirts of Antoine Redier, Georges Valois, and Pierre Taittinger. Fromentin declared, "After having swept the *Boches* from the trenches, it is incumbent upon our war veterans to sweep the political trenches clean."[58] Thus, even as SF speakers portrayed Nazi Germany in 1933 as a danger to France and called upon France to resist that threat, they expressed a hatred for parliamentarianism and a taste for paramilitary force that was all too compatible with fascism at home.

Moreover, even in 1933, *L'Ami du Peuple* praised Nazism for crushing Marxist labor unions and the Communist party in Germany. One article noted that France and Germany had the same enemies: "international finance and Bolshevism." In the period that followed, the titles of other articles reflected the shift in the newspaper's editorial policy: "In Ten Days, Marxism Will No Longer Exist in Germany," "Hitler Has Undertaken to Exterminate Marxism," "With Germany against Bolshevism." Coty's anti-Germanism was increasingly subordinated to a higher priority, anticommunism. Mussolini, on the other hand, was never a problem for Coty, who as early as 1928 paid homage to the Italian dictator for liberating Italy from communism.[59]

Renaud spoke much more kindly of Hitler in 1935 than Souchon did in 1933 but was no less patriotic in insisting that France should never "submit to any foreign . . . interference in the conduct of her internal affairs." In 1933 he accused Briand of being a naive pilgrim of peace who had dismantled France's military establishment at a time when Germany continued to rearm. Both in 1933 and 1935 Renaud supported a French military buildup as the best deterrent to a German invasion: "We want to show our power in order to not have to use it."[60] Renaud was just as nationalistic about his country as Hitler was about his.

This did not mean that Renaud was adverse to trampling on the nationalism of others should France gain the upper hand, especially if it benefited French imperialism. Renaud, a former colonial officer who had served in Indochina, shared Coty's dream of an empire of a hundred million inhabitants that would provide France with the raw materials needed to feed her industries and people.

He called for a strong French navy to preserve such an empire. In 1935 he accused leftist politicians, particularly Léon Blum, of sabotaging France's colonial efforts in Indochina, Morocco, and Senegal and for hampering her colonial officials in general, a policy, he said, that would one day produce a catastrophe. Renaud was also critical of Blum for demanding sanctions against Italy after Italy invaded "uncivilized" Ethiopia. Blum, he wrote, was "a man without a country," a Jew who sought to lead France into a "fratricidal war with Italy, our sister in Latin culture."[61]

Like Mussolini and Hitler, Renaud believed in exploiting other peoples to ensure prosperity at home. Although France became an object of plunder by the Germans during the Second World War, there is little reason to believe, given Renaud's own nationalistic and imperialistic attitudes, that he would have acted any differently had the situation been reversed. Imperialism was a major ingredient in fascist solutions to the Depression, and Renaud was one of its advocates.

To be sure, not all French imperialists were fascists in the 1930s. Indeed, most French Radicals and Socialists supported colonialism, some more benevolently than others, during the 1930s. And not all Frenchmen who supported an alliance with Nazi Germany and fascist Italy in 1935 were in favor of fascism in France. It is only when the SF's views on foreign policy are combined with its views on domestic policy that its fascism is fully revealed.

FASCIST REPUBLICANISM AND NATIONAL SOCIALISM

Like all of the other major French fascist movements of the interwar period (with the exception of the royalist AF), the SF claimed to be republican. The republicanism it had in mind, however, was meant to undermine political democracy, not fulfill it. For reasons of expediency, the SF hedged when it came to rejecting elections altogether. Between 1933 and 1936, the SF was torn between appearing too authoritarian, thereby running the risk of being banned by the government, and not authoritarian enough, thereby weakening its attraction to conservatives who wanted a more forceful response to Marxism. Its solution was to send a number of mixed messages, presenting itself as both democratic and anti-democratic.

In the wake of the February 1934 riots, the SF became increasingly vocal in its praise of the German and Italian dictatorships, its scorn for republican legality, and its threats of using the "guillotine" against leftist opponents. Earlier, however, in 1933, François Coty's proposed revision of the Constitution, his so-called Reform of the State, contained several democratic and even liberal features. It called for the president of the republic to be elected by direct universal suffrage (women were also to vote) and for a Supreme Court that would guarantee basic rights. According to Coty, France would still be republican, only it would practice a true republicanism, not the false republicanism of the Third Republic.[62]

On balance, Coty's Reform of the State was far more Bonapartist than democratic. It called for an immense strengthening of the executive at the expense of the legislature. Parliament would still be elected (the Chamber of Deputies by direct and the Senate by indirect suffrage), but its members would be restricted to one term in office, which Coty said would make them less demagogic, that is, less accountable to their constituents. Conversely, the president would be elected for seven years and be eligible for a second term. Parliament would have the power to vote taxes and control expenditures but not the right to initiate legislation, that task being reserved exclusively for the executive branch of the government. A Council of State appointed by the president would draft all legislation, which would then be voted on by parliament. Should the president dislike the outcome, he could dissolve parliament and call for new elections. All major reforms would be submitted to a national referendum for approval. The president would appoint all government ministers, half of whom would have to come from nonparliamentary backgrounds—one more feature of Coty's constitution that would make government officials less beholden to the public.

That Coty's Reform of the State echoed the Bonapartist tradition is no reason to deny that it was fascist, as some consensus historians have been wont to do. As William Irvine has pointed out,

> Claiming that movements cannot be fascist because they are "Bonapartist," a stock answer, really begs the question. What, after all, separates the Bonapartist tradition from the fascist one? René Rémond's answer would seem to be the absence of a mass party. This is true enough, although Bonapartism, especially in the early Third Republic, certainly had a popular base. . . . The real, although invariably implicit, significance of Bonapartism [for consensus historians] . . . is that it represents a traditional conservatism, and conservatism, once again, drives out any possible fascism.[63]

The first political rally held by the SF took place in June 1933 at the Salle Wagram in Paris and was notable for both its fascist symbolism and fascist ideas. With fascist uniforms and salutes contributing to what Coty called the grandeur of the evening, four speakers (Coty, Renaud, Fromentin, and Jacques Ditte) engaged in a series of anti-Semitic, anti-Masonic, anti-Communist, anti-Socialist, and antiliberal tirades—all combined with a call for the overthrow of the Third Republic by France's war veterans.

The first speaker that evening was Coty. He began by emphasizing that the SF was interested in more than mere oratory: "To speak is not to act." The SF, he declared, meant to provide a disciplined force, "ready for action but calm," that would oust the incompetent and greedy politicians of the Third Republic, who, as a result of their "complete absence of moral sense," had allowed France to become entangled in a "frightening web of internationalism." Italy, Germany, and England had become "solid" nations, while France had not.

Coty was followed by Jacques Fromentin, who also condemned "facile oratorical successes which led to nothing" and underscored the role that war veterans, men of action not just talk, would play in the movement. The best representatives of French nationalism, he said, were *les poilus*, the combat soldiers of the First World War. According to a police spy in attendance, these words were met by loud applause from the audience. Fromentin continued, "There is still time for our veterans to prove that they have guts (applause). It is up to the *poilus* to clear the political trenches (unanimous applause)." Perhaps concerned that such language might become grounds for a government ban, Fromentin added that the war veterans of the SF would not need rifles to do this job because "a sweep of the broom would suffice." He did not mince words, however, when it came to denouncing the alleged traitors who governed France, the "judeo-Germanic invasion" that was turning the nation into "an international ghetto," and French leftists who threatened to reduce the French taxpayer to rags.

The next speaker, Jacques Ditte, also complained of "crushing" taxes, which he blamed on excessive government spending. Behind this taxation were the Jews, "the avant-garde of internationalism," especially the "big Jews, the international bankers who fattened themselves off the people." The Jews were also linked to Marxism: "Against Marxist doctrine, against this judeo-German hodge-podge that reminds us of spoiled sauerkraut, we stand for a doctrine that is neat, clear, healthy, and French." Unlike "Blum and company," the SF was committed to low taxes and Christian civilization. Freemasons were also to blame, since they also supported creeping Socialism. Ditte also contrasted the good war veteran to the bad politician, while insisting that the SF had no intention of departing from legality.

The last speaker was Renaud, who also claimed that the SF was committed to "absolute legality." Renaud lamented the failure of the Third Republic to eradicate France's "number one enemy," the Socialists, from French political life.

Only Coty's Reform of the State, he said, could prevent politicians like Blum and Edouard Herriot (the Radical Socialist leader), from ruining the nation. All nationalists, "be they monarchists, republicans, or Bonapartists," needed to revive the sacred union of the First World War, only this time directing it against France's domestic enemies, the Socialist and Radical-Socialist parties. This new sacred union would be symbolized not by the "clenched fist" (the Socialist salute) but by the "open hand" (the fascist salute). Such was the flavor of the first public rally of the SF at the Salle Wagram in Paris in 1933.[64]

Two years later in *French Solidarity Attacks*, Renaud no longer paid lip service to legality. Referring to the riots of February 6, he hoped that a renewal of such demonstrations would lead to a "seizure of power." Action of this kind, he argued, was required by a moral imperative that overrode republican constraints, by a "return to the right, to the true Right, which is not the Right of . . . pettifogging legalists but the eternal Right which each man finds in his cradle at birth."[65] The parliamentary right, by contrast, was too liberal: "This is why the parties of the right do not think of engaging in combat against the reds. They prefer to compromise with them or to adjust to them. They accuse patriots, who consider more energetic and definitive means, of being violent and fanatic. They are gray beards or old masonic and cowardly republican types. They lack that sacred fire. They do not have the faith that arouses the masses, because they have the cold hearts of fat lawyers and not the vibrant hearts of apostles" (65). Renaud added that the SF would no longer be bound to the parliamentary right; the SF had "sympathies but not liaisons."

Renaud was critical of much of the French authoritarian right as well, chiding the CF, the AF, and the JP for limiting themselves to exhibitions, parades, and "speeches full of wind." He urged the followers of these organizations to turn to the SF, a movement that believed in "action and still more action" and that was ready to provide France, "if need be," with "a guillotine and not a bandage on a wooden leg" (41). If this was more bluster on Renaud's part (the SF was on its last legs in 1935), it was, ironically, the same kind of bluster that Vinceguide had directed at him in the spring of 1934. By 1935 Renaud had come to sound like an "adventurer" himself.

In 1935 Renaud also gave a more authoritarian twist to Coty's original Reform of the State. Coty's proposals had called for both houses of parliament, the Chamber of Deputies and the Senate, to be chosen by popular elections. In 1935 Renaud insisted that one of the houses of parliament be corporatist and that its members be chosen less democratically. Moreover, only the corporatist assembly would have the right to deal with economic matters, the Chamber of Deputies being restricted to strictly political issues. Each house was to be absolutely independent of the other, that is, the more democratically elected Chamber of Deputies would be forbidden to even discuss economic legislation! (111).

The corporatist assembly would be elected by the major industries and professions of France, with only the most "responsible" members of each profession being eligible for election (that is, with only those most connected with or loyal to management being able to serve in the corporatist assembly). Accountability would be to the top of the social pyramid, not to the bottom: "There must be no decisions taken by a majority but only by those who are responsible. In short, in our Reform of the State there will exist no representative body that will make decisions on the basis of the majority but only deliberative bodies that will be placed alongside chosen leaders who will distribute the work, these deliberative assemblies being responsible in each department to their leaders" (105). Renaud argued that this system would replace the incompetency of politicians, who were jacks-of-all-trades-but-masters-of-none, with the capabilities of technocrats who were proven experts in their fields.

However, not even such conservatively selected technocrats were to be totally empowered, Renaud stipulating that their corporatist assembly would be only a deliberative body, not a "concluding" one. "Final decisions would be taken exclusively by the President-Leader" (106). In a modest concession to democracy, Renaud proposed that the president-leader be chosen by an electoral college composed of members of the Chamber of Deputies and representatives of France's major industries and professions. Shamelessly professing to be a "resolute partisan of universal suffrage," Renaud claimed that only by a large infusion of professional and qualitative votes into a system that had previously been completely dependent on quantitative votes could the suffrage be renewed. Thus, while professing to believe in democracy, Renaud sought to gut it. The role of the masses in electing a president would be reduced, possibly by as much as a half, by corporatist representatives, and the people's representatives in the Chamber of Deputies would be denied the right to initiate or even approve economic legislation (111). This was republicanism with a fascist twist.

Because a president elected in the above manner would have to be well connected with the business community (a left-wing candidate could hardly expect to receive many "qualitative" votes), it was highly unlikely that any economic legislation he initiated would contradict this community's interests. No wonder Renaud believed that such a constitution would eliminate the Socialist threat from French politics. It would have given the "responsible" few, that is, representatives of management, more control over social and economic legislation and the "irresponsible" many, the workers, much less. By undermining political democracy, Renaud's reform would have undermined social democracy. It would have stacked the cards against labor with a politically loaded deck.

The integral relation between Renaud's political and economic views is further revealed in his complaint that under the Third Republic the state had become the manager of various factories, banks, and insurance companies as a result of the influence of the Socialists. According to Renaud, private firms were being replaced with government monopolies. The control of these businesses should be returned to their "natural managers," and the state should pursue a policy of economic decentralization, supporting private enterprise rather than government intervention (110, 211, 215). Thus, while Renaud strongly favored political statism, fascist statism, he was opposed to economic statism, socialist statism.

In *French Solidarity Attacks* Renaud praised the socially conservative and politically authoritarian AF, describing it and the SF as the two most advanced nationalist movements in France. Indeed, he suggested that the only serious difference between them was that the AF was royalist while the SF was republican (116).

In spite of its conservative socioeconomic goals and its support for a political system that favored business interests, the SF sometimes claimed to be a national "socialist" or national "syndicalist" movement. Like earlier French fascist movements, it described itself as a defender of the people, even of the proletariat—at least of those proletarians who were willing to abandon Marxism.[66] Like earlier French fascist movements, too, it was not above using mystifying rhetoric to win workers away from the Communist CGT and the Socialist CGTU. Its socialism, in effect, was no more genuine than its republicanism.

According to Renaud, the SF sought dignity and "material liberation" for the worker. There was "nothing more cruel" than the sight of the unemployed "with crossed arms and empty stomachs." The SF was dedicated to eradicating all the slums and "social scourges" in France, because everyone had the right "to rest, to sun, and to air." No movement could hope to bring these changes about without popular support: "Nothing good is ever achieved without relying on the workers and the peasants"; "We are of the people. We go to them, and they listen to us." The SF counted on the kind of Frenchmen who in earlier times had raised the "barricades" and made a "revolution." In 1789 their ancestors had rebelled against feudal privileges and "shocking fiscal inequities." It was up to their offspring to "take up again the great movement begun in '89, which was only the logical outcome of other revolutions whose sum total constitutes our history."[67]

Renaud insisted that the SF was no lackey of big business. He conceded that he often denounced left-wing politicians, but this, he said, was because they had not dealt with the social problem courageously. He claimed that he was equally critical of the parliamentary right when it failed to help the people. "No minister of the right," he wrote, had ever protected the workers. A society controlled by "plutocratic liberalism" would not last because it "pushed the workers from its breast." There was "nothing bourgeois" about the SF, for it was opposed to the great feudal barons who, sheltered by "the Trusts, the Banks, and the Stock Exchange," exploited the workers and treated the nation like a conquered country. The SF wished to end the servitude of the workers in the factories and fields of France, a servitude imposed by big business and international finance. The SF was "anticapitalist"; it opposed the concentration of riches that allowed unscrupulous financiers to carry out their antihuman designs. Only the "national syndicalism" of the SF could reintegrate the workers into *la patrie*.

Renaud even declared that the SF had a good deal in common with communism, not only with its desire to liberate the workers but also with its hatred of liberalism and plutocracy. However, he wrote, the rest of communism was "odious." Bolshevik organizations subsidized by Jewish international capitalism constantly sought to divide the nation. Workers who supported communism were honest but naive, which is why SF blueshirts were ordered never to attack their "Communist comrades," but rather only to defend themselves if they were attacked first. At the same time, the SF would be "merciless" toward Communist leaders who exploited workers for their own political purposes.[68]

In May 1934 Vinceguide, still a member of the SF, declaimed that "the Communists themselves are our brothers, and we invite them to enter our ranks to defend *la patrie*."[69] It was not a welcome, however, that extended to the communism in which these brothers believed. *Bolshevik* remained a pejorative term for Vinceguide, Renaud, and other SF speakers. In effect, the SF was employing the same tactic that the Faisceau had tried a decade earlier, appealing to Communists to join their movement while vehemently rejecting communism itself. In neither case did they have much success.[70]

The national syndicalism that Renaud had in mind was not Marxist. It was not even favorable to welfare capitalism, inasmuch as it wanted to lower taxes on the rich, not raise them, and cut social spending on behalf of the poor, not increase it. Coty's Reform of the State would have enhanced capitalist control of the basic means of production, not diminished it. Renaud attacked the trusts rhetorically, not seriously. For all of his allusions to the French Revolution of

1789, he was no advocate of class conflict. In 1935 he declared that the "number one goal" of the SF was "to make France live through the collaboration of classes."[71]

Renaud's answer to lower-class grievances was the same as that of previous French fascists: not social and economic justice for all, but upward social mobility for some. He supported neither worker control of industry nor a more equitable distribution of wealth, but rather the eventual "acquisition of property" by workers (212). The SF believed in careers open to talent, not social egalitarianism. The national socialism of the SF was the same as that of the Faisceau in this respect.[72]

Renaud acknowledged that social hierarchy would continue to exist under SF governance but maintained that SF leaders would display a greater sense of duty than the politicians of the Third Republic. And they would not shrink from employing harsh measures if the rich and powerful failed to meet their responsibilities to those beneath them, applying "the guillotine if necessary" to "the most highly placed persons."[73] Renaud failed to mention that the corporatist political structure he proposed would have made such retribution improbable.

In his vision of the good society, Renaud preferred to dwell on social harmony, not social conflict. Instead of French politics being characterized by a succession of fights between opposing forces, cooperation would rule. "The whole program of the Solidarité Française is to pay homage to this essential truth" (167). What Renaud did not spell out, of course, was that this cooperation would take place largely on management's terms because management would control the levers of political power, thanks to the SF's revision of the Constitution.

Renaud's dictum that each individual was "a cell that could not live without the life of the entire organism" was an expression not of socialist solidarity but of conservative nationalism (212). The organic society he described would have left the class structure—and the upper-class privileges that went with it— firmly intact. In short, Renaud's socialism was conservatism by another name.

Renaud's socialism was not compatible with the revisionist socialism of the SFIO, a party that also advocated class collaboration in 1935. What the SFIO sought was class collaboration between the workers and the most progressive sections of the bourgeoisie, not class collaboration between the workers and the most reactionary sections of the bourgeoisie. For the SFIO in 1935 class collaboration was a means of moving *toward* a socialist society, not *away* from it. Renaud was adamantly opposed to such an outcome. He repeatedly denounced Blum and the SFIO, condemned liberals who compromised with them, and demanded that Marxism in all its forms be defeated. Renaud summed up his attitude toward Blum and the SFIO in the title of an article he wrote for *L'Ami du Peuple* on November 16, 1932: "Blum, there is the Enemy."

In spite of such sentiments, Renaud maintained that the SF was "neither right nor left," that it would serve management and labor equally well. The corporatism of the SF, he said, was not the corporatism of constraint that was practiced in Italy, where Mussolini's prefects designated who would represent the various professions. Under SF corporatism, delegates would be freely chosen by each profession "without a gendarme around every corner."[74] "Freely chosen" did not mean, however, that Marxist unions would affect the voting, since under Renaud's plan both the Communist CGT and the Socialist CGTU would be abolished. The aim of the SF, Renaud said, was not simply to add a new set of unions to the thousands that already existed, which would only add to the "democratic disorder" oppressing France, but to eliminate all individualistic trade unions and business associations that undermined national solidarity. All Frenchmen would be required to join corporatist unions, which would be composed of both management and labor. The business associations of France would merge with these unions.

Within this framework, Renaud said, each local union would elect delegates to higher regional and national bodies representing their individual trade or profession—with the proviso that delegates of management and labor be elected in equal numbers. It would be up to these regional organizations, with half their members coming from management, to arbitrate all labor disputes. At the top of the corporatist pyramid would be a corporatist national assembly and above this a National Economic Council, half of whose members would be representatives of agriculture. In other words, the influence of workers, through the repeated watering down of their representation, would be largely negated at the highest level.

In one respect, however, Renaud in 1935 was more democratic than Coty in 1933 in that he stipulated that legislation prepared by the National Economic Council be sent to the Chamber of Deputies to be voted on, thus granting the chamber a modicum of power. (Coty, by contrast, had denied the chamber the right to even discuss economic legislation, let alone vote on it.)

Still, Renaud's formula clearly favored the right far more than the left. There was little chance that the new corporatist unions envisioned by Renaud would have adequately represented the interests of labor; management would have easily dominated them, especially at the local level, where management's power to hire and fire and promote and demote could be easily used to intimidate workers. Neither was labor's major weapon, the strike, likely to have been exercised by unions controlled by management and faced with a political system hostile to "class conflict." Finally, even should working-class protests, by some miracle, have managed to reach the National Economic Council, they would have encountered a body stacked with management representatives and conservative farmers unfriendly to their cause.

Renaud's notion of neither right nor left was to urge bosses to have "more heart" for their workers and workers to have more consideration for their bosses: "A boss is not necessarily an enemy; he is a man like anybody else. He also suffers. He undergoes crises. He faces impossible situations at the end of certain months. He knows the threat of bankruptcy. Be more understanding and don't think that a boss is always and above all an infamous exploiter! . . . We will never save our country if we do not save the bosses, the merchants, the industrialists, the workers and the peasants who are the immediate creators of prosperity for everyone" (156–57).

By making business associations and trade unions subject to the same corporatist system, Renaud sought to give the impression of evenhandedness. There would be no place, he declared, for *either* right-wing or left-wing instruments of class warfare: "In a corporatist France, . . . the General Confederation of French Production, the Steel Trust, and [other business associations], as well as the CGT and the CGTU, would be abolished" (144). But, of course, with management enjoying much greater power than labor throughout the whole system and with no independent working-class organizations to counteract that power, there would be little need for business enterprises to have their own counterassociations. In *Corporatism and the Reform of the State* (1935), Louis Mouilliseaux was more blunt than Renaud. Not only did he call for the abolition of the CGT, the CGTU, and other "revolutionary syndicalist organizations," but he noted that if it were impossible to convince workers of the "benefits of Order," then these benefits would have to be "imposed" on them.[75]

In sum, Renaud's claim that the SF was neither right nor left was simply untrue. Its corporatism would have drastically reduced working-class bargaining power and greatly increased management's authority. Labor would have been deprived of its own unions and probably deprived of its right to strike as well, given that the SF viewed strikes as a form of class conflict. Workers' grievances would have been submitted to corporatist arbitration boards dominated by representatives of management. At the highest level, the National Economic Council, half-composed of antiurban and antisocialist farmers, would have joined with other conservatives to block any serious reforms. If, as Renaud claimed, the national syndicalism of the SF was "simultaneously revolutionary and reactionary," serious elements of the former were hard to find.

ANTI-MARXISM

No doubt Renaud would have been astonished if he had been told in 1933 that French fascism was a revision of Marxism or that it was revolutionary in any Marxist sense. Certainly his was not. On the day the SF was launched, he declared, "Socialism, that is the enemy!"[76] Two years later he said that the SF pursued an antirevolutionary program of self-defense that aimed at suppressing both *L'Humanité* and the Popular Front.[77]

No doubt, too, most French workers would have been astonished if they had been told in 1933 that the SF was an offshoot of Marxism. Few proletarians were taken in by the SF's claims of national syndicalism. Most members of the CGT and the CGTU equated the SF with the fascism that had crushed Marxist unions in Italy and Germany. They saw it as a movement to be resisted, not supported.

And resist they did, sometimes violently. Following the riots of February 6, Communist and Socialist militants intensified their efforts to prevent the SF and other French fascist organizations from holding public meetings in Paris and the provinces. On several occasions these militants were so successful that SF members required police protection to return home, a turn of affairs that did little to enhance the SF's reputation as a virile barrier to communism.

Police reports in the wake of the February 6 riots recount how subsequent SF and JP meetings were repeatedly disturbed by local Communist and Socialist groups. When the SF or the JP announced in the newspapers that they were going to hold a public meeting at a certain time and place, *L'Humanité* and *Le Populaire* would often call upon leftists to protest. Although French Communists and Socialists were bitter enemies on a number of issues and although the spring of 1934 was months before the Popular Front was formed, when it came to antifascist demonstrations they often cooperated. This was especially true when the SF or the JP tried to hold meetings in working-class neighborhoods.

Police reported several incidents of left-wing attempts to disrupt such meetings. On March 29, 1934, at an SF meeting in the working-class suburb of Montreuil, Communists beat up several SF members and engaged in skirmishes with the police. Most of the SF audience left by a hidden exit and was escorted to the nearest subway by three police cars. On May 8, seven Communists entered an SF meeting at Saint-Quentin and threw rocks at the audience. On May 23, an SF meeting at a cinema in Cachan had to be protected from some four hundred to five hundred Communists by the police. On May 29, a group of leftists tried to enter a theater in Moulins where the SF was holding a meeting but were repulsed after clashing with the police. On June 5, the SF had to cancel a meeting set for the Communist stronghold of St. Denis because of intense local opposition. On June 9, police reported that when SF shock troops were sent orders to guard an SF meeting, the orders were sometimes marked with an X or XX. An X meant they were to come with a club, an XX with a revolver. On June 18, some six hundred to seven hundred Communist demonstrators in Lyon, singing the "Internationale" and throwing rocks, chairs, bottles, and paving stones, tried to break through a police barricade defending an SF meeting. On June 26, the mayor of Arras forbade an SF rally in his city for fear of a public disturbance, causing SF members to protest that they had been denied the right to freedom of assembly.[78]

Physical assaults by Marxists upon SF members were not the only reason Renaud hated them. Marxists, he wrote, were out to destroy the "fraternity of the classes" and also religion and the family. They were materialists who appealed to the lowest instincts of the people in their attempts to provoke civil war. Egged on by the Jews, they wanted to replace French patriotism with "international humanitarianism." Marx himself was a "Jewish pedant" and his followers "diseased dogs."

In denouncing Marxism, Renaud not only played to middle-class fears of a Bolshevik-style revolution in France but also exploited a more realistic and therefore perhaps even greater anxiety: that the Socialists and their allies might raise taxes if they came to power. According to Renaud, such leftists threatened a "taxation of folly" that would destroy the savings not just of the rich but of the ordinary people of France, "of you, the peasants, of you the small property holders or small merchants."

Renaud warned that just as French patriots in 1789 had had to deal with the internal as well as the foreign enemies of the nation, so French patriots in 1934 had to deal with subversives, only now instead of being royalists they were well-armed Communists acting on the orders of Moscow. Behind the Communists lurked the "sinister profile" of Léon Blum. The situation could be compared to a "tidal wave of mud," behind which could be heard the "howls of a whole pack of diabolical faces."[79]

At an SF meeting in April 1934, Vinceguide declared that France was entering a period during which "all the forces of the extreme left envisage a coming revolution." France was faced with another 1789, threatened once again from both within and without. "The bloody flag is raised. To arms, citizens!" Vinceguide exhorted. The shock troops of the SF were prepared to die fighting the "red tyranny" of the CGT and the CGTU: "Against force, we will respond with force." Vinceguide conceded that the SF possessed no great stores of arms, but he reminded his audience that many Frenchmen were hunters or had revolvers at home. If "all else failed," they "would not let themselves be assassinated" (a remark that, according to the police, was met with loud applause).[80]

In 1935 Renaud declared that a Marxist revolution must be prevented by "any means necessary" and that "revolutionary justice" should be meted out to the leaders of the Communist and Socialist parties should they attempt a coup. He remarked that it might not be necessary to erect guillotines in Paris if these leaders had already fled across the border. However, if any Marxist agitators were captured in France "justice would be done." The first to be punished would be Léon Blum: "If at seven o'clock in the morning the Solidarité Française attacks and takes power, at eight o'clock L'Humanité will be closed, Le Populaire banned, Freemasonry expelled, [and] the Popular Front dissolved. And at nine o'clock, Léon Blum will be taken before a council of war or a High Court."[81]

In Corporatism and the Reform of the State, Mouilliseaux attacked Marxism on various doctrinal grounds, beginning with its commitment to social democracy. Karl Marx, he wrote, had preached that "old, insane dream that stagnates in the soul of every Jew," the dream of society being reduced to a "single class of workers," to a "popular Moloch, the Proletariat, universal [and] sovereign."[82] Whereas the SF supported hierarchies dedicated to serving the nation, Marxism sought to level all classes.

Although Mouilliseaux was no friend of liberalism on many issues, he shamelessly exploited its principle of individualism when he found it useful in criticizing Marxism. He accused the Communists and Socialists of wanting to create a world in which everyone would be reduced to a cog in a machine, "scientifically proletarianized." Marxism, he wrote, ignored the importance of individual personality, which sprang from the exercise of free will. It deprived man of the right "TO BE HIMSELF, to remain his own master" (162). Marxist egalitarianism was the death of individualism:

How does one govern a herd of sheep? The animals are stamped with a red mark. They graze, reproduce, [and] sleep. . . . Such an administration is [seen by the Marxists] as legitimate. It suits the sheep, who is indifferent to the choice of his companion or his roof. His wool grows, his flesh increases, his offspring are born according to an eternal rhythm which is IMPERSONAL. . . . A sheep equals a sheep, which equals another sheep. . . .

[Whereas for us] one individual chooses to build the walls of his home against the flank of a hill, another prefers the protection of a valley. In the name of what dogma can other habitats be imposed on them? In the name of what [principle] should an egalitarian rope bind together what Nature is pleased to differentiate? . . . Marxism does not give a damn about fundamental [human] differences. It sees society as only a brutal mathematical sum of the same kind of units. . . . It is mass politics. (168–82).

Mouilliseaux had no difficulty, however, opposing proletarian choices, particularly their choosing of their own trade unions. He was also far more critical of Communist authoritarianism than of fascist authoritarianism, a double standard that ran throughout his thought. To be harnessed to a left-wing yoke under Marxism was "barbarianism"; to be harnessed to a right-wing yoke under corporatism was "cooperation." Mouilliseaux was not only more concerned with the personalities of middle-class than working-class Frenchmen, but also more attuned to the individual rights of gentiles, Catholics, and social conservatives than to those of Jews, Freemasons, and social radicals. Not all diversity was welcomed by Mouilliseaux. In short, like other French fascists, he extolled liberal principles when they served his cause and ignored them when they did not.

Mouilliseaux also waxed pious in contrasting SF "humanism" with Marxist materialism. Humanism, he said, was not opposed to progress, but neither was it in favor of epicureanism. Its goals were far more spiritual than those of Marxism, whose materialism and hedonism were decadent. The SF opposed mass production ("the machine without a soul") and supported artisans who crafted objects of quality, not quantity. Although the SF admired scientific methods, it did not want the French people enslaved by them. With Marxism, on the other hand, there was "too much science, too much of science only" (173, 167).

Mouilliseaux was no enemy, however, of a materialism that protected property rights, low taxes, and middle-class wealth. Although he complained about the "cult of the golden calf," about the "inhuman selfishness" of a society founded solely on capitalism, and about nouveaux riches who were the major beneficiaries of industrialization, his solution was a corporatist state that would disempower the labor movement and put all too materialistic conservatives in charge of society.

The last chapter of Mouilliseaux's book was entitled "Our Spiritual Revolution." In it, he emphasized that Marxism lacked any sense of the "transcendental, the supra-Human, the Divine." Its philosophical materialism and economic determinism rejected the "ancient moral values" innate in human nature— values, he might have added, that were conveniently compatible with the SF's social and economic conservatism.

Mouilliseaux also condemned Marxism for attacking nationalism. Marxism, with its internationalist principles and belief in class warfare, undermined national solidarity. The SF was inspired by the French Revolution of 1789, not by the Russian Revolution of 1917. "The 'Internationale' was not sung at Valmy or Jemmapes. The red flag did not float at the head of the armies of Marceau or Hoche." The SF was the party of the "Marseillaise" and the tricolor; the PCF and the SFIO were not. The SF was patriotic; Marxism was not (157–58, 162, 36).

ANTILIBERALISM

According to Mouilliseaux, France had not one, but two major enemies: Marxism and liberalism. Although liberals also "stigmatized, condemned and abominated Marxism," they were too philosophically skeptical and intellectually tolerant to combat Marxism effectively. For the formidable expansion of Marxism that had taken place in France, they had only themselves to blame. Whereas Marxism at least constituted an affirmation, liberalism was nothing but doubt (161). Liberals, in short, were too soft on Marxism, lacking the intellectual firmness to suppress it. They rejected, in other words, Mouilliseaux's double standard toward freedom in that they defended the right of everyone, leftists as well as rightists, to freedom of speech and association.

Mouilliseaux was no such liberal. Neither was Renaud or Vinceguide. For all three, the truths of French nationalism were absolute, and anyone who was "corrupt" enough to question them deserved to be repressed. To be sure, all three occasionally paid lip service to liberal values, only to contradict themselves later. In 1934, for example, Vinceguide declared that the methods employed by Mussolini in Italy would never work with a people as individualistic as the French. "The Solidarité Française," he declaimed, "struggles for individualism, property, and liberty."[83] Yet he repeatedly expressed his contempt for political democracy and the civil rights of his opponents.

Renaud was no different. In 1935, even as he complained that "judeo-socio-bourgeois tyrants" were "nibbling away at French liberties," he declared that in no way did he question the fundamental principle of government, which was that of authority. Neither did he believe that the major goal of the SF could be achieved solely through persuasion: "Class collaboration? Yes. But to achieve it, a force, an authority, a protective power is necessary." The benefits of order would be imposed on workers, and their membership in the new corporatist unions would be "obligatory."[84] Renaud's praise of Hitler and Mussolini for repressing the political left in Germany and Italy also suggests that his opposition to tyrants was selective.

Renaud and his collaborators objected to liberalism in education, too, particularly to anticlerical, left-wing liberalism. They denounced France's public school teachers for undermining the influence of parents and poisoning the souls of their children with Marxism, skepticism, antipatriotism, and anti-Christianity. According to Renaud, French education had become a fief of Moscow and could be saved only if a number of "anarchist, unionized, and revolutionary" teachers were fired. At an SF meeting in 1933, one SF speaker contended that French youth had been so brainwashed by their teachers that they no longer believed in anything, "not even in *la patrie.*" Another accused French schoolteachers of indoctrinating students with revolutionary ideas, blaming this on the fact that the schools were no longer Christian.[85]

These criticisms were sometimes accompanied by calls for violence against individual teachers. In 1935 Fromentin gave a speech in which he damned the French teachers' union for staging a national walkout, especially "certain teachers" who were involved in "revolutionary" schemes. His remedy was at odds with Vinceguide's earlier claim that the SF, respecting French individualism, recognized the unworkability of fascist methods in France. According to police, Fromentin told the audience, "We have created a special section [of blueshirts] . . . who have sworn upon the flag of our movement to execute without discussion the orders we give them and to die if need be in carrying them out. The first mission of these brave men will consist of punishing red teachers, a list of whom we have just carefully established. They will make themselves their masters, take their pants off, and make them ingurgitate and pass through their posteriors a minimum of ten grams of castor oil . . . to begin with."

One newspaper quoted Fromentin as saying, "We keep a public list of Freemasons and anticlerical teachers. They are all under surveillance. At the first insult that one of them delivers, we will go into his class, take his pants off and, in front of his students, inflict upon him the punishment he deserves, while our leader, Jean Renaud, gives the schoolchildren a lecture on their duties toward God."[86]

The reference to the Freemasons was a reference to the most hated of archliberals, the anticlerical Freemason being one of the major bêtes noires of French fascism in general. For Fromentin, it was a short step from condemning Freemasons as a "malodorous and cancerist gangrene" on the body politic to wishing physical violence upon them.

When Vinceguide declared in 1934 that "our base is Christian and Catholic," he was not referring to a liberal, leftist, or internationalistic brand of Catholicism. SF Catholicism was authoritarian, right-wing, and nationalistic. At one SF meeting, Vinceguide, evoking the memory of Joan of Arc as a symbol of French nationalism, stated that just as Saint Joan had resisted the English in her day the SF would resist the Germans in theirs.[87] His opposition to a German invasion of France, of course, made his brand of Catholicism no less fascist.

WOMEN

The sexual politics of SF males were as defensive as the rest of their politics, only here the threat was to a different kind of security. If Marxists threatened their economic security, Jews their ethnic security, Freemasons their religious security, and schoolteachers their parental security, feminists threatened the security they derived from their patriarchal authority in the home and their preferential treatment at the workplace.

Feminism seems to have aroused intense feelings in Renaud, judging from the shrill tone of his pronouncements on the subject. One reason he hated the Freemasons so much was because he associated them not only with Marxists, liberals, and Jews but also with feminists. To his mind, Freemasonry meant cultural liberalism, and one outcome of cultural liberalism was feminism. In 1935 he declared that although women had a major role to play in society their actions would be beneficial only if they refused to deliver themselves to the "dictatorship of the Freemasons or to the grip of Louise Weiss [a well-known pacifist and suffragist] or to other plumed mules."[88]

In *French Solidarity Attacks*, Renaud complained that, despite continuing male unemployment, more women were working outside the home than ever before, and he demanded that the government "partially suppress" salaried work for women. Most women, he said, took little pleasure in such work anyway, preferring to "be homemakers, have babies, [and] create health, beauty and elegance within the home" (130–43). The First World War, by causing women to replace men in the factories, and the Depression, by temporarily lowering the wages of men, had sidetracked women from their "millenarian" role. Women should return to their homes and become once again the "guardians of major traditions."

Many of these traditions, of course, were highly sexist, as were some of the arguments that Renaud used to defend them. He suggested, for example, that in the absence of paternalistic men to take care of them women had good reason to be frightened. Women who had lost husbands in the war were to be pitied, he wrote, for if after the war they were deprived of their jobs (a deprivation he supported!) they would have to write on an official form "no profession," which, in fact, meant "no protection." Thus even as Renaud expressed sympathy for the difficulties that war widows faced, he defended a policy that would have made it even harder for them, and for other women, to be more self-sufficient.

Like so much else in Renaud's politics, his sexism was justified partly on religious and patriotic grounds. Renaud called upon French women to reverse their country's declining birthrate, which, he said, violated both "the word of God and the needs of a powerful nation." In other words, one of women's divinely ordained tasks was to produce more eventual soldiers for France's military. Renaud did advocate that women be granted "simple equality before the law," but he did not mean by this that women's traditional gender roles or social attitudes should change (141, 143).

It was precisely because Renaud believed that women were generally more religious and conservative than men that he supported women's suffrage in 1933. Women should be given the vote, he said, because they were "the priestesses of Tradition."[89] Renaud advocated women's suffrage for the same reason that Pierre Taittinger, Colonel de La Rocque, and other French fascist leaders of the interwar period did: he assumed, as did many leftists of the era, that if women were granted the vote most of them would vote for right-wing candidates. Indeed, in 1934 one female supporter of the SF, Juliette Masse, writing in the party's newspaper, argued that women's suffrage was bound to benefit the political ideals of the SF: "The most proud, free and noble people in the world see themselves today enslaved by a 'parliamentary mafia' that takes its orders from an international of Freemasons. . . . Our politics as women centers on this major point: love of la patrie [which is connected to our role of] guardians of the family hearth. . . . It is up to us especially, as women, to accept the duty to awaken sleeping consciences to the patriotism among us."[90]

In 1935, however, with the Popular Front on the rise, Renaud had second thoughts about women's suffrage. No longer sure that most women would vote right wing, he described them as "the great unknown" of French politics. Women, he said, were still innocents who seldom thought of politics "except from the point of view of their vanity." Moreover, electoral democracy itself was fatally flawed. Women were foolish to shout "men vote thus we should vote," since under the Third Republic the vote itself was nothing but a trick and since the politicians who won were "almost as incompetent as the electorate in general."[91]

Renaud also worried that it was the wrong kind of women who wanted suffrage. "The only [women] who throw themselves upon the vote as a weapon of combat are those who belong to a feminine red army: Jewish lawyers, Socialist orators, and schoolteachers [who look forward to being] unleashed against *la patrie* and its traditions." These were not the kind of women, he declared, who would create a constructive feminism (134, 135). In other words, politically, socially, and culturally right-wing feminists were acceptable; politically, socially, and culturally left-wing feminists were not.

Renaud's proposed solution to the wrong kind of feminists was similar to his proposed solution to the wrong kind of workers, namely, to place their participation within a corporatist framework that would largely disempower them. Politically, rather than vote in national elections on a wide range of issues, women were to be represented by their own corporatist assemblies, in which they would be restricted to their own sphere of expertise "It will be much easier for shopkeepers . . . to send to [these] corporatist bodies women who are knowledgeable about matters whose inconveniences they have personally experienced than to elect a woman lawyer, an ambitious female teacher, or a ridiculous and cumbersome Jewess à la Louise Weiss" (136). Women, like workers, were to be politically contained.

PATRIOTISM, TRADITION, AND THE VETERANS' MYSTIQUE

Like other French fascisms, the SF attempted to monopolize patriotism, tradition, and the veterans' mystique for reactionary purposes. According to SF propaganda, only right-wing patriotism was patriotic and only right-wing traditionalism was traditional. Long-standing left-wing patriotism and long-standing left-wing traditions (anticlericalism, liberalism, socialism) were excluded. They were not part of "true" France.[92] Renaud not only wrapped his politics in the flag, but also attached a Christian streamer to it. His praise of "the generous spirit of Christianity," however, did not stop him from pandering to middle-class selfishness, defending colonial exploitation, and denigrating Jews.

According to Renaud, the patriotism of the SF was the same as that of France's war veterans. The war veterans of the SF had risked their lives for their country during the First World War and had therefore proved their patriotism. What Renaud failed to mention was that most of France's ex-servicemen in 1935 supported not the SF but other political movements, including liberal, Socialist, and Communist movements.[93] For Renaud to suggest that all French war veterans were fascists at heart was no more accurate than to suggest that all patriots were. Nevertheless, SF propagandists repeatedly sought to associate the veterans' mystique with their movement, contrasting the "cowardly" civilian politicians of other parties with the "brave" military combatants of theirs.

Jacques Fromentin went further when he urged France's war veterans to give left-wing "traitors" the treatment they deserved and to use their military experience to restore order in France.[94] Like other SF orators, Fromentin hoped that war veterans would play a major role in their movement, a paramilitary role. Not only were they to bar the road to communism but, it was more than once implied, when the time was ripe they would be used to overthrow the Third Republic itself.

In 1935, however, Renaud bitterly acknowledged the fact that most war veterans had not joined the SF. "They won the war with their military courage," he wrote, "but lost the peace with their political bankruptcy." They had allowed the government, which encouraged different veterans' associations to become "enemy sisters," to divide and conquer. Most veterans had also failed to transcend the material concerns that gave the government its hold over them: "They are impotent because the government has them in its grip. It holds them with pensions that are electorally distributed; it holds them with remarried war widows; it holds them with the positions and offices it grants; it holds them."[95]

In sum, the SF displayed several characteristics that were typical of European fascism during the interwar period. None of these characteristics in itself marks the SF as being fascist, but as a *cluster* of attitudes that formed a distinctive whole they presented a political alternative that was undeniably fascist in the context of the 1930s. The SF's political, social, and cultural authoritarianism, its application of the veterans' mystique to paramilitary politics, its disgust with electoral democracy, its exclusionary definitions of patriotism and tradition, its views on women, its hatred of decadence, its anti-Marxism and antiliberalism, its praise of fascist Italy and Nazi Germany, its pandering to anti-Semitism, and its taste for fascist symbolism were all parts of an ideological configuration that was highly fascist—its disavowal of the label *fascism* notwithstanding.

4 · The Croix de Feu /Parti Social Français

POLITICAL HISTORY

The Croix de Feu (CF, Cross of fire), which began as a politically insignificant veterans' association, eventually grew into the largest fascist movement in France. The CF was founded in 1928 with the financial help of François Coty. Coty also provided it with office space in the building where his newspaper *Le Figaro* was published. The CF originally restricted its ranks to decorated war veterans, choosing as its insignia a skull and cross surrounded by flames. In 1929 it extended its membership to nondecorated war veterans, whom it named the *briscards* (battle-hardened soldiers) of the CF. There followed other additions as well: the Sons and Daughters of the Croix de Feu, the Women of the Croix de Feu, the National Volunteers (males under twenty-one), the National Regroupment (adult nonveterans), and, in 1935, the French Social Movement (a charity organization to aid victims of the Depression).

In 1929 the movement had only five thousand members and was largely apolitical. Its cheaply printed weekly newspaper, *Le Flambeau* (The torch), had a small circulation and dealt mainly with veterans' benefits, mutual aid activities, and local reunions—only occasionally was an article devoted to denouncing communism, Germany, or the French evacuation of the Rhineland. The CF specialized in parading its troops on patriotic holidays and reminding the public of the veterans' mystique. In 1929 Winston Churchill spoke at one of its gatherings and called it a splendid association. Before 1934, the CF was considered to be of little political significance by the police and was the subject of few reports to the minister of interior.

In 1929 the first president of the CF, Maurice Hanot (pseudonym d'Artoy), had a falling out with Coty and was replaced with Maurice Genay. In 1930 Genay too broke with Coty but succeeded in taking the movement with him. One of the primary figures behind this action was the vice-president of the CF, François de La Rocque, a retired lieutenant-colonel with important business connections, especially with the electricity and petroleum industries. These connections made the CF less financially dependent on Coty and helped La Rocque become the president of the movement in 1931. La Rocque soon made himself the undisputed *chef* (leader) of the CF, assuming the role of a paramilitary commander and demanding of his troops a pledge of absolute obedience— which he characterized as "freely chosen discipline." Even in 1936 and 1937, when La Rocque came under intense criticism from dissidents within the movement, the bulk of his followers remained loyal to him, and thousands of new ones flocked to his banner.

La Rocque's charisma derived less from his public-speaking abilities than from his military demeanor. The image he projected was that of a stern but paternalistic commander who disdained the role of the traditional politician. Wrote one admirer, "[Colonel de La Rocque] who delivered thousands of speeches was never an orator. Without seeking easy effects, in a conversational tone, he moved an audience with his simplicity, his common sense, and especially his novelty."[1] In retrospect, La Rocque seems to have displayed more of the aristocratic aloofness of a Charles de Gaulle than the gutter magnetism of an Adolf Hitler. Bertrand de Jouvenel, who interviewed Hitler in 1936, found the German leader much warmer than La Rocque. According to de Jouvenel, La Rocque had a "petrified" face with "the consistency of a rock."[2]

Although La Rocque's speeches were as nationalistic as Hitler's, his style was more austere. La Rocque, who had a visceral dislike of unruly mobs, warned against rabble-rousers who might incite an audience to lose its self-control. He often urged his followers to remain, like himself, disciplined and calm, especially when they were awaiting orders to be sent into action. He was no less a fascist, of course, for having a stoic persona instead of a ranting one, unless one expects all fascists to have exactly the same personality as Hitler's—which would rule out such people as Heinrich Himmler, Adolf Eichmann, Albert Speer, Klaus Barbé, Valois, Taittinger, Doriot, Déat, and so on.

What *was* Hitlerian about La Rocque in 1931 was his insistence on the total obedience of his shock troops. In demanding blind faith in his leadership, he went further than previous French fascist politicians who, lacking La Rocque's military rank, implied that someone like General Weygand or Marshal Pétain, not themselves, would be the ultimate savior of France and that they were only preparing the way for such a "providential" leader to assume power.[3] La Rocque behaved as if he was quite capable of filling that position himself.

François de La Rocque was born in 1887 into an aristocratic family, the son of a general. (His two brothers later developed close ties with the French royal family in exile.) At nineteen, La Rocque entered Saint-Cyr, the French military academy, and at twenty-three he became a cavalry officer in Morocco, serving under France's famed colonial commander Marshal Louis-Hubert Lyautey. La Rocque led a company of native troops against Arab rebels and was awarded the Croix de Guerre for bravery. Seriously wounded in 1916, he was sent to France to convalesce. Volunteering for duty against the Germans, he again fought bravely and was wounded three times. He returned from the First World War a military hero, the recipient of the Legion of Honor and nine citations.

In 1919 he was assigned to the staff of Marshal Ferdinand Foch and soon afterward was dispatched to Poland to serve as Foch's liaison with Marshal Józef Pilsudski. Pilsudski, with the help of the French, was engaged at the time in repelling a Soviet invasion of his country. La Rocque's anticommunism was no doubt intensified by his witnessing of the Russian threat firsthand. When the Riff rebellion broke out in Morocco in 1925, a rebellion against French colonial rule led by the Arab chief Abd el-Krim and applauded by the French Communist party, La Rocque volunteered to return to Morocco, where he became head of French military intelligence in the colony. Following the defeat of Abd el-Krim, he returned to Foch's staff. When Foch died in 1929, La Rocque retired from the army, at the age of forty-two.

Soon afterward, he was hired by the Compagnie Générale d'Electricité (General electricity company of France) and became a member of its board of directors.[4] The head of this company was Ernest Mercier, the same Ernest Mercier who presided over the Redressement Français (RF, French recovery), an organization that subsidized various conservative political causes through its large slush fund. In 1926 the RF had contributed money not only to the electoral campaigns of several candidates for parliament but also to the antiparliamentary activities of Georges Valois, the leader of the Faisceau.[5] In 1931 the RF helped subsidize La Rocque's antiparliamentary crusade as well.

Under La Rocque, the CF became much more political. No longer limiting its appeal primarily to veterans, it sought to attract mass support and spoke out on a wide range of political issues. Like previous French fascist movements, the CF presented itself as a force that would bar the road to communism and defeat the French left in general through a mixture of authoritarian nationalism and para-military politics.

To attract public attention and new recruits, the CF resorted to the same tactic that the AF had employed on so many occasions: it disrupted a left-wing political rally. The target in this case was a public conference on disarmament organized by the French pacifist Louise Weiss and held on November 27, 1931, at the Trocadero auditorium in Paris. La Rocque and fifteen hundred of his fol-lowers joined the audience and proceeded to shout down the speakers, demand the microphone, and create such an uproar that the police had to be called in and the auditorium evacuated. The press coverage the next day brought La Rocque the publicity he wanted. His movement received a far greater boost, however, from the right-wing backlash that followed the elections of 1932 and the victory of a new Cartel des Gauches. CF membership, only 5,000 in 1929, rose to 25,000 in 1932.

The riots of February 6, 1934, brought the CF a flood of new recruits and financial support. The CF's show of disciplined force that evening was repeat-edly contrasted in the conservative press the next day with the rowdy behavior of some of the other demonstrators. Although conservatives were pleased that the riots had brought down the Daladier government, many were disturbed by the threat to public order that such rioting presented. The CF columns that had marched against the Chamber of Deputies on February 6 had not thrown rocks, slashed police horses, overturned buses, or set fire to government buildings. On the contrary, except for a brief assault by a few of La Rocque's troops on the rear of the Chamber of Deputies, they had not rioted at all. Avoiding the turbulent mob in the Place de la Concorde, they had operated on the opposite side of the Seine with military precision.

Overnight the CF won a reputation that distinguished it from the AF, the JP, the SF, and the other fascist leagues. While proving that it, too, was willing to mobilize its troops against a threat from the left, it showed that it could do so in a much more orderly way than its rivals. For many French conservatives, the disciplined force of CF war veterans was much more desirable than the sponta-neous violence of AF youths, even if the spontaneous violence was for a right-wing cause. At the same time, the CF's "maneuvers" on February 6 were viewed as a warning to the left that any insurrection on its part would be met with a paramilitary response. As a reporter for *Le Temps* wrote in 1935, "The demonstration [which members of the CF] gave of their discipline, during those somber days of February, did not fail to impress both the public authorities and the party of revolution which, from that moment forward, understood that the streets no longer completely belonged to it."[6]

Following February 6, the membership figures of the CF soared dramatically. According to police authorities, on the eve of the riots the CF had about 35,000 members in all of France, 18,000 of whom were in the Paris region. By August 1935, total CF membership had expanded sixfold to approximately 228,000 members. The explanation given by one police report for this enormous increase was simple: "The principal cause of the movement's success is obviously its fundamental antiparliamentarianism." Six months later, CF membership had doubled, rising to some 500,000 members.[7]

As the movement continued to expand, its ranks were swelled by persons who had not fought in the war but who supported CF ideology. As late as 1935, however, the CF continued to recruit war veterans. In June of that year, the police reported that around 40 percent of the membership of the Fédération des Associations Régimentaires et Anciens Combattants (FARAC, Federation of regimental and veterans' associations) had joined the CF. The FARAC consisted of 128 associations with some 130,000 members.[8] Between 1934 and 1935 La Rocque repeatedly suggested that the war veterans of the CF should replace the decadent politicians of the Third Republic with a new governing elite, an elite of war veterans.

The CF was organized in a military manner, authority descending from La Rocque at the top downward through a chain of command to the platoon leaders at the bottom. The paramilitary shock troops of the CF were called *dispos*, from the French word *disponible*, "available." These troops, sprinkled with war veterans, had sworn to be available for action on short notice. It was the dispos, particularly, who embodied the famed discipline of the CF. According to the police, on February 6 there had been only 1,200 to 1,500 CF dispos in Paris, a number that would increase sharply after that date.[9]

In 1933 La Rocque employed these dispos to launch a series of highly publicized paramilitary exercises calculated to win conservative support for the CF. Like previous French fascist movements, the CF presented itself as a movement willing to use any means necessary to defeat a Communist revolution. Like previous French fascist movements, too, it suggested that the same armed force could be used to overthrow the hated parliamentarianism of the Third

Republic, which it blamed for allowing communism to exist in France in the first place. La Rocque and his subordinates repeatedly told their troops that the movement's periodic mobilizations were in preparation for the D day and H hour that were sure to come.

The mobilizations themselves were conducted like military operations. Without warning, the dispos would be ordered to report to their assigned rendezvous points, where they would be picked up by waiting automobiles and driven to a destination—sometimes as far as two hundred kilometers away—that would be revealed to them only at the last moment. Here they would join their comrades from other car caravans dispatched from other parts of France. These mobilization exercises were carried out periodically until 1936, when the CF was banned by the government as a paramilitary organization.

Although René Rémond has dismissed these exercises as "political boy-scouting for adults," they were commonly led by combat-hardened war veterans with a fierce hatred of Marxism. Originally a movement of decorated war veterans, the CF included a number of men who had not won their medals through boy-scouting. True, the CF lacked military weapons (private ownership of weapons being severely restricted in France), but it hoped that sympathetic army commanders would supply it with arms if the Communists ever grew too threatening. Like previous fascist leaders in France, La Rocque portrayed his shock troops as an insurance policy against the Communists, as the embryo of a potential white army that would resist the reds should they try to revolt.

The CF was more than a paramilitary movement, however. Only a minority of its members were dispos. By the end of 1934, some 130,000 nonveterans and Frenchmen too old to fight had joined the Regroupement National (National regroupment). According to police, members of the Regroupement National, although fully in accord with the goals of the CF, were less committed to "descending into the streets with helmets on their heads."[10]

More militant than the National Regroupment was the youth auxiliary of the CF, the Volontaires Nationaux (VN, National volunteers). Consisting of males under twenty-one, the VN were officially assigned the mission of "extending the possibilities of the action of the Croix de Feu in public places during demonstrations."[11] They also participated in the paramilitary mobilization exercises of the movement. VN units were given the same numbers (as in fifth platoon, second regiment, and so forth) as the adult units of the CF and were trained to operate in concert with and under the "moral authority" of their elders. In the spring of 1934, police estimated that there were in the neighborhood of 50,000 VN in France.

Prominent among the ranks of the VN were a number of university students.

In 1934 a parliamentary commission investigating the February 6 riots became particularly interested in a large contingent of students from the Ecole Poly-technique, Saint-Cyr, and the French naval academy who had joined the VN. Of special concern to the authorities was the fact that these students came from three of France's *grandes écoles*, prestigious schools that prepared sons of the upper bourgeoisie and the aristocracy for high positions in France's military establishment and government bureacracy and that had close relations at the time with both of these seats of power. In November 1933, police reported that a group of students from these schools had asked if they could join the VN in "a massive and nonindividual" way.

On Armistice Day in 1933, about 350 of these students, with other forma-tions of the CF, marched up the Champs-Elysées to the Arc de Triomphe in their school uniforms. Three weeks later, many of these same students, during a ceremony commemorating the Battle of Austerlitz, passed in review before Colonel de La Rocque on the Esplanade des Invalides. That evening La Rocque addressed an audience of Saint-Cyr students, recounting his role in the campaign against Abd el-Krim. According to police, by 1936 the Students of the National Volunteers had approximately 1,500 members in Paris, of whom some 400 were from the law school and an equal number from the medical school, the rest being scattered throughout the other universities of Paris.[12]

Women also joined the CF. The females of the CF were just as committed to conservative nationalism and authoritarian politics as their male counterparts. The president of one of their sections spoke of the profound impression made on her by a parade of the Sons and Daughters of the Croix de Feu commemorating the birth of Joan of Arc. In March 1936, one-third of the 7,500 members of the CF in the sixteenth district of Paris were women. Assigned to spread the move-ment's ideas in their neighborhoods, some of these women boasted that they were far better propagandists than the men.[13]

In December 1935 a group of CF women founded the Mouvement Social Français (MSF, French social movement). The MSF was dedicated to social works on behalf of the poor. These works included charity balls and auctions and free meals for the hungry. In March 1936, the MSF claimed that its soup kitchens had doled out twenty-five thousand meals in Paris alone. The MSF also sought to recruit workers and young people into the CF, offering those who joined access to its recreational facilities and vacation camps. The MSF created leisure centers in both rural and urban areas, and in some cases offered to pay the entrance fee to local swimming pools for CF members who could not afford it. The MSF also organized what they called pilgrimages for children to the battlefields of Verdun and Metz as well as musical evenings for adults throughout France. In March 1936 an orchestra directed by a professor from the National Conservatory of Music played military marches for a CF audience in Paris, and this was followed by singers from the Paris Opéra, the Théâtre de Paris, and the Opéra Comique. That same month the MSF bought a twenty-room mansion that included a nursery for children and an auditorium that could seat four thousand.[14]

Although the MSF claimed that its social works were simply expressions of Christian charity, devoid of any political purpose, this was hardly the case. The MSF sought not only to wean a section of the working class away from the political left by using charity and sports facilities as enticements, but also to ward off increased government welfare spending and the increased taxes such spending would entail. Private charity was cheaper than higher taxes. The official program of the CF in 1936 praised social works as a way of "fusing classes through reciprocal mutual aid," while simultaneously calling for the elimination of a "succession of crushing taxes."[15] The social works of the MSF were in fact highly political, a conservative attempt to decrease lower-class discontent through upper-class paternalism, protecting their donors from the far greater loss to their wealth that might occur if the left came to power. By February 1936, police estimated that the MSF had some 500,000 members, 90,000 of whom were in the Paris region.[16]

Following the riots of February 6, 1934, all branches of the CF grew rapidly. At the end of February, CF headquarters in Paris announced the addition of 6,000 new members. In July it claimed that the weekly growth rate had gone from 7,000 to 8,000 to 10,000 and that its total membership was 150,000. Although these figures were doubtless inflated for publicity purposes, the increasing success of the movement was undeniable. On November 11, 1934, various formations of the CF marched from the Avenue George V to the Arc de Triomphe in ranks of eight for two hours. In January 1935 a reporter for *Le Temps* estimated that the CF and VN combined had grown to 160,000 (one-fourth of whom were in the Paris region) and that the Regroupement National had reached 100,000. In June 1935 police reported to the minister of interior that the CF had enrolled 25,000 members in one week. Police also noted that during one of its mobilization exercises that had ended at Chartres the CF had utilized 5,200 automobiles, an indication, in an era when few workers owned cars, of the middle-class backgrounds of some of its members.[17]

According to the police, by August 1935 in France and its colonies there were 81,000 Croix de Feu and Briscards, 77,000 Sons and Daughters of the CF, and 70,000 members of the Groupement National and its women's auxiliary: a total of 228,000.[18] In 1936 CF meetings throughout France attracted large crowds and packed the Salle Wagram in Paris. The movement's charity sales were well attended, including one at Kermasse that totaled 145,000 admissions and another at Berlitz that brought in 1,300,000 francs.[19]

Throughout 1934, 1935, and the first half of 1936 La Rocque continued to flaunt his movement's paramilitary capabilities and to denounce the politicians of the Third Republic for their decadence. Immediately following the February 6 riots, he characterized the conservative Doumergue government as merely "a poultice on a gangrenous leg."[20] Thus, he implied that it was not enough to temporarily remove the left from power; the Third Republic itself had to go. Yet, when the parliamentary commission investigating the riots called upon La Rocque to testify a few weeks later, he swore that he was a loyal republican devoted to republican legality, a disclaimer he had to make to avoid prosecution and prevent his movement from being banned by the government as a paramilitary organization (which it was anyway in June 1936).

During the summer of 1935, with the Popular Front on the rise, La Rocque ordered his troops to prepare for H hour, which he implied was imminent. When the Popular Front came to power in May 1936, however, his bark proved bigger than his bite. He attempted no coup and called upon his troops to remain calm even when the government banned the CF the following month. Instead of engaging in paramilitary violence, he bowed to the combined force arrayed against him, that of the police, the new Popular Front government, and the mass organizations of the left.

One month after the CF was officially dissolved, La Rocque founded the Parti Social Français (PSF, French social party). Like Jean Renaud of the SF, Pierre Taittinger of the JP, and Marcel Bucard of the Francistes, all of whose paramilitary organizations were also banned, La Rocque simply changed the name of his movement and claimed that it was now thoroughly democratic. The PSF adopted the statutes of a standard parliamentary party and announced its intention to participate in the very electoral system that it had previously condemned so vehemently. Rather than deny the continuity between the CF and the PSF, however, it emphasized it. As one PSF publication put it, "The French Social Party equals the Croix de Feu plus electoral politics."[21] Because of this admission, I often refer below to the post-1936 reincarnation of the CF as the CF/PSF.

La Rocque's alleged commitment to democracy in 1936 proved quite hollow in 1940, and it is difficult to believe that those who joined the CF/PSF after 1936 seriously thought that he had changed his views in any fundamental way. Before the CF was banned, La Rocque had repeatedly attacked parliamentary democracy and called for a government of war veterans. On the eve of February 6, he had informed his troops that the goal of the CF was to call to power a government "free of politicians of whatever kind," and on February 7 he had characterized the conservative (but still democratic) Doumergue government as a temporary bandage for gangrene. Anyone who supported the CF/PSF after 1936 would have had to have been gullible indeed, or a victim of political amnesia, to have assumed that La Rocque had suddenly become a democrat.

In June 1936 La Rocque chose to pursue the electoral path to power, a tactic hardly unprecedented in fascist politics. Hitler, after all, following the Munich putsch of 1923 and his subsequent imprisonment, had taken this path quite successfully. Nevertheless, some of the militant members of the CF, including Pozzo di Borgo, its vice-president, criticized La Rocque for responding so meekly to the government's ban and quit the movement in disgust. Di Borgo, as noted earlier, chose to enter the Cagoule, while other CF dissidents went over to Doriot. In 1936 La Rocque was aware that the Cagoule existed and that it was stockpiling arms as a terrorist organization. Although he forbade his followers to join the Cagoule, the self-described democrat La Roque did not share his knowledge of its existence with the authorities.[22]

In spite of the departure of Pozzo di Borgo and a number of other CF firebrands in 1936, the overwhelming majority of La Rocque's followers remained loyal to him. According to police, "In general, the members of . . . the Croix de Feu appear relatively moderate on the issue [of the government banning the CF as a paramilitary organization]. If some hotheads are talking of mobilizing the army of their followers throughout France to actively resist the government, little attention is paid to them. The general view is that the Colonel was right not to engage in such an adventure."[23] There was nothing notably unfascist, of course, about La Rocque's refusal to resort to force when the odds were against him. Between 1923 and 1933 Hitler had been equally prudent. La Rocque was no different from the German leader in turning to electoral politics when it was the only realistic option.

The CF/PSF lost some of its troops in 1936 but gained a host of new ones. In May 1936 police reported that the CF had received approximately 5,000 letters of resignation because of its failure to act, but that during the same period it had enrolled 31,584 new members.[24] By 1937 the CF/PSF was riding high. At one of its rallies, a speaker boasted that the movement had grown to 2 million members and that as the strongest party in France it would soon be in power.[25]

The historian Sam Goodfellow has pointed out that in Alsace, a CF/PSF stronghold, La Rocque attracted large crowds right up to the war. One village named a street after him. In 1937 the *Flambeau de l'Est* was the second largest weekly in Alsace, after the *Travailleur Syndicaliste*, published by the Popular Front. In 1939 the CF/PSF in Alsace had some 27,000 activists organized into 165 sections. This made it larger than the FR's major affiliate in Alsace, the Union Populaire Républicaine, which had 15,000 members.[26]

In 1938, the CF/PSF acquired one of France's major newspapers, *Le Petit Journal*, a mass circulation daily and one of the big five of French journalism. The purchase of *Le Petit Journal* was a sure sign of the movement's financial prosperity, few French political movements being able to afford such a newspaper.

According to the French historian Philippe Machefer, the CF had roughly 450,000 members when it was dissolved in June 1936. By November 1936, the CF/PSF had 600,000 members, making its party membership larger than that of the SFIO (200,000) and the PCF (200,000) combined. Machefer estimates that by 1937 CF/PSF membership was between 700,000 and 1.2 million.[27]

La Rocque's claim that by 1939 the PSF had 3 million members was no doubt an exaggeration, but the size of his movement was nevertheless imposing. William Irvine has written,

> The actual number may never be known, but by any standard the membership of the PSF was large and dynamic. The records of the local newspapers dealing with the activities of the PSF sections are consistent only with a very large membership. [The same is true] for the size of its provincial rallies. Remember too that political participation in France is low compared to, say, Germany— all parties, from the Socialists to the right, are a fraction of the size of their German counterparts. So, in this context, even 700,000 (an absolute minimum I would think) is simply gigantic.[28]

According to Machefer, by 1939 the PSF included among its members some 3,000 mayors, 1,000 municipal councilmen, and a dozen parliamentary deputies. Its Confederation of Professional Unions, the PSF's alternative to the CGT and the CGTU, comprised several thousand workers, many of whom either owed their jobs to pro-PSF employers or who simply took advantage of the PSF's widespread recreational facilities. Machefer believed that if war had not broken out in 1939 and if the national elections of 1940 had been held as scheduled, the PSF representation in the Chamber of Deputies would have increased to about 100.[29]

Although there is no assurance that the electoral strength of the CF/PSF would have been proportionally as great as its membership strength, it is clear that the major political parties of the period on both the right and the left viewed

La Rocque's movement with considerable alarm. As the British historian Julian Jackson has noted in his study of the Popular Front, after 1936 the PSF became "the largest and fastest growing party of the right" and "the main danger in the eyes of the left."[30] On the right, the FR, which previously had allied with La Rocque, now turned against him as it began to lose an increasing number of its members to his new electoral party. Indeed, some members of the FR in the Chamber of Deputies felt they had little chance of being reelected in 1940 if they failed to publicly associate themselves with La Rocque's party.[31]

A number of historians have attributed the spectacular rise of the CF/PSF after 1936 to La Rocque's new "moderation," to his acceptance of electoral politics, indeed to his *rejection* of fascism.[32] Yet the socioeconomic program of the FR was just as moderate and its political reputation far more democratic. After 1936, the FR, which had been an electoral party for years, was increasingly outdistanced by the CF/PSF, which was only recently electoral but whose past military mystique and authoritarian sentiments were well known.

It is no coincidence that the greatest surge in the growth of La Rocque's movement followed the electoral victory of the Popular Front in May 1936 and the sit-down strikes in June of that year. What the CF/PSF offered French conservatives was a more authoritarian response to the red menace than that proposed by the traditional parties of the parliamentary right. According to Irvine's *French Conservatism in Crisis*, the sit-down strikes, the Matignon accords, and the Popular Front social legislation that followed led many "beleaguered conservatives" to look to the CF/PSF as a potential savior.[33]

The rise of the CF/PSF was also due to its grass roots organization, which was much more extensive than that of the FR. As Irvine points out, this last feature separated the CF/PSF from traditional French conservatism and gave its brand of conservatism a more fascist cast. Whereas the FR and other right-wing electoral parties had relied on local notables and a minimum of demagoguery to get out the vote, "Fascists," writes Irvine, "eschewed elite politics in favor of mass mobilization. They, like their Marxist enemies, formed genuinely popular movements adept at the 'politics of the street,' at home with mass rallies, clearly attuned to the fact that 'revolution' could be stopped only by 'counterrevolution.' By this standard, the Croix de Feu was more fascist than any other formation of the Third Republic."[34]

Between the spring of 1936, when the Popular Front came to power, and the spring of 1937, when it fell, political circumstances were more favorable to fascism in France than at any time during the interwar period. The CF/PSF benefited from the conservative backlash to the Popular Front in 1936 just as the

Faisceau and the JP had benefited from the backlash to the Cartel des Gauches in 1924.[35] This time, however, the threat from the left was much greater, and thus the backlash to the left was much greater. Whereas in 1926 the Faisceau had achieved a membership of only 60,000, in 1937 the CF/PSF soared to nearly a million. Doriot's PPF, which had at least a quarter of a million members and sympathizers in 1937, made this backlash even greater. If one adds to these figures the considerable membership of Dorgères's Peasant Front (and adds the followers of the JP, the AF, the SF, and the Francistes as well), the size of the second wave of French fascism was greater still.

Although La Rocque continued to claim that he was a loyal republican, his appeal to authoritarian sentiments was all too transparent. His previous contempt for parliamentary politicians and electoral democracy was no secret, and even if he had to mute that contempt after 1936 to prevent his movement from being banned a second time, there was little reason to believe that he had truly changed his stripes. To be a democrat out of necesssity was one thing; to be a democrat out of conviction was another.

If La Rocque's politics were now ostensibly more moderate than before, the basic values that underlay them were not. Although professing a commitment to republican liberties and repeatedly denying that he was fascist, La Rocque praised Franco and Mussolini for their efforts against Bolshevism and suggested that the CF/PSF was engaged in a parallel struggle in France. He continued not only to criticize the Popular Front with inflammatory rhetoric (on October 1, 1936, for example, *Le Flambeau* declared that Blum's devaluation of the franc was part of a Communist plot to destroy Western civilization), but also to display the more combative side of his movement.

Like the CF, the PSF sought conservative support partly by presenting itself as an organization that commanded brave fighters who refused to be intimidated by the reds. When in late 1936, some 20,000 Communists held a rally at the Parc des Princes in Paris, 1,500 members of the CF/PSF contested the parade that followed, sparking a brawl that had to be stopped by the police. The next day La Rocque demanded the dissolution of the PCF. The government responded by launching an inquiry into his movement to see if it had reverted to its paramilitary practices.

On March 17, 1937, the CF/PSF again made headlines as a result of the "Clichy massacre." The CF/PSF had decided to hold a meeting in Clichy, a Popular Front stronghold that had elected a Socialist mayor and a Communist deputy. To schedule such a meeting was a bold move, sure to arouse Clichy leftists, but calculated to show French rightists that the CF/PSF was not afraid to confront the enemy on its own turf. On the evening of March 16, about 1,000 leftists marched to a local cinema where 400 of La Rocque's followers were conducting their meeting. When the leftists tried to break through a police barrier protecting the meeting-place, the police opened fire on the demonstrators, killing five and wounding about 300. The next day *L'Humanité* and *Le Populaire* called upon France's Communists and Socialists to hold a one-day general strike. They also demanded that La Rocque be arrested for provocation.[36] Although La Rocque's troops had been badly outnumbered on March 16 (and had to be spirited away from the cinema by the police), the fact that they were courageous enough to hold the meeting in the first place enhanced their reputation on the right.

Those who joined the CF/PSF were aware that its conservatism was more muscular than that of the FR. Its new Equipes volantes de propagande (EVP, (Mobile propaganda teams) consisted of members whose free time was available to the party and who were organized along the same lines as the CF's dispos had been. Divided into "hands" of five men, troops of five hands, clans of five troops, tribes of five clans, and legions of five tribes, these dispos by another name were expected to do more than simply dispense propaganda. Not only did they provide security guards for PSF meetings, but they were told in February 1937 that another right-wing parliamentary coalition government was unacceptable and the moment was near when the PSF would take power.[37]

La Rocque's pronouncements on foreign policy after 1936 also suggested a dubious commitment to democratic principles. In August 1936 La Rocque wished Franco success in his attempt to overthrow the Spanish Republic and declared that should Franco fail it would be a dreadful defeat for Western civilization. La Rocque not only opposed French intervention in Spain to save its new Republic but also denounced calls for France to go to war against Nazi Germany on behalf of the Jews. He was no pacifist, however, when it came to supporting Mussolini's actions in North Africa and criticizing England for condemning them.

In April 1936 La Rocque described the Italian dictator as serving the best interests of the West by establishing an outpost against the Soviet Union on the Red Sea, and he characterized the British as hypocrites for being scandalized by the same kind of imperialism that they themselves had practiced in India and elsewhere. Earlier, he had praised the "sacred egoism" of fascist Italy in expanding its empire into Ethiopia, derided the British for their "false humanitarianism," and insisted that France should not impose sanctions on Italy in order to protect British interests near the Nile or "to please the Bolsheviks."[38] In short, he portrayed fascist imperialism in North Africa and Franco's cause in Spain as extensions of the struggle against communism that was taking place in France.

In May 1937, two months after the Clichy affair, Jacques Doriot called upon French conservatives, and La Rocque specifically, to join in a Liberty Front against the Popular Front. Ignoring the fact that in November 1931, at the time of the Trocadero affair, the CF had first achieved notoriety by disrupting a left-wing meeting, Doriot spoke piously of defending freedom of speech and assembly against Communist attempts to disrupt right-wing meetings. Louis Marin's FR and Pierre Taittinger's National and Social Republican party accepted Doriot's invitation.

La Rocque declined, however, although hardly for ideological reasons (their party programs were virtually identical). Of more concern was his fear that by joining such an alliance he might lose more troops to Doriot than he already had. Indeed, according to police informants, in the wake of the Clichy affair there were rumors that should the government ban the PSF La Rocque himself might have to join the PPF in a subordinate capacity. As it was, La Rocque was able to retain his slogan: "One does not annex the Croix de Feu; one follows it."[39]

Publicly, La Rocque defended his decision not to join the Liberty Front on lofty democratic grounds, while at the same time implying that under different political circumstances he might not be so scrupulous. A PSF pamphlet in 1937 claimed that the PSF was too committed to republican liberties and to the Republic itself to become allied with the likes of the PPF, which it described as an irresponsible organization that might lead its followers into an adventure, that is, into an unsuccessful coup d'état. The pamphlet noted that the time was not ripe for such a coup, thereby suggesting that, were circumstances to change, the PSF's commitment to republican liberties might change as well. It also pointed out that because the Popular Front was in the process of disintegrating it was better to await its "amiable liquidation" than to launch a civil war that could lead to "bloody and vain battles between Frenchmen."[40] Thus the possibility was left open that if the Popular Front did not disintegrate, the CF/PSF might pursue a different course.

La Rocque's rejection of the Liberty Front disappointed not only Doriot, Marin, and Taittinger but other rightists as well. One of these was André Tardieu, a leading spokesman for French conservatism and a former premier of France who had retired from electoral politics. In 1937 Tardieu sought to discredit La Rocque in an interview he gave to Pozzo di Borgo (di Borgo having become an enemy of La Rocque after quitting the CF). Tardieu claimed that as France's minister of interior in the early 1930s he had helped subsidize La Rocque's movement with government funds. Because La Rocque had repeatedly proclaimed during those years that his movement was above politics and above electoral politicians in particular, the idea that he might have been Tardieu's "kept man" was potentially damaging. La Rocque denied the charge and sued Pozzo di Borgo for libel. The court ruled against La Rocque without commenting on whether the subsidies had in fact been provided. However, not only did most of La Rocque's supporters stick with him during the scandal, but, according to the police, some even thought it was fine if he had in fact accepted government funds: the funds had been used in the fight against communism.

Far more important than the Tardieu affair in slowing the growth of La Rocque's movement after 1937 was the parliamentary defeat of the Popular Front that year. Although the Popular Front made a brief comeback in 1938, it was soon replaced by a center-right coalition led by Daladier that ruled until 1940. Since the major cause of the spectacular rise of CF/PSF after 1936 was the image it projected of a more forceful response to the political left, once the threat from the left receded the CF/PSF's major reason for being receded with it. Just as Poincaré's defeat of the Cartel des Gauches in 1926 reduced the need for Valois's Faisceau, Daladier's defeat of the Popular Front in 1937 reduced the need for La Rocque's alternative. Still, as long as the Depression continued and a revival of the left remained possible, the CF/PSF was not without supporters. According to Philippe Machefer, the previously escalating membership figures of the CF/PSF leveled off at around a million in 1938.

In 1939, with war approaching, La Rocque argued that only by fashioning a political order as strong as Germany's could France hold its own against the Nazis. Following the signing of the Nazi-Soviet pact, he criticized the Daladier government for not going far enough in cracking down on French Communists (while saying nothing about cracking down on French fascists). In December 1939, he called for the arrest of Maurice Thorez, Jacques Duclos, and other French Communist leaders and for the repression of all Communist organizations in France, including Communist agricultural associations.[41]

LA ROCQUE AFTER 1940

When, in the summer of 1940, the German blitzkrieg broke through the French armies in the north, La Rocque left Paris for southern France, where he urged his compatriots to engage in "total resistance to the end." With Pétain's ascent to power, however, he called upon his followers to cease fighting and to support Vichy's national revolution.

In *Disciplines of Action* (1941) La Rocque went further, advocating "continental collaboration" with the Germans and praising the "ardent vitality of the fascist and Hitlerian regimes."[42] He warned his readers against the subversive designs of the Third International and the foreign designs of Gaullism and declared that a collaboration between "two great peoples like the German people and the French people" was "susceptible to recriprocal enrichments."[43]

He observed that parallels existed between certain Nazi doctrines and those of some of France's most famous conservative theoreticians: "Are not the results obtained by the National Socialist peasantry [in Germany] of the nature to inspire us, following the proper paths of our own traditions and temperament, to adopt the means to put into practice the doctrines of Le Play . . . and La Tour de Pin? The theory of 'families of good stock who have their roots in the earth' leads us to conclusions not far from [those of] Walter Darre, Minister of Agriculture for the Reich. We could cite other examples."[44] Similar thinking led *Le Flambeau* in December 1941, in an article recalling Napoleon's once intended invasion of England, to suggest that Hitler was a modern Napoleon.[45]

La Rocque's decision to collaborate with the Nazis was largely motivated by his desire to see the French left crushed once and for all. A lifelong French nationalist who in the 1930s repeatedly described the Germans as barbarians, he was willing to compromise his nationalism in 1941 for domestic political reasons. Although he maintained that Franco-German collaboration should not victimize either party, his hatred of Marxism, his disgust with liberalism, and his sympathy for the national "renovation" promised by the reactionary Pétain outweighed his dislike of the negative aspects of the German occupation. Significantly, he began *Disciplines of Action* by drawing a parallel between the riots of February 6, 1934, and Pétain's national revolution. Both, he wrote, were revolts against the "decadence of governmental and parliamentary morals" under the Third Republic and against the "shameful collusions" of leftist politicians who had encouraged "fratricidal struggles" on behalf of "foreign" causes.[46]

According to La Rocque, France's military defeat in 1940 was due not only to corrupt politicians but to the nature of political democracy itself: "Twenty years of degeneracy has led to this terrible catastrophe." "Parasites follow the masses," he wrote, whereas "true leaders guide them." Pétain, with his "military temperament," was far superior to the mediocre politicians of the Third Republic, and the French people should follow him with "total discipline." There was another reason members of the PSF should support Pétain: his doctrine was the same as theirs: "This doctrine was ours from the beginning of our movement, over the course of ten years of struggles and challenges" (104).

Thus the self-professed republican La Rocque now supported Pétain, a man who had ended representative government in France, repressed political liberties, and chosen to collaborate in Hitler's New European Order. To be sure, in

1940 others besides La Rocque, including many French liberals and Socialists, supported the establishment of the Vichy regime when faced with a national military disaster and the threat of German occupation—but not all did so with La Rocque's ideological zeal. In 1941 La Rocque placed himself squarely on the side of Nazi Germany and the Axis powers in the struggle, as he portrayed it, against Soviet communism. "Russia," he wrote, "that Asiatic empire in the hands of the declared enemies of Christian tradition, forms the antithesis of our civilization" (21). In *Disciplines of Action*, in a chapter on "the mortal vices" of France, he accused the Jews, along with the Marxists and the Freemasons, of being primarily responsible for France's military defeat (97–98).

Between 1940 and 1942 La Rocque portrayed democratic England as a greater threat to France than Nazi Germany. In 1941 he denounced de Gaulle for having "abandoned his post" and condemned England for attacking the French fleet at Mers-el-Kébir (which Churchill wanted to prevent from falling into German hands). La Rocque indignantly declared, "We do not want a 'Free France' that would be a [British] dominion. We do not want an enslaved France."[47] One reason he seems to have considered German enslavement less onerous was that he associated de Gaulle with the Communist threat. In May 1941 he wrote that Communists and Gaullists were "allied from the outset."[48]

When in December 1940 the Vichy regime outlawed democratic political parties in France, La Rocque responded by changing the name of the PSF to the Progrès Social Français (French social progress). The new PSF found the electoralism of the former PSF easily expendable: "Progrès Social Français equals Parti Social Français minus electoral politics. Well now, Progrès Social Français equals the Croix de Feu plus the mass of people of good will who joined La Rocque between the dissolution of the Croix de Feu in 1936 and the transformation of the PSF in 1940."[49] No longer were local delegates to the PSF elected, as they had been after 1936; rather, they were appointed by La Rocque, as they had been before 1936. Machefer has described the new PSF as a "veritable return to the sources," the movement having gone full circle, he says, from political authoritarianism to political democracy to political authoritarianism once again. There is much to suggest, however, that the movement never seriously changed its deepest beliefs.

It is true that in 1941 La Rocque refused to support Marcel Déat's idea of a single party, but this was due less to any serious commitment to democracy on La Rocque's part than to his fear of losing control of his followers to Déat, Doriot, and Bergery—especially since, as one Vichy official later recalled, they were "leaders without many troops." La Rocque's desire to retain control of his followers was also in evidence when the Vichy government asked La Rocque in

1940 to encourage his supporters to join Xavier Vallat's Légion Française des Combattants (French legion of fighters), an organization devoted to rooting out decadent ideas and combatting the Resistance. La Rocque agreed not to forbid his followers to join Vallat's organization but insisted that they not accept any leadership positions. In other words, he condoned their participating in political repression as long as they did not become dependent on Vallat himself. In 1941, when Pétain personally asked La Rocque to procure local leaders for the legion, he complied.[50]

Between 1940 and 1942, La Rocque tried to have it both ways, defending active collaboration with the Germans and French patriotism at the same time. In January 1941, he wrote, "There is no understanding possible, even with a victor, if there is an abdication of national dignity and the loss of a sense of honor."[51] Whatever the fascist elements in his thought, La Rocque always remained a *French* fascist, seeking partnership with the Germans, not subservience. The fact that the Germans chose to rule with an increasingly heavy hand was undoubtedly galling to La Rocque, but, in his eyes, to side against them meant backing the Russians and the British and thereby furthering the prospect of a postwar victory of communism or liberalism. Besides, in 1941 he may have believed, as so many did at the time, that the Germans would win the war.

By January 1942, however, the war had entered a new phase, one that made collaboration with the Germans look much less attractive. Not only had the British survived the Battle of Britain, but in December 1941 the Germans had also suffered a major defeat outside of Moscow. That same month the United States, with its enormous industrial might, had entered the war on the side of Great Britain. La Rocque, the veteran staff officer, may well have seen the handwriting on the wall.

Machefer dates La Rocque's entrance into the Resistance "from the moment when the entrance of the United States into the war seemed to announce the final triumph of the Allies and the increased power of the Germans over Vichy contradicted a certain idea that he had of collaboration."[52] Beginning in 1942 a number of collaborationists switched sides, going over to the Resistance or joining de Gaulle in London. One of these was Charles Vallin, the vice-president of the PSF, who claimed that he could no longer abide Pétain's support of Laval. Vallin arrived in London in September 1942 and offered his services to the Free French. Other PSF members followed suit, offering their support to the Gaullism they had previously denounced. La Rocque told friends that the news of Vallin's defection had struck him like a knife in the back, yet he himself had begun to abandon the Germans several months before.

Although La Rocque could never bring himself to back de Gaulle, a leader he had publicly excoriated since 1940, in January 1942 he offered to aid the British directly by creating an underground resistance organization that would pass on military information to British Intelligence. This organization, called Klan, began its operations shortly afterward. According to Jean d'Orsay, one of the editors of the PSF's *Le Petit Journal*, La Rocque asked him as early as September 1940 to begin collecting information that might help the Allies. If La Rocque was in fact playing a double game, it did not stop him in his public writings between 1940 and 1942 from damning the Allied cause and calling for continental collaboration with the Germans.

By the summer of 1942, however, La Rocque had indeed changed sides. He had not only formed his own secret resistance organization, but also now sent word to members of the PSF that they were to "remain French" and join neither the Milice, which fought the Resistance in France, nor the French Volunteer Legion against Bolshevism, which fought communism in Russia. In November 1942, the Germans, suspecting that La Rocque was aiding the enemy, banned the PSF. In March 1943, La Rocque obtained an audience with Pétain and urged him to reach an agreement with the Allies in order to avoid post-Liberation disorders in France (that is, in order to head off any left-wing uprisings or punitive measures against Vichy collaborationists). Two days later, La Rocque, along with 152 other PSF leaders, was arrested by the Gestapo.

La Rocque spent several weeks in solitary confinement in various French prisons before being deported to Germany, where he was interned with other French political prisoners in castles at Eisenberg and Itter. According to several prisoners who shared his captivity, he was exceptionally brave during this ordeal.[53] His health broken by harsh prison conditions that aggravated his wounds from the First World War, La Rocque was finally repatriated to France in 1945— where he was immediately imprisoned by the Liberation authorities for his earlier collaboration with the Germans. Released to house arrest in 1946, he died shortly afterward following an operation. In 1961 his widow's wish that her husband be posthumously awarded the Medal for Deportees of the Second World War was finally granted by La Rocque's former wartime adversary President Charles de Gaulle.

FINANCING

The CF/PSF was more than simply the career or charisma of one man. To understand why it became the largest and fastest growing political movement on the

French right after 1936, one has to look beyond La Rocque to some of the major political, social, cultural, and economic dynamics that fueled its success. Not the least of these was its financial backing.

Like other major French fascist movements of the interwar period, the CF/PSF was heavily dependent on big donors. François Coty provided much of the money that launched the CF in 1928. In 1930, after Coty broke with the then-president of the CF, Maurice Genay, other wealthy supporters filled the gap. One of these was Duke Pozzo di Borgo, a large landowner, former air force pilot, and director of the Anti-Marxist Institute of Paris who was vice-president of the CF. During the early years of the CF, di Borgo did much to keep the movement financially afloat. In 1934 police reported, "When the need arose, Monsieur Pozzo di Borgo certainly made new donations. For example, when [the CF] wanted to launch a new journal, *Le Flambeau*, Monsieur Pozzo di Borgo gave 80,000 francs. The journal was launched. Now it makes 126,000 francs a year from its advertisemennts, which largely permits it to subsist."[54]

As mentioned earlier, André Tardieu later testified that as minister of interior under Laval between 1930 and 1931 and as premier in 1932, he had used government funds to help La Roque expand his movement. He had done this, he said, on the recommendation of a "high military personality" and because he thought "it would be interesting to help in organizing the forces of order against the forces of disorder."[55]

When Laval returned to power in 1935, La Rocque may have curtailed his antiparliamentary mobilization exercises to repay Laval for his support. In June 1935 the prefect of the Eure and Loir informed Paris that La Rocque had informed his dispos in the region that there would be no large-scale mobilizations that summer because La Rocque had "temporary confidence in the Laval government." In August, a police informant reported a rumor in CF circles in Paris that La Rocque had adopted an attitude of "reserve" toward such mobilizations because "he was being towed along by Monsieur Laval."[56] A CF poster in July 1935 urged war veterans to accept cuts in their benefits proposed by the Laval government as a necessary measure to restore France's finances and ensure their future reimbursement.[57] La Rocque had not been so tolerant of similar cuts on February 6, 1934, when it had been a left-center government proposing them.

According to the police, the Banque de France was also an important donor to the CF. The treasurer of the CF was one of the bank's lawyers, the assistant treasurer one of its cashiers. Of the nine members of the CF's central committee in 1934, three worked in banks. By 1936, as many as 170 employees of the

Banque de Paris et des Pays Bas (which had formerly helped subsidize the JP) had joined the CF.[58]

Paul Chopine, a member of the CF's central committee who left the movement in disgust, claimed that the "flower of French aristocracy" had come to La Rocque's aid several times. Chopine insisted that the 16th arrondissement, "the most aristocratic quarter of Paris," had once provided the colonel with 750,000 francs within a few days to meet a political crisis. "Didn't a single charity sale at the Palais Berlitz," Chopine wrote, "bring in 1,200,000 francs?"[59] In 1935 police reported that the Banque Mallet Frères acted as a go-between for some of France's richest aristocratic families, including the royal family in exile: "We are assured that the Banque Mallet Frères . . . which administers the largest noble fortunes in France, notably those of the Guise family [which included the pretender to the throne], the Duchess of Uzès [a former supporter of the AF], [and] the Luynes family, has recently received large sums of money from Belgium [where the pretender lived]. These funds have been credited to the organization of the Croix de Feu or donated directly by this group."[60]

According to the police, the CF also received important subsidies from various electricity, railroad, and steel companies. In 1934 La Rocque was on the board of directors of a major hydroelectric company, the Compagnie Générale d'Electricité (General electricity company). Like other private utility companies in France at the time, this one feared the coming to power of a left-wing government that might lower electricity rates or even nationalize the industry (which eventually happened after the Second World War). Police reported in 1935 that Charles Laurent, who had large interests in several major electricity firms, including the Crédit Electrique, Union pour l'Industrie et l'Electricité, and the Société Centrale pour l'industrie électrique, had established a propaganda fund to "combat the projects of the parties of the left seeking the diminution of the sale price of electric currents and State takeover of the centers of [electricity] production." Laurent offered La Rocque support from this fund.[61]

One electricity executive, Ernest Mercier, became a member of the CF's central committee. Mercier, the head of the Compagnie Générale d'Electricité, was also the director of the Redressement Français (RF), which helped subsidize the Faisceau in 1926 and the SF in 1933.[62] In 1935 the Vigilance Committee of Antifascist Intellectuals, a left-wing organization, maintained that there was a connection between the CF and the electricity industry—and between the CF and other big business associations as well:

Colonel de La Rocque for three years belonged to . . . the board of directors of the *Union d'Electricité*.

Now, the latter is presided over by Ernest Mercier, electricity and petroleum magnate, honorary president of the Redressement Français, administrator of nineteen companies, distributor, according to Georges Valois, of the
subsidies of large capitalism. . . . If the concentration of fascist and capitalist
forces still escapes anyone, remember that the acting president of the Redressement Français is Maurice Champin, a heavy industry magnate, the director of
sixteen business associations; that the vice-president of the Croix de Feu is
Monsieur Pozzo di Borgo, [also] a director of several business associations, and
that the financial administrator of the Croix de Feu is an assistant bank manager.[63]

When in early 1936 Mercier withdrew from the CF in a huff after La Rocque
gave a speech criticizing the role of high finance in politics, the CF's treasurer, a
Monsieur Riché, piously declared at one of the movement's subsequent political
rallies, "People can no longer say that Monsieur Mercier is our financial backer;
moreover, he has never been, for the Croix de Feu have always been self-
sufficient."[64]

According to police, another source of funds for the CF was François de
Wendel, the steel manufacturer and president of the Comité des Forges (Steel
trust) from 1918 to 1940. In 1935 Wendel contributed money to both the premier
of France, Pierre Laval, and the paramilitary *chef,* Colonel de La Rocque: to the
first as a presiding republican obstacle to the left and to the second as a potentially dictatorial one. Wendel hoped that parliamentary conservatism could con-
tain the red tide, but if it were unable to he was prepared to turn to a more
authoritarian brand of conservatism.

Wendel had his doubts, however, about La Rocque's qualifications for dictator, preferring a more prestigious military figure. In July 1935 police authorities
reported to the minister of interior that

Monsieur François de Wendel supports Monsieur Laval with all his influence.
He considers [Laval] to be the last chance for the regime as it exists, and in case
the work now being undertaken fails what will inevitably come to pass,
doubtlessly with violence, will be a conflict between the Popular Front on one
side and the National Front and the Croix de Feu on the other.

Monsieur de Wendel does not neglect this hypothesis. At the same time
that he gives his support to Monsieur Laval, he is financially aiding Colonel de
La Rocque, for with all his energy he opposes the Popular Front coming to
power, whose projects for state intervention into the economy he dreads.

But, if Monsieur de Wendel considers the Croix de Feu disciplined and well
organized, representing the only force capable of matching the strength of the
left, his doubts about Colonel de La Rocque's qualities as a head of State are no

less, and he wonders if he would be up to resolving the difficult problems he would face after the installation of a dictatorial regime.

This is why it is said that Monsieur de Wendel intends, at the right moment, to replace the leader of the Croix de Feu with a man who enjoys great prestige in the country and who also has the favor of the army.[65]

The historian Jean-Noel Jeanneney has described how Wendel, although he valued the Croix de Feu as a paramilitary obstacle to a Communist revolution, preferred a parliamentary solution to civil war or dictatorship. Wendel subsidized politicians like Pierre Laval and Louis Marin more heavily than he did La Rocque and frowned on La Rocque's weakening of Marin's FR when the CF/PSF became an electoral party. Nevertheless, the victory of the Popular Front led Wendel to harden his position, and in September 1936 he had separate conversations with both La Rocque and Doriot, leading him to subsidize Doriot as well.

In effect, between 1918 and 1940, Wendel backed leaders of both the parliamentary and authoritarian rights, including a number of anticlerical "left republicans" between 1919 and 1924; in the latter enterprise he sought the support of Mercier and Coty. Between 1928 and 1932, Wendel granted regular subsidies to the JP and after 1934 began financing the CF. After a conversation with La Rocque in December 1936, he told a friend, "As for the PSF, it is on guard and says that it is rather confident that it can assure the protection of the center of Paris [should the left revolt]. La Rocque is not an orator nor even a propagandist, but he knows how to organize and perform a service, and it seems certain that he will do what is necessary to group the followers he has acquired and coordinate their effort."[66]

In 1937, however, Wendel was distressed when La Rocque refused to join Doriot, Taittinger, and Marin in the Liberty Front, thereby threatening to weaken the FR with his electoral competition. Wendel valued La Rocque for his paramilitary, not his parliamentary, capacities. For Wendel, La Rocque was a political last resort should the parliamentary option fail, someone who might defeat the left by force of arms if need be and establish a dictatorship of the right— however temporary La Rocque's role in that dictatorship might be.

In 1935 police reported that the CF was able to launch a daily newspaper owing to the support of six financial backers: Wendel, Schwof d'Hericourt, an industrialist, Ernest Mallet, a banker, Pierre Miraband, a banker, Jacques de Neuflize, a banker and railroad manager, and Otto de la Havraise, a major electricity company stockholder. Police noted that some CF members expressed surprise when La Rocque made a speech condemning the "directing role" that the "plutocracy" played in French politics, since "he is known to be in perfect accord with Messieurs Beghin, de Puyerimhooff, de Wendel, and Finaly [all industrialists and bankers]."[67]

In March 1936, La Rocque publicly denied that he had received any "outside subsidies, official or otherwise," and offered to make public his party's finances, which he estimated at five million francs. In a classic case of the pot calling the kettle black, he attributed the victory of the Popular Front to the actions of venal politicians whose support had been purchased with "contributions from capitalist, financial, and industrial powers." La Rocque even claimed that the French Intelligence Service had dispensed secret funds to the enemies of the CF, as had also the Soviet Union and Nazi Germany. According to the police, by March 1936 La Rocque had received fifteen million francs to finance CF candidates in the national elections of 1940, a war chest that had swelled because of gifts from "large economic groups."[68]

The official socioeconomic program of the CF in 1935 no doubt had something to do with the largesse of such donors, calling as it did for lower taxes, the "elimination of government intervention into areas belonging to free enterprise," the protection of family property, and respect for the "legitimate profits" from savings. No doubt, too, especially in light of the rise of the Popular Front in 1935 and its electoral victory in 1936, these donors approved of the movement's condemnations of class conflict and government social spending.

Economically threatened by a political system that had allowed the Popular Front to emerge, they subsidized a less democratic alternative for protection. The police report which stated that the obvious reason so much money was pouring into the CF's treasury in 1935 was the movement's "fundamental antiparliamentarianism" did not go far enough, inasmuch as it failed to mention the important economic interests that this antiparliamentarianism served. Much more revealing was the police report that described François de Wendel as someone who thought that the CF was "the only force capable of matching the strength of the left."[69]

MEMBERSHIP

Like other major French fascist movements of the interwar period, the CF/PSF was composed of largely middle, not lower, class people. As Julian Jackson has pointed out, in 1936 the PSF was out to win over sections of the middle classes that had been abandoned by the Popular Front: "And such evidence as exists suggests that the membership indeed consisted of peasants, shopkeepers, clerical workers, and so on frightened by the Popular Front."[70] The PSF itself declared in 1937, "We are essentially defenders of the middle classes, or, if one prefers, we seek a formula for national salvation by the middle classes and for the middle classes."[71]

One historian of the CF, Janine Bourdin, has described the mass base of the PSF as consisting primarily of small shopkeepers, small businessmen, peasants, traveling salesmen, white-collar workers, and managerial personnel in the private sector. Philippe Machefer found that most of the 670 local party headquarters of the PSF throughout France were situated in middle- or lower-middle-class neighborhoods and that La Rocque's claim in 1937 that 15 percent of his followers were merchants, 20 percent white-collar workers, 26 percent members of the liberal professions, 20 percent farmers, and 19 percent blue-collar workers roughly coincided with those fragments of the membership files that survived the Second World War.[72]

Sam Goodfellow, in his study of fascist movements in Alsace between the wars, reinforces the view that the mass base of the CF/PSF was largely middle class:

> Police reports noted that "engineers, factory directors, lawyers, reserve officers," and government employees figured prominently in the movement. Those farmers belonging to the Croix de Feu tended to be the "most important viticulturists" or prosperous farmers. . . .
>
> The Colmar Croix de Feu was led by "very cultivated and active people (engineers, factory managers, lawyers, reserve officers enjoying considerable sympathy among the military and administrative milieus." . . . Middle and upper-middle classes dominated the PSF, holding most of the key propaganda and leadership positions. The local leaders of the Croix de Feu/PSF bore a striking similarity to the leadership of the Faisceau in the 1920s. The editors of the *Flambeau de l'Est*, for example, were lawyers and industrialists. The party leaders were virtually all industrialists, lawyers, engineers, accountants, prosperous shopkeepers, and landed cultivators. Technocratic, well-to-do, and well-positioned socially, the PSF directors in Colmar and Mulhouse had no intention of fundamentally disrupting their situation except perhaps to improve it.[73]

Kevin Passmore in his study of the right and the extreme right in the Department of the Rhône finds that the PSF recruited from the same milieu as the PPF, that is, mainly from medium and small business enterprises in which proximity between employers and employees was greater than in larger firms. Many of these employers, who had had their authority as well as their profits challenged by the sit-down strikes of June 1936 and who were less willing than big business to compromise, welcomed the PSF's call for class collaboration. Workers who joined the PSF in Lyon were generally young and usually employed in small and medium firms located in areas of the city in which, Passmore writes, "there was a strong bourgeois presence." The possibilities of intimidation, in other words, were greater. Indeed, half a dozen PSF workers worked in small businesses owned by their fathers. Within the EVP units, the so-called mobile propaganda teams that provided security guards for PSF meetings, "youthful petty bourgeois males were numerous."[74]

Passmore notes that 30 percent of PSF activists in Lyon were white-collar workers who lived mainly in the bourgeois and petty bourgeois center of the city. They were also relatively young: 55 percent were forty years old or less. Here, too, the PSF was battling the PPF for recruits (24 percent of the PPF in Lyon were also white-collar workers): "White collar workers in the two parties [were] roughly similar in age, geographical origins, and in their residence in the bourgeois areas of the city. Where the parties differ is firstly in the greater appeal of the PPF to higher grade employees, and secondly in the presence of a significant white collar presence in working class areas. . . . Social polarization is . . . the best explanation, for supervisory personnel in proletarian suburbs must often have experienced isolation and perhaps attacks from communists" (338).

The PSF in the Rhône also competed with Lyon's leading Catholic trades union organization, the Confédération Française des Travailleurs Chrétiens (CFTC, General confederation of Christian workers). The CFTC generally remained faithful to Christian democracy and to the right to form free trade unions. Although it never approved of strike actions, it supported the reforms of the Popular Front and participated in joint demonstrations with the CGT—which was enough to arouse the hostility of employers. Following the sit-down strikes of June 1936, many of the rank and file of the CFTC went over to the PSF's union, the Syndicat Professionel Français (SPF, French professional union). Passmore explains:

> Often the main motive for joining was opposition to the CGT. . . . It is also possible to detect a shift to the right in the old core of the CFTC. Even in normal circumstances the attitude of conservative white collar workers to trades unionism was ambiguous, seeing it as a means both of collective self-defense and of protecting individual career structures. The popularity after June of the term "collaborateur" to designate non-manual workers after 1936 is illustrative of the attitude of many. The implicit threat to social hierarchy in June 1936 and the fact that CFTC members were disproportionately higher grade employees, led to suspicion of the CGT. . . . many CGT militants continued to associate Catholicism with the ruses of the patronat. . . . CFTC

members, often isolated in their workplaces, were vulnerable to the sort of treatment more often meted out to the SPF. Some were victims of the *conduit de Grenoble*, which involved ritual humiliation by female workers. (302)

In the midst of the sit-down strikes, Cardinal Maurin, who according to Passmore, had always been a reluctant supporter of Christian democracy, implied in a pastoral letter that the CFTC had failed and that the PSF's union was a legitimate option for Catholic workers. He announced that Catholics were permitted to join other unions than the CFTC, including new unions like the SPF, as long as these unions were not hostile to religion or the church. Other church leaders, however, insisted that Catholic workers remain within a confessional union, and Maurin backed down a few days later. After Maurin's death in November, his successor, Cardinal Gerlier, who opposed the deconfessionalization of Catholic trades unionism, refused to undermine the CFTC. Not all Catholic workers in the Rhône, however, followed his lead, many of them departing for the SPF and the PSF (302–04).

In the Rhône and throughout France, however, the PSF remained far more bourgeois than proletarian in the bulk of its membership. According to La Rocque's figures and Machefer's estimate, blue-collar workers—even higher grade Catholic blue-collar workers—composed no more than 20 percent of the PSF's rank and file. Sixty percent of the PSF were middle class (merchants, white-collar workers, members of the liberal professions), and the remaining 20 percent farmers—probably mainly landowning farmers rather than agricultural workers. If police reports on the financial backing and on the national and local leadership of the PSF are any indication, the party was controlled by men from upper- and middle-middle-class backgrounds—in many cases by engineers and other technocrats beholden to the industrialists who employed them. In this respect, the PSF's leadership structure was similar to that of the SF in 1934 or to that of the Faisceau in 1925.

In its propaganda, however, the CF/PSF went to great lengths to cater to members of the lower middle classes whom it needed in order to be an influential mass movement and not just a fringe party of upper bourgeois and aristocrats. Its subsidies from large corporations like the Comité des Forges and the general electricity company notwithstanding, it appealed to the anti–big business sentiments of the petite bourgeoisie. In July 1936, for example, *Le Flambeau* declared,

> Let us unite against our common enemies who exploit us: the trusts, the financial powers, the monopolies, the party of Moscow. The great trusts signed the Matignon accords. They have sufficient financial reserves. They will ob-

tain from the banks, their allies, the millions they need. All white-collar workers will become the employees of these trusts or [they will become] unemployed. There will be millions of new proletarians. It will be the dictatorship of one class, the suppression of [small] private property, everyone will become a proletarian of the anonymous trust.[75]

The same anticapitalism, however, defended the capitalism of small- and medium-sized businesses and denounced Marxism for threatening private property. It was also an "anticapitalism" that, in the official party program of the PSF in 1936 at least, favored big business by rejecting economic protectionism on behalf of free trade. Subsequently, however, some party spokesmen, emphasizing their support of the small enterprises, took a different view of protectionism. In 1937, for example, one PSF speaker told an audience that he was opposed to "the suppression of tariff barriers that would deal a mortal blow to French production by favoring foreign production."[76]

The CF/PSF also sought to win over the peasantry. In June 1935 La Rocque claimed that 40 percent of his movement's new members since November were farmers. Although he declared at that time that unlike an electoral party the CF did not play the game of promising peasants special benefits in return for their support, he denounced middlemen in the market towns of France for exploiting the peasants and called for more police inspections of their activities. The CF/PSF catered especially to Catholic sections of the peasantry. In 1937 one of its representatives, a Monsieur Pierrat, on a speaking tour through rural France, declared that "outside of God and the French Social Party nothing exists." Paul Chopine attributed the movement's peasant support to less religious causes:

Separated far from the large [urban] agglomerations, little affected by republican propaganda, still afraid of the large landowner and the local squire, [peasants] were ripe to be recruited into the troops of the PSF.

The propaganda tasks were assigned to men the peasants needed, for whom they often had respect. The notary in drafting a document, the doctor during the course of a visit, the salesman of agricultural implements, the veterinary in treating an animal, the miller or grain dealer would praise the PSF which they had joined themselves. The peasant was proud to be with these fine gentlemen.

. . . With articles, tracts, and meetings, the peasant was told: "If Marxism comes to power, it will take your land [and] your house." At big meetings, such as at Flers-de-l'Orne, the deputies of the PSF . . . would pit the peasant against the worker by pronouncing those impious words: "The worker makes fun of war, for they will not serve in it, while you, the peasants, will all go." They were told how State bureaucrats favored the worker.[77]

Apparently for the CF/PSF, the principle of class conciliation was flexible.

In their speeches to rural audiences, CF/PSF representatives argued that any social reforms that aided urban workers were at the peasants' expense. Popular Front legislation inaugurating the eight-hour day, the forty-hour week, and vacations with pay were said to benefit the proletariat, not the peasantry, raising the peasants' taxes without providing them with equal benefits. The CF/PSF also sided with peasant employers against peasant wage-laborers by opposing government limitations on the rural workweek. Critical of statism, it generally opposed government aid to farmers, even though it did advocate that farmers be given the same family allocations as urban workers. It urged farmers to form their own corporatist associations, free from government interference, and to set their own farm prices. The CF/PSF even condemned the wheat board, which the government had created to advance credit to the peasantry, because of its bureaucratic costliness to the taxpayer.[78]

In 1936 the CF claimed to have made enormous gains among the *colons* of French North Africa, that is, among its European landowners and merchants, who had a stake in keeping their Arab workers under control. This section of North African society had been perennially attracted to fascist ideas from the Dreyfus affair onward, and the 1930s were no exception. A CF speaker who had returned from Algeria in March said that the majority of French *colons* there supported La Rocque's movement and that they had succeeded in bringing with them a large number of native Algerians, "thus giving us a magnificent example of French reconciliation." According to him, the entire municipal council of Algiers, headed by the mayor, were members of the CF, and at Constantine six municipal councillors were members, streets were named after La Rocque, and stores flew the CF insignia.[79]

The working-class support that the CF/PSF enjoyed both in North Africa and on the mainland was probably due less to passion for "French reconciliation" than to employment considerations. Algerian farm laborers and French blue-collar workers could sometimes obtain jobs or curry favor with their bosses by joining La Rocque's movement. At CF headquarters in Paris in 1936, job vacancies were posted, and employers were told that they would be provided with "an elite personnel who would give them full satisfaction."[80] The implication was clear: such personnel would be not only skilled and hardworking but also opposed to Marxism.

Typical of the CF's approach to labor relations were the tenets voiced in a speech given in June 1935 by one of its spokesmen, Bertrand de Maud'huy, the son of the former military governor of Metz. According to police, de Maud'huy made a vibrant appeal on behalf of social peace and hard work. Afterward, the audience donated five thousand francs to aid the charities of the CF.[81]

The CF/PSF had a disproportionate share of upper-class supporters, including many who were highly educated. Not only was the movement heavily subsidized by big business groups and members of the aristocracy, but those who attended its charity balls and literary auctions were often from the most wealthy and cultivated sections of French society. *Le Flambeau* was sometimes ridiculed by the AF for its lack of literary polish, and PPF writers like Pierre Drieu La Rochelle, Bertrand de Jouvenel, and Raymon Fernandez had a greater reputation in French intellectual circles than the publicists who wrote for La Rocque's newspaper. Still, some prestigious names were associated with the CF/PSF, if only indirectly. In May 1936 the MSF held a charity auction at which the signatures of Paul Claudel, André Maurois, Paul Morand, and Henry Bordeaux were sold to the public—as well as those of Marshal Lyautey and General Weygand.[82]

One indication of the elite support that the CF/PSF enjoyed was the large numbers of students and faculty from the *grandes écoles* who joined the movement, most of whom came from upper-middle-class backgrounds. In May 1936 an audience of some fifteen hundred students, professors, and doctors turned out to hear La Rocque speak at a meeting of the university branch of the MSF. This was an impressive gathering (the university population in Paris being much smaller in 1936 than it is today), worrisome enough to warrant a police report to the minister of interior.[83]

As we have seen, the parliamentary commission that investigated the riots of February 6 was concerned with the relation between the CF and the *grandes écoles*, especially with the schools that produced officers for the military: Saint-Cyr, the French naval academy, and the École Polytechnique. Although military officers on active duty were forbidden by the government to join any political movement, reserve officers were free to do so. According to the police, not only did many reserve officers belong to the CF in 1934 but some of them, as well as students from Saint-Cyr and the École Polytechnique, were in direct contact with officers on active duty. Thus when students from the École Polytechnique paraded up the Champs-Elysées in 1933 as part of the CF column, they presented a disturbing spectacle to republican authorities—not because a few hundred students were about to overthrow the government but because their ties with the military raised the spectre of a more serious possibility.

When a member of the parliamentary commission investigating February 6 asked a police official, "Do you not know whether there are frequent contacts between reserve officers who belong to the Croix de Feu and officers on active duty?" the official replied, "Yes, there are. In certain cities there are [CF] groups in garrisons composed exclusively of officers and enlisted men." The official added, however, that he gave this information qualifiedly and needed to verify it.[84] The ensuing official record did not mention whether he had been able to do so.

The CF/PSF had some additional support in royalist circles, although it seems to have fluctuated according to circumstances. In June 1935, police reported that a number of CF members were either former or current members of the AF. At a time La Rocque was under increasing pressure from some of his militant followers to launch a coup d'état, it was rumored that a brother of his who had access to the count of Paris, the pretender to the throne who was living in exile in Brussels, was urging fellow royalists within the CF to leave the organization if La Rocque failed to act. In August 1935 La Rocque ordered that anyone within the CF known to be a member of the AF be put under surveillance, leading some AF/CF militants to resign in protest. Two months earlier, police had reported to the minister of interior,

> There are rumors rife in the highest circles of the Croix de Feu that cannot be verified but which are nevertheless interesting to take note of because they are at the very least either a manifestation of a certain state of mind or a sign of a certain [political] maneuvering. It is said that, despite appearances, Colonel de La Rocque is in permanent liaison with the Count of Paris through the intermediaries of his brothers, Pierre and Edouard, who belong to the Prince's entourage and with whom he is not as alienated as he lets on.
>
> It is also said that about a year ago there was an agreement reached with the House of France in terms of a collaboration. This agreement did not envision an immediate restoration. It would try, in the event that the Croix de Feu siezed power, . . . first to establish a "confidential relationship" between the House of France and the French State. It is pointed out in this regard that certain views held by the Count of Paris, who has a very great interest in social questions, are in accord with the tendencies manifested up until now by Colonel de La Rocque.[85]

In 1939 Paul Chopine claimed that in 1937 the count of Paris had believed that he had more to gain by allying himself with a mass party like the PSF than by remaining bound to the much smaller AF, a sentiment that had led the count to break with the AF in November of that year. According to Chopine, one had only to look at all the aristocratic names with ties to the PSF in parliament ("de Kérillis, de Pavant, de La Roche-Vernet, des Isnards, de Mortemart, de Saint-Just, d'Harcourt, de Clermont-Tonnere, d'Audiffret-Pasquier, de Montalembert, etc.") to discern the PSF's royalist connections.[86] Since Chopine had become one of the PSF's harshest critics by 1939, having fallen out with La Rocque earlier, he may well have been exaggerating these connections. That the CF/PSF received *some* support from royalist circles, however, seems likely.

On religious issues, the CF/PSF catered far more to Catholics than to non-Catholics, although it reiterated that it was ecumenical, that is, that it was not just a confessional movement. Nevertheless, it portrayed anticlerical Freemasonry as one of the great scourges of France and condemned secular education for de-Christianizing France. The CF/PSF was also a strong defender of traditional values, at least those that coincided with French conservative Catholicism.

Although the CF/PSF appealed primarily to the middle classes, white-collar employees, landed peasants, and higher grade Catholic blue-collar workers for the bulk of its support, it focused, like other French fascist movements of the era, on those sections of these classes that were the most religiously, culturally, and sexually conservative and the most politically, socially, and economically authoritarian, on people with a strong commitment to hierarchy in human relations. Secular, liberal, and democratic members of the middle classes, the peasantry, and the working classes did not find a home in the CF/PSF.

WAS LA ROCQUE'S MOVEMENT FASCIST?

Several historians have denied that either the CF or the PSF was fascist. According to René Rémond, the answer to the question of whether fascism had a significant following in France in the 1930s must focus on La Rocque's movement, the "centerpiece of the controversy." Rémond writes that the CF, being the largest nationalist league of the interwar period, is "the pivot of the debate" and that "the response to the question essentially depends on an appreciation of [the CF's] profound nature."[87]

Philippe Machefer has insisted that PSF doctrine was based not on fascism but on a "sort of 'patriotic, social Christianity,'" Zeev Sternhell that the Croix de Feu "was never a fascist movement" because "in France, real authentic fascism was always born on the left, never on the right," and Rémond himself that French leftists in the 1930s who saw La Rocque as the incarnation of fascism committed a "monumental" error. A number of scholars have agreed with these views.[88]

In 1988 Jacques Nobécourt asserted that there was no connection between Jean-Marie Le Pen's National Front and La Rocque's movement of fifty years earlier because, Nobécourt contended, La Rocque had been opposed to street violence, racism, and Vichy's Légion des combattants. Other proofs of La Rocque's nonfascism, according to Nobécourt, were the dissolution of the PSF by Vichy in 1942 and La Rocque's arrest by the Gestapo in 1943. Thus it was a myth that Le Pen's movement was a revival of La Rocque's, especially since Le

Pen's orientation was toward "national-populism" whereas La Rocque appealed to voters who were "fundamentally moderate."[89] Or, as a writer for *Le Monde* expressed it in 1985, La Rocque was simply "a link in the rather pragmatic evolution of French 'moderates' from Albert de Mun to Charles de Gaulle."[90]

For Rémond, La Rocque was a nationalist who, although he sought a strong government for France, was too legalistic to be a fascist. This was especially true, Rémond argues, after the CF was banned in 1936 and La Rocque replaced it with a PSF that "adopted the statutes, the organization, and the comportment of a party of the classical type." "In the eyes of the left," Rémond goes on, "this was purely a camouflage operation; in reality, it was a return—whose sincerity was shown by what followed—to the practices of pluralistic democracy." Although not all former members of the CF joined the PSF, hundreds of thousands of new members flocked into the party and underwent an "apprenticeship in democracy," creating grassroots organizations, running candidates for office, and forming a block of deputies in parliament.

Indeed, according to Rémond, by providing French conservatives with a viable *democratic* alternative, the PSF served to "immunize a sector of opinion against the fascist temptation." La Rocque denounced anti-Semitism and took measures against it when it cropped up in his movement. The PSF prepared the way for a similar nonfascist political movement ten years later, General de Gaulle's Rassemblement du Peuple Français (RPF, Reassembly of the French people).[91]

Julian Jackson too has denied that La Rocque's movement was fascist during the interwar period, either before 1936 or afterward:

> Even if the military style parades, the motorcades, the mysterious references to 'H hour' may have given some of its members a fascist *frisson*—Rémond talks of "political boy scouting for adults"—de La Rocque's ideology, as summarized in his book *Service Social*, was a collection of all the platitudes of traditional French conservatism: defense of the family, strengthening of the authority of the State, class collaboration, corporatism. None of this was necessarily anti-republican—although de La Rocque equivocated on the issue—and it was certainly not fascist. The inclusion of corporatism was in the best social-Christian tradition.

Jackson concedes that the CF was more authoritarian than the PSF (although still not fascist), but, like Rémond, he sees the departure of Pozzo di Borgo and his fellow militants from La Rocque's movement in 1936 as proof that the new formation was fundamentally different from the old. (Neither Jackson nor Rémond explains why a fascist like di Borgo, himself the movement's vice-president until 1936, belonged to the "republican" CF in the first place). Like Rémond, Jackson attributes the rising popularity of the PSF after 1936 to its rejection of extremism rather than to the reverse. "Even," Jackson writes, "if there was a degree of political opportunism in this rallying to the Republic, the significant point is that de la Rocque achieved his greatest influence when he appeared at his most moderate."[92]

Supporting the interpretation of Jackson, Rémond, Nobécourt, and others is the fact that throughout the 1930s La Rocque repeatedly criticized German Nazism and repeatedly denied that his movement was fascist. He emphasized that there was nothing foreign about either the CF or the PSF, especially where "German brutality" was concerned. In May 1933 *Le Flambeau* described Hitler's gangs as barbaric, and in July 1934 it condemned the Night of the Long Knives and Nazism's "regime of tyranny and inquisition."

When in April 1934 La Rocque was called to testify before the parliamentary commission investigating the riots of February 6, he said it was absurd to label him a fascist. When asked to be more precise, he replied, "If you look at everything that Mussolini and Hitler have written . . . and compare it with the modest things we have written, you will clearly see the differences." He added that the CF had never defended the "idea of a military state," that it "excluded a whole series of fascist ideas," and that it believed that the individualistic character of the French people "did not lend itself to fascist solutions." In 1936 he reiterated that the CF rejected "the statist servitude which foreign countries may accommodate to but which the ordered individualism of our race regards with horror."[93]

In 1936 La Rocque declared himself "firmly attached to republican liberties" and said that the results of French history excluded "fascist dictatorship, Hitlerian absolutism, and the inhuman slavery of Soviet Marxism." On April 11, he announced that supporting the CF was a way of avoiding fascism and Hitlerism—as well as a way of resisting the red revolution that would inevitably follow. On June 13, he wrote that the CF wanted "no fascist, Hitlerian, anti-Semitic, Semitic, capitalist [or] Communist dictatorship." Indeed, one of La Rocque's favorite tactics was to use the label *fascism* against his accusers, describing Blum's government and the Popular Front in Spain as a forms of "red fascism." By professing opposition to both the extreme right and the extreme left, he implied that the CF pursued a middle course. To readers of *Le Flambeau* he declared, "You do not want a Bolshevik dictatorship any more than you want an imitation for our use of fascist, Hitlerian behavior." In another article he proclaimed, "Your national character excludes servitude."[94]

On February 1, 1936, an article in *Le Flambeau* devoted to the third anniversary of Hitler's accession to power in Germany criticized the economic record of the Nazi regime. It noted that although unemployment had fallen, so too had the production of food and consumer goods—and that this decline had been accompanied by higher taxes and "increasingly heavier social charges." Articles on April 18 and 25 voiced additional criticisms. One took a swipe at Nazi racism when it observed that the German population was a "mixture of three races," the Germanic, Latin, and Gallo-Roman. Another article pointed out that the fastest growing industry in Germany was the armaments industry and that unemployed workers who could not find jobs in it were destined for careers in the army, a development that was described as a threat to European peace. *Le Flambeau* also faulted the Nazi educational system for dethroning elite culture and intellectual achievement in favor of mass culture and physical education. It was especially critical of German students in uniforms who intimidated their teachers.

In May 1937, La Rocque published an article entitled "No Fascism" in which he insisted that fascist attitudes were "contrary to the French temperament" and that the PSF was opposed to any "servile copy of fascist totalitarianism." In July and November 1937 he again denounced Nazism. Rejecting the slogan "Better Hitler than Blum," he said that his movement was against all dictatorships and declared, "Our ideal of liberty and our defense of Christian civilization rejects both the Hitlerian yoke and Muscovite tyranny." The PSF, he wrote, was respectful of legality, attached to republican institutions, and committed to the free exercise of individual rights. It was also "ferociously opposed to all copies of dictatorial regimes."[95]

In *Public Service* (1934), La Rocque criticized Nazi racial theory and accused Germany of indulging in "the worst follies," which he attributed to Germany's lack of a "Latin sense of measure." He reminded his readers that during the last days of the First World War the Germans had destroyed French orchards, mines, and cemeteries when they retreated. The Nazi taste for political violence, he said, was a sign of intellectual and social disorder. To employ such violence in France would lead "either to something odious or to buffoonery." La Rocque also criticized Italian fascism, saying that the CF shared neither its "debauchery of uniforms" nor its "quasi-religious" cult of the state. The CF, he said, believed that "absolute authority confided to the hands of one man or to one group of men who might install themselves in power without any controls or sanctions is the worst danger that a civilized country such as ours could run."[96] In light of such statements, one might indeed conclude that La Rocque was not a fascist and that to categorize him as such would be not only a monumental error but deeply unfair.

There is, however, another side to the story. La Rocque and other CF/PSF propagandists *did* criticize German Nazism and Italian fascism during the 1930s, especially when their movement was threatened with a government ban, but they also praised German Nazism and Italian fascism. In doing so, they took pains not to associate themselves too closely with fascisms abroad in order not to appear less nationalist at home, a consideration La Rocque candidly acknowledged in 1936 when he wrote, "We will inspire respect not by flattering foreigners and seeking their council but by holding fast to our own interests, while demonstrating the certainty of our moral solidarity as well as of our patriotic pride."[97] However, the CF/PSF also had something to gain by partially associating itself with foreign fascisms, especially where Hitler's and Mussolini's repression of Marxists was concerned. Nazism and fascism had been more efficacious than democratic conservatism in dealing with the reds in Germany and Italy, and the CF/PSF promised to be more efficacious as well.

The same article in *Le Flambeau* that criticized Nazism for putting German industry on a war footing and for undermining elite culture also lauded Hitler for "scooping up the pieces of a Germany that had been crumbled by defeat and socialism." Hitler, it said, was "intelligent, clever, energetic, audacious, and sincere" (one Junker, it noted, had called him "the shoemakers' Napoleon"). If Nazism was "a kind of Bolshevism in reverse," there was still a huge difference between Nazism and Bolshevism, and, compared to Russia, Germany was "happy." The author of this article, Constantin-Weyer, insisted on paying Hitler the "just homage" he was due, commenting that Hitler had raised the morale of the German people to new levels by achieving what even Bismarck had been incapable of, the full unification of Germany. Constantin-Weyer was "certain" that Hitler was "sincere" when he talked of peace. Constantin-Weyer also praised Mussolini for encouraging literature and the arts: "A party of the masses, Italian fascism strives to elevate crowds to the height of the elite."[98]

A month later another article in *Le Flambeau* spoke favorably of Rexism, Léon Degrelle's fascist movement in Belgium, describing it as a desirable alternative to the "rottenness" and "decrepitude" of the parliamentary regime in that country and taking heart from the fact that Rexism's recent electoral gains had demonstrated that in Belgium "there was a dynamism for reform stronger than Bolshevism."[99]

In *Public Service* La Rocque spoke of the "genius" of Mussolini and declared that "the admiration which Mussolini merits is beyond dispute."[100] The chief of the CF also expressed admiration for the "fifteen years of indefatigible reconstruction" that the Germans had carried out and called upon France to seek an entente with Hitler: "Should we therefore 'chat' with the Germans? Yes, a million times yes. But only on condition of being first of all masters of our own house, of having put an end in France to revolutionary enterprises, [and] of having established a solid and well-coordinated army, air force and navy." These words were written by the same man who a few months earlier, on the eve of the February 6 riots, had called for a government "free of politicians of whatever kind" and who, following the riots, had dismissed the conservative but politically democratic Doumergue government as merely "a poultice on a gangrenous leg."[101]

In 1935 La Rocque advocated an alliance between France and fascist Italy, two countries, he said, with "identical intellectual connections."[102] In September 1935 Le Flambeau called for "continental solidarity" with Italy and accused the Freemasons and the Communists of engaging in an international conspiracy to create a rupture between Paris and Rome by fostering a new Franco-German war.[103]

When La Rocque condemned Nazi brutality in 1934, he added a significant qualification. He did not mean, he said, that to disapprove of violence was to fear it: "To reject its usage is not to rule out the possibility of facing it and responding to it victoriously. Confronted with the criminal designs of the Popular Front, . . . it would be unpardonable for us not to create an effective defense with good Frenchmen [and] also an instrument capable of crushing attempts at revolution."[104] In other words, violence for violence's sake was reprehensible but violence to defeat the "criminal designs" of the Popular Front was not.

La Rocque maintained that the CF had acted quite "morally" on February 6 in demonstrating its physical strength vis-à-vis leftists who had engaged in "a plot against the security of the State." He added that the CF was prepared to perform such a "public service" again if the Popular Front and its "fomentors of subversion" posed a new threat to the nation (263–64).

In May 1936, on the eve of the Popular Front's coming to power, police reported that Pozzi di Borgo had said at a local CF meeting in Paris that Mussolini was a "great leader" who "despite the threats of the Masonic organizations, had realized his goal." At another meeting four days later, di Borgo praised Hitler as well. According to police, "After having reminded his audience that France was on the edge of a precipice . . . , [di Borgo] hailed the notion of la patrie and used as a symbol the work of Hitler, which had rapidly given the soul of a victor to a country that had been vanquished, beaten, [and] disoriented. . . . [Di

Borgo had declared,] 'Mussolini, like Hitler, has known how to make a great nation of his country and has succeeded . . . in accomplishing a tour de force that no one else has yet realized.'"[105] Police reported that this last remark was met with loud applause from the CF audience. Apparently they did not find it absurd (to use La Rocque's term) to associate themselves with fascism.

It is true that di Borgo abandoned La Rocque's movement in June 1936 for the Cagoule when La Rocque failed to act against the Popular Front, but the fact that di Borgo had found a home in the CF for several years indicates that the movement did not exclude members with fascist sympathies. Di Borgo, after all, had been the vice-president of the CF as well as one of its major financial backers.

Di Borgo, furthermore, did not take with him everyone in the CF who was attracted to fascism. Sam Goodfellow has found that after 1936, after the PSF had ostensibly turned in a more democratic direction, many of those who joined the PSF in Alsace had previously belonged to the Francistes, the JP, and other fascist organizations. Goodfellow says of this "fluidity,"

> Movement between Alsatian Francistes and the PSF was not uncommon. Ex-PSF members, for example, were among those listed as contributors to the German language edition of the *Franciste*. As the Franciste movement began to wane, many members switched to the PSF. Movement between the PSF and other fascist groups also took place. In January of 1939 the mayor of Niedernai, a PSF leader, held a joint meeting with the representatives of the Nazi-influenced *Bauerbund* on the issue of dairy cooperatives. . . .
>
> A thorough reading of local [PSF] party propaganda reveals little functional difference between the Faisceau, the Francistes, or any of the other fascist parties. . . . The national leadership [of the PSF] never fully repudiated the Alsatian PSF's links with the other fascist movements.[106]

According to Goodfellow, not only did the PSF's competitors, including the JP, "resent its success at their expense," but in 1937 the rivalry sometimes led to a confusion over salutes. "Everyone," writes Goodfellow, "wanted to use some form of the Hitler salute, although the Croix de Feu called it 'a gesture of reconciliation and frankness.'" Goodfellow is referring here to an article published in an Alsatian Franciste newspaper that raised the issue after pointing out that the *Parisian* had reported that on November 11, 1936, the fascist salute had been used at a PSF ball.[107]

On April 9, 1938, the *Flambeau de l'Est* praised Hitler for creating a national socialism that "bombarded the bourgeois cash drawer mentality and socialist homelessness and thereby created the unity of the German peoples." The article concluded, "Is it not our duty to reimpose national unity, if divisiveness and class hatred are to be ended?" Goodfellow finds such expressions of "thinly disgused envy" of Hitler not uncommon in both police descriptions of the Alsa-

tian PSF and in its local newspaper. According to Goodfellow, the fascist pro-
clivities of the PSF were also seen in its continuing military mystique, its criticisms of liberalism for promoting disorder, and in La Rocque's insistence in 1937
on "distancing himself from the parliamentary process by promising never to
head a republican government."[108] The PSF in Alsace was also, as we shall see,
quite anti-Semitic in 1938.

In 1941 none of La Rocque's previous criticisms of Hitlerism prevented him
from calling for "continental collaboration" with the Germans. To regard his
break with Vichy in 1942 and his arrest by the Gestapo in 1943 as proof of his
nonfascism simply ignores his active collaboration with Nazism between October 1940 and December 1941. If the "sincerity" of La Rocque's politics "was
shown by what followed" (to quote Rémond again), then his strong support of
the Vichy regime between late 1940 and late 1941 suggests that the La Rocque of
1936–39 was not sincerely democratic. And La Rocque's suffering at the hands
of the Germans after 1943, however heroic, did not make him any less fascist
two years earlier. If after 1942 his nationalism prevailed over his hatred of Marxism, Freemasonry, and decadence, it was hardly because of a lifelong commitment to democratic values. Between 1931 and 1936 La Rocque repeatedly expressed contempt for the basic principles of political democracy and encouraged
his dispos to believe that one day they would establish a more authoritarian
government in France.

Neither does the fact that La Rocque finally sided with the Resistance in 1942
(after the tide of the war had turned against the Germans) prove that he had not
been previously fascist in his domestic politics. As we have seen, not all French
fascists sided with the Nazis during the Second World War. Many were just as
nationalistic toward their country as Hitler and Mussolini were toward theirs.
Georges Valois, who founded the Faisceau in 1925, died at Bergen-Belsen for his
Resistance activities, and Philippe Barrès, one of his former lieutenants in the
Faisceau, served under Charles de Gaulle in London. In 1933, Barrès, the son of
the famous anti-Dreyfusard Maurice Barrès, had called upon French integral
nationalists to save France the way Hitler had saved Germany. As previously
mentioned, certain members of the Cagoule also served under de Gaulle or
fought for the Resistance during the Second World War. Eugéne Deloncle died
shooting at Gestapo agents who had come to arrest him. Sam Goodfellow tells
how French fascists in Alsace during the Second World War were "willing to ally
with the English, the Gaullists, or even the Communists, if, as one of them put
it, 'these people will be able to rid us of the Boche.'"[109] La Rocque was not the
only French fascist to eventually side with the Resistance.

Nor are the differences between La Rocque's personality and Hitler's of paramount importance. Not all fascists in the 1930s were as pathological as Hitler. To assume otherwise would be to blind ourselves to the danger of fascist ideas when they are expressed by people with seemingly respectable or moderate personas. La Rocque was no Hitler, but neither were Speer, Karl Doenitz, Joachim von Ribbentrop, Erwin Rommel, Mussolini, Galeazzo Ciano, Oswald Mosley, Valois, Taittinger, Renaud, Doriot, and a host of other European fascists.

It is also a mistake to assume that the thousands of French men and women who supported La Rocque between 1936 and 1939 were unaware of his previous political career. Between 1931 and 1936, La Rocque repeatedly attacked electoral democracy, denigrated politicians in favor of war veterans, and alluded to a D day when his dispos would seize power. As late as May 1936, the CF was presenting itself as a more forceful enemy of the left than the FR or the Radical party. It is difficult to believe that those who joined the PSF after June 1936 thought that La Rocque had abandoned his previous politics so completely, that he had become a born-again democrat overnight.

It is also difficult to believe that these new followers chose to support La Rocque's PSF instead of Marin's FR because they thought the PSF more moderate. The reputation of the FR was clearly more parliamentarian and less paramilitary than that of the CF/PSF. New members of the PSF after 1936 could hardly ignore their party's emphasis on the continuity between the CF and the PSF ("The PSF is the CF plus electoral politics"). To see the mass appeal of the CF/PSF after 1936 as residing in its moderation minimizes the intensity of the conservative backlash to the Popular Front and the desire of many French conservatives for a more authoritarian response to the threat from the left than that offered by either the FR or the Radical party. People who had read any of La Rocque's diatribes against Marxists and left-liberals in the 1930s could have hardly expected him to be moderate toward these "degenerates" should he come to power.

Certainly during the first few months of the Vichy regime and the German occupation of northern France, there was little that was moderate about La Rocque's political pronouncements. Freed of having to pay lip service to republican liberties, he insisted that the left be smashed once and for all—and without mercy. In *Disciplines of Action,* he called for harsh measures against anyone who opposed Pétain's goals as well as for punishment for those who had been, in his words, responsible for France's military defeat. To be sure, La Rocque also appealed for patriotic reconciliation and Christian harmony, which he said were to be based on a fraternal rejection of political hatred and a spiritual commitment to the "equality of souls." This did not prevent him, however, from advocating that such reconciliation be accompanied by the repression of Marxists, Freemasons, Jews, and other practitioners of the "mortal vices" of France.

According to La Rocque in 1941, France had entered a period that required "visible, pitiless, and justified sanctions" against its domestic enemies if it was to be saved. He illustrated his point with a chilling example from his military past:

> For two years [in Morocco], I commanded a post constantly harassed by the enemy. [My successor would be] massacred along with the majority of his native auxiliaries. Here is the method I used to generate security. Less indulgent than my [successor], I had any native convicted of treason or of passing intelligence to our adversaries shot by a firing squad. . . . And the number of those executed in two years did not reach a tenth of the French soldiers massacred by surprise in the six months following my departure. The abnormal circumstances in which we [presently] live [also] require . . . implacable and public examples of discipline which applies to everybody.[110]

The supposedly conciliatory La Rocque seized the opportunity in 1941 to condemn as "traitors" not only French Communists but also Blum, Daladier, and other non-Communist politicians of the Third Republic. In April 1941 he wrote Pétain complaining that Blum and Daladier had not yet been punished for their deeds by the Riom court and asked for swifter justice.[111] Significantly, he blamed Blum and Daladier not only for the fall of France in 1940 but also for the rise of the Popular Front in 1936. With no republican constraints to hinder him and ignoring his previous avowals of respect for these constraints, he sought revenge: "It is too easy to limit [our] anathemas to 1939 and 1940 when, since 1919, [politicians] founded their personal careers [and] built the fate of the country on manifestly degrading bases. . . . For they did not want . . . to transform the country and the people according to [the principles of the PSF]. Only [the PSF] would have been capable of turning aside the flow of the Popular Front, war, and defeat."[112]

La Rocque did concede that wrongdoers who had erred in good faith should not be punished, leaving it up to socially conservative Pétainistes to decide who was guilty of bad faith. If *Disciplines of Action* is any indication, La Rocque was not inclined to spare wrongdoers who had formerly been associated with the political left. He demanded that Freemasons and others with "decadent morals" be removed from the government because, he said, "an intermediate stage [was] inevitable during the course of which heavy sanctions would be applied against individuals who would be made examples of while awaiting the integral extirpation of contaminated elements." La Rocque maintained that unless "severe punishments" were meted out to certain individuals "disorder" would result.[113]

La Rocque's double-talk was sometimes breathtaking. Although he avowed that *Disciplines of Action* was not a polemical book, that Vichy should not engage in political vendettas that might be viewed by the populace as reprisals, and that the national revolution was to be waged *"for* ideas and not *against* men," he labeled Blum and Daladier traitors and complained that the French police, "who had previously protected elements of the Popular Front," were allowing Communists like Thorez and Duclos to escape arrest. Calling for "total discipline" under Pétain, he insisted on French "unanimity." "No dissidence," he wrote, "will be legitimate [or] supportable. . . . We must fuse French diversity, *under the pain of death* [italics mine], into a flexible and vigorous harmony."[114]

Apparently, La Rocque found no contradiction between his critique of Bolshevism in 1936 for "killing all liberty," regressing "to the intolerance of the Inquisition," and treating its political leaders "like divinities" and his own support for repression, his own intolerance, and his own sanctification of a leader, Pétain, in 1941. In 1941 La Rocque opposed releasing Spanish prisoners from French concentration camps on the grounds that they had been contaminated by Communist propaganda and urged that doubtful bureaucrats in the French civil service be replaced with men who were distant from politics (that is, from democratic politics).

Finally, as previously mentioned, in 1941 La Rocque expressed his admiration for the "ardent vitality of fascist and Hitlerian regimes," compared Nazi theories of "families of good stock who have their roots in the earth" with the doctrines of Pierre Le Play and René La Tour de Pin, and asserted that collaboration between "two great peoples like the French and the Germans" could lead to "reciprocal enrichments." He also defended collaboration with the Germans on the grounds that the Second World War was a crusade to save Christian civilization from "demon Russia" and that de Gaulle and the British had chosen to side with this "Asiatic empire."[115] La Rocque was no antifascist in 1941.

But what of his politics before the war, between 1931 and 1939? Was he fascist during this period as well or was he only a mildly authoritarian republican, a political and social moderate who was in fact, as he himself often said, strongly opposed to fascism? Should any French politician, after all, have his earlier career judged by his later career, especially when the circumstances were so different? Many Socialist and Radical politicians supported Pétain in 1940, hoping that Pétain would be able to negotiate better peace terms with Hitler. This did not mean that they supported fascist ideas either before or during the war. Was La Rocque any different?

On a number of important counts, the answer is undoubtedly yes. Not only in 1934 did La Rocque express his admiration for Mussolini's "genius," seek a government free of politicians of whatever kind, and call for an entente with Nazi Germany and an alliance with fascist Italy, but also both before and after 1936 his views on domestic politics contained many of the same doctrines and values that were central to fascist ideology elsewhere in Europe during this period as well as to the fascist tradition in France from 1924 onward. One has only to compare La Rocque's basic social, economic, political, and cultural ideals with those of earlier French fascists like Antoine Rédier, Valois, and Taittinger to see their continuity with that tradition.[116]

The similarities between La Rocque's ideology and those of the SF and the Francistes are also striking, which is one reason many of their members went over to the PSF when the two organizations faltered. Ideological commonalities help explain in addition why some members of the CF joined the PPF in 1936 when La Rocque backed off from attempting a paramilitary coup.

As La Rocque repeatedly indicated in his writings before 1936 and after 1940, democratic ideology violated his most deep-seated convictions. Where a fundamental commitment to democracy was concerned, La Rocque was more than conservative; he was reactionary. The transformation of the CF into the PSF in 1936 was more cosmetic than substantive. Even as the leader of the allegedly republican PSF, La Rocque spoke of dealing with the left in an authoritarian manner. The paramilitary dimension of the CF/PSF was never completely scrapped, as the organization of its EVP shows.

As many of La Rocque's own words reveal and as police reports of the era confirm, the attitudes and actions of La Rocque and his lieutenants throughout the 1930s were never as democratic, liberal, and legalistic as they have been portrayed to be. Although CF/PSF propaganda employed some republican rhetoric for safety's sake, it engaged in the same kind of double-talk and employed many of the same code words that were the stock-in-trade of other French fascist movements of the interwar period and that were all too familiar to contemporaries who had heard fascist discourse before.

True, in the 1930s La Rocque denied that his movement was fascist, but so, too, did Renaud, Vinceguide, and Doriot regarding theirs. And even Valois and Bucard, who did label themselves fascists, as well as Taittinger and Doriot, who accepted fascist salutes from their followers, repeatedly affirmed that they were republicans. To take La Rocque's disavowals of fascism at face value is to mistake mystifying language for political substance. Like Taittinger, Renaud, Bucard, Dorgères, and Doriot after 1936, La Rocque had to profess some support for republican institutions and liberties if he was to prevent his movement from being banned by the government. French fascists, well aware that they were much more vulnerable to government reprisals after the Popular Front came to power in May 1936 than they had been in February 1934 during the Chiappe affair, shifted their rhetoric and shifted their tactics. La Rocque did so too.

Before the riots of February 6, when the French right was in full backlash against Socialist influence in the government, and before the elections of May 1936, when the Popular Front posed a massive new threat to the French right but had not yet come to power, La Rocque was openly critical not only of the particular deficiencies of Third Republic parliamentarianism but of electoral democracy itself. Immediately following the riots, however, when the very existence of his movement was endangered by the government, and immediately following the victory of the Popular Front, when the CF was outlawed as a paramilitary organization, La Rocque sang a more republican tune. Political context may not be the whole story, but it is an important part of it. Many of the contradictions in CF/PSF ideology between 1928 and 1939, especially those surrounding issues of political democracy and civil liberties, were due largely to changing circumstances. The less constrained the CF/PSF was by circumstances, the more authoritarian it behaved.

La Rocque was not the only European fascist to tailor his authoritarianism to changing circumstances. Hitler, after all, before he came to power, implied that he would crush leftists, not rightists, defend Christianity, not attack it, curtail Jews, not exterminate them. Again, this is not to suggest that La Rocque was identical to Hitler but only that he could be equally flexible in pursuing his goals, as he sought to appear more moderate at times than he actually was.

As we have seen, after Hitler began in 1934 to repress opponents on the right as well as on the left, it was inexpedient for any French political leader, La Rocque included, to associate his movement too closely with fascism, especially the German variety. At least this was the case until June 1936, when the growing right and right-center backlash to the sit-down strikes and the Popular Front led the French conservative press to display an increased appreciation of Nazi Germany as a bulwark against communism.[117] It was precisely between 1936 and 1938, the years during which the Popular Front posed the most serious threat to French conservatism, that La Rocque's movement enjoyed its greatest growth. It did so not because it was more democratic than the FR but because it was more authoritarian. Although La Rocque was forced to walk a political tightrope (if he rejected republicanism his organization could be banned a second time), his social conservatism was clearly more muscular than that of the FR leader, Louis Marin. Marin commanded no dispos/EVP and had supported parliamentary democracy in 1934 when La Rocque had proclaimed that all politicians should be removed from government.

La Rocque's call for "harmony" between 1936 and 1938 was intransigent when it came to the political left and left-center. *Le Flambeau* hardly lived up to the slogan on its masthead, the "Organ of French reconciliation." Instead, it sought to heighten conservative fears and right-wing recalcitrance with inflammatory language denouncing the "criminal" schemes of the Popular Front. La Rocque told his readers that no illusions were possible toward the Popular Front, since it included "unpatriotic" Socialists and Communists. The Socialist party, he wrote, was "inspired" by the Communist party and was therefore in league with Moscow. La Rocque's concept of reconciliation was narrow at best.

In 1936, after condemning the French left for its "appeal to hatred," La Rocque urged that there must be "no indulgence" toward the forces of disorder. True, in March he called upon his followers to display sangfroid, discipline, and calm in the face of their opponents' verbal attacks but implied that this was the way that soldiers behaved toward an enemy whom they would eventually crush, not spare. He warned his followers not to be deceived by the Communists when they talked of reconciliation. One had only to recall the massacre of a million moujiks in Russia to realize the danger that the Popular Front presented.[118] In other words, Blum and Daladier were no better than Stalin.

In June 1936, La Rocque defended a reconciliation that would "eliminate" "noxious" forces in French political life, "punish" those who robbed the people of their savings, and "outlaw" those whose private life did not conform to their public declarations. Reconciliation would remove from power all those "worm-eaten cadres" who were responsible for French decadence. There was to be no reconciliation with a Popular Front whose "immorality" could only lead to "anarchy" and "catastrophe" and whose ties with the Soviets posed a threat to Western civilization itself.[119] This was not the language of one who was offering an outstretched hand.

In 1936, even as La Rocque claimed to oppose civil war in France, he sought to encourage more, not less, hostility toward the Popular Front. It was the supporters of the Popular Front, he argued, those "apostles of dissension, tumult, and civil war," who were the real threat to social peace and who therefore had to be thoroughly defeated. La Rocque was alert to public fears of civil war and sought to appease them, but he did so in a way that was uncompromising. Reconciliation for La Rocque meant reconciliation on right-wing terms.

La Rocque's immediate response to the election of the Popular Front in May 1936 was not to respect the will of a democratic majority but to claim that this left-center victory was the work of "leaders sent from Moscow" and of "gold squandered by the Soviets." Although he acknowledged that legitimate social discontent existed in France, he warned that the Popular Front was threatening to deliver France, "tied hand and foot, to Asia and its mercenaries." On May 9 *Le Flambeau* ran a cartoon picturing Marianne, the symbol of France, her hands tied above her head, being whipped by a Russian soldier.

Significantly, the allegedly moderate La Rocque placed much of the blame for the victory of the Popular Front on the weaknesses of democratic conservatism and on the *bien-pensants*, or respectable conservatives who supported such conservatism. The Communists and Socialists, he wrote, had exploited the failure of French conservatives to respond more vigorously. " 'Nationalist' politicians, in whom too often our citizens have placed their confidence, have opened the gate to a new invasion of the Barbarians."[120] There was no escaping La Rocque's implication that stronger medicine was needed than that prescribed by the parliamentary right. Indeed, La Rocque suggested that this was the reason the membership of his movement had undergone such a dramatic rise since the election. Moreover, on May 9, the same day *Le Flambeau* published La Rocque's first response to the Popular Front's victory at the polls, it ran an interview that one of its staff had obtained with Marshal Pétain. Although the marshal said that he made it an absolute rule not to speak of politics, he characterized the CF as one of the "healthiest" movements in France.

Following the Popular Front's electoral victory in May 1936, La Rocque ruled out a coup d'état, yet he did so not because he was a political democrat but because he believed a coup would not have been successful. He was held back by political realism, not by republican idealism. "The country," he declared, "would not understand if the [CF] engaged in street battles contrary to the will apparently expressed in the last elections. It would disapprove of an adventure that would be fatal to our hopes." He could not resist insinuating, however, that if worse came to worst the CF was prepared to resort to force. In typical military fashion, he told the readers of *Le Flambeau* on May 30, 1936, "Be calm, united, vigilant. All the necessary dispositions have been taken."[121]

Nor was La Rocque's supposed moderation in 1936 the kind that respected the civil liberties of his enemies. In 1936 the PSF published a pamphlet that advocated "the most serious administrative and penal sanctions" for French schoolteachers who undermined "civic responsibilities and national loyalty." It also called for "severe punishments" for any groups, parties, or newspapers guilty of conducting a campaign against "military duty, civic duty, or loyalty to the country or its institutions."[122] Both before and after 1936, the CF/PSF called for the complete repression of the PCF and portrayed the SFIO as a pawn of Moscow. In spite of occasional language to the contrary, La Rocque was no defender of pluralistic democracy.

La Rocque's own loyalty to republican institutions in 1936 was questionable. In 1935 he asserted that France needed "healthy" institutions and an "orderly" people in order to compete effectively with Germany. In 1938 he observed that France would never be secure until it was as "politically strong" as Germany.[123]

Between 1936 and 1939 La Rocque continued to judge French foreign policy in terms of French domestic policy, emphasizing that fascist Italy and Nazi Germany were enemies of the Soviet Union and warning that any siding with the Soviet Union against them would be abetting communism in France. Although he insisted that France strengthen its military might to deter Germany from attacking, he repeatedly linked fascist Italy and Nazi Germany with the anti-Communist cause in France, suggesting that to support Italy and Germany against Russia was a way of resisting the left at home.

In 1938 La Rocque criticized "bellicists" in France who objected to appeasing Hitler at Munich and opposed a war against Germany because it would lead to "the collapse of the franc, the invasion of our skies, . . . [and] the deliverance of our cities to the bloody orgies of a long-planned uprising following the rites of Lenin and the instructions of Stalin." In 1939 he wrote that no durable peace could be achieved without the establishment of an entente between France and Germany, claiming that it was Stalin's desire to drag Europe into a war against Germany. La Rocque also maintained in 1939 that "hostility between Rome and Paris is contrary to the nature of things."[124]

Finally, as the following will show, the domestic ideology that La Rocque espoused was fascist in important respects, echoing as it did many of the central tenets of mainstream fascism in Italy, Germany, and France. Not only did this ideology express the same dislike of Marxism, liberalism, parliamentarianism, and democracy and seek to replace workers' unions with yellow unions, but it also displayed a strong taste for military values and a great disgust for the "decadence" that undermined them.

Contained in La Rocque's "platitudes," which were indeed shared by many French conservatives of the era, were a number of dangerous implications—as would become all too evident after 1940. Even between 1936 and 1939, when La Rocque professed to be a born-again democrat, his hatred of decadence remained a major feature of his thought; and when in 1940 an opportunity arose to attack this decadence more fascistically than democratically he did so without mercy. To say that he "equivocated" about his republicanism is also a considerable understatement. To say that he was never anti-Semitic is even less accurate.

ANTI-SEMITISM

In the 1930s, La Rocque welcomed right-wing Jews into the CF/PSF, but so too did other fascist movements of the era. As we have seen, it would be unhistorical to make racism a litmus test for all fascism. Whereas the Hitlerian variant of fascism was deeply racist and assigned Jews a central role in its demonology, Italian fascism was neither racist nor anti-Semitic during its first fifteen years in power. And most French fascist movements were not racist either during the interwar period. In the 1920s Georges Valois and Pierre Taittinger criticized anti-Semitism, and in the 1930s even Charles Maurras and Jean Renaud, leaders of two of the most anti-Semitic fascist movements in France, claimed that they were not racists, that is, that they did not advocate biological anti-Semitism. Jacques Doriot was not an anti-Semite when he founded the PPF in 1936, although he became one later. Marcel Bucard's Francistes rejected anti-Semitism before 1936. The major bonds between German, Italian, and French fascism before 1940 were anti-Marxism and antiliberalism, not racism and anti-Semitism. Therefore, La Rocque's acceptance of Jews in the CF/PSF during the 1930s was not at odds with all varieties of fascism, particularly Italian fascism.

Moreover, La Rocque was not always as pure on the Jewish Question as some historians have suggested. In 1934 he was less anti-Semitic than Hitler but more anti-Semitic than Mussolini. La Rocque did indeed object to *racial* anti-Semitism during the 1930s, but, like Maurras, Renaud, and others, this did not prevent him from indulging in cultural and political anti-Semitism. And it did not prevent many of his supporters, particularly those in Alsace and Algeria, from being more anti-Semitic than he. As a movement, the CF/PSF grew increasingly anti-Semitic in the late 1930s, and in 1941 La Rocque himself pronounced Jews a major source of corruption in France.

In 1934 La Rocque asserted that the CF rejected racial conflict on behalf of racial collaboration just as it rejected class conflict on behalf of class collaboration. Jews were officially welcomed into the CF from the beginning. One of the major financial backers of the CF in 1935 was Ernest Mercier, the electricity magnate who was denounced by the anti-Semitic Henry Coston in 1944 as "one of the Jewish financiers-industrialists who controlled France."[125] Ferdinand Robbe, another leading member of the CF, was also Jewish. Rabbi Jacob Kaplan, the socially conservative chief rabbi of Paris, held patriotic ceremonies in his synagogue in conjunction with the CF. The AF more than once accused La Rocque of being a philosemite.

In a chapter of his book *Public Service* devoted to what he called the ethnic problem, La Rocque warned his readers against mediocre attempts at imitating the German regime at the expense of French originality. Racism, he said, was a "disgraceful neologism" and an "artificial conception" that ignored the fact that the French people were the product, from Roman times onward, of a series of ethnic invasions that had led to an amalgam of races. Racial antagonisms had no place on the "amiable soil" of France. The French population comprised peoples from many foreign countries who, "forgetting their ethnic and linguistic origins," had "melted" into France. The Germans, on the other hand, had arrogantly created a racial "Gott mit uns" (God with us) to justify "the most inhuman acts."[126] Racism was practiced by nations that were still primitive and that achieved unity only by invading others, whereas France's "diverse vitality" had been enriched by Greco-Roman influences. "Hitlerism and its excesses," La Rocque wrote, "[would] soon come to grief under a wave of condemnation and ridicule" (160–61).

In 1934 La Rocque asserted that racism not only contradicted common sense and nature, but was an affront to the Jewish soldiers who had given their lives for France during the First World War: "Our dead would protest from the bottom of their heroic tombs if governments gone mad dared to tear from the French community those who [had] given their blood [and had been] incorporated into its substance. The French race is a magnificent synthesis. . . . It forms a whole. No linguistic research, no hereditary analysis can prevail against this fact. No consideration of geographical origins or religious beliefs is applicable. Only French quality and devotion are important, *on the condition that they are sincere, tested and confirmed*" [italics mine] (157).

This last qualification was to prove fateful, for it became the basis of La Rocque's denunciation of left-wing Jews under the Third Republic and of so-called unpatriotic Jews under the Vichy regime. In *Public Service*, in the same chapter in which he criticized Nazi racial theory, La Rocque warned of the dangers of excessive immigration, especially of foreigners escaping Germany who espoused Marxist ideas: "France is the sweetest of adoptive mothers, on the condition that her new children give themselves to her without reservation. . . .

It remains true that we have to protect our loyal hospitality against the abusive unfurling of foreigners who come to dispossess our manual workers of their jobs and transmit to our citizens the germ of insurrection and revolution. . . . We refuse to classify our citizens according to their [ethnic] origins from the moment that they submit to French unity . . . [and] bow to the absolute imperative of patriotic sentiments and reflexes" (160–62).

Because La Rocque equated "patriotic sentiments and reflexes" with social and economic conservatism, what this meant in effect was that left-wing Jews were not welcome. Racial anti-Semitism was benighted, but political anti-Semitism was not. This was the same distinction that the anti-Semitic SF had made when it insisted that it was not racist. As early as 1934, La Rocque distinguished between good Jews and bad Jews, good Jews being those who wanted to be assimilated not only into French culture but also into the political right. Bad Jews were left-wing Jews who were too Marxist or godless to ever be French. Thus, while ethnic origin was ruled out as a qualification for French citizenship, ideological outcome was ruled in.

Moreover, on the immigration question La Rocque blurred even this distinction. He warned that if too large a mass of immigrants entered the country, rather than enriching French culture they would overwhelm it. Cities like Paris and Marseille, he wrote, were becoming saturated with foreigners who had been expelled from their homelands, and a lax French naturalization policy had led to the inundation of these cities by a rising multitude of undesirables. La Rocque even blamed Hitler for driving refugees into France, while sneering at French "sentimentalism" for accepting them. France, he said, had become the shepherd of "a swarming, virulent mob of *outlaws,*" some of whom, under the pretext of fleeing Nazi persecution, were really infiltrating France as spies. La Rocque stressed that he was not being anti-Semitic in pointing out this danger because he knew a number of assimilated French Jews who regarded this "insidious" invasion as a threat to their established positions in France and who feared that the onslaught of Jews from Germany would spark an anti-Semitic reaction against themselves as well (159).

Still, the fact remained that so-called patriotic Jews, that is, assimilated, right-wing Jews, were free to join the CF. In 1933 La Rocque informed Bernard Lecache, a leader of the International League against Antisemitism and editor of *La Droite de Vivre* (The right to live), that the CF would participate each year "at Notre Dame, an Israelite Temple, and a Protestant Temple" in religious services dedicated to the memory of France's war dead. La Rocque added, "As to the numerous Jewish war veterans enrolled in our ranks, they can tell you that no confessional question has ever been brought up in our association."[127]

On June 14, 1936, Rabbi Kaplan presided over a religious service in his synagogue on the rue de la Victoire that was organized by the Jewish Central Consistory of Paris in collaboration with the CF. The ostensible purpose of the ceremony was to commemorate the patriotism of Jewish soldiers who had died for France in the First World War, but many contemporaries, including several Jewish critics of Kaplan, saw the event as the rabbi's bestowal of a political blessing on La Rocque's movement. For some of these critics, Kaplan was abetting fascism in France at a time when fascism was persecuting Jews in Germany. For the politically right-wing Kaplan, however, La Rocque's movement was not anti-Semitic, and the ceremony in his synagogue only demonstrated that Jews could be just as patriotic and conservative as other Frenchmen.

According to police, La Rocque arrived ten minutes before the ceremony began, accompanied by a member of the Rothschild family. Rabbi Kaplan commended the contingent of CF members who attended the service for demonstrating "their respect for all religious confessions and their aversion for all doctrines of hatred which threatened to divide Frenchmen." He called for a renewal of the sacred union of the First World War in which instead of Jews, Protestants, and Catholics there was "no one but Frenchmen." The ceremony ended with an organ playing the "Marseillaise." Two days later, the AF described La Rocque's role in the ceremony as repugnant.[128]

Not all CF members, however, rejected anti-Semitism. In March 1936 police reported that some CF activists were recruiting Algerian Moslems in Paris by appealing to the anti-Semitism aroused by the Cremieux law, which had given political rights to Algerian Jews but not to Algerian Arabs.[129] (In 1940, under Vichy, La Rocque supported the abrogation of this law.) The International League against Antisemitism declared in the wake of the Rabbi Kaplan affair that the CF's flagrant anti-Semitism in North Africa made the action of the Jewish Consistory of Paris a provocation.

La Rocque sometimes tried to discourage the anti-Semitism that he encountered at PSF meetings. At one such gathering in Algeria in 1937, he was interrupted by a shout from the audience, "Down with the Jews!" to which he replied, "Leave me alone. It is not a question of religion here." One French anti-Semite who witnessed this exchange characterized La Rocque's response as scandalous.[130]

In 1937 the PSF's major rival on the extreme right in Algeria, Doriot's PPF, tried to make political hay by accusing La Rocque of being too soft on the Jews. Victor Arrighi, the chief of the PPF in Algeria, led the attack. However, as the historian William Irvine has pointed out,

> In fact, Arrighi's charges of philo-Semitism were, so to speak, perfectly unfair both to the PSF of Algeria and to Colonel de la Rocque. The local PSF had always been, as its organ admitted, partisans of an 'electoral anti-Semitism.' They had been no less willing than their PPF counterparts to qualify the Jewish propensity to vote en masse for left-wing parties as 'racist.' Nor was La Rocque insensitive to these concerns. Under pressure from the PSF of Algeria he declared: 'I absolutely insist that henceforth our friends in Constantine abstain from all relations, commercial or political, with members of [the Jewish] community.' No one was allowed to go about crying 'death to the Jews,' of course, (a point also made routinely by Arrighi), but for all that there had to be 'a complete end to all relationships of any kind with that community.' In short, La Rocque wanted no pogroms against the Jews of Constantine—merely an economic boycott. For the last ten months of 1938 the PPF of Oran (but not Algiers) was more explicitly and more virulently racist than the PSF. With Arrighi's departure from the PPF at the beginning of 1939, the anti-Semitic tone of the Oranais PPF became less pronounced. The PSF, by contrast, continued to hammer away at Jewish 'racism' and, significantly, highlighted every Jewish story (and virtually every issue of its newspaper had one) with a star of David upon which a clenched fist had been superimposed.[131]

By 1937 the PSF had grown increasingly anti-Semitic in France as well. With the Popular Front in power, led by the Jewish Léon Blum, and with the PSF being challenged within the extreme right by Doriot's PPF, some PSF leaders in the provinces began to escalate their Jew-baiting under the guise of anti-immigrationism. In doing so, they echoed La Rocque's earlier merging of the two. William Irvine writes,

> Spokesmen for the party were fond of rejecting "Hitlerian racism," a favorite and convenient phrase that suggested indignation about the brand of anti-Semitism practiced by France's hereditary enemy without taking a very firm stand about the home-grown variety. Local newspapers of the PSF displayed no scruples about reproducing articles from the rabidly anti-Semitic *Gringoire* purporting to show Jewish influence in the Popular Front government. Nor did the party make a secret about its serious reservations concerning the influx of "foreign" Jews or the "intrusion of a scandalous proportion of intriguing and unscrupulous 'metèques' [aliens] into the liberal professions." *Le Flambeau de Flandre* condemned anti-Semitism but wondered: "Does this mean that we must welcome with open arms the children of Israel and just let them take over all the most important positions in the land?" After reminding readers about "Jewish racism," which could be a "permanent danger for the life of the na-

tion," the newspaper called for "an organization of the professions laying down some regulations concerning nationality and professional antecedents." Marcel Vigo, head of the PSF in the Pyrénées-Orientales, noted: "In the PSF we refuse to fall into xenophobia, anti-Semitism, or race hatred of any kind." His definition of race hatred and xenophobia seems to have been fairly narrow, however, since he quickly added: "We also firmly believe that France can live without the foreign gangrene." What prompted this observation was the spectacle of all the "asiatic faces," "Germans with odd profiles" who had left Germany after Hitler took power.[132]

In 1938, as Sam Goodfellow has discovered, the PSF in Alsace also exploited anti-Semitism. Goodfellow recounts,

[On April 2, 1938, the *Flambeau de l'Est*] contained a tasteless cartoon depicting Léon Blum, France's first Jewish head of state, in a Nazi uniform ornamented with a star of David instead of a swastika, giving a Nazi salute to thousands of Jackbooted Jews who were shouting: "One Volk! One Reich! One Fuhrer! Heil Blum!" In the following issue, the editors argued that Jews were fundamentally inferior because "the Jew" was an "economic vulture." These were not isolated expressions of anti-Semitism. In the 1936 elections, the PSF had put up placards in Mulhouse warning Alsatians that "the Jew kills your parents," "steals your goods," and "poisons your race."

Goodfellow also points out that La Rocque himself was not above pandering to local anti-Semitism even when formally rejecting it. In the *Flambeau de l'Est* of September 19, 1936, La Rocque's defense of the rights of "non-Christians and foreign races" did not prevent him from referring to the "Jewish rabble" headed by Léon Blum. Goodfellow comments, "It is no wonder that Alsatians believed that La Rocque would support their anti-Semitism."[133]

If La Rocque was more accommodating toward anti-Semitism in Alsace and Algeria in the late 1930s than he had been earlier, it may have been owing to the fact that Doriot's PPF had begun to use anti-Semitism to boost its appeal. After 1940, the Vichy regime made anti-Semitism even more expedient, and in 1941 La Rocque abandoned more of his scruples. In a chapter of *Disciplines of Action* devoted to the "mortal vices" of France, he condemned Jews for the inordinate and nefarious role they had played in French politics and financial circles under the Third Republic. He justified this anti-Semitism, as he had in 1934, on anti-immigrationist and antileftist grounds, but now added two further reasons: the Jews had sought to "de-Christianize" and "despiritualize" France and had used their "money powers" to turn French politics into "something rotten." Although La Rocque remained troubled by the unfairness of anti-Semitism when applied to Jewish war veterans and suggested that these veterans merited special treatment, he attacked Jews in general, linking them to the hated Free-masons:

> The influx of stateless Israelites chased out of Central and Eastern Europe has had a serious impact on French morality, on French health. People blame the excessive number of Israelites brought into the councils of government and into the command posts of French existence. . . . All [these criticisms] are justified. None of them denies the fact that patriotic Jews shed their blood mixed with ours on the battlefields of 1914–1918 . . . [and] 1939–1940. They won the right to be adopted into France's fraternity.
>
> But the virulence, the purulence of doubtful elements which massively infiltrated the French organism found a favorable terrain. Hasty naturaliza-tions introducing treason had their instigators, their protectors. A dangerous monopoly of government positions was accorded them, thanks to certain ac-complices. Who prepared this favorable terrain? Who were the sponsors of so many undesirables? Who conceded to them these scandalous monopolies? I have asserted, and maintain it here, with absolutely certainty: Freemasonry and its leaders.[134]

Defenders of La Rocque have argued that, compared to the excesses of the French press in the Nazi-occupied zone, La Rocque's wartime writings on the Jewish Question were moderate. They point out that his personal secretary at the *Petit Journal*, Ferdinand Robbe, was Jewish and that, according to one confi-dante, La Rocque privately expressed outrage when he heard that Vichy intended to exclude Jews from French universities.[135]

La Rocque's *public* stance, however, was less indignant. His association of Jews with the mortal vices of France, especially at a time when Vichy was anxious to show its good will toward the Germans by persecuting Jews in France, was nothing less than callous. If La Rocque was indeed less extreme on the Jewish Question than some of his contemporaries, the fact remains that as early as 1934 he publicly indulged in political and cultural anti-Semitism, and in 1941 he joined in the general hue and cry against a highly vulnerable minority.

ANTIDEMOCRACY

A major characteristic of fascism was its hostility toward political democracy, a hostility La Rocque shared. To condemn the more dysfunctional features of the Third Republic in the 1930s was not in itself fascist (some democratic liberals and socialists did this as well), but La Rocque's objections were more fundamen-tal, attacking electoral democracy itself and denouncing politicians in general for being corrupted by it. When La Rocque declared in 1934 to the parliamentary committee investigating the riots of February 6 that "the Croix de Feu is republican as I am myself," he was being less than candid.[136]

In *Public Service*, the hollowness of La Rocque's republicanism was glaringly revealed when he stated that to make a fetish of electoralism was to confuse the means with the ends. One had to realize, he said, that the means might have to be subordinated to the ends if France was to be saved: "The end is that of national existence. A regime is a means. . . . Before shouting 'Long live the Republic!' or 'Long live the Emperor!' or 'Long live the King!, we demand that everyone shout 'Long live France!'"[137] In other words, if the ends required it, a republic was dispensable.

In 1934 and 1935 La Rocque insisted that he was apolitical, using the term in the same way that other fascists had used it before, that is, as a euphemism for rejection of a particular kind of politics, electoral politics. In fact, of course, La Rocque was highly political, pursuing the goals of authoritarian conservatism through mass propaganda and mass organization. He repeatedly implied that the CF's scorn for "electoralism" made it more moral than its democratic adversaries. In 1934, not mentioning the financial subsidies he had received from big business sources, he spoke proudly of the CF's "ferocious separation in regards to politics," of its refusal to "submit to any partisan influence." He even declared, "Our mystique and our rectitude are so pure that any proceeding against our [cause] is condemned in advance" (247, 267–68, 254).

It was a highly antidemocratic form of purity. La Rocque wrote in *Public Service* that an election was not a "supreme, quasi-sacred instrument of civil virtue" but rather an exercise in "collective decadence." The election of the second Cartel des Gauches in 1932, he said, had led France to the "precipice" in February 1934 (93): "At the risk of being accused of neology and of having an *idée fixe*, I will not cease throughout this book to incriminate electoralism. I mean by that a widespread deformation which sees in the verdict of the suffrage, whether it is universal or limited, a superior aim. 'Good elections' are preached as a salvation; an electoral seat is desired like a dream. . . . The word 'electoralism' will recur herein like a leitmotif. The state of mind which it represents explains the lack of productivity in our mediocre times" (91). La Rocque recalled the reaction he had had when a dinner host, after vilifying the parliamentarians of the Chamber of Deputies for their corruption, had asked him whom the CF was going to support in the next election. La Rocque said that he had responded with a smile of disdain, implying that he regarded all elections with contempt and would not debase his movement by involving it in the electoral process (103–04).

Between 1931 and 1936, La Rocque repeatedly contrasted the probity of the war veterans of the CF with the corruption of France's parliamentary politicians: "The [moral] capital of the Croix de Feu must not be dilapidated in secondary operations. The pasts of our comrades forbid them from entering into shady contacts with political clienteles" (12). Only by withdrawing from the "virus of the politician, destroyer of energies, creator of decomposition" could the CF maintain its purity. One reason the war veterans of the CF were "an instrument par excellence of national Salvation" was that they eschewed electoral politics (12, 20).

La Rocque also blamed France's military weakness on her "slavery to degenerate parliamentarianism," sprinkling his speeches with words like *disgust, revulsion, mediocrity,* and *impotence* when speaking of France's democratically elected representatives. Typical was a comment he made in 1934:

> Our past . . . separates us from the politicians. We have measured their impotence. We experience toward them the same repulsion, simultaneously contemptuous and ironically admiring, that soldiers feel toward those they are about to ambush. . . .
>
> In 1926 . . . I had the occasion to attend a noisy session of the Chamber of Deputies—the only one I have ever seen. It was one of those decisive nights. Nothing can capture the disgust I felt at this burlesque tragedy. There arose from this assembly the same atmosphere of collective mediocrity that I recently found again during my appearance before the [parliamentary] investigation committee. (70–71)

At one CF meeting in 1935, a former military pilot named Verseburg called France's parliamentary deputies scum, imbeciles, and bastards and, noting that "France [was] dying because of this breed," said that something had to be done about it "at all costs."[138] Verseburg's indignation was not totally spiritual, however, since he worried that these same politicians might spur higher taxes by increasing government spending. Verseburg was indulging, in effect, in a favorite CF pastime: expressing moral outrage at parliamentary corruption while defending middle-class selfishness with no sign of shame.

In 1936 Pozzo di Borgo was also moralistic when he lamented the effects that serving in the Chamber of Deputies had had on his father ("For my father to have changed in so little time, the atmosphere of parliament had to be truly pernicious") while praising Mussolini for spreading virtue. To a meeting of CF militants, di Borgo proclaimed, "Parliamentarianism is not worth much. What we must do above all else is reform the morality of our country and inculcate in our people a love of justice, honesty, family, and country. . . . Mussolini has known how to revive his country and return it to a position that it had lost."[139]

Although di Borgo, Verseburg, La Rocque, and other CF spokesmen were hardest on left-wing politicians, notably their bête noire Léon Blum, they were also critical of conservative politicians who refused to resist the left more forcefully. In 1935 La Rocque faulted not only the left-center parliaments of 1924 and 1932 but also the more conservative "blue horizon" parliament of 1919, which, he said, had returned to the failed democratic practices of the past, allowing two Cartel des Gauches governments to eventually come to power. Instead of doing more to prevent such disasters, parliamentary conservatives had "jealously protected their portfolios and their solidarity with their enemy colleagues, to the last breath of their parliamentary majority."

Even Poincaré, acclaimed by French conservatives in 1926 for defeating the first Cartel des Gauches, was dismissed by La Rocque as a politician who had only delayed the march of the left to power rather than eliminating it for good.[140] Following the victory of the Popular Front in 1936, Pozzo di Borgo blamed the election results "partly on a bourgeoisie who, due to their customary egoism and nonchalance, have favored a push to the left and partly on the quite understandable nausea that the masses feel toward the rotten and decadent parliamentarians who have allowed the country to sail along without a rudder."[141]

Although there were moments when the CF protested that it did not reject all parliamentarianism but only corrupt parliamentarianism, the distinction was often ignored. On April 25, 1936, an article in Le Flambeau stated that while the CF was opposed to the "present degeneration" of parliamentarianism it had never said that it wanted an end to parliamentarianism. However, another article in the same issue was less compromising: "We have no need for parliamentarians, even for those elected thanks to us. We do not count on their gratitude; they cannot count on our indulgence." The writer added that even if a new blue horizon parliament were elected in May, it could be assured of "our criticisms and sarcasm." For the CF itself to benefit from an election "would simultaneously undermine its moral value, sacrifice its prestige, [and] profane its mission." This was no brief for political democracy, even right-wing political democracy.

If, for the CF, electoralism was bad enough when the right controlled parliament, it was an absolute disaster when the left did so. La Rocque wrote in April 1936, "Universal suffrage, *incapable of procuring our salvation*, can determine our shipwreck" (italics mine).[142] The victory of the Popular Front in May confirmed La Rocque's worst fears about electoral democracy. This did not stop him, however, from turning his own movement into an electoral party two months later after the CF had been banned as a paramilitary organization. It is doubtful that he did so out of democratic convictions.

Still, even prior to 1936, when La Rocque denounced electoral democracy and the politicians who participated in it, he was careful to deny that the CF was completely antidemocratic. He claimed that the CF only wanted a stronger and more moral form of republicanism. Notwithstanding his comment in 1934 that it would be fruitless to draw up a blueprint for political reform without first eliminating "the parliamentary gangrene [and] establishing a provisional order," he presented a plan for such a reform—one that included an electoral component.

In *Public Service* he proposed a constitutional revision that would still be republican in that a democratically elected legislature and an independent judiciary would continue to play a role in the French government. The "leader of the nation" would also be elected, but the executive branch of government would be strengthened so that it would no longer be "invaded" by the legislative branch and so that the leader would have the "rude authority" he needed to fulfill his responsibilities. The leader would appoint his own ministers, have the right to dissolve parliament and call for new elections at any time, and could be prevented from completing his term in office only by a two-thirds' vote in parliament.[143]

Thus, like Taittinger, Coty, Bucard, Doriot, and other French fascists of the interwar period who, unlike Hitler and Mussolini, were never able to seize control of the state and therefore had to continue to operate within a framework of political democracy, La Rocque called for a revision of the constitution that fell far short of totalitarianism while at the same time advocating a political mystique that would bring "notions of authority back to power." In November 1935 La Rocque published an article in *Le Flambeau* that dealt with the nature of that authority: "[Chaos] will come to an end only under a reconstructed State capable of imposing controls and sanctions, strong enough to reduce its expenditures, [acting as] the servant of its citizens without being a slave to their caprices."[144]

In 1936 the platform of the PSF included a proviso to ensure that outcome, one reminiscent of Coty's legislature-diminishing Reform of the State of 1933. The platform specified that the Chamber of Deputies be deprived of any power to initiate legislation requiring expenditures.[145] It also proposed that a National Economic Council be created alongside parliament as a "sort of Council of

State" representing the corporatist organizations that were to be created in every profession. The council's task would be to advise the government on what economic initiatives it should or should not take. Given the nature of PSF corporatism, this advice doubtless would have been highly conservative. In light of its socioeconomic goals, it seems clear that what the PSF was proposing were structural changes that would enable the "rude authority" to overrule the "caprices" of the masses in a way that would reduce government spending on the lower classes and prevent higher taxes on the upper classes.

The role that La Rocque assigned to the chief executive was considerable. The ideal state, La Rocque wrote, would "call forth and complete the authority of the leader," "concentrat[ing] present and future responsibilities on him."[146] If La Rocque's own leadership style is any indication, this executive would have behaved in a more military than democratic manner. As La Rocque commented in *Public Service*, "Having always occupied command positions, . . . I never communicate my intentions until the time comes to present them to a final war council or to put them into execution. When that phase begins, I must resign myself to the loss of secrecy. . . . A leader is formed, overwhelmingly, by silent reflection and indefatigable study" (95–96).

If in 1934 La Rocque did not rule out electoral democracy altogether (he claimed that the CF was committed to a form of "popular representation" that would be "equitable for the entire people"), he left little doubt that his heart lay elsewhere. Expressing contempt for "the mediocre game of electoral competitions" and his dislike for the "inconvenient" aspects of universal suffrage (noting that the latter were "acknowledged today in all the countries of the world"), he sought to reduce the role of the electorate and their representatives in the political process (9, 204). He advocated limiting the prerogatives that devolved from the vote, reducing the number of deputies elected, and establishing a system of proportional representation that would weaken the influence of local party organizations (204–05). He did propose that women be given the vote and that a family vote be instituted so that men with children had more votes than others. Again the assumption was that the women's vote and the family vote would be a boon to the Catholic right.

Above all, La Rocque damned a system in which politicians sought benefits for their local constituencies at the expense of the general good. A politician, he said, could get elected and preserve his seat in the Chamber of Deputies only by promising the electorate "everything they asked of him." This led to cabinet ministers and other politicians being inundated with constant requests for favors. Such "degenerate *electoralism*" had to be stopped. As for those who thought it chimerical that parliament would ever accommodate itself to a more Spartan morality, La Rocque replied that a "few severe sanctions, renewed from time to time" could achieve this result (206–08).

According to La Rocque, the CF pursued a flexible middle course between discipline and freedom. There was nothing fascist or totalitarian about the government it envisioned (only demagogues, he said, accused the CF of that). The CF desired a France that was "generously and intelligently liberal but rid of the indisciplines of 'Liberalism'" (215–16, 255). The French people were individualistic and idealistic, but they would accept discipline from above if it were fair and did not interfere with their private lives:

> To enclose France in an iron corset would be a mistake which would be quickly paid for by an explosion of the armor itself. . . . To impose a "totalitarian state" on her would be to crush her living personality. . . . To subject her to a kind of civic mutism would not only be opposed to the most elementary psychology but contrary to the collaborative spirit of our compatriots. To leave her the license to throw into the forum, without any classification or control, all the desires, all the suggestions of its passionate crowds, would be to unleash a destructive individualism. France wants to make use of all the resources that derive from the nervous influx of its multiple and spontaneous temperament under the solid and elastic guardianship of a state that is a protector of liberties and a manager of disciplines. (201–02)

La Rocque therefore cultivated the appearance of moderation while advocating that the state prevent the passionate crowds of France, that is, left-wing political constituencies, from wielding their former influence. This moderation was rendered further suspect by the fact that in *Public Service* La Rocque's bows to liberty and diversity were only pages, sometimes only sentences, away from his denunciations of electoralism and destructive individualism. It was also a moderation that would have resulted, had La Rocque's constitutional proposals been put into practice, in the disempowerment of the many on behalf of the few.

After June 1936, when the CF was banned and the PSF was founded, La Rocque professed to be even more moderate, as his movement plunged into the very electoral politics that it had previously vilified. (If the CF lost its purity at this point, La Rocque failed to mention it.) Like the CF, the PSF insisted on its loyalty to republican institutions and republican legality even as it continued to honor an authoritarian mystique.

The advent of the Vichy regime in 1940 led La Rocque to abandon even the pretense of republicanism. In *Disciplines of Action*, he expressed his "aversion for electoral mandates" and for democracy as a whole.[147] France's military defeat in 1940, he said, had been the result of twenty years of political "degeneracy." Since the First World War, French political life had been marred by laziness and intrigue, the fall of France in 1940 having been presaged by "the revolutionary wave" of 1936. The Vichy regime should not appoint the discredited politicians of the Third Republic to governmental positions because a "parliamentary dosage," rather than stimulating the energy of the masses, would suppress it. Government by the people should be replaced by government for the people.

La Rocque insisted that although the Vichy regime needed to have the confidence of the nation it must not revert to the failed democratic practices of the past. He posed what he called the "problem of the masses," that is, how to achieve the support of the masses without submitting to their control. He expressed concern that his even raising the question might cause him to "be suspected of democratic convictions," a charge that he said he prevented by noting that he had spoken out against democracy even before the fall of France at a time when democracy still "exercised its dictatorship" in France. He was referring to an article he had published in *Le Petit Journal* in April 1940 in which he had contended that the excessive use of the word *democracy* in the French press was "pure and simple demagoguery" and that this practice could create some "regrettable misunderstandings in Rome, Madrid, and elsewhere."[148]

La Rocque's solution to the supposed problem of the masses was in tune with that of a long line of French reactionary writers stretching from Hippolyte Taine to Gustave Le Bon to Charles Maurras. Like them, he argued that hierarchies were necessary to keep the masses under control, that democratic mystiques and revolutionary crowds were a threat to the social order, and that social morality had to be based on the principle that "duties had priority over rights." The masses, La Rocque wrote, should not be dismissed as a "negligible quantity" because the danger they presented was real. When the masses obeyed only their instincts, they threatened to provoke disorder and disunity.[149] They were also given to making excessive wage demands:

> One only has to have had the responsibility of dealing with crowds, even with those inspired by the highest ideals, to realize how uncontrollable and noisy a multitude can become the moment the least unexpected emotion passes through it.
>
> The crowd needs not to be penned in but judiciously assigned its place, partitioned, oriented. The crowd, abandoned to itself, reverts to its lowest reflexes: it becomes chaotic, an avalanche, a tidal wave. The masses must not absorb power and, voluntarily or involuntarily, make it its prisoner.
>
> Or else the democrat becomes a tramp and the demagogue becomes a tyrant. Passions dominate; demands and quarrels surge up: it is the triumph of materialism directed against the forces of morality. . . .

> We have known too well the regime of workers who have grouped together solely in behalf of their professional interests, procuring the highest stipends, indeed even portfolios, for their apostles who have feathered their own nests. (128–29)

Indeed, La Rocque's distrust of crowds was so great that, unlike Hitler, he was opposed to whipping up audiences, even right-wing audiences, with theatrical displays of unbridled passion lest he lose control over their actions. He said that the kind of public support he sought had nothing to do with the "excitements of a crowd listening to a tribune." He associated himself not with the demagogues of ancient Rome who pandered cleverly to the emotions of the mob but with the Christian apostles of the same era who guided their followers with calm instruction:

> The applause directed at the speakers' platform is essentially harmful to morality . . . [and to] a strict sense of duty. . . .
> I have known . . . some celebrities renowned for their hold on the masses. On several occasions, I have been astonished by this hold, which nothing, when looked upon "coldly," seemed to justify. After examining it, the explanation, always the same, is that it is the result of an undeniable, but exclusively carnal magneticism, which can be described as electric. . . .
> Historical periods that are troubled and nervous are fertile in sorcerers, conjurers, magicians, and mountebanks. [But] the renaissance of a country demands ascetics, apostles. (139–40)

In this regard, La Rocque preferred Salazar, the dictator of Portugal, to Hitler, a preference suggested by several favorable articles in *Le Flambeau* devoted to Salazar in November and December 1941.

Such distinctions, however, did not erase La Rocque's profound dislike of democracy. Indeed, at the heart of his answer to the problem of the masses in 1941 was a military analogy that equated leaders with officers and followers with enlisted men and that assigned to the masses the "role of fighting troops." Although La Rocque conceded that such troops, when properly commanded, wanted not merely to obey their officers but to accompany them into action, this was hardly a brief for political equality. Another analogy he employed was even more undemocratic, a nostalgic return to a medieval ideal that deprived the lower orders of even a military role: "I have read some very touching chronicles," he wrote in 1941, "about the relations between the lords and the peasants during the time of chivalry long ago" (132, 129–30). He noted that unlike the decadent rich of a later era, these lords had rendered services to the peasants in return for their obedience. Thus La Rocque glorified noblesse oblige from the top down rather than self-determination from the bottom up, declaring that only parasites followed the masses whereas true leaders guided them (132, 6, 21, 54). So much for La Rocque's republicanism.

PARAMILITARISM

Another fascist trait of La Rocque's movement, evident especially but not solely before 1936, was its paramilitarism. Mussolini and Hitler had shown the way with their squads of blackshirts and brownshirts, and various French fascist movements sought to emulate them. Unlike the Faisceau, the JP, the SF, and the Francistes, however, the CF eschewed blue shirts for its dispos—probably to avoid being too closely identified with foreign fascisms. This decision did not make its shock troops any less paramilitary in their intentions. Like other French fascist movements, the CF subscribed to barring the road to communism by any means necessary and touted its war veterans as the best-qualified group for the job. On ceremonial occasions, La Rocque stood alone, very much the commander, reviewing his troops as they marched by in well-ordered columns, some prominently displaying their war decorations on their lapels. Only their clothing was civilian.

In 1934 what primarily distinguished the ideology of the CF from that of its democratic counterpart, the FR, was not its socioeconomic program but its military ethos. Had the CF tried to compete with democratic conservatism on its own grounds, it would have had nothing substantially new to offer. What it did offer was the framework for a French *Freikorps* willing to fight the Marxists should they launch a revolution. Because it was illegal for civilians to possess military arms in France, the CF's paramilitary potential, especially its organizational potential, mattered more in 1934 than its military capability. Hoping that sympathetic conservatives within the French army would provide it with arms in the event of a civil war, the CF not only offered to fight alongside regular army units against a Communist revolution but also hinted, more than hinted, that its troops might one day overthrow the Third Republic by force.

Between 1933 and 1936, the CF repeatedly threatened a coup d'état against a parliamentary regime that had permitted the growth of Marxism. At various CF meetings, both in Paris and the provinces, La Rocque and local CF leaders told their dispos to be prepared for action at any time, suggesting repeatedly that it was only a matter of weeks before they would move against the government. When questioned by the parliamentary commission investigating the riots of February 6, 1934, La Rocque denied that he had any such intention, but he and his lieutenants had conveyed a different message to their troops.

For one member of the commission, Laurent Bonnevay, the deception was obvious: "Prodigious one day with affectionate and fraternal affirmations, the next day [the CF launches] violent and acerbic calls to violence. Affirming its republican loyalism at the same time that it disdains free institutions, [the CF proclaims its respect for] legality and authority even at the hour that it secretly organizes veritable mobilizations throughout [French] territory . . . as if [it] was preparing for a 'March on Rome.'"[150]

In 1937 Guy de Hauteclocque wrote about several CF meetings he had attended: "Speeches about national reconciliation, a social program, and some sentimental or demagogic proposals only served to cloak the announcements about 'D day' or 'H hour' or [such comments] as 'in shedding the least blood possible' we will get rid of those 'bastards' and send on vacation 'a parliament rotten to the core.' Meetings of regional leaders, repeated to satiety, where a delegate from party headquarters would develop, each time, the following leitmotiv: everything is ready; in *n* days, the Colonel will take power."[151] The final report of the parliamentary commission on the February 6 riots also underscored the paramilitary character of the CF:

> [The CF] is preoccupied with organizing war veterans. Organized in a military fashion, it controls groups for combat and defense which are organized throughout all of France and particularly in Paris. The combat groups consist of dispos, or *disponibles*. . . . They must respond to all convocations.
>
> The dispos are constituted in "hands," groups of five men. Three hands form a group of fifteen. Groups of several hands form a division. In Paris there are three divisions. The aim is to be able to bring together these men as rapidly as possible and to complete a mobilization with the briefest delay.[152]

The commission worried about the "blind obedience" La Rocque expected of his dispos in carrying out his orders as well as the lack of democratic participation in CF decision making. As one deputy said to La Rocque at the hearings, "I find that what gives your organization a military character is that one man makes the decisions. We know other organizations that are based on democratic principles. . . . In your organization, the men know nothing; nor do their leaders immediately above them. There are only men who execute orders and a leader. And that appears to us as a military organization" (25).

La Rocque's reply was disingenuous. He maintained that his movement was not organized militarily because its units acted on a regional basis whereas a truly military organization would be more centralized. He also pointed out that the CF had not carried arms on February 6, as they would have had they intended a military coup. What he failed to mention was that this might not always be the case if sympathizers in the army ever chose to provide the CF with weapons. Neither did La Rocque mention that Mussolini's blackshirts and Hitler's brown-shirts had also been short on military hardware before they came to power. When asked how he expected to see the CF's program for France put into effect if he rejected both electoral politics and paramilitary overthrow, La Rocque lamely replied that it would come about because of the moral force of its ideas.

The commission concluded that the CF and the other paramilitary leagues of the nationalist right, "comprising dozens of thousands of followers who obey the will of a single person or of a small number of leaders," were not only organized in an undemocratic fashion but posed a threat, if not yet to the repub-lic itself, at least to republican legality: "The commission acknowledges the existence of groups which, whatever the political goals they pursue, by their authoritarian organization, by their discipline, by the framework they impose, by the quasi-absolute power of their leaders, constitute powerful means of ac-tion whose forceful interventions in the streets, on behalf of a political aim, can present a danger to public order" (27, 155).

In *Public Service* La Rocque sounded far less devoted to republican legality than he did before the parliamentary commission. He defended the riots of February 6 and presumably the violence that occurred as the revolt of decent people against the machinations of the Socialists. What February 6 had demon-strated, he said, was not only the moral force of the CF but also the need to replace the decadent politicians of the Third Republic with a more spiritual elite, an elite of war veterans. This imperative remained inasmuch as nothing new had happened since February 6 to oust these politicians. The Depression had created a "state of receptivity" for a transfer of power from the old elite to a new. It was only a matter of time before some shock—a suspension of treasury payments, a collapse of the stock market, the sudden closing of several banks— would set off a deflagration that would bring the CF to power. It had been the "total bankruptcy" of France's parliamentary politicians that had led to the events of February 6, and as long as those politicians continued to rule the "powder" could explode again.[153] These were not the words of a man who condemned all street violence or thought only in terms of an electoral or parlia-mentary transfer of power.

At a private meeting of the VN at Metz in June 1935, La Rocque traced the history of the CF. In contrast to his testimony before the parliamentary commis-sion, in which he had emphasized his commitment to republican legality, he noted that it was the events of February 6, 1934, which had given the CF its notoriety: that is, it was precisely its illegal threat of violence, its threat of using paramilitary force, that had made the movement popular. Three weeks later, police reported to the minister of interior that La Rocque's followers were convinced that "new times" were near and that they would be the "primary beneficiaries of this new state of things."[154]

In retrospect, it is easy to dismiss La Rocque's threats of a coup as political hyperbole since he never in fact attempted one. Some historians have even seen his failure to do so as proof of his commitment to republican legality. This last conclusion is difficult to square with the repeated threats, however veiled, that La Rocque and his lieutenants made against the Third Republic between 1934 and 1936, with the enthusiasm with which their followers responded to such talk, and with the many practice mobilizations the CF carried out in preparation for "H hour" and "D day."

A reporter from *Le Temps* described one of these mobilizations in 1935: "Disciplined, they had come together at Chantilly where, up until the last moment, secrecy had been maintained by all involved about an expedition which had to, in a few hours, move 15,000 men from one place to another." As La Rocque repeated endlessly, the key to the success of the CF, especially where the mission of its dispos was concerned, was discipline. In 1934 he praised his troops for their willingness to obey "an exact discipline" and for giving renewed value to the words *En avant!* (Forward!), the same words used by French soldiers in the First World War before they launched an assault against the enemy.[155] It was also the French equivalent to the political rallying cry that Mussolini had adopted for his movement in Italy. La Rocque's preference for military language in the communiqués he dispatched to his troops was itself indicative of the spirit of the movement.

In 1935 the CF even had a few aircraft at its disposal. These planes belonged to members of the movement and, sporting the CF's insignia, were flown occasionally over left-wing rallies to intimidate their adversaries. More important were the number of aviators, some of them military pilots, who belonged to the CF. According to police,

> The Croix de Feu movement has made marked progress among the personnel of commercial and military aviation. Its sections at Bourget, Drancy, Blanc-Mesmil, and Dugny are composed, in a very large proportion, of aviators. As for the Air France Company, we estimate that 50 percent of the flying personnel are Croix de Feu or Volontaires Nationaux. A good many officers and non-commissioned officers of the 34th Aviation Division at Le Bourget [airport] have joined the Croix de Feu. The ground personnel are much less sympathetic. It can be estimated that about 1,200 is the number of the members of the aeronautical group of the Croix de Feu.[156]

At a CF meeting on June 27, the section leader, a Major Loste, announced that flying lessons would be available to members, although he preferred at that time not to give the name of the company that owned the airfield.

The CF's behavior in the summer of 1935 was hardly reassuring to the authorities. At a rally in Algiers, airplanes marked CF on their wings flew over the crowd; next, a motorcycle parade of local dispos rode past, and this was followed by an announcement that the CF had created its own women's hospital corps! La Rocque told those assembled, "Today, I come to speak to you in *the language of decision, of an offensive decision* that nothing will stop, and which in a period of time that history will find very short and which for us is close, will lead us to a French France!"[157]

Two weeks later, according to local police, Major Debay of the CF's executive committee for North Africa told an audience of some six hundred in Algiers (one hundred of whom were women) that "the time for merely amusing ourselves is finished and the hour for passing to action is about to sound." He declared that H hour could occur that summer or during the last trimester of 1935 and that, consequently, all CF members should stay in contact with one another. He claimed that in Algeria the "levers of command" belonged to the CF and declared that all public officials who wished to keep their posts should, "above all, obey." He added, "Everything is foreseen, . . . the different services— automobile, aviation, etc.—know the tasks that have been assigned to them, . . . the leaders of the Croix de Feu know where they must act, . . . with force if obligated by necessity." Debay concluded his speech with the cry "Long live La Rocque!"[158]

In France, La Rocque too was fanning the flames. At a CF meeting in Metz on June 13, he announced that the end of the present parliamentary regime was near. He predicted that a crisis would occur in October or November when parliament would have to vote on the budget, which, he said, it could not balance because the deficit was too large. "It will be then," he declared, "that the H hour of the Croix de Feu will sound and that our association, its ideas once in power, will take action to reorganize the country according to its needs."[159] These words were met with extended applause.

On June 29, 1935, police reported that La Rocque was far less interested in finding collaborators in parliamentary circles, "even if they were on the right," than he was in seeking people in the army and the bureaucracy who would serve in the directory he intended to establish after he came to power. Another police report a few days later said that La Rocque was in the process of creating a technical committee that would "form the core of government in case the Croix de Feu seizes power." Individuals were being selected to head the police, the Ministry of War, the Ministry of Foreign Affairs, and so on. With the exception of Messieurs Ybarnegaray and Marquet, no parliamentary politician was to be considered for a high government post. On July 8 police reported that supporters of La Rocque believed that their movement was on the verge of taking control of the government.[160]

August came and went, however, as did September, October, November, and December, and no paramilitary coup was attempted. For all his hyperbole, La Rocque never gave the order to act. Like other French fascist leaders before him who had threatened to overthrow the government by force, he backed down in the end, bowing to reality. Recognizing that he lacked sufficient mass support and military backing for a successful coup in 1935, he decided that wisdom was the better part of valor. La Rocque was no democrat, but he was no fool either. An experienced military man, he understood the odds against him. Like Valois and Taittinger in 1925, he tacked his sails to circumstances—and in 1935 circumstances were still not favorable enough for a successful coup.

Although many army officers, including Pétain, may have been sympathetic to La Rocque, few were willing to engage in such a risky adventure. The fact that they had to deal with a citizens' army that included thousands of liberals, Socialists, and Communists in its ranks no doubt gave them pause. Such an army was not a reliable instrument for antidemocratic politics.

And neither was the political climate in the summer and fall of 1935 ripe for a successful coup. Most members of the Radical party at that time, that is, of the vital center of French politics, were still more inclined to resist fascism than to accept it. The Communist and Socialist parties were even more antifascist. By August 1935, the Popular Front, formed largely to defeat the sort of threat La Rocque represented, was well on the way to achieving the mass support that would bring it to power less than a year later. To challenge the supporters of this coalition with paramilitary action would have been a formidable and probably disastrous undertaking. On August 17, La Rocque wrote in Le Flambeau, "Vis-à-vis the masses of the Popular Front, we remain in a defensive position."

Looking back on this period six years later, La Rocque claimed that he had desisted from launching a coup out of fear that it would have led to a civil war, which would have benefited the Germans. His next comment, however, was more telling: "We would have had to overcome the double shock of masses of people drunk with [Popular Front] demagoguery and of public authorities [the police, army, etc.] obedient to the orders of the government: the victory of the 'reds' would have been certain."[161]

In the summer and fall of 1935, La Rocque took a hard look at the superior government forces arrayed against him as well as at the rise in public support for the Popular Front and refused to bite the bullet. He made the same decision a year later when the Popular Front came to power. To have attempted a coup in June 1936 would have been to gamble against even lower odds. To view La Rocque's caution in 1936 as proof of his commitment to republican ideals is a benign interpretation indeed. As he explained to a PSF audience in 1937, "Do you understand today that if in the month of June I had ordered you to descend into the streets, you would have been crushed?"[162] This was not the argument of a democratic liberal committed to republican legality but of a realistic authoritarian afraid of paramilitary defeat. La Rocque's not having launched a suicide attack in 1935 or 1936 made him no less fascist than Hitler, who, following the Munich putsch in 1923, also played it safe.

Indeed, what is surprising about La Rocque in the summer of 1935 and again in June 1936 is not that he shrank from ordering his troops into action, but that he had led them to believe that H hour was so imminent in the first place, causing him to lose face when he failed to fulfill his promise. La Rocque's decision not to launch an assault upon the government must have been embarrassing for him, as he had led his troops for weeks to expect the opposite.

Nevertheless, unlike Jean Renaud of the SF, who lost many followers when he had failed to act following the February 6 riots, La Rocque not only survived the crisis but prospered afterward. For many conservatives, the political left posed an increasing threat after 1935, and they continued to value the CF for its paramilitary potential. Moreover, unlike the SF in 1934, the CF's financial backing remained strong, and no staffers went unpaid. La Rocque's calls for discipline and calm were welcomed by rightists who feared that an attempted CF coup might lead to public disorder and even civil war, while his references to a future H hour continued to offer hope to his more militant supporters.

After 1935 La Rocque continued to bluster, vowing in 1936 that if the Popular Front went too far and if the public authorities proved to be too feeble he would take "instantaneous efficacious initiatives" to protect France from harm. On May 17, 1936, he told a CF audience that the day was near when the war veterans of the CF would join with other war veterans to save France "for the second time."[163] Again his bark was bigger than his bite. When in June the Popular Front banned the CF as a paramilitary movement, La Rocque acquiesced. Instead of launching an armed revolt, he founded the PSF. This turned out to be a highly successful move, as large sums of money and a host of new recruits poured into a movement that had only recently been dissolved as a threat to the republic.

Although La Rocque said that his movement was no longer a paramilitary organization, he not only created the EVP but continued to remind the public in other ways that his brand of conservatism was more muscular than most. In June 1936, during the sit-down strikes, police reported that members of the VN had visited a number of shopkeepers, telling them, "Should you need us, give us a sign. We are in the street." (The report added, however, that most of these shopkeepers preferred to rely on the police for protection.) On September 5, 1936, *Le Flambeau* told its readers, "Each attack on your persons, on your legitimate property, on your right to work, merits an immediate sanction. If the public authorities do not do their duty, do it resolutely yourself. And if you need to be protected, counseled, supported, [or] brought together, come to any PSF headquarters."

In 1937 the PSF held a series of public meetings throughout France that it called congresses, even though certain aspects of the meetings resembled the former mobilization exercises of the CF more than the behavior of an electoral organization. In April a number of automobiles filled with PSF members departed in the middle of night for an undisclosed destination with instructions not to open their sealed orders until they were eighty-three kilometers from Nevers. Paul Chopine, a former member of the PSF, subsequently asked rhetorically, "Does this resemble a [democratic] political party, or are not these secret convocations, these motorized trips toward an unknown destination, this passive obedience to the orders of their leaders an exact reflection of Hitler's mobilizations before Munich?" Although Chopine's assessment was overblown, he was not the only one who found the PSF reverting to CF practices. In December 1937 La Rocque was fined three thousand francs by a French court for maintaining an organization with a military structure (the court referred to the EVP). In May 1938 the PSF was charged again with the same offense.[164]

On February 17, 1937, a PSF audience at the Salle Wagram in Paris did not protest when La Rocque reverted to some of his old language. Predicting the collapse of the Popular Front, La Rocque warned against counting on another parliamentary coalition of the right to save France. Another Union Nationale government, he said, would be "just as disastrous as all those that preceded it." Although the PSF, having only a dozen deputies in parliament, was in no position to win a majority vote, La Rocque told his followers to hold themselves ready for any eventuality: "The time is near when our party will come to power and save France." Two days later at another rally, La Rocque said, "People are now talking of a movement toward a new government led by Flandin. That would be hardly any better [than another Blum government]. What is necessary is a rapid dissolution [of the Chamber of Deputies], because Parliament is not responding to the spirit of the people."

He added that the major reason the Communists had not already opted for violent revolution was that they knew the PSF would throw its weight against them. He claimed that the Senate, too, "misunderstanding neither our intentions nor our force," had taken the sensible path and voted against the Blum government.[165]

In 1937 nearly a million French men and women were members of a movement that continued to allude to antiparliamentary solutions and paramilitary scenarios.

ANTI-MARXISM

Like other French fascist movements of the interwar period, the CF/PSF regarded Marxism as the number one threat to the nation. La Rocque even acted as if this were the case between 1940 and 1941 under the German occupation. Marxism was associated in La Rocque's mind not only with revolutionary Communists and nonrevolutionary Socialists but also with liberal fellow travelers who he believed abetted them with their tolerance.

The CF/PSF was one more fascist attempt to destroy the red menace. It was dismayed by the successes of the left in the elections of 1932 and 1936, the victory of the Popular Front arousing its worst fears. A police report a few days after the election of 1936 said that the mood in CF circles was one of discouragement.[166] Spirits revived, however, as the conservative backlash to the Popular Front gathered steam and as the CF/PSF went on to launch an extensive propaganda campaign against the appeal of Marxism in a Depression era.

The CF/PSF's socioeconomic alternative to Marxism was typically fascist: class conciliation rather than class conflict, corporatism rather than socialism, "cooperative" rather than "revolutionary" unions, social peace rather than sit-down strikes, hierarchies rather than equalities, and upper-class paternalism rather than lower-class bargaining power. Like previous French fascisms, the CF/PSF portrayed itself as more "social," more caring toward the lower classes, than it actually was. It even claimed in 1936 that the Popular Front had stolen its program, a particularly egregious piece of double-talk.

Its socioeconomic program not only opposed increased power for workers but called for the elimination of their traditional sources of leverage, free trade unions and the right to strike. Like the Faisceau, the JP, the SF, the Francistes, and the PPF, the CF/PSF sought to replace working-class solidarity with subservience to management.

This scheme was sugarcoated with offers of private social assistance to the worst victims of the Depression. The CF/PSF surpassed other French fascist movements of the period in the amount of aid it provided to the down-and-out through its widespread charity activities—activities that had much more in common with the Salvation Army than with the Popular Front. The CF/PSF's answer to poverty was voluntary upper-class paternalism, not government welfare programs financed by involuntary taxes.

CF/PSF ideology was no revision of Marxism. It was full of violent diatribes against Communists and Socialists alike. A mass-produced CF postcard in 1935 contrasted three red arrows carrying the words *Hate, Disorder, Trickery* with three tricolored arrows that read, *Motherland, Family, Work.* When in May 1936 the CF was accused of having backed the Communists in the previous election as a tactical maneuver, La Rocque replied, "That is false, and if by chance any member of the CF did it, he will be dishonored and immediately expelled." That same month Pozzo di Borgo decried the election of the Popular Front, praised "the work of Mussolini," and told a CF audience to be prepared to prevent by all possible means the catastrophe that might occur. He hoped this could be done "without recourse to brutal force" but added, "We do not fear this, and if it is absolutely necessary, well then, too bad."[167]

The presumptively moderate PSF of 1936 was seldom restrained in the language it used to describe the Popular Front. In July, turning the language of its critics against them, the PSF called the Popular Front Hitlerian for its "state seizure of all branches of activity and especially of finances." It damned Blum for assaulting the financial institutions of France, which were "responsible for [the country's] prosperity." In October *Le Flambeau* ran the headline "DOWN WITH TYRANTS!" and asserted that Blum had banned the CF "to protect the red hordes of Stalin."[168]

The PSF was no more conciliatory toward the Popular Front than the CF had been. Condemning the "Marxist ideal" and "foreign doctrines" of the Popular Front as alien to French traditions, it blamed Blum for allowing the revolutionary masses to foment social disorder and destroy economic stability. Blum was not only threatening to increase the deficit, but also wished to sabotage capitalism in order to further his own "revolutionary adventure."

In 1937 at a PSF rally in Paris, Paul Creyssel, a deputy from the Loire and a member of the PSF's new block in parliament, attacked the Popular Front's foreign policy as well. Creyssel criticized Blum for permitting French volunteers to go to Spain to fight against Franco, for refusing to form a military alliance with fascist Italy, and for maintaining France's ties with the Soviet Union (which Creyssel feared would drag France into a war with Nazi Germany).[169]

According to a PSF pamphlet from 1936, "The danger par excellence which our country now faces is Communism." The demonic machinations of Moscow were leading France toward "insurrection, subversion, catastrophe." La Rocque told an anecdote from his days as a colonial officer in Morocco: "Bolshevik Communism is a frightful spectacle of the worst savageries. It was in 1925, during the revolt of the Riff, and the memory is still horribly present in my mind, [that I saw] French soldiers buried to the neck, their heads covered with honey so that, bitten by wasps, their death was more cruel."[170]

French Communists and Socialists responded physically as well as verbally to the CF/PSF, attacking its meetings in Paris and the provinces. French police reports of the 1930s describe numerous left-wing attempts to intimidate La Rocque's supporters. In June 1935, for example, when it was learned that the CF planned to hold a meeting at Romainville, local Communists and Socialists organized a counterdemonstration that massed some 1,000 of their followers against 400 CF members. To get to the hall where the meeting was to be held, the rightists had to pass through a hostile crowd held back by the police and face shouts of "Down with fascism!" "La Rocque to the stake!" "Chiappe to prison!" A month later at Jenlain, police prevented some 200 leftists from blocking access to a CF meeting. In September some 250 members of the Caen CF were ambushed by a dozen Communists who threw "diverse projectiles" at their column of sixty cars driving toward Paris. The result was several broken windshields, some flat tires, and three injured riders.[171]

Similar attacks were reported in 1937. In January, the PSF ran into opposition in Nice. As one local newspaper described it, "[At 8:00 P.M.] more than 300 members of the [PSF] paraded through the city singing the "Marseillaise," applauded by the majority of onlookers. However, the Communists had sounded the alarm. At 8:30 several hundred of them were massed before the offices of the newspaper *L'Eclaireur de Nice.* Their arms raised in clenched fists, they loudly sang the "Internationale." When the nationalists reached their street, they brutally assaulted them. Numerous blows were exchanged. A squadron of mounted police then intervened and dispersed the demonstrators." On February 28 at Vrigne-aux-Bois, an industrial center near Sedan, the PSF held a meeting in a factory. As the attendees were leaving, leftists met them with rocks, bricks, and gunshots, killing one PSF member. The rest of La Rocque's supporters retreated into the factory, where they stayed until they were rescued by the police.[172]

La Rocque would take his revenge under Vichy, describing the Popular Front as having been not just ideologically mistaken but politically diseased. France, he wrote in 1941, reached the bottom of its degeneracy in the elections of 1936.[173]

"NEITHER RIGHT NOR LEFT"

In spite of its big business financing, union busting corporatism, and red-baiting diatribes against the Popular Front, the CF/PSF repeatedly insisted that it was "neither right nor left," that it served neither capitalism nor Marxism. La Rocque asserted that his movement brought together people from all classes and professions, "labor and management, industrialists and farmers, economists and workers, without forgetting professors and military men" and that it was "the only movement that [could not] be classed a priori, a posteriori right or left." It had achieved, he said, a fusion of all classes in which individual wealth had no bearing on the choice of its leaders: "One sees generals, great artists, great scholars, [and] high dignitaries of the Legion of Honor proud to obey workers and clerks who wear the Military Medal or the Croix de Guerre."[174]

"Neither right nor left" also implied that the CF/PSF was somehow *both* right and left, that it included doctrines and followers from both camps, that, to use its own terminology, it was both national and social. In 1934 La Rocque declared, "We have made men of good will understand that one can be social without ceasing to be national and that one can be national without abandoning the search for social progress. The sign of resurrection is the spontaneous conjunction of the ardent forces of the left with the reanimated forces of the right, once both have been stripped of their false leaders." A CF tract in 1935 even proclaimed to workers, "Your aspirations are ours. Those who have portrayed us as your adversaries have lied. We are your brothers. We will prove it. Join the Croix de Feu."[175]

Behind the scenes, such brotherhood was less evident. In June 1935 police reported that dissidents within the CF were worried that the movement would never attract enough mass support because of La Rocque's "inertia" on the social question. In August leftist politicians were predicting the decline of the CF because it was too conservative in a Depression era. La Rocque responded by multiplying CF soup kitchens for the poor and creating a free job bureau for unemployed workers who joined the CF. According to the police, this new bureau had promise because La Rocque "could count on commercial and industrial circles" to help him.[176]

In May 1936, following the electoral victory of the Popular Front, the CF tried to steal some of the opposition's thunder by purporting to be leftist itself, even going so far as to claim that the Popular Front had derived its social program from the CF's.[177] Some CF speakers told their audiences that on the social question the CF was "much like Communism and Socialism," except that, unlike them, it was not controlled by Moscow. They said that the CF was in a position to "tip the balance to the right or to the left" and that it extended its hand to the parties of the left "on condition that they adopted a program that was essentially French."

CF speakers also attacked hidebound conservatives for resisting measures that would benefit the workers, an intransigence, they said, that could profit only the Communists. At a church service on May 18 attended by some 150 CF members, a Catholic priest asserted that the choice was between constructive Christianity and devastating communism. At a CF rally on May 15, Pozzo di Borgo criticized French businessmen who made money their king. Observing that some bien-pensants had recently joined the CF "now that their 'banknotes' [were] threatened," di Borgo told the story of how, in reply to one of these new converts who was pleading with him at a cocktail party, "You are our last chance; will you support us?" he had said, "Yes, like the rope that supports the hanged man."[178]

La Rocque was more careful than di Borgo to play to upper-middle-class fears of the Popular Front without threatening the upper middle classes themselves. In a speech on May 20, he criticized wealthy Frenchmen for failing to comprehend their social role, pointing out that they would be condemned forever "if they fell into the hands of the Muscovites. . . . If they fall into ours, they must follow us and know how to understand us." On May 21 Le Flambeau criticized "selfish" conservatism for having led the nation to ruin and contended that the old parties were no longer capable of assuring workers the renumeration and dignity they deserved. However, a police report on May 28 remarked that few CF members took such rhetoric seriously: "[La Rocque has] repeated in vain that his ideas have arrived in power since the Popular Front has taken his program. That assertion has provoked a certain malaise and triggered large smiles from some of the younger members who are not ashamed to say that the Colonel himself is quite embarrassed by it."[179]

It is true that prior to the May elections Le Flambeau expressed its support for a minimum wage law, paid vacations, and a shorter workweek—thus seeming to agree with the Popular Front on these matters. However, the qualifications it tacked onto these proposals were another story. In effect, what the CF/PSF gave with one hand it took away with the other. While insisting that each worker be guaranteed a salary that would enable him to "maintain a household with dignity," it added that the salary should take into account the special conditions of each enterprise, the local cost of living, and the type of product produced. In other words, some workers would receive a smaller minimum wage than others. Moreover, benefits were to be allocated not by the government but by each profession at the local level and awarded only to workers who demonstrated their "fidelity to the enterprise."[180]

Any shortening of the workweek was to be similarly flexible. A PSF pamphlet said that although the forty-hour week was desirable in some cases in general it was harmful to national productivity and to France's foreign trade balance. All limitations on the workweek should be "determined within the framework of the profession and the region." Translated, this meant that the protection intended by the forty-hour-week law could be negated by local management. Two years earlier La Rocque had opposed shortening the workday on the grounds that it would create "half-unemployed" workers.[181]

The PSF also purported to be in favor of paid vacations for workers—but here, too, it stipulated that professional and regional variations should be taken into account and that only workers "faithful to their companies should benefit." If faithfulness were judged by PSF standards, it would have excluded not only CGT and CGTU members (who were regarded by management as notoriously unfaithful) but *any* workers not servile to management.

It was a formula, in effect, that would have enabled management, through the granting and withholding of paid vacations, to reward workers who abandoned working-class solidarity and to punish workers who did not. Indeed, the PSF pamphlet suggested that one test of a worker's fidelity was whether he would leave his former union for a corporatist one, something that it implied when it spoke of "reliable" workers for whom vacations with pay would be a "point of departure" for "associating" them with the companies that employed them.[182] In other words, the PSF sought to transform one of the Popular Front's most popular reforms into a mechanism for union busting.

Thus the CF/PSF plan offered much less to labor in general than the Popular Front's did. In June 1936, confronted with the sit-down strikes, *Le Flambeau* claimed to support the workers even as it strove to limit their success and cut the losses of management. Declaring that many of the demands being made by workers were legitimate and reflected long-standing preoccupations of the CF, it added that "the character of these demands, when they ignore the factor of fidelity to the enterprise, is purely demagogic."[183]

The CF/PSF's position was far more right than left, far more national than social, in its efforts to restore managerial authority, water down union demands, restrict benefits to faithful workers only, and encourage a corporatist approach to labor relations that destroyed collective bargaining. In short, it tried to *appear* proworker while *being* probusiness, hoping to siphon off in the process some of the Popular Front's left-center support.

The PSF pamphlet left little doubt as to where the movement's real sympathies lay. It condemned the sit-down strikes as a form of terror and the strikers as unpatriotic because they had replaced the French tricolor with the red flag. Signs of decadence, it said, were everywhere, both in Communist calls for brutality and bourgeois displays of "pusillanimity." Workers had been tricked by Communist propaganda, but employers were also at fault for their failure of nerve. "Under the disguise of legitimate demands, the mass of workers, persuaded to leave their factories as the result of obscure intrigues, abandoned their machines, consented to the violation of their individual liberty and to the temporary abandonment of their families. Across from them, the employer class, embarrassed, passively submitted to conditions that were disastrous for the future of the national economy, for labor, for the family, and for peace."[184] The PSF pamphlet concluded with an appeal for more national discipline and responsibility in labor relations, that is, for a return to managerial authority and working-class submissiveness.

The CF/PSF in 1936 did call for larger and earlier retirement pensions for the elderly, for more insurance protection for workers in hazardous industries, and for the extension of such benefits to the peasantry. However, in keeping with La Rocque's long-standing opposition to statism, it urged that such programs be managed not by the government but by mutual aid associations and private insurance groups. It spoke sympathetically of the right of workers to better housing and hygiene, but without specifying how this right was to be achieved (something of a problem since the PSF also demanded that taxes on French industry be reduced). It decried the massive unemployment created by the Depression but insisted that people collecting government unemployment insurance be carefully screened for cheaters and that payments to foreign workers be rolled back as a matter of "public morality." It also demanded that government employees, including French schoolteachers, be denied the right to strike.

Somewhat surprising, in light of La Rocque's big business financial backing, was the PSF's proposal in 1936 that the state monitor the Bank of France to ensure that investment capital not be monopolized by the trusts at the expense of smaller French business enterprises. This was consistent, however, with the PSF's propaganda effort to expand its mass base within the lower middle classes. Far more surprising was the PSF's demand that gas and electricity rates be lowered to reduce the consumer's cost of living, something that might well have upset Ernest Mercier, the energy czar who had provided La Rocque's movement with major funding. (Indeed, Mercier did abandon the PSF in a huff in 1936, although it is not clear that he left for this reason.)

It may be that the PSF's call for lower gas and electricity rates was simply a way of blunting growing public criticism of the utility companies, of staving off nationalization of the energy industry (a nationalization that did occur after the Second World War). The same tactic may also explain the PSF's criticism of capitalist "excesses," even as it defended capitalism itself. By siding partially with the critics while preserving an essentially conservative agenda, the PSF may have hoped to head off more drastic measures by the left. This was certainly the tactic it employed in promoting the forty-hour week and paid vacations.

In one area the PSF refused to display even a semblance of compromise, taking a position that was not just conservative but reactionary. This was the issue of management's power vis-à-vis labor's in future industrial disputes. Here the PSF put forth what it called the centerpiece of its socioeconomic program, the "organized profession," a corporatist attempt to replace the troublesome CGT and CGTU with new unions that could be controlled by management. On May 23, 1936, *Le Flambeau* described these unions as "chambers of commerce, of agriculture, of corporatist groups" that would no longer be infected by "the virus of politics" but that would be established on a "strictly professional basis," that is, that would be right wing, not left wing, and the enemy of separate working-class trade unions.

Thus the CF/PSF, even at the height of its supposedly leftist phase in 1936, even when it maintained that the Popular Front had stolen its social program, sought to undermine the labor movement and the reforms it pursued. In addition, its repeated assertion during this period that the spiritual was more important than the material and that the "passion for [economic] well-being and good living" was a source of decadence did not leave the impression that it was deeply committed to improving the standard of living of the lower classes.[185]

The CF/PSF was also more right than left in 1936 in its defense of free enterprise capitalism. Not only did it condemn Marxists for threatening private property, private enterprise, and the profit motive, but it also rebuked left-wing liberals for proposing higher taxes, increased welfare spending, and more statism. In 1934 the CF had called for tax reduction, an end to government interference in the economy, the defense of interest from bank savings, the right to the legitimate profits of family property, and the restriction of immigration to "the strict needs of production." In *Public Service* La Rocque attributed the Depression not to maldistribution of wealth, market forces, or insufficient government regulation but to "a collapse in morality." France, he wrote, had been ruined by "a frenzy for rapid gain," by "incredible self-indulgence," by an "abusive use of credit," and by a "casual attitude toward paying one's creditors," not by any systemic flaws in capitalism itself. The economic crisis was basically a moral crisis, and the solution, therefore, was not more statism but more morality.[186] It was not a solution that was likely to upset France's business community.

In 1936 Paul Creyssel, a major spokesman for the PSF on economic affairs, published a tract that was also far more right than left, proposing a classically conservative solution to the Depression. According to Creyssel, most of France's economic problems stemmed from the influence of Marxism and the results of the Matignon accords. The nation's economic crisis could be solved only by lowering wages and reducing government spending. Intervention into the economy by government bureaucrats could lead to the death of capitalism and the ruin of freedom. "At the risk of forgoing electoral opportunism and of shocking the taste of many," Creyssel wrote, "I will undertake a partial defense of capitalism."[187] The suppression of free competition would reduce both the quality and quantity of industrial production. It was precisely because capitalists were driven by the profit motive that they constantly improved production techniques. Moreover, they invested most of their gains in creating new enterprises that helped raise the standard of living for all.

Creyssel conceded that capitalism was essentially "amoral" and incapable "by its very nature" of concerning itself with "all the weak, with all who fail, with all those whom it crushes along the way." To leave capitalism without correction, he said, would be to accept the misery of the majority. The solution, however, was not state ownership, which would reduce everybody to misery, but state intervention only where it was absolutely necessary. The public should beware of demagogues who, pandering to their electoral clienteles, promised more pensions and more subsidies "without concern for the taxpayers." To resist the "mortal tendency" to raise taxes in return for such benefits required a great deal of virtue, for "it is against yourself that you have to struggle." The Communists loved to cry, "Make the rich pay," and no tax increase was ever too high for them. But all Frenchmen paid taxes, the poor as well as the rich, and therefore expensive new programs harmed everyone (38–40, 45).

According to Creyssel, the state should never interfere in strike negotiations on behalf of labor, as it had at the time of the Matignon accords. In return for accepting the risks of economic competition, employers should have their profits, their property, and their authority respected. Workers should renounce the use of force and the occupation of factories. In return, employers should guarantee them the right to work as well as the right to health, unemployment, and old age insurance.

Creyssel maintained that for workers to engage in class struggle was "a crime against French fraternity." A French worker and a French employer had more reason to join hands than a French worker and a Japanese worker because the first two had a common interest in ensuring that their product outcompeted that of their foreign competitors. Class hatred violated this solidarity and led to economic ruin. Workers should reserve their hardness not for their employers but for the false prophets of Marxism. Socialism "stifled the individual under the tyranny of the State, sterilized initiative with bureaucratic conformism, [and] destroyed civilization without improving the condition of the workers" (44, 46–47).

Creyssel did blame the Depression, at least partially, on unorganized and uncontrolled capitalism, on an economic liberalism that had led to a good deal of misery and despair. The cure, however, was not socialism but corporatism, not government organizing and controlling the economy but each profession organizing and controlling itself. What must *not* be done, Creyssel emphasized, was to let the state take over the factories and businesses of France, for "free enterprise and its legitimate profits must be maintained and defended as the source of progress and collective wealth" (47–48). Thus, even as Creyssel criticized uncontrolled capitalism, he defended capitalism itself, proposing only that each corporatist association, dominated by management, do its own controlling.

Creyssel also described the PSF in 1936 as a staunch supporter of free trade abroad. He rejected the protectionist argument that France could withstand the Depression by retreating into a closed economy and stressed that it was indispensable for France to "import and therefore export." To pay for imports and maintain its balance of payments, France had to make its products cheaper than those of other countries, an eventuality that was prevented by the "brutal and systematic" application of the forty-hour-week law. This law was an economic folly and an act of treason: "*The forty hours law is going to dangerously increase the rise in prices*" (66). Making France less competitive in the world market would result in higher unemployment at home. Under the Popular Front the general interest had been sacrificed to particular interests, to the interests and "appetites" of the unions. The wage gains won by the workers in June had hurt everybody because they had led to higher prices for manufactured goods, and this in turn had brought about a general increase in the cost of living. In terms of real wages, the workers were worse off than they were before the Matignon accords (63–67, 69–71, 74–76).

There were a number of gaps in Creyssel's analysis, not the least of which was his failure to assign any responsibility for the conservative flight of capital abroad that had followed the advent of the Popular Front to power. Apparently if any sacrifices were to be made for *la patrie,* better they be made by French workers than by French investors. Creyssel made no mention either of investors' favoring their appetites at the expense of the general interest when they deprived French industries of capital or of their being any less patriotic for doing so. He also failed to explain how the misery of the weak under economic liberalism was to be corrected, other than to leave it up to corporatist associations to grant them the help they had denied them before.

Neither did Creyssel dwell on what would happen if the new corporatist unions did not produce the new harmony in labor-management relations that he predicted, that is, if unfaithful workers chose to engage in strike activity in spite of corporatism. He merely remarked that a judge or a legislator might become an arbitrator in such a situation; he provided no details. Given Creyssel's dislike for the kind of negotiations that had led to the Matignon accords and his opposition to wage increases, which might weaken French competition in foreign markets, he probably would not have favored arbitration that bent to labor's "appetites." In 1934 La Rocque had declared that under a CF government, with the state's right to "arbitrate, control, and apply sanctions restored," strikes and lockouts "would tend to disappear."[188] Apparently, right-wing statism would do the job. Certainly La Rocque had little difficulty supporting probusiness statism under the Vichy regime.

Like other fascist movements of the era, the CF/PSF saw corporatism as the primary means of restoring discipline in labor relations. It, too, wanted red unions replaced with management-dominated unions. In 1934 La Rocque deplored the fact that so many of France's trade unions were political and that they exerted so much influence on a national scale: "Their attachment to the CGT and the CGTU has led them into a perpetual attitude of demagoguery and subversion. Unions, to play their proper role, must remain exclusively professional and regional. Their sole basis must be the enterprise. And if technical coordination is required on a national level, in no case must it take on the character of a coalition."[189] La Rocque knew, of course, that the bargaining power of workers would be reduced if they were denied the right to act in solidarity with each other nationally. La Rocque preferred to sugarcoat the pill with talk of class conciliation, telling a gathering of workers and managers at a Renault factory near Versailles in 1937 (after announcing that the PSF had launched a new weekly, *The Free Worker*) that it was up to them to come up with common solutions to their problems "while keeping in mind the general interest as much as your particular interests."[190]

Like the SF, the CF/PSF envisioned the establishment of a corporatist National Economic Council whose advice would be sought by the state. In 1934 La Rocque conceded that the "builders of tomorrow" might have to appeal to existing unions for help at the outset, whether they be "revolutionary, Christian, or independent"—although he followed this statement with another diatribe against the CGT and the CGTU, contending that many workers, "even those called 'reds,'" were looking for a non-Marxist alternative to their unions.[191]

Nevertheless, in 1936 the PSF insisted that its corporatism was fundamentally different from Italian fascism's in that under the PSF's plan each profession would operate "not under the absolute tyranny of the State" but only within its own narrow domain and only with the collaboration of management and labor. On the other hand, it noted that only in a country where "order reigned" and "authority was obeyed" would Frenchmen stop hating one another.[192] In other words, PSF corporatism defended a capitalist economy and a disciplined work force—all backed up by an authoritarian government hostile to strikes.

Why would any French worker have supported this kind of corporatism and joined the PSF's Confederation of French Professional Unions? A partial answer has already been suggested: by signing up, some workers had a chance of obtaining or retaining jobs from employers sympathetic to La Rocque's movement. Paul Chopine cited other reasons as well:

> If it was learned that a worker's wife had gone to a hospital to have a baby, a woman of the PSF would go visit her. [In a factory] a PSF worker . . . would say to someone he was trying to recruit: 'You see, the CGT has abandoned you; with [our union], it will be different. Would you like me to send you a lawyer, a doctor?'
>
> Another approach was that of intimidation: 'If you join, you will always have work, you will be well-regarded [by management].' If the man is young and courageous, he will refuse, but if, on the contrary, he has three or four children at home, he will sign in order to keep his job, so that his kids will have what is necessary.[193]

La Rocque put it differently, praising the "responsible" worker who was loyal to his company and who believed in the "fraternal interaction of all social groups."[194]

In the end, PSF rhetoric, favoritism, and arm-twisting met with only limited success among French blue-collar workers. According to René Rémond, the PSF's French Professional Unions were composed "principally of white collar workers, management personnel, and members of the middle classes." Such a profile is consistent with the PSF's support of the traditional elitism of the white-collar workplace, of "the necessary hierarchies" of each profession.[195]

The PSF's answer to what it called the proletarian problem also assumed necessary hierarchies, although it spoke of them as being open to newcomers. The PSF maintained that through hard work and thrifty habits blue-collar workers or their children could move up the social ladder, into the lower middle classes to begin with and even higher eventually. "We want to put an end to the proletariat," declared *Le Flambeau* in 1937. Like previous French fascists— Valois and Taittinger, for example—La Rocque extolled upward social mobility and careers open to talent over class solidarity and social egalitarianism.[196] His call to *arrivisme* complemented his rejection of class warfare (at least of proletarian class warfare, since he had no objections to bourgeois dispos fighting for *their* class interests). The upwardly mobile proletarian, who left *his* class solidarity behind, was praised for practicing class conciliation instead of class conflict. Individual competition, not red revolution, was the way to better one's condition.

La Rocque was unwilling, however, to guarantee that every child would have an equal educational opportunity at the outset to make the competition fair. Although a PSF pamphlet agreed that education should not be a privilege of the rich and urged the state to devote part of its budget to subsidizing poor students, it rejected the notion that education should be free for everyone because the taxes this would require would "weigh unjustly" on all classes of society.[197]

Besides, according to La Rocque, what ultimately counted was not equality of wealth or equality of opportunity but "the equality of souls," that is, spiritual equality. The PSF vowed to "equalize the efforts" of the rich and the poor on the "spiritual and moral plane," but not on the material plane. Neither, La Rocque declared in 1934, should the CF focus on the worker as the only type of Frenchman worth defending: "The friends of the people should not waste time celebrating the worker, appealing to the worker, saluting the worker, embracing the worker, following the worker." It was one thing to help the less privileged; it was another to succumb to the Marxist cult of the proletariat to the detriment of the bourgeoisie.

In 1941 La Rocque backtracked even further as he underlined the "super-natural" basis of the PSF's mystique and expressed contempt for those who wanted to transform the social into "some kind of universal panacea."[198] The PSF's alleged concern with working-class grievances, expressed so ardently in the face of the Popular Front's victory of 1936, was easily disregarded once Vichy came to power.

In the 1930s the CF/PSF had adopted the slogan "Social first," a deliberate contrast to the AF's "Politics first." Even then, however, it was not to be con-fused with socialism first, since the CF/PSF's social program offered little more than private charity, recreational activities, managerial paternalism, employer favoritism, and the hope of upward social mobility as solutions to the prole-tarian problem. In 1934 La Rocque did call for more public housing projects for working-class families but then criticized such projects if they attracted "shady" types and became part of the red belt encircling Paris, a red belt consist-ing of "barracks" and "fortresses" for the "army" of the Popular Front. Appar-ently here, too, faithful workers deserved decent housing; unfaithful workers did not. Even in 1936 some CF/PSF writings faulted working-class demands for reflecting the "egoism" of the times. Creyssel pointedly remarked that whereas the Germans, Italians, and Japanese had accepted the need for sacrifice with enthusiasm, the French were still undergoing a great moral crisis.[199]

In 1937 La Rocque warned that although French workers should be given a dignified wage they should not be "crazily paid" because this would make their companies uncompetitive in the world market. In 1939 he urged the Daladier government to increase the workweek to sixty or seventy hours if necessary to hasten France's preparations for a coming war against Germany, a call to sacri-fice that might have been even more patriotic had he demanded a sharp increase in the taxes of the wealthy for the same purpose.[200]

If the content of CF/PSF ideology was far more right than left, its rhetoric was sometimes less so, particularly after 1936, when it sought to detach lower-class and lower-middle-class voters from the Popular Front. Following Blum's ascen-sion to power, it criticized wealthy bourgeois who displayed no concern for the sufferings of the poor and condemned the selfishness of factory owners who refused to acknowledge that some of the aspirations of the working classes were "perfectly legitimate."[201]

La Rocque often combined appeals for Christian charity with appeals to class interest, bourgeois class interest. He argued that the indifference of the upper classes to the plight of the lower made it easy for Marxists to exploit working-class discontent. This left France with two equally bad choices: either a conservatism blinded by egoism or "a regression towards the paleontology of Internationalism and Marxism." The "elegant" right lacked both the compassion and the virility that was required to defeat the political left.[202]

La Rocque claimed to be disgusted at the autocratic behavior of certain trusts "whose uncontrolled power had led to excesses and scandals." The anonymous trust, he wrote in 1936, was a "hideout for corruption, an antichambre for statism, [and] an enemy of social works." He went on to damn the stock exchange and international finance as well, and, in 1941, he added "the plutocracy of nepotism" to his indictment.[203] The CF/PSF proposed no specific curbs, however, on the activities of either big finance or big business, while its official socioeconomic program denounced government interference with laissez-faire capitalism. Neither did the large financial subsidies that the CF/PSF received from big business groups, especially the electricity and steel trusts, square with the movement's leftist rhetoric.

Still, the rhetoric continued. At a PSF meeting in 1937, one speaker, a Monsieur Pinçon, blamed France's bourgeoisie for not providing France with the leadership it needed. According to police, "[Pinçon] was particularly critical of sons of the bourgeois after the war 'who, concerned only with the lure of gain and the luxurious and easy life, gave free reign to their desires with contempt for even the most elementary morality.'" He declared that the hatred of the workers for their bosses was accentuated by the actions of the bourgeoisie. But instead of calling for a socialist revolution to overthrow the bourgeoisie or for the Popular Front to tax them more heavily in order to increase social spending, Pinçon urged businessmen to hire only members of the PSF.[204]

In 1941 La Rocque laid part of the blame for France's military defeat on the *embourgeoisement* of France. France, he said, had gone soft in the 1920s and 1930s, and bourgeois hedonism was one of the reasons. Such criticism did not lead him, however, to condemn the bourgeoisie as a class or to question its social and economic privileges. The antibourgeois elements in his cultural thought made him no less probourgeois in his economic thought. Here, too, his claim that his movement was neither right nor left was largely spurious.

ANTIDECADENCE

Like other fascists of the interwar period, La Rocque loathed decadence. Fascists throughout Europe often applied this term to any political, social, or cultural phenomenon that they deemed soft, hedonistic, or undisciplined. Their antidote was a spiritual virility that was deeply military in nature and that in La Rocque's case tapped some of the ascetic traditions of French Catholicism. In defining decadence and virility in this fashion, La Rocque echoed such antidemocratic writers as Hippolyte Taine, Charles Maurras, and Maurice Barrès as well as such fascist politicians as Antoine Redier, Georges Valois, and Pierre Taittinger.[205] All favored using "virile," or authoritarian, means in the defense of a conservative social order. Thus, even their criticisms of bourgeois decadence served bourgeois economic interests.

In 1941, as a supporter of the Vichy regime, La Rocque attacked middle-class decadence but not middle-class privileges, bourgeois hedonism but not bourgeois wealth. Although he attributed France's defeat in 1940 partly to *bourgeoisisme*, he was careful to distinguish his criticism from that of Marxists, pointing out that the lower classes were just as prone to seeking "paltry comfort" as the upper classes. "I do not protest the fact of someone being bourgeois," he wrote. "I attack the bourgeois spirit in its pejorative sense."[206] Substituting cultural and spiritual analysis for social and economic analysis, he had no quarrel with bourgeois who remained austere. Neither did he challenge the property rights of those who did not.

In *Public Service*, La Rocque had damned "paralyzing bourgeoisism" while defending conservative economic interests. Bourgeoisism, he said, had begun to afflict France prior to the First World War, a sickness that Paul Morand had described so well in his novel, *1900*. Since the war, the appearance of bald heads and potbellies on so many French youths made one doubt the possibility of a "virile dawn." The nation faced a moral crisis caused by the unlimited pursuit of material pleasures. France could be saved only by adopting the "rude asceticism" practiced by the war veterans of the CF: "Our physical, moral, and spiritual asceticism helps raise us to the height of our ideal."[207]

In 1937 La Rocque praised Jean Mermoz, a celebrated aviator who had joined the CF, as a model of virility. Mermoz, having been deprived at an early age of the coziness of a bourgeois home and having triumphed over a number of life's obstacles through sheer force of will, was someone to admire: "Launched into a struggle for his own subsistence without anyone to support him, he . . . [hurled] himself against all the egoisms of society. . . . Imagine . . . his fiery temperament, absolute in nature, unafraid of risk. He had received much less than you. . . . He succeeded. But at the price of what efforts, what ordeals, what revolts!"[208] No decadent bourgeois Mermoz!

In 1939 La Rocque warned that even the French army was becoming bourgeoisified: "One feels less intensely the grandeur of voluntary servitudes. [For] a [superficial] discipline can . . . camouflage a mortal softening. . . . It is necessary to choose: immediate, radiant enthusiasm or else—even after a victory— decadence and death."[209]

In 1941 La Rocque's disgust with decadence became punitive. The French people, he said, should collaborate with the Germans, for whatever the risks involved they were preferable to "the acceptance of decadence and *merited* servitude" (italics mine). A period of heroic abnegations was required, during which the French people should bow to the moral necessity of inevitable suffering: "National rebirth will be accomplished through suffering; it will be achieved only through suffering." French politicians whose private lives had been notorious before the war should be replaced with moral leaders who would punish them for their wrongdoing: "If anyone objects to the Spartan character of this last recommendation, I will respond that we are living in exceptional times. These exceptional hours justify the strictest severities toward those responsible. An illustrious contemporary once said: 'One does not administer a country with rosaries.' The reply he received was: 'One does not confide one's house to prostitutes.' We would add: the National Revolution, a harsh task carried out in cruel circumstances, can only be accomplished by ascetics."[210]

In *Disciplines of Action*, La Rocque, complaining about French adolescents who were devoted more to joie de vivre and amusing themselves than to fulfilling their patriotic obligations, declared that France must choose between decadence and regeneration. He criticized France's schools for neglecting the role of athletics in building the nation's future, a position that echoed the PSF's official party program of 1936. This program decried the fact that foreigners often said that France was not sportive and advocated that France offer more physical education classes. Like defenders of the Strength through Joy movement in Germany, CF/PSF spokesmen emphasized the connection between sport and warfare. At a CF meeting in 1936, Mermoz argued that French national security made the practice of sports indispensable, inasmuch as a strong and healthy youth was necessary to safeguard the nation. La Rocque declared to the children in the audience, "By practicing sports, which will make you morally and physically strong, you will assure the continuity of our eternal France, which will shine in the world on condition that we give the impression of being strong."[211]

In 1941 La Rocque extolled Nazi Germany and fascist Italy for prizing students not just for their academic abilities but for their moral and physical strengths—and for giving virile youths their due when it came to allocating leadership positions:

In the [French] program of encyclopedic instruction, too cluttered to not harass the brains of our students, too burdensome to leave room for the assimilation of a true culture, the part that fell to corporal exercises was viewed with regret. . . .

Innumerable generations were allowed to stew in an excess of examinations [and] certificates . . . . [Also later in life, the highest salaries and honors went to those with the highest seniority.] Between one's schooldays and the years of later advancement, the rising generations were stifled: access to the greatest responsibilities coincided with the closer one came to retirement. We acknowledge and admire the ardent vitality of the fascist and Hitlerian regimes. Both have relegated seniority schedules to the realm of social security statistics for the elderly. Both have preferred [to give leadership positions to] persons who have proved themselves [in real life situations] rather than to [those who merely excel on] exams.[212]

However, La Rocque also insisted in 1941 that the young in general be placed firmly under the control of their elders, first under the control of their parents and then under the control of Marshal Pétain. Only in this way, La Rocque maintained, could the energies of youth be channeled into idealism. In practice, what La Rocque objected to under the Third Republic was not that old men were in charge of French youth (Pétain, after all, was an octogenarian) but that old men with decadent ideas were in charge of French youth.

In La Rocque's opinion, some of the most pernicious of these ideas stemmed from the Enlightenment. The Encyclopedists of the eighteenth century (Diderot and Voltaire and others) had spawned a mentality that had led to the "degeneracy" of the Third Republic. France had grown decadent because of the emphasis French schools placed on rationalism, humanitarianism, and egalitarianism. At the heart of the problem was a corrosive liberalism which taught that happiness was to be found in an egoistic pursuit of material pleasures rather than in an unselfish acceptance of spiritual duties. The hedonistic values of the *philosophes* underlay the social radicalism of the 1930s: "The cult of reason caused any notion of the reasonable to be lost. Parlor room speculations and the ramblings of endless talk made people forget the limits of terrestrial possibilities and obliterated all sense of effort, of duty. The excesses of humanitarianism stifled the spirit of humanity. Dissertations on 'the self' stifled the call to altruism. The glorification of equality led to jealousy, then to hatred between the classes" (88).

To counter such decadence, La Rocque proposed a return to spirituality, to the "France of the crusaders, the France of builders of cathedrals, the France of 1789 even, as long as the courtesans, the encyclopedists, and the instigators-profiteers of revolution do not vitiate this spirituality with their egoism, their vanity, and their base calculations." This formula for order, he said, was conceived in suffering and would succeed only when society replaced its selfish quarrels with national reconciliation and social peace (158). La Rocque's critique of decadence, in other words, was part of his critique of social radicalism, an attempt to replace that radicalism with a spiritual vision of society.

A theme La Rocque repeated endlessly throughout the 1930s was "the primacy of the spiritual in human affairs." In 1941 he associated this primacy with a return to traditional values:

> Materialism is at the origin of all our misfortunes. Those who believed in "extinguishing the last stars" sterilized in advance the victory of 1918 and prepared the defeat of 1940. The sectarianism of Monsieur Homais [Flaubert's positivist in *Madame Bovary*] had as its first victim the mystique of patriotism. Dechristianization replaced love for a large and united family with a mediocre concern for [self-advancement]; it has subordinated a vocation of service to the vain culture of the superman, to a pretentious and exclusive preoccupation of each individual with maximizing his gains.
> We must return to traditional values, protecting and encouraging religious fidelities.[213]

La Rocque's attacks on what he referred to as the selfishness of working-class economic demands were part of his indictment of materalism. In 1935 he combined his plea for spiritual equality ("the equality of souls," "equality toward the high") with a warning that the alternative was Marxist materialism and "bloody class struggle."[214] Some of La Rocque's left-wing critics argued that such pronouncements masked a defense of upper-class material interests and the acceptance of social evils. A brochure published by the Vigilance Committee of Antifascist Intellectuals in 1935 concluded, "In giving precedence to the moral problem over the economic problem, in placing itself, as La Rocque says, 'outside the lowly tyranny of demands for more food,' [the CF] gives the appearance of disinterestedness. And yet it intends to maintain social injustices."[215]

In July 1940, following France's defeat by Nazi Germany, La Rocque accused democracy of being a source of decadence because of its encouragement of hedonism: "The world situation has put a halt to the trampling of so-called democracy; we have condemned the thing as well as the word. The abuse of pleasure and ease has killed our elites [and] led our people astray. We preach the harsh law of suffering and mutual help. Above everything, we place the Christian ideal."[216]

In 1941 La Rocque paid homage to the role of mystiques in political life and noted that all true mystiques transcended merely material concerns. Too, he added, the sufferings of the world would always be with us. They might be ameliorated by Christian charity, yet they could never be eliminated: "Intellectual, corporal, and material differences are inevitable; it is folly to expect them to disappear. This apparent injustice has no other solution than mutual respect and reciprocal assistance. . . . There are . . . ineluctable miseries. . . . Adversity, if it does not kill a person, offers him a precious stimulant."[217]

La Rocque now replaced the slogan "Social first" with "Mystique first," although mystique had always been paramount in his political thought. During the first months of the German occupation, he spoke of the spiritual as not only a source of comfort for those who were now faced with increasing physical hardships but also an antidote to the hedonism that, he said, had brought France to such a pass in the first place. The answer to the nation's problems, he wrote, would be found in "a religious mystique, a mystique of intellectual and spiritual progress [and] a mystique of tradition" (138).

La Rocque's attacks upon hedonism, materialism, and decadence in general also reflected his allegiance to a severe brand of Catholicism. Although, like Valois, Taittinger, and Renaud, he presented his movement as ecumenical ("each member [of the PSF] practices his own religious faith and respects the religious faith of his neighbor"), La Rocque made no secret of his commitment to Catholicism.

Neither did the CF/PSF as a movement refrain from publicizing its Catholic connections. French police reports of the 1930s are full of accounts of CF/PSF members attending ceremonies in Catholic churches commemorating the French war dead of the First World War and of officiating Catholic priests manifesting sympathy for the CF/PSF. Typical are the following two examples:

> On November 18, 1934, a mass was celebrated at the Church of Saint Laurent in memory of the war veterans of the tenth arrondissement of Paris who fell on the field of honor.
>
> The tenth section of the "Croix de Feu and Briscards" had asked its members, the "Volontaires Nationaux," and their families, to attend this ceremony, and there was a large turnout. About 600 persons answered the call. . . . I noticed eight flags belonging to the associations of the "Croix de Feu and Briscards," the "Volontaires Nationaux," and the "Solidarité Française." . . . Father Martin, the head priest of Notre Dame des Victoires, a member of the Croix de Feu, delivered the sermon. . . .
>
> On May 24, 1936, the Croix de Feu organized a religious ceremony at Notre Dame cathedral in memory of France's war dead. Some 800 members of the Croix de Feu, with flags and banners, paraded to the Cathedral. . . . The sermon [before 5,000 persons] was delivered by a chaplain who, after praising the vir-

tues of sacrifice displayed by the war dead, asked the members of the Croix de Feu to conserve preciously in their hearts the religious beliefs and old traditions of their country so that France would live healthily and beautifully. He also counseled them to piously conserve the cult of the [war] dead "who, like Christ, sacrificed themselves on the cross that the Croix de Feu has chosen as its symbol."[218]

Although groups of CF/PSF members sometimes attended similar ceremonies at Protestant churches and Jewish synagogues as a way of advertising the movement's commitment to national reconciliation, the bulk of the party membership was doubtlessly Catholic. Throughout its existence, the CF/PSF paraded its religiosity, as in 1930, when *Le Flambeau* described CF visits to various war monuments in France and Italy as pilgrimages, and in 1936, when the PSF called its members "the great defenders of Christian civilization," and in 1941, when La Rocque compared Christ's sacrifice on the cross to the efforts of the "apostles" of the PSF to save humanity.[219] One reason the CF/PSF hated the Freemasons so much was their anti-Catholicism.

If the CF/PSF was strongly Catholic in orientation, the *type* of Catholicism it practiced was distinctive, though not unusual. Opposed to left-wing Catholicism—the Catholicism of, say, Emmanuel Mounier—it was a politically authoritarian, socially conservative, and highly ascetic brand of Catholicism as well as a Catholicism heavily laced with military values.[220] It extolled not the Franciscan friars but the Christian knights of the Middle Ages, not the Socialist "worker-priests" but the religious right of the 1930s.

It was a type of Catholicism that, however spiritual it claimed to be, was prepared to defend middle-class economic interests with paramilitary force. To be sure, the CF/PSF sought to prevent class warfare by encouraging Christian charity, but it made it clear that should this fail to stave off a Marxist uprising counterrevolutionary violence was desirable. CF/PSF Catholics also opposed increased government spending on the poor, tax hikes for the rich, and strikes by workers by linking Christian values with military values, particularly with those that subordinated egoism and hedonism—especially working-class egoism and hedonism—to discipline and self-sacrifice.

La Rocque's martial definition of spirituality was typical of French fascism in general. Like Antoine Redier, Georges Valois, Pierre Taittinger, François Coty, Jean Renaud, Marcel Bucard, Pierre Drieu La Rochelle, Bertrand de Jouvenel, and other makers of the fascist tradition in France, La Rocque taught that if military values were extended to French society at large the decadent mores of the Third Republic and the social conflicts they engendered could be overcome. Paramilitary Christianity would negate not only Marxist materialism but also working-class insubordination. There was a great contrast, La Rocque wrote, between the "cult of the Golden Calf," which corrupted civilian life, and the spirit of self-sacrifice that characterized the army and the CF. A soldier obeyed those above him and devoted his life to spiritual, not material, gain. Civilian values were decadent; military values were not. In 1941 a headline in *Le Flambeau* put it succinctly: "THE ARMY: MODEL FOR THE NATION."[221]

ANTILIBERALISM

Opportunistic disclaimers notwithstanding, La Rocque regarded both political and cultural liberalism as decadent, as part of a generalized threat to authority—to social, economic, religious, parental, and marital authority. Cultural liberalism undermined traditional values by undermining the authoritarian foundations on which many of these values were based. One reason Marxism, Freemasonry, and feminism were linked in CF/PSF demonology, in spite of differences between them, was that they all challenged authority in one way or another and thus contained a liberal component.

Like other French fascist movements, the CF/PSF was a purveyor of hyphenated reasoning. Looking at the primary villains in CF/PSF propaganda—Marxists, liberals, Freemasons, and (eventually) Jews—one sees that they are repeatedly described as working together to destroy the nation, either as direct co-conspirators or as indirect fellow travelers. From a socially and religiously conservative point of view, there was a certain rationality to this linkage. Liberals, including Masonic and Jewish liberals, might, because of their commitment to intellectual freedom and civil rights, abet the rise of Marxism and atheism. Freemasons were known for their strong support of the "Rights of Man," even of the rights of Marxist men. They represented not only uncompromising liberalism but militant anticlericalism as well.

Members of the CF/PSF thus found compelling economic and religious reasons for detesting political and cultural liberalism: liberals were soft on Marxism and atheism. It was easy, therefore, to go from anti-Marxism and anti-atheism to antiliberalism. Even strongly *anti*-Marxist liberals were considered pernicious if they were willing to tolerate the proselytizing activities of Communists and Socialists, thereby opening the floodgates to Bolshevism.

Along with hyphenated reasoning went hyphenated feeling, especially where issues of authority were concerned. Repeatedly, La Rocque implied that what all the domestic enemies of France had in common was an opposition to authority.

(By *authority*, of course, he meant right-wing authority, because he had no qualms about challenging left-wing authority.) In La Rocque's terminology, to challenge authority was to challenge traditional values, *traditional* connoting discipline, *liberal* connoting indiscipline. Marxists undermined managerial authority, liberals religious authority, and feminists marital authority. At stake was not only economic but psychological control. Part of La Rocque's appeal was his promise to restore order in private as well as in public affairs. Left-wing liberals, he suggested, contributed to decadence not only by tolerating strikes by workers but by encouraging wives and children to rebel.

In the last chapter of *Public Service*, entitled "Authority," La Rocque noted how "from the beginning to the end of this book" he had emphasized the need for more responsibility at the apex of French government. "But," he added, "responsibility, in order to be effective and fruitful, requires as its counterpart a solid authority." He also applied this principle to family matters: "To maintain the family is to consolidate the authority of the parents over the children and to suppress the interference of the State in the instruction of children, until they pass from the control of their parents to that of judicial sanctions. It is to recognize the responsibilities of the father and his rights as the head of the household."[222]

La Rocque's views on the family were part of a belief in tradition that, he said, had to be repeatedly transmitted to the young, for it was the "immutable disciplines" of tradition that had kept France strong (and, he might have added, maintained paternal authority as well). "The cult of tradition," he wrote in 1934, should be the mainspring of national education (117). In 1941 La Rocque called his philosophy disciplines of action, a philosophy based on a hyphenation of authority-tradition-discipline that had been a recurring theme in his writings since 1934.

La Rocque not only extolled the well-disciplined family headed by a patriarchal authority, but also dubbed the PSF itself "the great family." In 1941 he called Pétain the father of the nation and urged the French people to support the Vichy regime with the "indivisible and multiple cohesion of an immense family." It was in this context that La Rocque urged the creation of a "flexible harmony" "*under the pain of death*" (italics mine). He insisted that just as there should be a Labor Charter that placed workers under certain necessary hierarchies, so there should be a Youth Charter that placed young people under the control of their parents. Youth should be seen not as an "independent entity" but as members of a family. Youth too should adhere to the slogan "Work, Family, Country," a slogan launched by the CF in 1934 and adopted by the Vichy regime in 1940. Like Georges Valois in 1925, La Rocque advocated grounding an authoritarian state in authoritarian religion and authoritarian families.[223]

All three were to be reinforced by a traditional work ethic. In 1937 Charles Vallin, the vice-president of the PSF, maintained that political and economic reforms alone would be useless without a revival of previous attitudes toward work: "We intend only to return France to her natural climate, to a love of work and of work well done, to respect for the family, to a taste for effort, and to a sense of honor. When France has found [this climate] again, then 'structural reforms,' to use the current jargon, will be easy. . . . Return France's soul to her—and all the rest will be given in surplus." In 1941 La Rocque warned that if French youth did not dedicate themselves to the "rehabilitation of the family and of work" they would be doomed to decadence.[224]

According to CF/PSF ideology, women were also expected to submit to the necessary hierarchies of life, that is, to their husbands. The CF/PSF was no more democratic on gender issues than it was on political, social, and economic issues. In yet one more example of hyphenated reasoning, Vallin, in a speech to a group of women of the PSF in 1937, equated feminists with insubordinate proletarians:

> I owe you a confession that may seem maladroit before such an assembly: I am not a feminist. Why not? For the same reason, doubtlessly, that I will never be a socialist. There are in these kinds of religions, in these caricatures of religion, a fanaticism, an exclusiveness, a sectarianism that turns truth into error.
> . . . The place we give to women in society, the respect that we vow to them, and . . . the cult that we surround them with, turns us away, quite naturally, from a vulgar feminism. It is not with class struggle that the social question will be resolved. Yet, it is toward a sort of class struggle, opposing the feminine "proletariat" to the masculine "capitalist," that feminism is leading us. This is not how we will resolve the great human problem that preoccupies us this evening. . . . [The solution] is not struggle; it is collaboration and mutual aid. It is not hatred but harmony.[225]

In effect, the CF/PSF proposed the same solution for women's grievances that it proposed for workers' grievances: that subordinates and superiors seek harmony, not equality. Here, too, the superiors, in this case the husbands, would control the bases of that harmony, undemocratic corporatism between management and labor being matched by an equally undemocratic corporatism of sorts between men and women. The CF/PSF was responding to another attack upon authority, this time upon male authority, and once again its tactic was to preserve authority by shifting the focus of the debate from the injustices involved to a lofty appeal for collaboration, however disparate the power exerted by those engaged in this collaboration. As for the ideal of womanhood that Vallin left his audience with, it was not one—to use Vallin's terms—of fanatical, tasteless, and vulgar feminists but rather one of ladies who understood that true greatness came from simplicity (6). One reason Vallin and other CF/PSF males despised Freemasonry so much was that they believed its secular liberalism also spawned feminist revolt.

This is not to say that the CF/PSF was opposed to all the interests of women. As it did in regard to workers, it sided with some of women's social and economic needs as long as they were satisfied within a paternalistic framework. In contrast to the SF, the CF/PSF supported a woman's right to work outside the home. In 1934 La Rocque objected to men who met women's "just demands" with silence or dismissed them with a few "insipid gallantries." Since the First World War, he said, the social and professional role of women in France had grown considerably, and it was a mistake to reduce that role to being solely a mother or a wife—particularly when the death of a million and a half soldiers had left so many widows.[226] Women's presence in the workplace should be respected: "The old expression of ridicule, 'a working woman,' is out of date."

At the same time, La Rocque asserted that women should not be deprived of their traditional prerogatives within the home. Women with husbands and children who entered the workplace remained mothers and wives, with obligations not only to the family but to the nation at large. The latter included raising large families so as to guarantee France's military strength against Germany. A higher birthrate, La Rocque wrote, would ensure the full flowering of France's spiritual forces (115).

According to La Rocque, a wife should have the same legal rights as her husband in all matters regarding their children, but in all other matters the husband was to be viewed as the *chef*, the boss. Women should be granted the vote, starting at the municipal level, but female suffrage should be accompanied by the family vote (whereby the *chef* would be given more votes than his wife, one for each child). The sexual behavior of a wife should be exemplary: "One does not confide one's home to prostitutes" (116). In 1941 La Rocque blamed the "abuse of divorce" on prewar hedonism.

It could be argued that one aspect of La Rocque's view of the family that was highly anti-Nazi was his insistence that the loyalty of children to their families be greater than their loyalty to the state, a principle that contradicted Nazi teaching that children should denounce their parents if their parents criticized the regime. The trouble with this argument is that it overlooks the fact that not only was Italian fascism less fanatical than German Nazism in this respect but also that even Nazism professed to be a strong supporter of the traditional family *before* it came to power.[227] It was only after Hitler had consolidated his power that he challenged parents' authority over their children.

Still, the CF/PSF repeatedly defended the rights of parents against the rights of the state, at least when the state and its educational institutions were viewed as too liberal or too Marxist. In 1934 La Rocque objected to the state's centralizing education, a criticism he failed to make after 1940 of the equally centralized educational system of the Vichy regime. In 1936 the official party platform of the PSF attacked educational statism and called for giving more support to private schools and to the "diverse spiritualities" of France, a euphemism for encouraging the establishment of more Catholic and conservative schools. Under this system, "the family would decide the choice, for the child belongs to [the family]." Thus, conservative families would be able to send their children to schools that were free of the secular liberalism and political radicalism of the public schools. According to La Rocque, whatever the drawbacks of decentralization, they were preferable "to State control or to anarchy."[228]

In fact, what La Rocque objected to was not so much educational statism per se but educational statism that was politically incorrect, that is, educational statism that was anticlerical and left wing, that violated the doctrines of the PSF. In May 1936, following the election of the Popular Front, he condemned a school system that, he said, sought to standardize French citizens by indoctrinating them with class hatred and antipatriotic sentiments. At the same time, he called for a different kind of standardization, one that would place a higher value on physical education and on the spiritual and moral forces of the nation. When the ideas of the CF came to power, he wrote, their "first objective" would be education.[229]

However, with the Popular Front in power, a PSF pamphlet in 1936 called for a freer, less politicized educational system. Although its rhetoric was liberal, its intent was repressive. It warned that revolutionary parties were using the schools to brainwash the nation. Far from being neutral, as they claimed, these schools had become the "victims of the reigning ideology." The state monopoly of education had created a "war machine against religious education" and a "demagogic weapon" against the "so-called ruling classes." It sought to deprive the latter of as many of their functions as possible while adding to the proletariat of the factories and the fields a growing intellectual proletariat who would prepare the way for revolution. France's schools, from the primary to the university level, had become forums for propaganda, producing "apostles of class struggle, conscientious objectors, and antifamilial agitation." The prevailing sociology in France's universities "attacked the foundations of religion and served as a preamble for political socialism."[230]

According to the PSF pamphlet, the state had so democratized education that intelligence no longer transcended ideology: "But of what importance to the State is an intellectual elite who is not concerned with the politics of numbers?" (152). The politicization of learning had gone so far that there were "literary sects of the right and literary sects of the left, an art of the right and an art of the left," sterile rivalries that could not produce the kind of durable works that sprang from serenity, not conflict (152–53). The state, "ungrateful toward Intelligence," had added to its temporal authority a spiritual authority over education, which it was misusing for its own ideological purposes. The left-wing politicians who governed France were not true leaders but "high priests of ideology."

And yet the same PSF pamphlet that denounced using education for political indoctrination rejected the principle of educational "neutrality," calling it a "trap": "Even if [neutrality] were possible, it would not be desirable. Why would one want the soul of a child to be abandoned, naked and stripped of its heritage" (151, 155). Neutrality would reduce learning to a "colorless documentation" that would leave the student "licensed with diplomas but lacking in principles." For in the end, it was the moral education of the student that was of paramount importance, and it was the responsibility of the state to "forbid" all teaching likely to harm the health of the nation, especially the student's sense of his or her patriotic and moral obligations. The negligence of the state in 1936 was truly criminal in this regard. No cult of neutrality must be allowed to negate France's spiritual forces.[231]

The PSF denied that it wanted to give the state in France the kind of power over education and culture that the Nazi state exercised in Germany. The Nazi state not only controlled the educational system totally, but also censored artistic views that contradicted Aryan theory, a practice that reflected a serious prejudice against one of the essential elements of any national patrimony, "its works of the spirit."

However, if intellectual dictatorship was wrong, so too was intellectual license: "Too much intellectual liberty is sometimes a source of anarchy." The best policy was to encourage intellectual diversity through educational decentralization, while insisting that the state ensure the morality of all schools throughout France.[232] Although the PSF failed to explain how this morality would be implemented by a "freer," more decentralized educational system, it seems clear that its aim was to remove secular liberalism and left-wing ideas

from the schools and to replace them with its own religious and political principles. Certainly, PSF educational theory, like PSF ideology in general, was
strongly opposed to any policy that allowed voices of decadence to propagate
their ideas with the same impunity that they had in the past.

The antiliberalism of the CF/PSF was most prominent in its hatred of the
Freemasons, those archdevils of liberalism, especially when they "conspired"
with the Marxists. In September 1935 *Le Flambeau* spoke of a "plot by Freemasonry and the Third International" to take over the country, and in April it
linked Marxist "blackmail" and "Freemason schemes." In June, a CF speaker at
a rally in Algiers ended his address, according to the police, with "a violent
diatribe against Freemasonry and [the cry] 'Long live La Rocque!' "[233]

Second only to the Marxist in CF/PSF demonology was the Freemason. Even
in 1941, when La Rocque was more anti-Semitic than he had ever been before, he
condemned the Freemasons more than he did the Jews. Some Jews, he wrote,
could be assimilated into *la patrie* but a Freemason, never. It was a mistake to
blame Jews alone for France's defeat, as it was the Freemasons who had prepared
a "favorable terrain" for them. Freemasons had long been in league with the
Marxists; they were co-conspirators with the Jews as well. "In each place and on
each occasion where Jewish purulence has manifested itself," La Rocque re-
viled, "Freemasonry was the introducer, the protector, the co-conspirator. To try
to regulate the Jewish question without crushing forever the Lodges and their
antennas would be chimerical. . . . The principal causes of our misfortunes will
be eliminated only when the work of Freemasonry has been not only condemned
but also destroyed in every domain where it operates, in every spot on our
territory."[234]

For La Rocque in 1941, the Freemasons were to be rejected even more harshly
than the Jews, for some Jews, if properly assimilated, could be just as patriotic as
their Catholic counterparts (as Rabbi Kaplan had demonstrated in 1936). But the
Freemason could never be truly French because he scorned religion and colluded
with Marxism. (That many French Freemasons were, in fact, quite socially and
economically conservative failed to dissuade La Rocque and other French fascists from portraying them as Communist fellow-travelers.) CF/PSF publica-
tions and speeches were filled with attacks upon the Freemasons; their lodges
and secret ceremonies were depicted as sources of political corruption and endless machinations. It was alleged that Radical and Socialist politicians were
often Freemasons and that they conspired with one another as members of the
same clan. La Rocque's talk of a plot by Freemasonry and the Third International
was a recurring theme in *Le Flambeau*.

In October 1940 La Rocque seized the opportunity offered by the establishment of the Vichy regime to demand the complete repression of Freemasonry in
France and the removal of former Freemasons from all government posts, down
to the municipal level, as well as from all other positions of political and cultural
influence in France. Their detection, he wrote, must be pursued relentlessly.
Freemasonry was one of the mortal vices of France, having contributed to the
decadent mores that had led to the nation's military defeat: "Its furtive reign had
infected little by little the French organism with all kinds of moral failings."

According to La Rocque, Freemasons should not be allowed to return to
government positions even if they promised to mend their ways because for a
Freemason "the recognition of, even contrition for, his errors of the past does not
constitute a right to the future. He cannot be assimilated into the good and loyal
services of Frenchmen who have submitted to their spiritual ideal and their
patriotic duty." When in 1941 La Rocque recalled the "dear refrain" of his youth,
"We want France French," he was complaining not about the German soldiers
occupying France but about the "unpatriotic" Freemasons.[235]

5 · The Parti Populaire Français

JACQUES DORIOT: THE COMMUNIST YEARS, 1920–36

Just as Pierre Taittinger's JP and Georges Valois's Faisceau were founded in 1925 as part of the conservative backlash to the electoral victory of the Cartel des Gauches of 1924 and just as François Coty's SF and Colonel de La Rocque's CF emerged in 1933 as part of the conservative backlash to the election of another left-center coalition government in 1932, Jacques Doriot's Parti Populaire Français was launched in June 1936 as part of the conservative backlash to an even more severe threat from the left, the Popular Front, which had come to power the month before.

The PPF's first political rally was held in Saint-Denis, a working-class district of Paris, and was organized by Doriot, the mayor of Saint-Denis, who, like many of his original followers, was a former Communist. Some historians have been led by these facts to portray the PPF as a form of left fascism. Doriot was indeed a Communist between 1920 and 1936, but the party he founded in 1936 abandoned the authoritarian left for the authoritarian right. Denouncing both the PCF and the SFIO and losing a crucial election to the Communists in Saint-Denis in 1937, Doriot turned to lower-middle-class constituencies for the bulk of his support and proposed a socioeconomic program crafted to favor not the proletariat but the bourgeoisie, especially the big business associations that primarily financed his movement.

By 1937 Doriot was very much an *ex*-Communist. To suggest that he was still a Communist in 1937 because he had been a Communist in 1933 and that therefore the PPF was more an expression of ideological continuity than of ideological change is highly misleading—although such a notion has been repeatedly implied by historians who insist that French fascism was essentially a left-wing phenomenon. Doriot's passage from communism to fascism entailed a sharp break from his ideological past and was largely the result of personal opportunism, not Marxist revisionism. When developments within the PCF in the mid-1930s blocked Doriot's career prospects, he turned first to the political left-center, then to the political right-center, and finally to the political far right in order to revive his political fortunes.

In doing so, he practiced the same kind of ideological flexibility that he had demonstrated previously within the PCF, only this time to the point of abandoning Marxism altogether. By 1936 Doriot was no longer the dedicated Communist he had been in his earlier years. By 1937 he had replaced the social ideals of his youth with their opposites, becoming a proponent of the very fascism that he had previously denounced.

In 1920, at the age of twenty-two, Doriot had joined the PCF. Coming from a working-class background (his father was a blacksmith and his mother a seamstress), he had begun working in a factory at the age of fifteen. Soon afterward, he had taken a job at a local dairy, where he survived on free milk and two francs a day. Twenty years later he bitterly recalled the hardships of the young worker: the eleven-hour days, the verbal abuse from supervisors, the fines deducted from low wages, and the general "absence of humanity."[1] In 1915, at the age of seventeen, he moved to Saint-Denis, where he worked in various factories as a metalworker. Saint-Denis was a Socialist stronghold, and in 1916 Doriot joined the Jeunesses Socialistes (Socialist youth), even though his major interest at the time was boxing, not politics.

In 1917 Doriot was drafted into the army. Four months later he was at the front, and in 1918 his unit was decimated by the Germans at Chemin-des-Dames. He later received the Croix de Guerre for carrying a wounded comrade on his back for some two kilometers. Following his discharge from the army in 1920, he joined the recently founded PCF and played an active role in the party's campaign against French militarism and colonialism. In 1923, at the age of twenty-five, he was sentenced to a year in prison for a series of articles he had written calling for military disobedience. Later, as head of the PPF, he opposed

French intervention in the Spanish Civil War and defended an appeasement policy toward Nazi Germany.

To suggest, as some historians have, that he was against war with Franco and Hitler in the 1930s because of his earlier pacifism ignores his collaboration with the highly unpacifistic Nazis after 1940, including his service at the Russian front after 1941 with the French Volunteers against Bolshevism, a French unit of the German army.[2] Doriot's antimilitarism following the First World War did not prevent him from supporting Nazi militarism during the Second World War. Moreover, as a Communist militant between 1920 and 1934, he displayed no qualms about engaging in *domestic* political violence. As the head of the Young Communists in the early 1920s, he was renowned for his fighting prowess in the street battles of the day. The PCF at the time opposed bourgeois militarism and bourgeois warfare but not Marxist militarism and Marxist warfare. On the contrary, it readily accepted violence on behalf of class struggle, anticolonialism, and revolutionary overthrow. Repeated Communist assaults on French fascist political rallies of the era were certainly not inhibited by Communist pacifism.

Neither as a Communist before 1934 nor as a fascist after 1936 was Doriot ever an opponent of all violence, all militarism, or all war. For Doriot, whether one engaged in violence or not depended on whose political cause was being served and on whether one supported that cause or not. Although he reversed himself ideologically after 1936, damning Marxism instead of supporting it, it was not out of abhorrence for violence per se. Indeed, temperamentally Doriot was very much a fighter, whether as a Communist throwing a cafe table at riot police in Paris in 1925, as a sergeant battling advancing Germans in 1940, or as a fascist opposing the Communists on the Russian front in 1942.

The First World War, while doubtless a horrible experience for the young Doriot, did not determine his political thought any more than it did that of right-wing *anti*pacifists after the war. Just as most French soldiers, following the Armistice, returned to their prewar political affiliations—conservatives, liberals, and socialists joining their respective veterans' associations—Doriot retained his prewar commitment to the left. After 1920, applying a Marxist perspective to what he had experienced, he both defended and denounced violence, depending on whose class interests it served: revolutionary violence was good; counterrevolutionary violence was bad.

After joining the PCF in 1920, at the age of twenty-two, Doriot moved rapidly up the party ranks. The Italian Communist Ignazio Silone remembered meeting him in 1920 and found him to be not the enfant terrible of the PCF that he would later become but rather a young man who was "modest, good-natured, and sentimental."³ In 1920 Doriot was sent to Moscow to attend the Third Congress of the Communist International. After the congress was over, he spent several months in the Soviet Union, traveling extensively and speaking at more than five hundred political meetings. He met and venerated Lenin and in 1924 sobbed at the news of his death. In 1921 he also admired Trotsky but later sided with Stalin in condemning him as a traitor. When Doriot returned to Paris in 1922, he was made the head of the Jeunesses communistes (Communist youth). In 1924, he became a member of the central committee of the PCF, was elected to the Chamber of Deputies, and became a leading spokesman for the PCF in parliament. His political career was soaring.

In 1925 he denounced French imperialism in Morocco and accused French banking interests, specifically the Banque de Paris et des Pays-Bas, of machinations against Abd el-Krim, the Arab leader. When the Riff rebellion broke out a few weeks later, Doriot and the PCF sided with Abd el-Krim against the French government. Some members of the French extreme right, including Colonel de La Rocque, would never forgive Doriot for this "betrayal," even after Doriot became a fascist and a strong defender of French colonialism.

Doriot became a hero in Communist circles for his role in the rue Mathurin-Moreau affair. On October 12, 1925, police tried to prevent him from participating in a political rally protesting the Moroccan war. He charged into their ranks and badly injured a police sergeant in the brawl that ensued, thereby making a name for himself as a man of prodigious physical strength. Pierre Drieu La Rochelle later wrote of this event, "Those who saw Doriot then, alone, before two hundred policemen, plunging into the mass [of them], wheeling a café table above his head, carrying a cluster of police agents atop his powerful shoulders, succumbing only after complete exhaustion, knows that there is at least one political leader in France who is a man."⁴ According to the historian Dieter Wolf, Doriot became the declared favorite of Parisian Communists after this incident.⁵

Doriot's popularity with rank and file Communists in 1925 made him a top prospect to head the PCF one day. His ambition was thwarted, however, by rivals within the party, a development that eventually led him to abandon the PCF, first for his own brand of communism in 1934 and then for full-blown anticommunism in 1936. In 1925, aware that it was the Comintern that would determine whether he would become chief of the PCF or not, he tried for the next two years, as he had done previously, to curry favor with the powers-that-be in Moscow. His opportunism was all too transparent: after Lenin's death he first supported Trotsky, then Zinoviev, and finally Stalin. Doriot joined his major rival in the PCF, Maurice Thorez, in denouncing Stalin's enemies and was invited to a private dinner with Stalin as a reward. The Soviet leader declined, however, to make Doriot general-secretary of the PCF, eventually appointing Thorez instead.

Between 1926 and 1928 Doriot suffered two further setbacks. In 1926 the Comintern dispatched him to China for several months, and when he returned in 1927 he was no longer the leader of Jeunesses communistes in France. In his absence, Thorez had maneuvered to remove him from his power base within the party. Doriot was also arrested by the French police shortly after his return from China and spent several months in prison for his support of the Riff rebellion and for writing antimilitary articles.

Nineteen twenty-eight marked a major turning point in Doriot's career. After his release from prison that year, he was no longer as docile toward the party leadership as he had been. Thorez and the PCF politburo had deprived him of his position with the Jeunesses communistes and now blocked his climb to the top. In spite of the two prison terms and other personal sacrifices he had undergone for the party, he had been treated shabbily and had had plenty of time in his cell to think about it. The Doriot who emerged from prison in 1928 was no longer the "modest, good-natured and sentimental" young man he had been in 1920, no longer a grateful youth on the way up but an embittered veteran on the way down. He had no intention of submitting meekly to Thorez's dictates.

In 1928 Doriot publicly challenged the official party line of the PCF for the first time. At issue was the relation between the PCF and the SFIO and between communism and socialism in general. It was the Comintern's position and hence the position of Thorez and the Communist leadership in France that the Socialists undermined class struggle by collaborating with the bourgeoisie and were not only enemies of the proletariat but "social fascists." Doriot called for an end to such recalcitrance, pointing out that in the recent legislative elections many Communist and Socialist candidates had been defeated because they had refused to support one another during the runoff elections. He argued that in order to better defeat fascism cooperation between the PCF and the SFIO was desirable. Moscow, however, rejected his plea, as did Thorez and the party leadership in France. Doriot was accused of rightist deviation, and when he reiterated his dissent at the PCF's annual party congress in 1929 Thorez responded by assigning Henri Barbé, the new head of the Jeunesses communistes, the task of discrediting Doriot. In 1930, while on a trip to Moscow, Doriot was also reprimanded by Comintern officials for his failure to toe the party line.

Having lost his leverage within the PCF as a spokesman for the Jeunesses communistes, Doriot spent the next four years concentrating on another political base, an electoral one, in Saint-Denis. Although he had spent much of the previous six years either in prison, underground, or abroad, in the elections of 1930 he was easily reelected to the Chamber of Deputies by the voters of Saint-Denis, winning more votes than any other Communist candidate from that district. Although such a success would have normally entitled the winner to be the mayor of Saint-Denis as well, the PCF appointed a lesser candidate, Gaston Venet, to the position. Not until 1931, when Venet's incompetence proved embarrassing to the party, was Doriot allowed to replace him.

In the next three years, Doriot turned Saint-Denis into a Communist showplace, overseeing the construction of new public baths, a sports stadium, a municipal library, and child care facilities for working-class mothers. In 1933 some twenty-five hundred children were sent off to vacation camps at municipal expense. In the elections of 1932 Doriot was reelected by a comfortable majority as the deputy-mayor of Saint-Denis, that is, as its representative in parliament as well as its mayor. In the Chamber of Deputies, he called for a seven-hour workday and national unemployment insurance (to be paid for by employers and the state), proposals that further enhanced his popularity in the "red fortress" of Saint-Denis. Dubbed the king of Saint-Denis, he was once again a power to be reckoned with within the PCF.[6]

In 1934 Doriot denounced the fascist threat posed by the riots of February 6 and, again challenging the party leadership, called for a coalition with the Socialists to defeat this threat. He was hardly the only leftist in France in 1934 who felt that the division between the Communists and the Socialists in Germany had worked to Hitler's benefit and who wanted to avoid the same mistake in France. In calling for a truce with the Socialists, for a Popular Front against fascism, Doriot was advocating a policy in February that the Comintern would adopt in June. In February, however, Doriot's call for a reversal of the party line was regarded by Thorez and the Comintern as a breach of party discipline. Thorez used *L'Humanité* (which Doriot was denied access to) to smear Doriot and distort his position.

Doriot fought back. On February 8, seizing upon the left-wing backlash to the February 6 riots and ignoring PCF orders, he began direct negotiations with SFIO leaders in Saint-Denis. His goal was to hold a joint demonstration to protest the riots of two days earlier. The SFIO, confronted with a government ban on all demonstrations, backed out at the last minute. The PCF announced that it would hold a demonstration of its own on February 9 in spite of the government ban. Rather than participate in the demonstration themselves, however, Thorez and the rest of the PCF leadership spent February 9 in hiding in order to avoid possible arrest, letting their followers do the fighting for them. Doriot, by contrast, was in the forefront of the demonstration, a bloody affair in which six men were killed and several hundred wounded in clashes with the police. Once again Doriot was acclaimed for his physical courage. In the weeks that followed, he continued his efforts to unite Communists and Socialists in a common effort against fascism and was instrumental in creating the Antifascist Vigilance Committee of Saint-Denis, headed by eight Communists and five Socialists. A member of the PCF's politburo complained that this committee was "a crime against the working class" and called for its dissolution.[7]

Soon afterward, Thorez called a meeting of Communist leaders from northern Paris, including Saint-Denis, to bring Doriot to heel. Doriot's challenge to the party line was debated and a vote was taken: eighty-four delegates supported the PCF's official policy and fifty-four Doriot's alternative. When Thorez subsequently denounced Doriot's supporters as heretics, Doriot resigned his post as deputy-mayor of Saint-Denis in protest. Two days later, on April 11, Doriot published an open letter to the Comintern again defending his call for a united front against fascism. Significantly, he noted that such an effort would entail not only cooperation with the Socialists but with the middle classes and the landed peasantry as well, in effect a policy that would at least temporarily replace class struggle with class collaboration.

The Comintern summoned Doriot to Moscow. He refused to go. In May he was reelected deputy-mayor of Saint-Denis by an even larger majority than before. Thorez responded by attempting to limit his influence to Saint-Denis, sending Communist militants to disrupt Doriot's speaking engagements elsewhere. At Rouen in June, blows were exchanged when some 150 Thorez loyalists disrupted a meeting at which Doriot was about to address an audience of 2,000. Even though Doriot was still officially a member of the PCF, he was already being treated as if he were a fascist.

The issue in 1934, however, was less one of ideology, or even strategy, than of party discipline. In June the Comintern itself adopted Doriot's previously heretical position, changing the party line to allow collaboration with the once-hated Socialists. Doriot dryly noted that "what had been in January a crime and opportunism had become in June inevitable and revolutionary."[8] His mistake, as Dieter Wolf has pointed out, was to have been politically correct six months in advance. What neither PCF nor Comintern leaders could tolerate was his refusal to obey orders, especially his refusal to go to Moscow. At the PCF's annual congress in June, Thorez proposed that Doriot be dismissed from the party, and the motion was passed by the standard unanimous vote. In Saint-Denis, however, Doriot held on, fighting off the challenge in the 1934 elections of the official PCF candidate, who accused him of being a renegade. Doriot won again, garnering 75.9 percent of the vote.

Between 1934 and 1936 Doriot continued to call himself a Communist despite his break with the PCF. In 1934 he still advocated the nationalization of French industry and supported the Soviet Union in foreign policy. In 1935 he accused Gaston Doumergue of being a "pre-fascist braggart" and the neo-Socialist Marcel Déat of presenting a "bad copy of fascism." In December 1935 Doriot voted in parliament for the dissolution of the CF, the SF, the JP, and the Francistes, and in February his Saint-Denis Vigilance Committee against Fascism condemned members of the Action Française for their physical assault on Léon Blum. In 1935 Doriot called Hitler "the executioner of the German people" and "the most formidable enemy of the German and international working class."[9] In April, he again tried to form a local electoral alliance with the Socialists, but they turned him down. In the elections of May 1935, he was victorious once more, although the opposition of the PCF was beginning to take its toll. Doriot's portion of the vote, 56.9 percent, was down from the 75.9 percent of 1934.

Rebuffed by the SFIO, cut off from the PCF, his financial resources dwindling, Doriot sought to capitalize on his foreign policy differences with the PCF and the SFIO as a way of attracting support, especially in Saint-Denis, a pacifist stronghold. He accused the Soviet Union and its lackies in France of wanting to drag France into a war against Germany and proposed negotiations with Hitler to prevent such a war. Although he continued to condemn fascism as a domestic evil, criticizing Nazi repression of workers in Germany, he opposed a war against Germany. While such a stance no doubt pleased many French conservatives—who by 1935 had gone from hawks to doves in their willingness to appease Nazi Germany[10]—Doriot was not in a position, either politically or financially, to abandon communism altogether and retain his electoral majority in Saint-Denis.

Prior to the elections of May 1936, Doriot was still a man of the left. *L'Emancipation Nationale*, the local newspaper he controlled, displayed a hammer and sickle on its masthead, and audiences at his political rallies sang the "Internationale" and gave the Marxist salute. Doriot supported most of the reforms proposed by the Popular Front, including the forty-hour week, and he continued to denounce fascism.[11] By June 1936, however, at the time he founded the PPF, his ideology, though still in flux, was no longer Communist, not even that of a dissident Communist. Indeed, before the year was out he went from the extreme left to the extreme right, proposing an alternative to Marxism that, in effect, would have replaced the CGT and the CGTU with management-dominated corporatist unions. He also adopted a number of other positions that were in tune with French fascism.

DORIOT'S SHIFT TO FASCISM

The turning point came following the elections of May 1936. No longer did Doriot agree with conservatives only on foreign policy; his position on domestic policy, particularly regarding the social and economic policies of the Popular Front, began to move rightward as well. By 1937 the former antifascist had become a fascist in all but name, advocating many of the same doctrines, values, and attitudes that spokesmen for the Faisceau, the JP, the SF, the Francistes, and the CF had. The former Communist became a fierce anti-Communist, denouncing the Marxism he had so long defended, placing class collaboration, not class conflict, at the center of his social ideology; extolling capitalism, not socialism, as the best economic system for France; and looking to the petty bourgeoisie, not to the proletariat, for the bulk of his support.

In October 1936 Doriot said to his friend Victor Barthélemy, "For a long time I believed in class struggle as the essential factor in revolution. I no longer believe in this." He also told Barthélemy, "[In 1934] I was already a renegade; I remain one. And as everyone knows it is appropriate for renegades to burn down what they have previously adored. But I know Communism well. . . . And it is because I know Communism well that I have become its implacable adversary."[12]

The primary spur behind this remarkable shift was the outcome of the elections of May 1936 in Saint-Denis and what it portended for Doriot if he continued to rely primarily on Communist voters. As Wolf has noted, the results of that election revealed how precarious Doriot's position had become. Although Doriot won the election, his percentage of the vote had continued to drop (from 75.9 percent in 1934, to 56.9 percent in 1935, to 51.4 percent in 1936). Moreover, in the 1936 elections, even though he had outdistanced his PCF rival in the first round by 10,875 to 8,899 votes, in the runoff election the SFIO had backed the PCF candidate and Doriot had been able to win only with centrist and conservative support. Indeed, during the electoral campaign Doriot had even asked the CF to use its influence on his behalf, despite his having once condemned La Rocque's movement as fascist. By May 1936, according to Jean-Paul Brunet's estimate, perhaps 50 percent of Doriot's electoral support still came from working-class voters.[13] The rest, in other words, was middle class. Doriot must have realized that as long as the PCF and the SFIO continued to band against him, his electoral base on the left would be threatened and that to survive politically he would have to increase his support on the right, especially among middle- and lower-middle-class voters.

Soon after the 1936 elections, Doriot was approached by Gabriel Leroy-Ladurie, the head of the Banque Worms. Leroy-Ladurie represented important business interests who wanted to undermine the Popular Front. He asked Doriot to form a new political party to help in this effort. Doriot, short of funds and seeing his political star on the wane, accepted the offer, and the PPF was launched—thanks to generous subsidies from Leroy-Ladurie and his friends.[14]

For the next few months, Doriot walked a political tightrope, trying to retain his blue-collar supporters in Saint-Denis while moving to broaden his appeal beyond this constituency. When all the major factories in Saint-Denis were shut down in June by some 15,000 workers engaged in sit-down strikes, Doriot supported the strikers with material aid while urging them to spare small businesses and accusing the Communists of trying to foment a revolution. As mayor of Saint-Denis, he used municipal funds to provide some 130,000 meals for workers occupying the factories, aid that stopped only when the strikes came to an end in July.

Although Doriot described most of the workers' demands as legitimate, he cautioned that a "brutal" application of the forty-hour-week law would wreck a number of small enterprises. He denounced the "big bourgeoisie" for "provoking" the strikes by lowering salaries and being "selfish." At the same time, he implied that the strikes had not been spontaneous at all but were the result of Communist machinations. PPF leaders acted as mediators between management and labor in Saint-Denis, helping to forge settlements in several factories, backing the workers in many of their demands while warning that they would lose their independence to the Communists if they became too political. Even in June and July, PPF spokesmen were touting the benefits of class collaboration over class conflict. As Brunet has pointed out, such pronouncements did not go unappreciated by besieged bourgeois in Saint-Denis: "On its side, management and a large fraction of the middle classes, who had been plunged into anguish by the social subversion of June, considered Doriot's organization more and more as a possible rampart against Communism."[15]

Six months later, Doriot was openly critical of both the sit-down strikes and the Popular Front. Ideas that he had expressed cautiously in June and July, he now stated more forcefully, to the point that his view of social conflict began to mirror that of the French right in general. Rather than praise the workers for the gains they had achieved (which one might expect from a supposedly proletarian leader), he portrayed their actions as a great mistake. The wage increases they had won, he said, had been wiped out by inflation. The strikes had hurt production, which ultimately hurt the workers themselves. As a weapon, the strike was a disastrous tactic and a betrayal of class collaboration. The forty-hour week "risked becoming a remedy worse than the sickness." Marxism had proved to be a "bankrupt" philosophy, especially its doctrine of class struggle. Doriot no longer advocated proletarian revolution and a Marxist takeover. On the contrary, he paid homage to the middle classes and the peasantry as the guarantors of social stability.[16] In March 1937, he called upon the major right and right-center parties in France to form a Liberty Front against the Popular Front.

When new elections were held in May 1937, Doriot lost his position as mayor of Saint-Denis. A majority of the electorate voted for his Communist rival, Fernand Grenier, the candidate of the Popular Front. Doriot received only 37.9 percent of the vote. According to Brunet, by that date the PPF inspired widespread "repulsion" in Saint-Denis, and Doriot was "literally crushed" by his opponent. Bertrand de Jouvenel remembered seeing Doriot the night of the election sitting in a chair, his two arms dangling before him, like "a boxer in the corner of a ring after having taken his punishment."[17]

There were signs in the months that followed that Doriot paid an additional price for rejecting his former ideals. However opportunistic he had been as a member of the PCF, communism had given a certain meaning to his life, had made the battles he had fought and the imprisonments he had endured seem worthwhile, even noble. Following his abandonment of communism after 1936, his personal habits began to change. According to some of Doriot's closest associates, toward the end of 1937 he became hedonistic and self-indulgent, spending less time with his family, frequenting brothels, and eating enormous meals in Saint-Denis's best restaurants. Bertrand de Jouvenel recalled that Doriot would often spend three hours in a restaurant consuming large amounts of food and wine; by 1938 he was sagging with obesity.[18] Whereas the earlier Doriot had been stocky but muscular and renowned for his strength as a street brawler, in 1937 he went to fat. Brunet attributes this transformation to the political setbacks Doriot suffered in Saint-Denis that year, his loss of the mayorship and his failure to win La Rocque's support for the Liberty Front. But as a Communist Doriot had suffered greater political reverses than these without going to seed.

The emotional losses Doriot suffered during this period may have been deeper than Brunet suggests. After June 1937 Doriot no longer had the left to fall back on for either psychological or financial support, at least not nearly to the extent that he had before. The political and emotional home he could repair to in hard times was no longer so welcoming. The loss of his previous political identity may have also been depressing to a man whose new political identity, at least when judged by his previous social ideals, was sorely lacking. Indeed, from the point of view of the cause he had served for almost two decades, he had sold out to the enemy, betrayed what he had fought for in the past, chosen to serve the oppressors instead of the oppressed. Psychologists like Erik Erikson tell us that a healthy identity is normally based on a morally satisfying life commitment and that the lack of such an identity can lead to a sense of existential emptiness. There is reason to believe that Doriot may have sought to compensate for his identity loss by increasing his physical gratifications. It may have been a coincidence that Doriot grew obese after his break with the political left, but more likely the change was a result of that break.

What is clear is that Doriot was neither a Communist nor a Socialist after June 1936, as the successive socioeconomic programs he proposed repeatedly demonstrated. By 1937 Doriot had become a staunch defender of capitalism, the middle classes, and the landed peasantry, an opponent of class conflict, sit-down strikes, and proletarian revolution, an enemy of the Communist party, the Socialist party, and the Popular Front, and a critic of French intervention on behalf of the left in Spain. He now supported an entente with Nazi Germany and fascist Italy against the Soviet Union, while himself heading a political movement that increasingly adopted the doctrines and trappings of domestic fascism, including the fascist salute. The Doriot who had previously pleaded for reconciliation between the PCF and the SFIO was now a declared enemy of both. The former harbinger of the Popular Front was now one of its harshest critics; the former Marxist was now an anti-Marxist; the former antifascist was now a fascist.

When a number of former members of the AF, the JP, the Francistes, the SF, and the CF joined the PPF in 1936, it was not a Communist but an anti-Communist they were backing.[19] Doriot, having failed in his previous attempts to strike an alliance with the Socialists, had moved sharply to the right. Although political survival seems to have been Doriot's primary motivation, this does not explain the support that he received from others after June 1936, including the lavish funding he was granted by various big business groups. As Jean-Paul Brunet writes, "The case of Doriot singularly transcends the history of an individual. For Doriot was never alone or only the head of a small group. Dozens of thousands of Communists and former Communists followed him and his dissidence into the PPF, and even some into the sad adventure of collaboration [with the Germans during the Second World War]."[20] Brunet might have added that eventually dozens of thousands of *anti*-Communists also joined the PPF, a movement that had gone far beyond Communist dissidence by 1937.

Although the majority of the PPF's political constituency in June 1936 came from left-wing, working-class backgrounds and although the PPF's original central committee was dominated by former Communists, the composition of both groups changed considerably over the next two years. At the time the movement was founded, however, its membership presented a considerable contrast to previous French fascist movements, whether one compares it to the membership of Valois's Faisceau in 1925 or to that of La Rocque's CF in 1935. A majority of the PPF's first members came not from conservative and Catholic sections of the middle classes and the peasantry but from Communist and anticlerical sections of Saint-Denis's working class. Some contemporaries thought it appropriate, therefore, that one of the leading intellectual supporters of the PPF, the novelist Pierre Drieu La Rochelle, had written a book in 1934 entitled *Fascist Socialism*. (Had they actually read the book, they might have questioned the socialism of an author who engaged in an extensive critique of Marxism and extolled the virtues of American free enterprise capitalism.)[21]

Consensus historians have viewed Doriot's communism and that of his original followers as partial proof of the PPF's fascism. Having defined fascism from the outset as fundamentally left wing, they have suggested that the only significant fascist movement in France in the 1930s was the PPF, precisely because of its previous Communist connections. However, a close examination of what the PPF's national "socialism" actually amounted to does not support this conclusion.

The PPF differed from the PCF and the SFIO in a number of fundamental ways, particularly in its rejection of egalitarian principles. To be sure, in 1936 the PCF and the SFIO were also opposed to a Marxist revolution (in the immediate future) and also defended class collaboration. Their motives, however, were quite different from those of the PPF. Doriot opposed a Marxist revolution and class conflict *not* because, like the PCF, he worried that social turmoil in France might endanger the Soviet Union by weakening France as a military ally against Germany or because, like the SFIO, he was committed to preserving political democracy against the fascist menace, but because he needed Leroy-Ladurie's financial support to survive politically.

To retain that support, Doriot had to expand his political constituency beyond the proletariat of Saint-Denis, where he was losing ground in 1936, in a way that served the interests of his conservative financial patrons. Thus, unlike

Blum and Thorez in 1936, Doriot sought middle-class and peasant votes not in order to strengthen the left-center in French politics, the Popular Front, but in order to strengthen the right-center, the backlash to the Popular Front. Doriot's criticisms of the sit-down strikes, the PCF, the SFIO, the forty-hour week, the Matignon accords, and the Soviet Union were all designed to serve this purpose.

Whereas the PCF and the SFIO temporarily muted their anticapitalism in order to win the support of French centrists for the Popular Front and the struggle against fascism (with the intention of returning to more Marxist programs under less pressing circumstances), the PPF not only accommodated itself to capitalism but extolled it. The PPF took issue with Marxism itself, attacking its basic principles and seeking its elimination from French politics. Not only did the PPF call upon France to enter an anti-Communist entente with Nazi Germany, fascist Italy, and Franco Spain, but its approach to domestic policy was typical of fascism. So, too, was much of its symbolism and style.

FASCIST SYMBOLISM

Privately, according to his friend Victor Barthélemy, Doriot "did not deny [in 1936] that he wanted to make the PPF into a fascist party."[22] Publicly, however, Doriot refused to call his movement fascist, doubtless for many of the same reasons other French fascists of the era disowned the label. Like the SF and the CF, the PPF insisted that it was not fascist. Robert Loustau wrote in *L'Emancipation Nationale* in 1936, "We are far from being fascists," and Raymon Fernandez added a similar disclaimer in 1937.[23]

In 1936 Doriot told Barthélemy, "I don't know if I am fascist. Fascism can't be copied. I don't want to copy either Hitler or Mussolini. I want to make the PPF a party with a new style, a party like no other in France."[24] After April 1937, however, with the Popular Front no longer in as strong a position to crack down on the extreme right as it had been before, Doriot flaunted the fascism of his movement even as he continued to reject the label.

The PPF borrowed a number of symbols and practices from German and Italian fascism, although it was careful to give them a French twist. Members of the PPF were required to take an oath of loyalty to Doriot. The PPF adopted a fascist salute, one that distinguished itself from the German version by slightly bending the hand and holding it at face level (a nuance that photos of PPF meetings indicate was largely ignored). Brunet has written of the function that this salute performed at PPF meetings: it "implied a collective upsurge, a displacement of energy, an electrifying contact between the Leader and his followers."[25] Doriot replaced the Marxist anthem, the "Internationale," with a new party hymn, "France, Liberate Yourself," with lyrics denouncing class struggle—"shake off the yoke of fratricidal struggles"; "Out with the makers of quarrels"—and music that reminded listeners of the nationalistic "La Marseillaise."

Like NSDAP ceremonies in Germany, PPF ceremonies in France often centered on the party's flag. The PPF flag, replacing the swastika with the Celtic cross against a background of French red, white, and blue, served a liturgical as well as an ideological purpose. Writes Brunet, "With the PPF, the flag, symbol of the party and of the 'Leader,' captured the exaltation which emanated from the crowd of activists. When the 'Leader' gave it to a federal or local party official, it was the sign of a transfer of command, a delegation of authority by the 'Leader,' and whoever brandished it launched a sort of cry toward the sky which projected the instinctive *élan* of the crowd."[26] It was a symbolism, in other words, more conducive to authoritarian leadership and paramilitary obedience than to parliamentary democracy and universal suffrage. Authority descended from the top down, not from the bottom up; the crowd was to be aroused, not convinced.

Like the NSDAP, the PPF paid homage to party martyrs who had lost their lives in the street battles of the movement. By 1938 at least three PPF members had died in this manner, each allegedly shot by a "militant syndicalist." At ceremonies commemorating their sacrifice, Doriot or one of his representatives would call out the name of the fallen hero as if the absent figure were a soldier at roll call, and at each name the crowd would reply, "Present!" The crowd would also sometimes shout, "Attack! Over the graves!" According to Brunet, the roll call sometimes created a "quasi-mystical" effect, arousing in the participants a feeling that was both "funereal and transcendent."[27]

The public meetings of the PPF, however, were not as militarized as some Nazi rallies, at least not those held by Hitler after he came to power. Most members of the audience did not wear uniforms, and they were not formed into soldierly columns. There were attempts to emulate Nazi staging in some respects. At one meeting, Doriot spoke from a huge podium overlooking the audience against a backdrop of a massive party flag that covered the auditorium wall behind him. Below Doriot stood a phalange of security guards in party uniforms. The party uniform differed only slightly from that of other French fascist movements of the period: light blue shirts with armbands, dark blue trousers, brown shoulder belts, and basque berets.

Doriot made no secret of his troops' readiness to use physical force, which was unavoidable, he said, as long as the Communists continued to attack PPF meetings. He was not overstating the attacks. Soon after the PPF was launched, its meetings and personnel were frequently subjected to Communist violence, just as previous French fascist movements had been. Doriot was the object of a half-dozen assassination attempts between 1936 and 1939, including one in which his automobile was machine-gunned.[28] These episodes enhanced Doriot's reputation for personal courage.

By the end of 1936 the PPF had demonstrated a definite fighting capacity of its own, with the result that the PPF's meetings went relatively undisturbed after that. In October Doriot traveled to Montpellier to give a speech. A band of Communists attacked his security guards outside his hotel (one guard fired a pistol), and Doriot was hit by a rock in the clash that followed. The following day L'Humanité ran the headline "THE INDIGNANT POPULATION BESIEGED THE HITLERIANS IN THE HOTEL WHERE THEY TOOK REFUGE."[29] A week later in Nice, several thousand Communists and Socialists tried to prevent Doriot from speaking at a rally, but some seven hundred of Doriot's supporters fought their way through the crowd, wounding scores and killing two. The rally took place as scheduled.

In Nice a few days later, the PPF's Joseph Darnand retaliated by leading an assault on some Communists who were leaving a meeting of their own. In November, the PPF went on the offensive in Paris as well, dispatching "combat groups" to beat up Communists after their gatherings. Barthélemy proudly recalled that "this time it was the Communists who were sent to the hospitals of the city [and who suffered] a much larger number of wounded than we did. A salutary lesson, and one which bore fruit: after that, our rallies took place with practically no attempts [by the Communists] to sabotage them."[30] Thus the PPF was able to respond to Communist attempts at intimidation more successfully than any other French fascist movement of the period, an accomplishment that no doubt enhanced its appeal to conservatives looking for a tougher response to the red threat. The PPF's reputation for action, not just talk, led some of the more militant members of the CF to desert La Rocque for Doriot after 1936.

Like previous French fascist leaders, Doriot emphasized that any violence his troops employed was counterviolence only, that is, right-wing violence in response to left-wing violence. It was to be understood, in other words, that conservatives had nothing to fear from such violence because it was reserved strictly for their adversaries. These assurances may have been unconvincing to some French rightists in 1936: they knew that across the Rhine Hitler had not stopped with crushing the left alone, that he had employed violence against conservative opponents as well. Still, the fact that the PPF had proved more physical than past French fascist movements in responding to assaults from the left was doubtless one reason for the continuing flow of conservative subsidies into the PPF's treasury.

Like the SF and the JP, the supposedly nationalist PPF did not shrink from recruiting some of its shock troops (about a hundred) from unemployed North Africans in Paris. Most of the PPF's streetfighters, however, were native Frenchmen. The leader of the PPF in Marseille, Simon Sabiani, a former mayor of the city known for his ties with local gangsters, launched his toughs against leftists on more than one occasion. In southern France, Joseph Darnand, a former member of the AF and later chief of the collaborationist Milice, organized some five hundred men into a PPF combat force.

Imitating the CF, the PPF created its own brigades of dispos who were prepared to respond to any "convocation" on short notice. Brunet writes, "From the central assembly point, a special car convoy took the brigade 'to the place where its presence was deemed necessary, a place which was not revealed until the moment of departure.'"[31] Some of these dispos were former Communists, but others were former members of the CF, the AF, the JP, the SF, and other right-wing organizations. Doriot was careful to deny, of course, that he had any intention of creating a paramilitary organization, since this would have made the PPF vulnerable to a government ban. According to police, Doriot's dispos were not as disciplined as La Rocque's. Their hatred of the Communists, however, was no less intense.

The PPF also shared the CF's taste for authoritarian leadership. Although Doriot had not been an army officer like Colonel de La Rocque and although the military mystique played a less prominent role in the PPF than it did in the CF/PSF, Doriot perpetuated a French fascist version of the *Führerprinzip.* Doriot was more than a spokesman for the PPF; he was its *chef.* His troops took an oath of allegiance to him with their right arms extended in a fascist salute. Like the CF/PSF in 1936, the PPF formally adopted the statutes of a democratic political party (party leaders were to be elected and its politburo was to be a collegial body), but its spirit was highly undemocratic. Doriot called for strict obedience from the rank and file, emphasizing the importance of party discipline. At the first annual congress of the PPF in 1936, he declared, "Discipline is discipline. You accept it or you don't accept it. If you don't want it, what's the use of bothering others?"[32]

Above the rank and file, however, there were important limitations on Doriot's personal power, especially within the PPF's highest councils because he had to take the wishes of his major financial backers into account and could not afford to alienate his closest collaborators on the PPF's central committee without facing serious repercussions. When he broke with Pierre Pucheu in 1938, he literally paid a heavy price. The exodus of several central committee members and party intellectuals that followed dealt a considerable blow to his prestige. Doriot differed from Hitler and Mussolini, of course, in that he never came to power and therefore was never able to impose the kind of discipline a dictatorship could demand.

Doriot also differed from Hitler and Mussolini as a public speaker, his style being much less theatrical and rabble-rousing than theirs. The notion that all fascist leaders are necessarily bombastic orators is an all-too-comfortable illusion. One can advocate the basic beliefs of fascism in other styles as well, as was demonstrated by Georges Valois, François Coty, and Colonel de La Rocque. By all accounts, Doriot tried not to whip up his audiences with passion but to persuade them with logic, presenting his ideas in a calm, reasoned, yet forceful way. His delivery, although vigorous, tended to remain that of a Marxist dialectician even after he rejected Marxism itself. Sabiani in Marseille, on the other hand, a veteran politician who became vice-president of the PPF in 1938, was a much more exciting speaker than Doriot, less didactic and more colorful.

Some of Doriot's listeners were impressed, however, by the naturalness of his style, by his rejection of the verbal conceits that were in vogue with politicians of the era. Doriot created a mild sensation with some audiences when he removed his coat and spoke in shirtsleeves and suspenders. This gesture, along with his tendency to sweat profusely during his often lengthy speeches, only enhanced his image as a man of the people. For conservative backers of the PPF who wanted "the people" on their side, this image was an asset.

Some who came to hear Doriot speak were especially impressed by his robust physique. At least before he put on weight, he *looked* like a blacksmith's son. The novelist Drieu La Rochelle, who placed a high value on physical virility and who would later define fascism as a "revolution of the body," wrote of Doriot, "We have watched this son of a blacksmith, this former metallurgical worker, in the swell of his shoulders and back, in the bristling of his thick head of hair, in the vast perspiration of his forehead, continue to expand before us the work of fifteen years. Before our eyes, he has taken the destiny of France in his arms and has lifted it high above him like a great herculean brother."[33] Years later, a former PPF militant, Eric Labat, would remember Doriot as "a miracle of physical power in the service of the word." As a public speaker, Labat said, Doriot hammered his arguments in a muscular cadence, to the point that the audience felt that they were witnessing "an enormous and collective rape by a power [which expressed] an elemental virility."[34]

According to some of Doriot's closest associates, however, the leader of the PPF was not simply a primitive brute. Indeed, he was something of an intellectual, although largely self-taught because his formal education had come to an end when he was twelve. Pucheu was impressed by Doriot's cultural depth, that of a serious autodidact, as well as by his political astuteness: "The man impressed us with his youth, his rough and extensive political experience, . . . his familiarity with the working masses, his incontestable physical courage. In all truthfulness, I have never known anyone of our generation so blessed with the qualities of a statesman."[35] Friends described Doriot as a voracious reader and as a man of immense curiosity. Barthélemy, who spent a number of long, "unforgettable" evenings with Doriot discussing various subjects, was amazed by his intellectual breadth:

> [Doriot] had acquired a wide culture, not only politically but in many other domains: artistic, literary, religious. . . .
>
> One day we discussed diverse interpretations of certain passages of The Divine Comedy and also of Leopardi and Carducci. He told me he greatly regretted not having learned Latin, so he could read the ancients in the original. However he knew the translations well, so much so that he had a profound knowledge of the Church fathers and of the great theologians. During one long evening he launched into a captivating discourse on the relative merits, from a philosophical point of view, of Karl Marx and Saint Thomas.[36]

That Doriot's personality was not identical to Hitler's did not prevent him— just as it did not prevent La Rocque, Renaud, Bucard, Taittinger, and other French fascists—from finding much to admire about the revolution Hitler had carried out in Germany. In 1938 Doriot wrote in The Remaking of France,

> The Hitlerian revolution has given back to Germany her authority, her prestige, her liberty, her force. . . . This popular national revolution, like all revolutions, is proud of its work. . . . It practices a foreign policy of prestige. It seems that France has not completely recognized the considerable event that the Nazi arrival in power has been: victory over Bolshevism, a slower but no less decisive victory over the old, traditional forces in Germany, a pacifist victory over [the Treaty of Versailles]. This triple victory has made Hitler and his party the uncontested master of Germany.
>
> For the ordinary German, Hitler is the man who has erased defeat, internal colonization by Bolshevism, and, in part, social injustice. This is enough to ensure the solidity of his regime.[37]

These words were written well after Hitler's crushing of the trade unions in 1933, the Night of the Long Knives in 1934, the murder of dozens of Hitler's opponents, the elimination of political democracy in Germany, the crackdown on all oppositional newspapers in Germany, the establishment of concentration camps for political recalcitrants, the passage of the anti-Semitic Nuremberg laws, the humiliation of Jews in the streets of Germany and Austria, the book burnings, and numerous other onslaughts on German civil liberties. Confronted with these events, Doriot did not allow his knowledge of Thomistic theology to outweigh his hatred of communism and his desire to forge an equally successful political movement in France. He once confided to Barthélemy that he admired both Stalin and Hitler for their will to power and extraordinary ability to manipulate men.[38] Although Doriot opposed Stalin's goals in 1938, he was no enemy of the means Stalin had used in pursuing them.

Doriot's admiration for Hitler did not mean, of course, that he desired a German conquest of France. Like other French fascists of the 1930s, he argued that the best way to protect France from the German threat was to create a French state that was just as strong as the German state. When France declared war on Germany in 1939, Doriot joined the French army in spite of his previous pacifism and was later decorated for bravery for commanding a French military unit that held up the German advance. It was only after the fall of France and the establishment of the Vichy regime in 1940 that Doriot chose to collaborate with the Germans. Between 1936 and 1939, he was as nationalistic about France as Hitler was about Germany.

What made Doriot a fascist both before and after 1940 was not simply the stylistic features of his movement. Far more important was his adoption of fascist ideology. Before turning to the ideology of the PPF, however, it is important to consider who financed, led, and supported the PPF—information that tells much about whose interests that ideology was meant to serve.

FINANCING

As previously mentioned, the PPF was heavily subsidized at the outset by Gabriel Leroy-Ladurie, the general manager of the Banque Worms. Without Leroy-Ladurie's financial support, Doriot might well have sunk into political oblivion after 1936; with his support, he was able to revitalize his career. Leroy-Ladurie was a political reactionary who, according to Dieter Wolf, was "impregnated with the political ideas of the Action Française." In May 1936 Leroy-Ladurie asked Claude Popelin, a former member of the CF, to recommend a political leader who, if sufficiently financed, could strip the Popular Front of some of its mass support. Popelin suggested Doriot.

Although Leroy-Ladurie had originally hoped that Colonel de La Rocque would accomplish this task, the failure of the CF to deter the Popular Front from coming to power in 1936 led him to look for additional help. Wolf recounts that Leroy-Ladurie was much impressed by a police dossier he had obtained that described Doriot as the most serious menace to the republic at the time. At the beginning of June, Leroy-Ladurie met with Doriot to discuss the establishment of a new political party. He subsequently arranged for large subsidies to be delivered to the former Communist.[39]

A few weeks later Leroy-Ladurie's role was taken over by Pierre Pucheu, a former member of the CF who had close ties to Leroy-Ladurie and the Banque Worms. Pucheu transmitted funds to the PPF from various business groups, one of the most important being the Comité des forges [the steel trust]. The Comité des forges was the same association that earlier had helped finance the Faisceau, the Redressement Français, and the CF.

Once again, François de Wendel, the president of the Comité des forges and one of the CF's major financial backers, was involved in the negotiations. In September 1936, after meeting with Doriot for the first time, Wendel had this reaction: "The man is . . . powerful. He is well-balanced and has a great deal of composure. He is obviously disgusted with Communism and knows what is necessary to fight it. But is this sufficient to make him a great leader?" A year later, after dining with Doriot at Pucheu's home, Wendel concluded that ideologically Doriot had joined the troops of the modérés (Wendel's own camp) and that "he was only interesting to the degree that his methods were different from ours."[40]

For the most part, however, Wendel left it up to his subordinate Pucheu to keep tabs on Doriot and to see that the interests of big business were served. Pucheu was employed by the Comptoir sidérurgique de France [Metallurgical bank of France], a branch of the Comité des forges. According to Brunet, Pucheu provided the PPF with abundant and regular subsidies until the autumn of 1938, when he broke with Doriot. The fact that Pucheu's departure reduced the PPF to a perilous financial state indicates the importance of his previous support.

In 1936 Pucheu acted as a financial middleman for heavy industry, dispensing funds to political movements (the PPF was only one of them) that might contribute to the defeat of the Popular Front. The leader of the peasant movement of the extreme right in Alsace, Joseph Bilger, later recalled how Pucheu had promised him an annual subsidy of one million francs if he would enlist his greenshirts in

Doriot's cause.[41] In 1937 Pucheu became a member of the PPF's inner circle, first of its central committee and then of its politburo, a position that enabled him to monitor the political results of big business financing and to ensure that the PPF remained loyal to his patrons' wishes.

As a member of the PPF, Pucheu was certainly no Communist, national or otherwise. Before joining the PPF, he had been the head of the CF's Volontaires Nationaux. On several occasions he had lectured to business audiences, proposing a new economy that would ensure industrial discipline through corporatist hierarchy and, if necessary, the intervention of the police. Later, as the minister of interior for the Vichy regime, he used his position to crush the political left and to expand his business opportunities. The historian Henry Ehrmann writes,

> He frightened his own colleagues in the Ministry by the ruthlessness which he used to introduce a French brand of totalitarianism. In his dealings with the Germans he sought to profit from the connections he had established before the war and counted on the support not only of French heavy industry but also of the German industrialists and generals who, behind the broad back of Goering, had established their niche in the nazi system. General Weygand considered Pucheu one of the "principal agents of Berlin"; he is probably described more correctly as having believed with a perverse fanaticism in the virtues of a Continental "new order" in which the common interests of European business would eventually prevail over the stratagems of political amateurs. He coldly assumed responsibility for the shooting of Communist hostages by the Gestapo. His subsequent attempt to use business contacts in the United States to win the favor of the Allies did not save him from a Free French firing squad.[42]

A friend of Pucheu, also a member of the central committee of the PPF in 1937, was Bertrand de Maud'huy. Like Pucheu, he had belonged to the CF before defecting to the PPF, and like Pucheu he had close ties with several big business groups. (After the Second World War, de Maud'huy continued to serve on the boards of several important industrial and financial associations.)

The Comité des forges was not the only sector of French big business to finance the PPF. Once the movement was launched, money poured in from other sources as well. Brunet points out that when the treasurer of the PPF, Emile Masson, was arrested in 1945 he possessed a list of some 240 donors, business enterprises, and business associations that Pucheu had given Doriot in 1937 or 1938: "The list mentions eight large banks (including the Verne, Rothschild, Dreyfus, Lazard, BNCI banks and the Bank of Indochina), big business associations (such as the Center for Industry and Commerce), establishments in the metallurgical and automobile industries, etc." Brunet concluded that "the major part of the funds received [by the PPF] emanated from *le patronat* [industrial management]."[43] The police reported that Doriot also received important subsidies from such organizations as the Central Committee for Coal Mining, the Circle of French Business Associations, the National Association of Economic Expansion, and the Union of Economic Interests as well as from such individual enterprises as Mazda Lightbulbs and Violet Frères.

Between 1936 and 1937 Doriot also benefited monetarily from his position as mayor of Saint-Denis, receiving kickbacks from local contractors and merchants who did business with the municipal government. Brunet states that "the Leroy and Walter companies, for example, sent regular subsidies to *L'Emancipation* [Doriot's newspaper] and poured large sums (announced as anonymous) into the subscription campaigns launched by the newspaper." According to Emile Masson, the PPF's war chest grew from 4,367,000 francs in 1937 to 5,713,000 francs in 1938 but dropped to 1,593,000 francs in 1939, the last figure coinciding with the PPF's political decline that year.[44] Brunet attributes the large sums given to the PPF before 1938 to fear of the Popular Front. Once the Popular Front was decisively defeated in parliament in 1938, the funding receded. This same pattern is found in the financing of previous French fascist movements, whose rise and fall also correlates with the rise and fall of political threats from the left.

Brunet relates how the regional branches of the PPF also raised money. Simon Sabiani in Marseille had been subsidized since 1934 by "the rich bourgeoisie and the shipowners of the city." Among Sabiani's major financial backers in June 1936 were a shipowner, an admiral, and the head of Marseille's gas and electricity company. In Lyon, the industrial enterprise Rhone-Poulenc paid one of its chemical engineers a large salary to leave his job and work for the PPF. The leader of the PPF in Bordeaux was Jean Le Can, the owner of a large construction company (it had built the new port of Bordeaux). When Le Can finally broke with Doriot in 1938, he estimated that the whole experience had cost him a million francs. Brunet concludes that a major reason for the PPF's political success in these regions was the financial backing it received from local sources; where such backing was absent the PPF failed to implant itself.[45]

The PPF also received secret funds from fascist Italy. One of Doriot's lieutenants, Victor Arrighi, returned from Italy in 1937 with three hundred thousand francs that had been given to him by Count Galeazzo Ciano, Mussolini's foreign minister. Ciano later wrote in his diary that Arrighi had returned later to ask for more money—and for arms as well. Ciano's comment was, "To Doriot, we will give money, not arms."[46] Brunet states that from 1936 onward the PPF received regular payments from Italy. There is no evidence, however, that Doriot was subsidized by Nazi Germany before 1940, in spite of numerous Communist accusations to that effect. Morever, even the funding from Italy was quite small compared to that from French sources.

The rise of the PPF after 1936 was primarily fueled by the conservative back-lash to the Popular Front in France rather than by fascist governments abroad. In its financial dynamics as well as in its social, economic, and cultural dynamics the PPF was an overwhelmingly French affair. It was only after France's military defeat in 1940 that Doriot, like La Rocque, collaborated with the Germans.

In 1936 the social and economic ideology of the PPF, its socialist rhetoric to the contrary notwithstanding, complemented the material interests of its major financial backers. Some of the original members of the PPF, however, seem to have taken the party's purported socialism more seriously. In 1937 one PPF intellectual, Pierre Andreu, quit the movement when an article he had written in the party's newspaper criticizing the antisocial behavior of a Clichy business-man was revised by an editor—no doubt, according to Brunet, because the busi-nessman was a generous donor to the party.[47]

The results of such generosity were physically evident. Doriot was able to move into better offices, to establish several local headquarters in the provinces, and to mount a number of speaking tours throughout France (one weekend in 1938 he traveled by airplane to speaking engagements at Toulon, Marseille, and Lyons). Another sign of financial prosperity was the PPF's purchase of several newspapers, including *La Liberté*, a journal whose circulation rose to ninety thousand in 1937.[48] In 1938, Fernand Grenier, Doriot's old Communist foe in Saint-Denis and a parliamentary deputy, wrote a letter to the minister of inte-rior. After lodging a protest against acts of violence committed by Doriot's gangs against Communists in Saint-Denis, Grenier pointed out that the PPF "disposed of resources out of proportion to its number of followers." Millions, he said, had been spent to cover the deficits of the PPF's daily and weekly newspapers and the costs of several regional headquarters.[49]

According to Fernand Légey, a disaffected member of the PPF who had served on the party's federal committee as a delegate from Algeria, large sums of money had been donated to the PPF by conservative businessmen and landowners who felt that Doriot had a better chance of attracting the lower classes to fascism than did Colonel de La Rocque. These financial backers believed that La Rocque had "neither the audacity nor the cleverness of a Hitler or a Mussolini," while Doriot knew how to talk to the masses in their own language. With the election of the Popular Front and the sit-down strikes that followed, "the upper bour-geoisie finally understood that they could no longer ignore the anger of the people." Some of these bourgeois chose to support a man who would "install a dictatorship in France by making use of the working masses and by making fools of them." They hoped that the PPF would both undermine working-class solidarity and become a paramilitary obstacle to the Communists by combining Communist techniques for mobilizing the masses with shock troops composed in part of former CF members. The PPF was *populaire* in name only, since it was "in sum the exact program of the monarchists of the Action Française" and based on the "same system of corporatism that is dear to Maurras." Consequently, Légey noted, it was not surprising that an editorial of December 1936 in the AF's newspaper had expressed sympathy for the PPF.[50]

Légey recalled that when he was member of the PPF it never lacked money, that its headquarters and offices were handsomely furnished, that its leaders traveled first class wherever they went, and that there was no way that the membership subscriptions and the sale of party insignias could cover a budget that ran into millions. The movement was subsidized, he said, by "big industrialists, big businessmen, [and] bankers, that is, by capitalism and management." In Algeria the propaganda budget of the PPF was paid for by "the biggest industrialists, *colons*, and businessmen." (9, 10).

Légey also noted that because members of the central committee of the PPF were not elected and because their meetings were not open to the party's rank and file, deals with the *patronat* were easily made. Légey remembered receiving a letter from Victor Arrighi of the PPF central committee instructing him to give certain sympathetic industrialists the names of PPF workers whom they could hire when vacancies occurred. These workers were to be told to support the CGT and its local unions on wage demands and other grievances, but to oppose any calls for strikes. "In return," Arrighi had written, "the owners to whom you have rendered service will thank you with a financial contribution" (10).

Some owners, Légey wrote, sent their workers free copies of the PPF's newspaper, *L'Emancipation Nationale*. Légey found it ironic that a party that was "subsidized by industrialists, businessmen and managers" would "pretend to struggle against the social conservatism of these people." He concluded that only two hypotheses could explain this contradiction: either the PPF was betraying its bourgeois financial backers on behalf of the working class or it was betraying the working class on behalf of its bourgeois financial backers. Légey believed that it was the workers who were being victimized (11).

Although Légey acknowledged that Paul Marion, one of Doriot's closest lieutenants, had declared that the PPF would ally itself with the devil and his grandmother to defeat communism (the implication being that one could become allied with rightists and still remain a non-Communist leftist), Légey pointed out that such a compromise was not necessary for a large number of party activists, "for example, the royalists," since they agreed with the political right in the first place. The same was true of "the big colonial bourgeoisie," who approved of Doriot's plan for an electoral system in Algeria that would give seven hundred thousand Europeans more voting power than six million Arabs. In taking this position, Légey wrote, "the big colonial bourgeoisie, sister to the continental, has pushed its selfishness to the limit against the indigenous population" (14).

Police reports of the period lend credence to Légey's account. One stated that at a PPF rally in 1937 Doriot insisted that "workers and bosses must cooperate without . . . having to resort to strikes." Another speaker at the same rally, having declared that the principal objective of the PPF was to combat communism by all possible means, praised Doriot for admitting that he had made a serious error as a young man in joining the Communist party. Conveniently ignoring the big business financing of the PPF, the speaker went on to describe the PPF as an enemy of the trusts:

> In 1936 Doriot totally abandoned the Communist Party and created the Parti Populaire Français with the aim of grouping around him the middle classes, [people] who are pressed on one side by the large trusts and on the other side by the Communists. The politics of the Soviets cannot be applied in France where there is a large number of small merchants, small artisans, small investors, and workers. The situation of the Russian worker has perhaps been ameliorated, but it is far from being as good as that of the French worker. Bosses there will always be, and they are indispensable.
>
> We want neither a dictatorship of the right nor a dictatorship of the left, but the middle class Frenchman who represents two-thirds of the population must live.[51]

Like the PSF, the PPF presented itself as taking the middle of the road between two extremes; it too was allegedly *modéré*. At an earlier rally, another PPF speaker sounded the same theme: "Between the two hundred families which represent capital and the two hundred families which represent Stalin, there are other people in France. We are ready to welcome [all those opposed to communism], whether they be Croix de Feu or Radical Socialists or even disillusioned Socialists."[52]

Thus it was possible at PPF meetings to have former members of the CF, the AF, and other right-wing organizations speak alongside former Communists. At one party gathering in the ninth district of Paris in April 1937, two of the speakers were Joseph Delest and Georges Lebecq. Delest was one of the editors of the AF's newspaper and a member of its veterans' organization, and Lebecq—the same Lebecq who had helped organize the demonstrations of February 6, 1934, against the "socialist menace"—was the head of France's largest conservative veterans' association, the UNC.[53] The nature of the PPF's socioeconomic program may help explain why men like Delest and Lebecq would rub elbows with Doriot's supposedly Communist supporters.

When Doriot launched the PPF in June 1936, he fashioned a movement that reflected the special interests of his financial backers on the strike issue. Otherwise they would not have supported him. They also wished to divide the labor movement and create an alternative to the Popular Front that was less threatening. These backers hoped that Doriot would mobilize sections of the lower and middle classes against the Popular Front. More than money, however, was necessary to make such a movement succeed; Doriot had to prove that he could win popular support outside of Saint-Denis. Because the socioeconomic program he proposed in June 1936 was no longer Marxist (and by 1937 not even left-centrist) and because many of his original proletarian supporters eventually abandoned him, he ultimately turned to less blue-collar constituencies for the bulk of his support.

The original members of the PPF politburo no doubt understood this imperative quite well. Precisely because many of them were ex-Communists, that is, men habituated to viewing politics in class terms, they focused their propaganda efforts on increasing the social bases of their movement—only this time aiming less at the lower classes, at industrial and farm workers, than at the lower middle and middle classes, at small and intermediate businessmen, farm owners, white-collar workers, engineers, and so on. To be sure, the PPF tried not to alienate the proletariat entirely, especially in Saint-Denis, claiming that the PPF was neither right nor left and that it was still socialist in spirit. But as the specific social and economic programs put forth by its leaders indicate, the PPF was intent on broadening its class support even if this meant sacrificing much of its initial blue-collar following (which was rapidly eroding anyway). By 1937 the original politburo and central committee of the PPF as well as its propaganda staff were joined by men from much more conservative backgrounds, extreme rightists who welcomed the new direction Doriot had taken.

LEADERSHIP

In June 1936, when the PPF was founded, ex-Communists were prominent in both its leadership and rank and file. Seven of the eight members of the party's original politburo, its highest governing council, were former Communists. Only Yves Paringaux, a former member of the CF and a spokesman for Pucheu and other CF dissidents who joined the PPF, came from the extreme right. The seven ex-Communist members of the politburo were Doriot, Henri Barbé, Victor Arrighi, Paul Marion, Jules Teulade, Alexandre Abremski, and Marcel Marchal. Most of these men were longtime associates of Doriot in Saint-Denis. All seven, like Doriot, had severed their ties with the PCF at least two years before they joined the PPF.

Henri Barbé had once been the head of the Jeunesses communistes, having succeeded Doriot in that position. Between 1929 and 1934 Barbé had specialized in writing antimilitary propaganda for the PCF, and in 1933 he had spent eight months in prison for refusing to serve in the French army. In 1934 he had sided with Doriot against Thorez and had been expelled from the PCF. When Doriot was reelected mayor of Saint-Denis in 1936, Barbé became the assistant mayor.[54]

Victor Arrighi had also been a Communist. The former manager of a Communist bank, Banque ouvrière et paysanne (Workers' and peasants' bank), he had quit the PCF in 1930 to join the Radical-Socialist party, which he left in 1936 to join the PPF. Described by one contemporary as an "authentic scoundrel," he was known for his taste for "the agreeable life without material worries" and his habit of "never losing sight of the financial side of things."[55]

Paul Marion had joined the PCF in 1922 at the age of twenty-three, had become a writer for L'Humanité, had taught at Marxist propaganda schools in Bobigny and Paris in 1924 and 1925, and had been elected to the central committee of the PCF in 1926. In 1927 he had traveled to Moscow to work for the Comintern, and in 1928 had attended the World Congress of the Communist International. In 1929 he had resigned from the PCF and joined the Union Socialiste et Républicaine, a left-center party. When he joined the PPF in 1936 he was the editor of the newspaper Le Quotidien, which had once been the official organ of the Cartel des Gauches. He also wrote for La République, an anti-Marxist, pacifist journal. He was a friend of Claude Popelin, the journalist who recommended Doriot to Leroy-Ladurie. It was Marion who personally introduced Leroy-Ladurie to Doriot, paving the way for their collaboration.

Less influential members of the PPF political bureau were Jules Teulade, Alexandre Abremski, and Marcel Marshal. Teulade was a former construction worker who had resigned from the PCF in 1929, had rejoined in 1932, and had resigned again in 1934. On one occasion, Teulade had struck the brother of a top PCF official during an altercation in the offices of L'Humanité. Abremski was a former Communist who had once worked in a gas factory in Clichy. Elected to the municipal council of Saint-Denis in 1935 on the Communist ticket, he had followed Doriot into the PPF in 1936. Marchal was another Saint-Denis municipal councilman. A Communist activist since 1929, he had headed the Saint-Denis section of the Jeunesses communistes and had presided over the ninth district of the Paris region of the Communist party. In 1934 he had quit the PCF in support of Doriot, and in 1936 he joined the PPF.[56]

Between 1937 and 1938 the PPF's politburo was enlarged to include several authoritarian conservatives, the most important being Pierre Pucheu. Being a major source of campaign funds, Pucheu no doubt exerted a weight in the group's deliberations that few of the ex-Communists could match. In 1937 Jean Le Can, the Bordeaux construction millionaire, also joined the PPF's politburo, along with Claude Popelin and Robert Loustau. Loustau, who would draft the socio-economic program of the movement, was a Catholic mining engineer and a close friend of Pucheu. He and Pucheu had been leading figures in the CF's Volontaires Nationaux before joining the PPF.[57] By 1938 the politburo had added a number of other staunch anti-Communists as well: Pierre Drieu La Rochelle, Bertrand de Jouvenel, Raymon Fernandez, Claude Jeantet, Emile Masson, Maurice Touze, and Simon Sabiani.

Beneath the politburo was the central committee, which was composed mainly of local party leaders, journalists, and intellectuals. It met less frequently than the politburo and had less say in the major decisions of the party. In 1937 the membership of the central committee, like that of the politburo, was expanded to make room for more conservatives. Among the newcomers were Jacques Martin-Sané, a former member of the JP, and Jean-Marie Aimot, a former member of the Francistes. On social and economic issues, they agreed with one of the original members of the central committee, Bertrand de Maud'huy, who, as previously mentioned, was a former member of the CF and friend of Pucheu who sat on the board of directors of several industrial and financial associations. Also added to the central committee in 1937, perhaps to help perpetuate the fiction that the PPF was neither left nor right, were three ex-Communists: Georges Deshaires, Marius Paquereaux, and Maurice Lebrun. More likely than not, the motives of these three were more mercenary than principled. Even if they retained some of their Communist convictions, it is difficult to believe that their views would have counted more than those of de Maud'huy and other rightists on the central committee.

By 1938 the PPF's politburo was no longer dominated by former Communists. Several of its recent members came from right-wing backgrounds. Pucheu,

Popelin, and Loustau were all former members of the CF. Claude Jeantet had been the leader of the Students of the Action Française and had later written articles for such right-wing journals as *Candide, Je suis Partout,* and *Le Petit Journal.* Le Can, one of the wealthiest members of the politburo, obviously had no desire to see his Bordeaux construction company submerged by Marxism. Loustau's engineering background led him to prefer technocratic leadership to collective bargaining, as did a score of other engineers, managers, and white-collar workers who poured into the PPF after 1937. One of the original members of the politburo, Yves Paringaux, was an engineer.

Three well-known intellectuals who joined the politburo in 1938 were Bertrand de Jouvenel, Pierre Drieu La Rochelle, and Raymon Fernandez. De Jouvenel was one of France's leading political scientists, and Drieu La Rochelle and Fernandez were novelists. All three were political journalists as well. Passionately anti-Marxist and extreme right in their socioeconomic views, they touted a "third way" between capitalism and communism that, they claimed, would avoid the errors of both. They wrote regular columns for *L'Emancipation Nationale,* providing its readers with intellectually sophisticated arguments on behalf of fascism.

Four other prominent intellectuals who supported the PPF were Alfred Fabre-Luce, a political journalist, Abel Bonnard, a man of letters elected to the Académie Française in 1932, Alexis Carrel, a Nobel Prize winner, and Maurice Duverger, who twenty years later would teach at the prestigious Ecole des Sciences Politiques in Paris. Long after the PPF was defeated as a political organization, the ideas that these writers propagated would continue to surface in French intellectual circles.[58]

If the official socioeconomic ideology of the PPF in 1938 is any indication, the views of men like Pucheu, Le Can, Loustau, Popelin, de Jouvenel, Drieu La Rochelle, and Fernandez negated any lingering attachment to communism within the politburo, so much so that the *Program of the French Popular Party,* published that year by the ex-Communist Paul Marion, not only defended capitalism but also preached a brand of corporatism compatible with that espoused by the CF, the Francistes, and other fascist movements of the era. This was also true of the PPF's original program, summarized by Loustau in his book *Social Justice* (1936).[59] The fact that Loustau had been a member of the CF before joining the PPF makes this program (one supported at the time by a politburo composed largely of ex-Communists) less surprising.

One of the most important members of the PPF politburo in 1938, as well as the party's new vice-president that year, was Simon Sabiani. Sabiani had joined the Communist party following the First World War but had left it in 1922. In 1932, as a member of the non-Communist left in Marseille, he had been elected to the Chamber of Deputies. Before joining the PPF in 1936, he had been the mayor of Marseille, the head of his own Socialist Action party, and, between 1935 and 1936, a member of the Antibolshevik Front. As late as 1936, Sabiani posed as a defender of the working classes, although, as Dieter Wolf has pointed out, his political career after 1934 was largely financed by "the rich bourgeoisie and shipowners" of Marseille.

Sabiani had a reputation for surrounding himself during his electoral campaigns with gangs of toughs, some of whom were criminals from Marseille's underworld, men willing to respond to Communist violence with violence of their own. According to Wolf, "Sabiani, of Corsican origin, [was] one of the most disturbing and discussed figures in Doriot's entourage. For his adversaries, he [was] the chief of a band of gangsters or assassins who wanted to make Marseille a little Chicago."[60]

In 1936 there were striking parallels between Sabiani's situation in Marseille and Doriot's in Saint-Denis. Both men were former Communists who had previously won elections with the help of working-class votes but who were seriously threatened by the electoral alliance of the Communists and the Socialists after 1935. Rejected by the Communists and the Socialists and faced with declining support from blue-collar workers, both Sabiani and Doriot realized that they had to increase their appeal to the middle classes and refashion their ideology accordingly if they were to restore their political fortunes.

As the historian Paul Jankowski has shown, it was precisely because Sabiani was losing support on the extreme left in Marseille in 1936 that he turned to the PPF as an alternative. In the municipal elections of 1935, his fears had proven justified. In the first round of voting in the working-class sections of his electoral district, his Communist rival had won 32 percent of the vote to his 19 percent. Thus, writes Jankowski, Sabiani was faced with "a class-based Communist conquest of his legislative constituencies."

The elections of May 1936 marked a major turning point for Sabiani just as they did for Doriot. Although in 1935 Sabiani had described himself as being bound to the culture of socialism and had continued to criticize the political right, in 1936 he expended most of his polemical ammunition against the political left, accusing the Communists of subversion and the Socialists of fraud. When he attempted to hold a political rally in Marseille, local Communists tried to disrupt the meeting. Sabiani's supporters responded with blows of their own. In the days that followed, there were other clashes. Jankowski writes, "The campaign was rough in Sabiani's constituency, a dead heat with at least one murder a side by the Socialists and the Communists and one attempted murder by the *Sabianistes.*"[61]

The results of the elections of 1936 were a disappointment for Sabiani. His vote in working-class neighborhoods had declined even further, which was only partially compensated for by his stronger showing in some middle-class neighborhoods. He lost the election and with it his seat in the Chamber of Deputies. Jankowski describes Sabiani's reaction: "From now on the Communist Party was the enemy. It was 'bolshevism invading,' 'Muscovite enslavement,' an occult power working on the Socialists, Léon Blum, and all of France. Above all it was foreign. . . . The danger was not the worker on strike nor even the ideology of Marxism but the cosmopolitan mercenaries in the pay of 'the Russia of the Comintern.' . . . Communism became an obsession" (53).

In the meantime, the sit-down strikes of June 1936 had sparked a conservative backlash in Marseille. One of the major beneficiaries was the CF, whose support among the middle classes in Marseille began to rise sharply. Sabiani considered allying his party with La Rocque's, but, according to Jankowski, he feared that his smaller organization would be engulfed by it. By joining the PPF, Sabiani saw a chance to steal some of the CF's thunder, increase his appeal to middle-class voters, and play a major role in a well-financed national movement (a role not guaranteed by the CF, whose local leadership was already in place) (46–52). Joining the PPF rather than the CF also enabled Sabiani to retain some of his original blue-collar support, since the CF had not been successful in the working-class neighborhoods of Marseille while the PPF still had a reputation in 1936 of being a proletarian party.

In fact, the differences between the PPF's socioeconomic goals and those of the CF were minimal, which helps explain the ease with which some CF militants in Marseille abandoned La Rocque's movement for Doriot's following the elections of 1936. As one local police report observed, "a fairly large number from the [CF] have decided to leave it for the [PPF], which is more audacious and above all more combative" (57). Under Sabiani, the PPF in Marseille became quite combative indeed, one of the trademarks of Sabianisme being the willingness it displayed in engaging in physical encounters with its political opponents, a trait it shared with Doriotisme as well.

According to Jankowski, the main reason Sabiani converted to the PPF in July 1936 was simple: "*Sabianisme* was facing extinction" (54). Squeezed by the Popular Front on his left and by the CF on his right, Sabiani was in danger of losing his political base altogether. Doriot saved his political neck. Writes Jankowski, "For Sabiani and his diehards, the creation of the PPF could not have come at a more propitious moment. Doriot's new party delivered them from oblivion: it promised to breathe new life into a moribund organization, to give it national and ideological identity and to recruit all sorts of new members, set against Communism and conservatism alike" (57).

Ideologically, both Sabiani's Socialist Action party and Doriot's PPF were far more set against communism and socialism in 1936 than against conservatism. As Wolf has observed, Sabiani's organization had already created an ideological identity quite similar to that of the PPF before the PPF was founded, an identity that was socialist in name only. One of the consequences of this new identity was that in the elections of May 1936, both Sabiani and Doriot lost votes to the Communists and Socialists while gaining votes from conservatives and moderates.

In July 1936, one month after the PPF was founded in Paris, the PPF was launched in Marseille. Sabiani was one of the main organizers of the inaugural rally at which Doriot spoke. Jankowski relates how Doriot, before an audience of fifteen thousand, "attacked Stalin, called for peace, trivialized the distinction between right and left, spoke of a mystical faith in nationhood, [and] pledged himself to fight the Communists with their own weapons." Following this speech, Sabiani took a public oath of loyalty to Doriot. Thanks partly to Sabiani's organizational talents, the PPF grew rapidly in the region, soon stretching from Marseille and Toulon to Cannes and Nice. Algeria, which had strong commercial ties with the region, also became a PPF stronghold. In 1938, as a reward for his recruiting successes in southeastern France, Sabiani was made vice-president of the PPF.

As for local leaders of the PPF throughout the rest of France, in 1936 a minority came from the political left or left-center. The 740 delegates who attended the first national congress of the PPF in November 1936 were asked to fill out questionnaires dealing with their past political affiliations and social origins. Of the 625 who replied, 207 came from parties of the left (133 had been Communists, 54 Socialists, 12 Radical-Socialists, 6 Neo-Socialists, and 2 Unity Proletarians), and 176 came from parties of the right (91 had been CF, 32 AF, 23 politically conservative Christians, 10 SF, 8 JP, 7 Francistes, and 5 Democratic Alliance). Further, 242 delegates, the largest block, specified no previous political commitment at all.[62] Thus, roughly 33 percent came from the left and left-center, 28 percent from the right and right-center, and 39 percent from no previously declared political allegiance. Of the total number of respondents, less than 8 percent came from Communist backgrounds. If any of them clung to their former social and economic ideals, they must have been quite disappointed by the party's official program of 1936, which repeatedly contradicted those ideals.

MEMBERSHIP

After 1936 the rank and file membership of the PPF in France and Algeria came increasingly from middle-class backgrounds, as did the local cadres of the movement and their leaders on the politburo and the central committee. Working-class support declined as the socioeconomic conservatism of the PPF rose. Not only did blue-collar workers throughout France overwhelmingly reject the PPF during its existence, most supporting the Popular Front instead, but even within Saint-Denis, Doriot's personal stronghold, the majority of working-class voters deserted the PPF in the elections of 1937. Although many of Doriot's original followers were employed in the large factories of Saint-Denis and were therefore literally proletarian, by 1937 most of them had returned to supporting the PCF.

One indication of this shift is the declining percentage of blue-collar workers who attended the annual national congresses of the party. Responding to a questionnaire circulated at the first party congress in November 1936, 49 percent of the delegates listed themselves as workers, 22 percent as white-collar workers, and 21 percent as engineers, businessmen, or members of the liberal professions. At the PPF's second party congress in 1937, only 20 percent of the 736 delegates listed themselves as workers (metalworkers or industrial workers), while 35 percent classified themselves as shopkeepers or businessmen, 20 percent as white-collar workers, 13 percent as members of the liberal professions (journalists, lawyers, doctors, teachers), and 8 percent as farmers or landowners. In 1938, 58 percent of the delegates came from the middle classes (engineers, lawyers, doctors, teachers, businessmen, white-collar workers, and civil servants). As Jean-Paul Brunet has observed, a definite bourgeoisification of the party cadres took place between 1936 and 1938.[63]

The rank and file of the PPF also grew more bourgeoisified after 1936, especially outside of Saint-Denis. Zeev Sternhell has estimated that, nationwide, former Communists "never made up more than ten per cent of [the PPF's] simple rank and file," even when former Communists comprised 90 percent of the party's politburo. Brunet reports Doriot's claim that as late as March 1938, in Saint-Denis at least, most members of the PPF were proletarians. According to Doriot, of the PPF's 2,973 members in the municipality, 70 percent were blue-collar workers, 1 percent white-collar workers, 13 percent shopkeepers and artisans, and 3 percent entrepreneurs or members of the liberal professions. In these percentages, writes Brunet, "the PPF thus came rather close to the sociological profile of the great workers' city."[64] However, even if Doriot's statistics were accurate, they applied to only a minority of the working class in the district because most Saint-Denis workers voted for the Communist or Socialist parties after 1936, not for the PPF.

Not only was Doriot crushed by his Communist opponent, Fernand Grenier, in the 1937 elections, but also, if one takes into account that of the 37.9 percent of the vote that Doriot received not all of it came from blue-collar workers, his lack of proletarian support becomes even greater. Doriot had appealed to right-wing voters during the 1937 election (which is one reason La Rocque's PSF had backed him at the time), most of them probably being more middle class than proletarian, although their numbers may have been small. What does seem clear is that the Communist Grenier's 54 percent of the vote was more purely proletarian than Doriot's (it being unlikely that many middle-class voters would have voted for a Communist) and, therefore, that most of those who deserted Doriot for Grenier in 1937 were workers.

In 1937 the PPF had had little success in the factories of France, including those of Saint-Denis, when it tried to establish political sections to compete with those of the Communists and the Socialists. Accused by the CGT of trying to establish management-dominated unions, the PPF encountered considerable hostility. Dieter Wolf comments,

> Concerning the evolution and number of these factory sections, there is practically nothing to be found in the [PPF] press, which only rarely provides any precise information on the subject.
>
> This reserve may be attributed to the fact that PPF groups formed a small minority in the majority of factories and had to avoid, for tactical reasons, open conflicts with unions that were much more influential and infiltrated by the PCF. They had to limit themselves to a sort of clandestine activity. Furthermore, the factory sections of the PPF had, from 1937 onward, the reputation of working for management and of being camouflaged "yellow" unions. A report that the head of the PPF received in October 1938 from a leader of the Renault Federation, which was a typical organization of the party, spoke only of modest partial successes and contained this characteristic phrase: "We have achieved a unanimous opposition against us." Opposed to 400 members of the PPF, of whom 100 had proved themselves to be very active, were 7,500 members of Communist cells.[65]

Like previous fascist movements in Europe, the PPF failed to win over to its cause more than a small fragment of the country's proletariat. As Kevin Passmore writes, "Doriot's support from ex-Communists has been exaggerated by historians. Local research in Lyon, Marseille, and the Alpes Maritimes shows the failure of the party to bite into Communist support and its reliance on petty-bourgeois and bourgeois individualists, often previously sympathetic to conservative movements."[66] Jean-Paul Brunet states that of the 12,500 members of the PPF in the Marseille region in March 1937 some 78 percent were workers "in the largest sense" of the term.[67] The trouble with "the largest sense" of the term is that it encompasses such nonproletarian types as white-collar workers, self-employed artisans, and municipal employees, that is, persons whose political views usually differed from those of industrial workers. Moreover, Paul Jankowski's meticulous study of the PPF in Marseille repeatedly contradicts the notion that the PPF was largely a movement of ex-Communists dedicated to a revision of Marxism. Not only had Sabiani lost most of his former Communist followers by 1936 but many lower-class individuals who did continue to support him after that date seem to have done so more for employment than for ideological reasons.

Jankowski estimates that there were between 4,000 and 7,000 PPF party members in the city of Marseille between 1936 and 1939. He analyzes a sample of 426 of these from fragmentary records that survived the war: "408 can be identified and traced, 173 of them from post-Liberation trials or investigations, and 95 of these in turn give some motives for their membership: a partial sample, but a sample nonetheless."[68] Jankowski found that only 6 percent of this sample were workers, while 7 percent were artisans ("the most 'proletarian' element of the middle class"), 9 percent shopkeepers, 11 percent office workers, 20 percent civil servants, and nearly 25 percent "merchants, managers, industrialists, journalists, and lawyers and doctors and other members of the liberal professions." The last figure, if representative, was a sharp rise from the less than 6 percent of bourgeois who supported Sabiani before 1936, a shift that, according to Jankowski, raised the PPF's "social center of gravity" from the lower classes to the middle classes. Sabiani himself claimed that 78 percent of his followers in the spring of 1937 were workers. According to Jankowski, this was "sheer fantasy": "Only 28 of the 426 members of the sample are workers, skilled or unskilled—a steep drop from the level of the earlier *Sabianiste* organizations" (60, 63–65).

Jankowski asks not only who joined the PPF in Marseille, but also why they joined. Regarding the working-class supporters of the PPF in Marseille, he concludes,

None of them joined to expurgate and rejuvenate the France of PPF rhetoric. At least four joined looking for work: an occasional rag collector, 32 years old and unemployed—"I did it because I had been promised work"—who eventually left the party after finding work independently as a dishwasher; a mechanic, also 32, on the strength of a friend's word that he might find work through the party; a 28-year-old illiterate Algerian day-laborer, who had somehow met Sabiani and through him found a job at the *Raffineries de Sucre Saint-Louis*. . . . And the political 'ideas' of a 25-year-old jack-of-all-trades, sometime plumber and stonemason, were not ideas at all: "I joined the PPF in 1936. Before, I had belonged to the Communist party, but I had changed [my] ideas because I found myself at one point without work and the CGT took no interest in my situation. I [therefore] joined the PPF." They are the only skilled or unskilled workers to reveal their motives, and conviction is not one of them. . . .

The other members of the "lower class"—domestic and service personnel, . . . sailors and dockers . . . —tell the same story. . . . Some joined out of personal gratitude, like the 50-year-old Corsican sailor of the Boulevard de Paris— "I paid all [my] dues in order to please Sabiani who had rendered numerous services to my family". Some joined in the hope of finding a job, like the unemployed seamstress . . . who left in disappointment 18 months later, [or] the illiterate Corsican sailor . . . who . . . hoped for a job in municipal tax collection.

Sabiani, in short, had lost many of his lower class supporters and those who remained, or those who joined, had little interest in the ideals of the PPF. They were clients as before. (61–62)

One wonders whether similar considerations may have motivated many of Doriot's working-class supporters in Saint-Denis, given that Doriot, like Sabiani, had also been the mayor of a municipality and may also have benefited politically from the gratitude of those who had received his patronage.

Jankowski's study of the PPF in Marseille suggests that many of Sabiani's lower-middle-class supporters (small merchants, office workers, lower civil servants, and so forth) were also more concerned with jobs and favors than with ideology, as in the cases of a Corsican who was "bound by friendship forever to Simon Sabiani" because he had once found him a job in customs and of a drysalter who was persuaded that a shipping company would buy his insecticide if he joined the party (62). Civil servants made up one-fifth of the PPF sample, which, writes Jankowski, corresponded to the fact that "about one-sixth of all municipal employees in Marseille—1,280 out of 7,603—belonged to the PPF in 1938." Several of the white-collar workers in Jankowski's sample had been the recipients of patronage: "I joined the PPF in 1937 out of gratitude for its leader Simon Sabiani who had found a job for me as a fireman in the city of Marseille"; "Sabiani had got me in as a tax-collector in 1928, and in gratitude I followed his politics"; "I was taken on at the Mairie in 1934, and to be agreeable to Sabiani I joined the PPF"; "I joined the PPF because it was almost obligatory for municipal employees to join the party which Sabiani led" (63, 62).

In contrast to such favor seekers were the wealthy, educated members of the PPF, its upper-bourgeois members, people who were not dependent on Sabiani for their livelihoods. According to Jankowski, "They joined the PPF for a different motive: they joined out of conviction." These were merchants, managers, industrialists, doctors, lawyers, and journalists who totaled nearly 25 percent of Jankowski's sample. Although their convictions were no doubt also affected by economic interests—in their case, a desire to protect their wealth and status from encroachments by the Socialists—they were more ideological in recognizing the need for a broader view of politics if those interests were to be safeguarded. As Jankowski points out, "For a securities broker '[the PPF] seemed to represent the party of order,' and employers were undoubtedly impressed by the party's anti-Communism, like the technical director of a factory—'I joined the PPF in 1937 because of its social doctrine'" (95).

Jankowski concludes that the PPF in Marseille soon evolved into a two-tiered party, with "a new, ideological, largely *bourgeois* layer grafted onto an older, clientelistic, largely popular base." Where the bourgeois layer was concerned, the PPF "hoped to exploit the charged climate of the slump and the Popular Front and rally all who were frightened by the times" (66, 70).

Once the Popular Front was defeated, bourgeois panic declined. By 1939 most of the PPF's original middle-class supporters in Marseille had deserted the movement because they no longer needed it. Jankowski comments,

> In the summer of 1936 [the PPF] could exploit real fears in Marseille, the fears reported by police as late as March 1937: "political anxiety, notably among the middle classes and the right wing parties, [is growing]. They say in these milieux that our country is moving with big strides towards bloody revolution". But by 1938 and 1939 most voters probably thought that the PPF was tilting at windmills. The decline of the Communist vote in the cantonal elections, the formation of the Daladier government in April 1938 and its final break with the Popular Front later that year, the failure of the general strike of November 1938, the drop in May Day attendance, from 25,000 in 1937 to 13,000 in 1938 to 4,000 in 1939—the threat of upheaval, real or imagined, lost its hold. (62)

On the other hand, many of Sabiani's lower-class clients remained loyal to the end, leaving him with a rump membership of 3,000, about half of the PPF's local following in its heyday. Presumably, the half that departed was more middle class.

Still, between 1936 and 1938 the PPF—in Marseille, Saint-Denis, Algeria, and elsewhere—had managed to extend its support beyond the lower classes to sections of the lower, middle, and upper bourgeoisie.

Regionally, the PPF made its greatest inroads where anti–Popular Front sentiment was strongest, where local business financing was most forthcoming, and, in the case of Algeria, where ethnic divisions served to aggravate the backlash to the Popular Front. Indeed, as Wolf has written, "Algeria and the Mediterranean coast became, along with the Paris region, [the PPF's] principal zones of influence."[69] Algeria, fertile ground for French fascism in the past, was also responsive to the PPF in 1936. In 1936, many French *colons*, fearing that the Popular Front meant to extend political rights to Arabs, welcomed the "patriotism" of the PPF with open arms. Since many of these *colons* were businessmen or large landowners, they also found the PPF's economic program attractive. Doriot, a critic of French colonialism during his Communist years and a former supporter of the Riff rebellion, now defended French colonial rule and opposed the Arab cause.

Overall, in France and Algeria combined the PPF's recruitment efforts were much less successful than those of its major competitor, the CF/PSF. Wolf estimates that in 1937 the PPF's "zone of influence" was 300,000, with no more than 50,000–60,000 active members. Philippe Burrin speaks of 300,000 sympathizers and 60,000 activists in 1937. Jean-Paul Brunet estimates that in early 1938, when the PPF was at its peak, it had as many as 100,000 active members.[70] Thus, even at its height, PPF membership was no more than a seventh to a tenth of the size of the CF/PSF's, which had between 700,000 and 1.2 million party members in 1938 (although some of these may also have been less active than others). If one includes PPF sympathizers in the count, the PPF was still only a third to a half as large as the PSF. Still, the PPF numbers were not insignificant, particularly if one keeps in mind that the membership of the PCF in 1936 was about 80,000.

Between 1936 and 1938, when the conservative backlash to the Popular Front was greatest, the PPF made its largest gains nationwide—its loss of support in Saint-Denis was compensated for by membership gains elsewhere, especially in southern France and Algeria. In 1938, however, the PPF lost its major raison d'être when the Daladier government abandoned the Popular Front and allied itself with the right-center. Without Daladier and the Radicals, the Popular Front was dead. Just as Poincaré undermined the Faisceau in 1926 by defeating the Cartel des Gauches, Daladier undermined the PPF in 1938 by abandoning the Popular Front. Daladier, in rolling back a number of Popular Front reforms and cracking down on the Communists, made Doriot less useful to conservatives, who no longer felt so beleaguered. Before 1938 the national membership of the PPF had risen steadily; after 1938 it began to recede.[71]

In October 1938 a major conflict within the PPF leadership led several of the party's most prominent members to resign, including its major financial backer, Pierre Pucheu. Others who departed were Henri Barbé, Paul Marion, Victor Arrighi, Bertrand de Jouvenel, Pierre Drieu La Rochelle, Robert Loustau, and Alfred Fabre-Luce. One of the reasons Pucheu gave for leaving was his disagreement with Doriot over the Czech crisis the month before. He maintained that Doriot should have opposed Hitler's annexation of the Sudetenland more strongly than he did because the Munich Settlement had weakened France against the German threat. Pucheu, Marion, and others complained that Doriot had betrayed the "intransigent") nationalism of the PPF.[72]

However, since most of the French right supported the appeasement of Nazi Germany during the Czech crisis, it seems strange that Doriot's concurrence with appeasement would have been the main reason for conservatives within the PPF to desert him. One PPF dissident who criticized Doriot in October for his stand on the Czech crisis, Pierre Drieu La Rochelle, had himself counseled appeasement a month before. A more likely explanation for the exodus was the withdrawal of conservative financial support from the PPF as a result of the defeat of the Popular Front. Pucheu, a representative of the Comité des forges, may have used foreign policy as an excuse for departing when he was actually spurred by domestic considerations. The collapse of the Popular Front made the PPF less valuable to big business. The Munich Settlement may have been a convenient pretext for a departure that would have taken place in any case.

In justifying their departure, Pucheu, Marion, Drieu, and others also attacked Doriot on spiritual grounds. They faulted him for consorting with prostitutes and overindulging in gourmet meals and for his growing obesity—even though Doriot's hedonistic private life had been in evidence long before the fall of 1938. Marion now complained that Doriot refused to accept the minimum of asceticism that leading the PPF required, and Victor Arrighi accused Doriot of no longer being a true *chef*. Doriot replied that he had no intention of changing his personal habits to please his critics or of trying to become a political idol.

It is difficult to say how sincere these criticisms were; as Victor Barthélemy later pointed out, a man like Pucheu knew history too well to believe that a less-than-exemplary private life prevented a leader from becoming a great statesman.[73] For writers like Marion, de Jouvenel, and Drieu La Rochelle, however, Doriot's increasing physical "decadence" may have been taken more seriously.

All three extolled fascism as a revolution of the body that would turn French-men into flat-bellied soldier-athletes. Doriot had blatantly violated this ideal.

PPF dissidents also accused Doriot of using secret subsidies from Italy to finance his personal pleasures, of protesting too little when Mussolini spoke of annexing parts of southern France, and of being hostile even to amiable criticisms from his associates. Arrighi objected to Doriot's undercutting his authority in Algeria, and Marion claimed that Doriot's leadership methods were so Stalinian that no one could tolerate them indefinitely without degrading himself.[74] Pucheu later wrote, "What we ignored was [Doriot's] absence of any faith, his total cynicism, which had only retained from Communism the most odious tactical maneuvers, and his lack of will power which gave way to a dissolute life paid with easy money, bereft of all great and true ambition." Pucheu thought that Doriot's "indelible vices" had been spawned by his "sliding" from a working-class, revolutionary constituency to a conservative, "facile" one. Pucheu also accused Doriot of receiving funds from fascist Italy, which, Pucheu implied, was connected with Doriot's support for the Munich Settlement.[75]

And yet the critics themselves were hardly boy scouts. It was Arrighi who had solicited funds from Italy in the first place, the same Arrighi who never lost sight of the financial side of things and who himself enjoyed "the agreeable life." De Jouvenel and Drieu La Rochelle were notorious womanizers, and Drieu especially was no stranger to brothels.[76] Between 1936 and 1938, these men had themselves defended a strong alliance with Italy as a means of resisting the Bolshevik threat. And the former Communists among Doriot's critics—Marion, Arrighi, and Barbé—were not unfamiliar with Stalinian methods or Doriot's authoritarian ways.

It seems equally strange that Doriot's financial corruptibility in 1938 would have bothered the deserters that much. A year and a half earlier, in May 1937, Doriot had been charged by the French minister of interior with taking kickbacks while mayor of Saint-Denis, an accusation that led no one on the PPF politburo at the time to abandon him. Marion, Drieu, and others may have broken with Doriot in 1938 partly for moral reasons, but it seems unlikely that these were primary. (Drieu, for one, returned to the PPF in 1939 in spite of his previous complaints about Doriot's shortcomings.)

Furthermore, Pucheu had not stopped being a conduit for big business funds to the PPF in 1936 because Doriot was soft on fascist Italy or Nazi Germany. By late 1938, however, with the Popular Front in disarray, Pucheu and his patrons could stop subsidizing the PPF without endangering their economic interests.

Pucheu's superior, François de Wendel, was less concerned in 1938 about

Doriot's stand on the Czech crisis than he was about the possibility that Doriot might turn the PPF in an anti-Semitic direction, which Wendel opposed. The steel manufacturer was also troubled by the rumor that Doriot was receiving money from Mussolini and made a trip to Doriot's headquarters to ask him directly about it (he returned unconvinced by Doriot's denial). Thus, according to Jean-Noel Jeanneney, Doriot was not only less useful to Wendel in 1938 than he had been when the Popular Front was at its height, but also suspect in his patriotism.[77]

When Drieu, de Jouvenel, and Marion—writers who were paid for the columns they produced for the party's newspaper—became aware of Pucheu's departure, perhaps they saw the financial handwriting on the wall and chose not to go down with a sinking ship. If so, it was nothing unique in the annals of French fascism: numerous supporters of the Faisceau, the SF, the JP, and the Francistes had left these movements when the flow of money decreased. Pucheu was quite right when he said that the PPF was "touched with death by our departure, which amputated a major part of its leadership"—and, he might have added, a major part of its funding as well.

The PPF was not extinquished overnight, however. Indeed, in spite of declining membership figures, the majority of the PPF's leadership and rank and file remained loyal to Doriot until 1940. Some even followed him into collaboration with the Germans. The anti-Marxist and antiliberal sentiments that had fueled the PPF from the beginning continued to sway followers, and even in late 1938 there was no guarantee, short of fascism, that as long as the Depression persisted the left would not rise again.

After 1940, Doriot supported the Vichy regime's concerted attack upon the political left in France and called for active collaboration with the Germans to repel the Soviet threat. In both instances, he claimed to do so on behalf of national socialism. Yet, as Reinhold Brender has pointed out, of the 4,485 party members who remained loyal to Doriot after 1940, only 9.6 percent were industrial workers, 64.9 percent coming from the middle classes.[78]

NATIONAL SOCIALISM AS ANTI-MARXISM, CULTURAL TRADITIONALISM, ANTIFEMINISM, AND IMPERIALISM

Some historians view Doriot as a fascist leftist because he defended national socialism. Even Jean-Paul Brunet, who has described the conservative turn in Doriot's politics after June 1936, concludes that the PPF leader was a Communist at heart: "Until the very end, Doriot remained a Bolshevik, a Bolshevik gone astray no doubt, but a Bolshevik. The fight to the death between Communism and fascism, between the PCF and Doriot, has had the effect of masking this ideological and political kinship. . . . Doriot's friends always underscored the ideal of social justice which motivated him. . . . In fact, Doriot never succeeded in accepting his rupture with Bolshevik ideology."[79]

Brunet contends that Doriot reflected his former communism after 1936 not only by continuing to believe that the ends justify the means but also in wanting "to make a clean sweep of the past and fundamentally destroy this senescent and incompetent society in order to create another society on a new basis." Brunet agrees with other consensus historians that French fascism was neither right nor left but a genuine fusion of the two, that indeed in many respects it represented a revision of Marxism. Brunet maintains that fascism and communism shared the same hatred for capitalist economics, bourgeois society, and social injustice, making it inevitable that the two ideologies should have had "a mass of points in common." Brunet also argues, somewhat contradictorily, that Doriot's fascism was "less an ideology than a referential system which gave free reign to instinct."[80]

In fact, however, the PPF had developed a quite elaborate ideology by 1938, one whose basic socioeconomic program was similar to those of Louis Marin's Republican Federation and Colonel de La Rocque's French Social Party. Like other French fascist leaders before him, Doriot claimed that his movement was neither right nor left. But again the claim was dubious. Certainly, neither the official PPF programs of 1936 and 1938 nor Doriot's own writings on specific social and economic issues after 1936 were Communist by any stretch of the imagination. Had the PPF's program been implemented, it would have allowed the political right in France to bring the political left to its knees, as fascism had done so effectively in Italy and Germany. "Our politics are simple," Doriot declared in 1938. "We want a union of the French people against Marxism. We want to rid France of the agents of Moscow."[81] Typical of the front-page headlines in the PPF's newspaper, L'Emancipation Nationale, were the following: "SINCE BISMARCK, THE GREATEST ENEMY OF FRANCE IS STALIN." "ARE THE PREFECTS OF THE REPUBLIC AT THE ORDERS OF MOSCOW?" "THE COMMUNIST ARSENAL IN LYON." "IN LYON THE COMMUNISTS ARE MANUFACTURING ARMS, AT AIX THEY STEAL THEM!"[82] The PPF attacked not just the Communists but also the Socialists for indulging in "anticapitalist demagoguery."

In The Remaking of France, Doriot claimed that the message of the Popular Front to the workers was, "Work less, you will earn more. Do less, you will have more."[83] France, he said, had entered a period of tragic decadence as a result of the Popular Front. Blum's government had only confirmed the axiom "No happy working class in a nation where one no longer produces" (50). Should workers resort to the "strike gymnastic" again in order to raise their wages, any victory they gained would be meaningless as long as production remained low.

Doriot's call for a Liberty Front against the Popular Front in 1937 was a striking example of how far he had moved toward the right. He not only defended "freedom of commerce" but also wanted the major parties of French conserva-tism, including the CF/PSF, to enter into an alliance with the PPF. La Rocque rejected Doriot's invitation not because Doriot was a national socialist but be-cause Doriot's authoritarian conservatism was too much like his own—and therefore presented a threat to La Rocque's leadership on the extreme right. Doriot had already stolen some of his troops, and La Rocque feared that a closer relation between their two movements might lead to further losses. La Rocque wanted to defeat his rival, not strengthen him. As for Doriot, the very fact that he was eager to enter a political alliance with men like La Rocque, Marin, and Taittinger demonstrated how far he had traveled since his Communist years.

Nevertheless, as late as 1938, in *The Remaking of France,* Doriot insisted that he had not sold out to the right, that his party was social as well as national and that it was situated "between" communism and reaction. "If we do not want Communism," he declared, "it is because it is the most formidable instrument of human exploitation. If we fight social conservatism, it is because it generates discord and hatred" (108). Doriot maintained that the old divisions between the right and the left were misleading because some rightists were more revolution-ary than some leftists (24, 35, 45).

By *revolutionary,* however, Doriot did not mean a proletarian assault on the class structure. On the contrary, he presented the PPF as a party of "social peace" (106). This peace, Doriot emphasized, required an end to class conflict, whether such conflict was manifested in working-class insurrections or industrial strikes. Only cooperative relations between management and labor could save France from ruin: "The essential characteristic of the Parti Populaire Français [results from its having been born] at the moment of great social battles. A few months earlier, a union of former Communists of Saint-Denis and young Volon-taires Nationaux would have seemed impossible [and] that of workers and bosses improbable. It was the great social ordeal of June 1936 [that is, the sit-down strikes] that made it necessary to gather all these men and all these move-ments behind our flag. Together, we agreed that we must seek the means of preventing social warfare, civil war" (107).

Doriot maintained that the PPF's mystique of social peace differentiated it from all other political movements—a claim that ignored, of course, the existence of the same mystique in every other conservative political movement of the era. Neither was Doriot's critique of Marxist egalitarianism, of Marxism's failure to take into account the "profound inequalities between human abilities," particularly socialist in a society in which the disadvantaged had much less of a chance to fulfill their abilities than the advantaged (24).

Like Valois, Taittinger, Renaud, Bucard, and La Rocque before him, Doriot offered a corporatist solution to class struggle, emphasizing that class solidarity be based on "the common good of the enterprise." Like his predecessors, he urged labor to cooperate with management on the grounds that "without profits for capital there would be no work for the worker" (98). And like them, too, he called for the replacement of Marxist unions, especially the CGT and CGTU, with corporatist unions that would banish political questions from their deliberations.

In 1938 Doriot acknowledged that he had asked PPF workers in 1936 to stay within the CGT in order to oppose the Communists, a position to which he no longer subscribed. He demanded that PPF unions be independent of the Communists and that these unions, which welcomed Christians as well as management into their ranks, devote themselves to holding the Communists in check. He insisted that the PPF brought "workers, bosses, and technicians" together, especially workers who had had enough of "strike culture" and wanted to return to work (110–16).

An important departure from previous French fascist corporatisms, however, was Doriot's proposal that management's share of the profits be limited by the government to a "legitimate" profit only and that the surplus be placed in a social fund to aid the less fortunate. This plan, he said, was "a hundred times more anticapitalist" than that of a Popular Front that favored big business at the expense of small business. The PPF would challenge the big corporations and financial institutions that used capital "without social responsibility" (46, 47, 50). On the face of it, Doriot's proposal was quite radical indeed, especially the talk of restricting profits and redistributing wealth through a social fund.

Doriot was conveniently vague, however, when it came to specifics. At what point would the line be drawn between legitimate and surplus profits? Who would determine what the limit on profits would be? Would the decision be made by corporatist unions (which management would dominate) or by a corporatist national council (which management would dominate)? If labor was to forgo resorting to strikes, how would it exert any pressure on management, especially if management controlled the trade unions? With traditional unions replaced by corporatist ones, what would prevent management from seeing to it that the surplus that went into the social fund remained small—or, for that matter, what would dissuade management from holding down wages even when productivity increased? If class cooperation was not to be a one-way street, with workers doing all the cooperating, why was not the surplus simply shared with labor in the first place? Doriot answered none of these questions.

As a Communist in the 1920s and early 1930s, Doriot had taken for granted that one could not count on capitalist paternalism to protect workers' interests, that the defense of those interests depended on the ability of workers to exert bargaining power through their own unions and the threat of strikes. He now reversed himself, relying on the very paternalism he had previously dismissed. Neither would the earlier Doriot have been reassured by the later Doriot's statement that, should the PPF come to power, at the apex of its corporatist organizations, its national council, would sit the most "responsible" members of the industrial triad: workers, management, and technicians (100). Doriot did not stipulate what percentage of this council would represent the working class (an impotent third?) and, above all, who would determine who was responsible?

Nevertheless, in *The Remaking of France* (1938) Doriot painted a rosy picture of what life would be like for workers under PPF corporatism. Whereas "class unionism" had led to social warfare, lower productivity, and a decline in real wages, class collaboration would lead to social peace, higher productivity, and an increase in real wages. Under the economic liberalism of the past, in which the only rule was profit, workers had had good reason to rebel. But under PPF corporatism, in which surplus profits would fall into a government social fund (thus becoming "an element of social progress for the working class") and in which higher production would lead to higher wages, there would be no need for the class conflicts of the past. "Under French corporatism," Doriot wrote, "social disorder [and] strikes will no longer be helpful, because the worker will realize that any increase in production is to his advantage" (99). It was the same argument that Georges Valois had used in 1926 on behalf of a similar brand of national socialism.

As a Communist, Doriot had denounced capitalism and called for the nationalization of the basic means of production; as a fascist, he defended capitalism and said government-owned industries were "superprotected." In 1938 he berated the Popular Front for wanting to nationalize the banks, insurance companies, utility companies, railroads, and armaments industry. The Popular Front, he said, wanted to "completely suppress the risks of capitalism," which would lead to the "bureaucratization of production." Under a PPF government, individual profit would remain "the motor of production." Indeed, some of the surplus profits placed in the social fund would be used to finance new machines and new technology (46–47, 98, 100). Doriot did not say what percentage of the social fund would be devoted to industrial development, that is, how much would be subtracted from social welfare spending. The key was trickle-down capitalism, not trickle-down government.

Like other French fascists, Doriot professed to be a defender of small and middle-sized businesses against the large corporations and anonymous trusts. He promised these businesses that he would "render the great trusts less powerful" by undertaking "certain measures" that would decentralize industry and democratize capital (99–100). This was as specific as he got. Clearly, nationalizing the trusts (that is, "bureaucratizing" production) was not part of the solution. Doriot's heavy reliance on big business contributors to finance his movement was no doubt one reason his anticapitalist rhetoric remained so nebulous.

At the same time, like all fascist politicians, he realized that no mass movement could be based on the upper–middle classes alone (who composed less than 10 percent of the French population) and that it was therefore vital to attract lower-middle and middle-middle class support. In the absence of such mass support there was little reason, other than the gangs of anti-Communist toughs Doriot commanded, for his big business backers to continue financing him.

Rhetorically, Doriot sided with the petite bourgeoisie against the big bourgeoisie. In criticizing the Matignon accords, he noted that big business was in a much better position than small business to absorb the losses incurred. Big business had greater profit margins, economic reserves, and access to credit. Small firms, less economically cushioned, risked bankruptcy when they were forced to raise their employees' salaries or lower their employees' working hours. Too long, Doriot wrote, had the free sector (that is, small business) been sacrificed to the protected sector (big business). The closest he came to saying how he would rectify the situation was to assert that the PPF would reject competition in "its most stupid forms." Yet one of his major criticisms of the Marxist left was that it wanted to "completely suppress the risks of capitalism" (44, 46–47, 99–100).

By 1938 Doriot's alleged socialism was aimed far more at the middle classes than at the lower classes. His opportunism was all too transparent. France, he wrote, was essentially a middle-class country, a "standard country [pays type] of the middle classes." To succeed politically, it was not enough to talk only about the proletarian condition. The middle classes represented "a social situation different from [that of] the proletariat" and "a state of mind, a state of the soul equally distinct from the proletarian spirit and soul" (30).

Doriot made it clear that the PPF was no enemy of the middle-class soul. Describing "the crisis of the middle classes, especially in the big cities," as frightful, he condemned the Popular Front for disrupting production with the sit-down strikes and for raising working-class wages through the Matignon accords (32). In 1938 he noted that PPF corporatism included national unions for the artisanat, commerce, and small industry and that the defense of these groups was one of the PPF's "essential preoccupations." Doctors, lawyers, and teachers would also have their corporatist organizations, as would journalists and writers who wished to oppose the "Bolshevizing house of culture" with a "French house" (118, 119).

Doriot also appealed to the peasantry for support, especially to rural landowners being pressured by their agricultural workers for higher wages. Declaring that the PPF would fail in its duty if it thought only of the proletariat and their bosses and not of the middle classes and the peasantry, he praised Dorgères's Greenshirts for aiding the PPF in Rennes and Leroy-Ladurie's peasant movement for bringing agricultural workers and their bosses together in Lorraine, thus achieving a "beautiful realization" of the PPF's own doctrines (116–17). (Leroy-Ladurie, as noted earlier, had been instrumental in financing the PPF in 1936.)

Doriot praised Dorgères's and Leroy-Ladurie's movements for their anticommunism. The PPF, he said, unlike its Marxist adversaries, opposed not only the collectivization of agriculture but also the exodus from the farms, which had led to a frightful concentration of people in large cities and had generated misery, unemployment, and social troubles. The PPF would work to preserve the small private farm by creating new credit facilities, helping peasants to specialize in products of quality, and expanding the market for their products in France's colonies. As for the traditional values of the French peasantry, "the peasant is the essential support of a society such as ours" and represented "the best virtues of our people."[84]

The nationalist part of Doriot's national socialism was also more conservative than revolutionary. When Doriot declared in 1938 that "our credo is *la patrie* and nothing but *la patrie*" and emphasized that the PPF was dedicated to "intransigent" nationalism, he was referring as much to the Marxist threat at home as to the German threat next door.[85] Like La Rocque, Renaud, and other French fascists, Doriot espoused a type of nationalism that portrayed French leftists as less patriotic than French rightists. In 1938 he wrote that the history of

France had been a series of glorious combats against foreign invaders and that, "in raising the flag against the *domestic enemies of France,* we have the impression of continuing the glorious history we have inherited from our ancestors" (96, italics mine). When Doriot said that France had grown decadent, he was not being antinationalist but antileftist. It was not all of France that he was condemning, only the France of the Popular Front.

For the PPF, internationalism stood for Marxism and class conflict. Internationalism divided Frenchmen; nationalism united them. The uniting, of course, was to take place under the existing social order, PPF nationalism serving to preserve, not to overthrow, that order. In 1937 the PPF paid homage to one of the favorite heroines of French right-wing Catholicism, Joan of Arc. Members of the AF, the JP, and other French fascist movements had often extolled Saint Joan as a symbol of French nationalism, but for former Communists and atheists within the PPF to do so was something new. Paul Marion proudly observed that the PPF was the only party in France to lay wreaths at the statue of Joan of Arc and at the Mur des Fédérés (a Communard memorial).[86] In honoring Joan of Arc, however, Marion made a point of condemning "fratricidal hatreds." Here, too, nationalism was used to bolster social conservatism, not social radicalism.

The PPF further reinforced the established social order by linking French nationalism with provincial traditionalism. "A nationalism only understands itself," Doriot wrote in 1938, "if it finds its sources in the old traditions of the French provinces."[87] The old traditions of the French provinces, of course, were more conservative than those of the industrial centers of France.

PPF national socialism was also traditionalist in regard to women. Doriot sounded much like La Rocque when he declared that "the family is the fundamental cell of the nation" and attributed the declining birthrate in France to moral causes. He did acknowledge material causes as well, for he advocated giving married male workers higher salaries than bachelors (97, 5, 3). In 1936 Paul Marion declared that one of the major objectives of the PPF was "the woman in her home" and proposed that government subsidies be given to women with several children as a way of encouraging large families.[88]

Pierre Drieu La Rochelle wondered whether the shop girls of Saint-Denis would vote Communist or fascist and thus become either the "flirts" of the quarter or childbearing mothers. Drieu's novels portrayed emancipated women as sources of decadence, while in his diary he noted that one reason he had joined the PPF in 1936 was to end his "enslavement" to women by participating in a movement that represented the greatest possible masculinity. For Drieu the essence of fascism was its cult of male virility. Bertrand de Jouvenel also denounced the spread of feminine softness throughout society and also called for a more manly ethos to combat it.[89]

Although the PPF was much less Catholic than other French fascist movements of the era, especially at the outset of its existence, its propagandists eventually played the spiritual card quite shamelessly, using it as one more weapon in their battle against Marxism. Drieu saw a connection between the "unanimous faith" that inspired the cathedrals of the Middle Ages and the nationalistic élan that characterized the PPF in 1936, a unanimity and an élan that rested on class collaboration.[90] In 1942 Doriot stated that the PPF worked "in a materialistic world to create a spiritual world" and faulted Marxism for believing in the primacy of economics. "The fundamental error of Marxism," he wrote, "is to believe that the economic milieu completely forms the social milieu, that man is the exclusive product of the economic milieu."[91]

In 1934, two years before he joined the PPF, Drieu La Rochelle condemned Marxism for being "saturated with matter, the material, and materialism." Fascism, he said, was dedicated to "the restoration of the spiritual." Having visited Germany that year, he praised the Nazi leadership not for raising the standard of living of the masses but for *lowering* it! "At bottom," he wrote, "they are moving toward a more spiritual, aesthetic conception of society."[92] The book in which this was written was entitled *Fascist Socialism*.

The PPF's views on foreign policy were also more fascist than socialist, being in large measure an extension of its views on domestic policy. In *The Remaking of France* (1938), Doriot's major concern was how to defeat Marxism at home and the Soviet Union abroad. He proposed that France ally itself with Nazi Germany and fascist Italy against the USSR, even though this would have further upset the balance of power in Europe in Germany's favor and would have left France militarily more vulnerable. Although Doriot loved to present himself as taking a realpolitik approach to foreign policy, he supported, for ideological reasons, the prospect of Germany's expanding into both Russia and Asia. It is hard to imagine how this would have enhanced France's national security. That it would have dealt a crushing blow to Soviet communism seems to have been enough for Doriot, whatever the eventual cost to French nationalism.

In 1936 the PPF opposed intervention in the Spanish Civil War against Franco, and in 1938 it supported the appeasement policy toward Hitler. In both cases, it appealed to pacifist sentiments. In 1937 *L'Emancipation Nationale* lamented the fact that twenty-five thousand young Frenchmen were risking their lives in Spain. "Mothers," it urged, "reclaim your children." Another issue carried a photo of a Catholic church in Spain with the caption "Destroyed by the reds."[93] In 1938 Paul Marion warned that the Soviet Union was trying to drag France into a war against Germany. France, he wrote, should not give Russia the least support. He called for an end to the Franco-Soviet pact and reconciliation with nationalist Spain. Reconciliation with the Soviet Union, however, was out of the question.

In 1938 Marion was not as pacifistic toward Communist Russia and imperialistic Japan as he was toward nationalist Spain and Nazi Germany. He called upon France to join with Hitler in a "defense of the West," not only against the Russian threat in Eastern Europe but against the Japanese threat in the Far East. France, he wrote, should establish a virile peace with Germany and then, together with Italy and England, expel the Japanese from China.[94] Presumably, this would have required an unpacifistic resort to arms.

In *The Remaking of France,* Doriot went even further, advocating that Germany be included as a full partner in a global alliance against the "yellow peril," an alliance that would benefit the West by appeasing Hitler with spoils in the East. Apparently, for Doriot, waging war against Asians was less reprehensible than waging war against Germans, especially if it helped destroy communism and strengthened the French Empire. Doriot wrote,

> Hitler said the other day that the victory of Japan over China was less serious than that of Bolshevism. For the moment, that is true. The victory of Bolshevism would be the end of civilization, [creating] chaos, servitude, [and] misery for the whole world. But the victory of Japan over China [will one day threaten our children] with a mass of Asian products and Asian men.
> . . . Only . . . a united Europe . . . can prevent Japan from continuing her expansion into China. A united Europe could find in China markets that would provide Germany . . . with great satisfactions and also with some possibilities for calming her colonial appetite.
> Resolve the problems . . . between England, France, Italy and Germany . . . [and] open the door to the Orient. Once again we would achieve the great white prestige, the European prestige. It is up to us to once again send our best men to the colonies.[95]

Doriot sought to allay fears that an end to the Franco-Soviet pact would make Germany more threatening to France by suggesting that Hitler's ambitions could be diverted eastward, not only toward Asia but toward Russia. In his response to the Czech crisis of 1938, Doriot argued that Poland, Romania, and Yugoslavia were ready to join Germany in its *Drang nach Osten* [drive toward the East]—which meant that they were also ready to turn against France if France continued to side with the Soviets. The fact that Poland, Romania, and

Yugoslavia were already engaged in "domestic struggles against Bolshevism" made a reversal of alliances all the more imperative. France's toleration of communism, both at home and abroad, could be its downfall:

[At the moment that Poland, Romania, and Yugoslavia abandon France for Germany] Hitler will tell Stalin that he is going to chase Bolshevism from Europe. He will take up, again in the name of Germany, the ancient torch of that old civilization against Asian barbarism, and the countries neighboring the USSR, particularly sensitive as they are to Stalin's threats, will rely on this rampart. Faced with a choice between an anti-Bolshevik Germany and a Bolshevizing France, they will choose the Berlin-Rome axis, and since they will understand the weaknesses of the Soviet giant, they will tell themselves that its collapse will permit them to take a little space from the immense plains of White Russia or the rich territories of the Ukraine. (78)

In 1938 the centerpiece of Doriot's foreign policy was an entente with anti-communist Germany. "The future of the world," he wrote, "depends on Franco-German relations" (190). At the same time, he insisted on the PPF's nationalism, declaring that France should never allow itself to be conquered by Germany. During the Czech crisis, Doriot even declared that if Germany attacked France's ally, Czechoslovakia, "France would not accept it." These tough words were immediately followed, however, with the caveat that should France decide to go to war against Germany it would be "left alone with the USSR at the beginning of the conflict" and because the Russian army had been severely weakened by Stalin's purges France would be risking a war it could not win (62).

Doriot did advocate maintaining France's alliance with England as a counterweight against Germany, although not if it meant alienating fascist Italy. "Let us go to Rome," he wrote, praising the Italian poet Gabriele d'Annunzio for having said that he had two countries, Italy and France. Doriot justified Mussolini's invasion of Ethiopia on the grounds that Italy needed a larger empire to absorb its surplus population (83, 85). France needed Italy and Germany to help destroy communism in Europe and the East, and if such allies required colonial gains in return for their support, then so be it. Doriot had traveled a long way from his anti-imperialist days of the 1920s, now favoring both Italian and German *lebensraum* as a corollary to an anti-Soviet foreign policy.

Doriot was also a strong defender of French imperialism in 1938. He praised French colonial authority "in all its plenitude" and warned against "acts of weakness," such as extending voting rights to Moslems in Algeria. "France," he wrote, "commands the colonial countries; it cannot, it wants not, it must not share its authority and power." France's role was not to "transform Moslems into Frenchmen" but to permit old civilizations to develop under French authority (76, 102, 108). No wonder many *colons* in Algeria supported the PPF.

After the fall of France in 1940, anticommunism continued to dominate Doriot's political thought. In 1942 he published *France Is Not a Country of Slaves*, the title referring not to the enslavement of France by Nazism but to the enslavement of France by communism should the Germans lose the war. Doriot called upon his readers to collaborate with the Germans against the Bolshevik-Anglo-Saxon alliance and criticized the Vichy regime for not pushing harder for a national socialist revolution like that of the Nazis'.[96] The socialism he had in mind, of course, was not to be confused with communism. After 1942 Doriot fought with the Germans on the Russian front as a member of the French Volunteer Legion against Bolshevism. In 1944 he fled with other collaborators to Germany. In February 1945 he was killed by machine gun fire from an unidentified airplane.

NATIONAL SOCIALISM IN THE WRITINGS OF PIERRE DRIEU LA ROCHELLE, RAYMON FERNANDEZ, AND BERTRAND DE JOUVENEL

Three of the PPF's most prominent intellectuals were Pierre Drieu La Rochelle, Raymon Fernandez, and Bertrand de Jouvenel, men who wrote regularly for *L'Emancipation Nationale*. Although Jean-Paul Brunet is correct to point out that these writers exercised little power in the top councils of the party and were very much the subordinates of men like Doriot and Pucheu, they were nevertheless important propagandists for the movement and played major roles in elaborating its ideology and transmitting it to the public. They also helped give an intellectual respectability to the PPF and to French fascism in general, which added to its attraction. Today, it is the writings of these men, not those of Doriot and Pucheu, that are most often cited in the French press.

In 1934 Drieu's book *Fascist Socialism* attracted a good deal of attention in intellectual circles. Its provocative title has subsequently been cited by various scholars as evidence that French fascism had its roots in the political left, even though the book characterizes Marxism as decadent and rejects the egalitarian aspects of French utopian socialism. Drieu's early models were not Marx and Engels but Georges Sorel and Fernand Pelloutier; his interest in the two French writers was directed not at their economic theories or their concern for the poor but at their calls for heroic action and their contempt for bourgeois hedonism. The most important influence on Drieu's early thought was not a socialist at all, but the fierce antisocialist Friedrich Nietzsche, who would leave an indelible mark on Drieu's concept of fascist socialism.

Drieu's critique of bourgeois decadence, like Nietzsche's, differed from a socialist critique in that it took pains to distinguish between bourgeois who were virile and bourgeois who were not. As it turned out, most bourgeois, in Drieu's eyes, were more virile than most proletarians, particularly in political matters. Moreover, as Drieu wrote in 1922, "If one withdrew from the capitalist camp, in truth there would be no other support for one's ideas, no other social category to fall back on."[97]

In *Fascist Socialism* Drieu called not for a revolution of the proletariat but for a revolution of the bourgeoisie. He challenged the presumption that the proletariat was the revolutionary class of the future. One of the great myths of Marxism, he said, was the idea that the proletariat was more vigorous, dynamic, and revolutionary than the bourgeoisie. In truth, the opposite was the case:

> Those traits of working class life that are supposedly the basis of a school for courage are not decisive if one looks at them closely. The worker has a more demanding economic life? The worker has a harder physical life? But how many bourgeois have an undemanding economic life, from the top to the bottom of the ladder? The comfort which the bourgeois has is always threatened with ruin. As for the hardness of the work, it varies radically from worker to worker depending on his trade. The machine tends more and more in a number of cases to make the worker into a seated and inert figure like the bourgeois. For the bourgeois, however, sports restore his physical force.
>
> All these considerations can cause us to doubt that central ideal of Marxism: that [the proletariat] is better prepared than others by their living conditions for that war which is revolution and that because of this they are predisposed to victory.[98]

According to Drieu, the Marxist view of class struggle was also a myth. There were several major classes, not just the bourgeoisie and the proletariat. Any successful politics had to take this complexity into account. One of the reasons the Old Regime was overthrown by the French Revolution in 1789 was that it had failed to achieve a satisfactory balance between classes. The primary thrust of history was not toward class struggle but toward class collaboration: "The governments that have succeeded one another since 1789 have had to work constantly to achieve an equilibrium among the rich bourgeoisie, the middle and lower bourgeoisie, the peasantry and the proletariat, among industry, commerce, agriculture, and the liberal professions. All those who have neglected or miscalculated this equilibrium have perished" (161).

There was no such thing as a ruling class. A social class was composed of a large number of people, but political power was wielded only by a few. The primacy of the nobility in the Old Regime was social, not political, as demonstrated by the ease with which they were overthrown in 1789. The present bourgeoisie was not a ruling class in the Marxist sense: it administered the economies of Europe, not its political life, as the fascist revolutions in Germany and Italy had shown. Economic and political power were separable.

Although Drieu conceded that an economic class might support a governing political elite, he insisted that government itself was never simply a committee of that class. A governing elite had an autonomous life independent of class interest. The great revolutions of the past did not replace one governing class with another but "one governing elite with another elite, animated by a new spirit, armed with a new technique" (17–18). This was true of the fascist revolutions in Italy and Germany. They represented not the overthrow of one class by another but the adoption of a new political philosophy and new methods of government. The Marxist view that class struggle was the primary motor of historical change was erroneous: "A class cannot exercise the political power which always belongs to an elite independent of classes. . . . The class struggle imagined by Marx for the conquest of power is therefore without purpose" (41–42).

Nothing could have been less socialist, of course, than Drieu's attempt to separate analytically political power from economic power. Whereas Marxists taught that political developments were largely determined by underlying socioeconomic developments, Drieu reversed the formula. For him, revolutions depended less on socioeconomic conditions being ripe than upon ideas being ripe. Although Marxists in the 1930s acknowledged that subjective factors (vigorous leadership and political consciousness) played a vital role in revolutionary action, none were willing to dismiss objective factors (material conditions and class interests) as cavalierly as Drieu. If Marx had turned Hegel upside down, Drieu sought to set him aright again. In formal philosophical terms, Drieu was much more of a historical Idealist than a historical Materialist. He counted on the spirit of fascism, not on class conflict, to regenerate society.

Consequently, when Drieu spoke of fascist socialism, it was not economic socialism that he was referring to but spiritual socialism. By this he did not mean greater compassion for the poor, a fairer distribution of wealth, or more social egalitarianism but rather the emotional subordination of each individual to something larger and more powerful than himself, something that in turn would make him feel stronger and more virile. For Drieu, fascist socialism was a military mystique that was metaphysically deeper than simply indulgence in creature comforts.

Fascist socialism was opposed neither to capitalism nor to class stratification. It had no intention of nationalizing the basic means of production or of depriving the bourgeoisie of their privileges. "Our socialism," he wrote, "will succeed better than the socialism of the Socialists or the Communists because it cannot be reproached for serving the foreigner or for wanting to cut the throats of the bourgeois. We will leave the bourgeois their skins, we will leave them their positions in the economy, and we will leave them at first their money. We will only demand that they forswear their little individual souls. At the same time we will deprive them of the spirit of their system which has begun to slip slowly toward [Marxist] socialism."[99]

All this was consistent with the position that Drieu had taken in 1928 as an advocate of the Young Right. Defending hereditary wealth against the threat from Marxism on the one hand and from monopoly capitalism on the other, he had praised the heroic qualities of early free enterprise capitalism and had debunked the bureaucratic nature of later corporations. He had had no qualms about economic individualism, especially when it was rugged: "The American pioneers in crossing the Atlantic left the Middle Ages behind. . . . The road was open to individualism. . . . The most virile qualities emerged again, higher in America than in Europe. How could it be otherwise, living perpetually on guard in the isolated wilderness, waging war against Indians, struggling against Nature."[100]

Ultimately, what concerned Drieu most were not the economic benefits of fascism but its promise of a higher spirituality. Thus he returned from a trip to Germany in 1934 full of praise for its relative poverty: "I found, after having been away two years . . . that Berlin seemed poorer, Germany seemed poorer. . . . Fascism facilitates the open acknowledgment of one fact: universal impoverishment, the necessary reduction of the general standard of living. But this poverty can be a richness. . . . I ask myself whether the poverty which is mounting in Germany does not hide a moral richness? The answer is yes: there is in Hitler's Germany a moral force as there is in Mussolini's Italy."[101] Thus, in *Fascist Socialism*, Drieu contrasted Marxism, which was "saturated" with materialism, with fascism, which sought a "restoration of the spiritual." Fascism was anticapitalist, he said, because it rejected a society based on "the appetite for lucre."[102]

His self-styled socialism notwithstanding, Drieu had no wish to destroy what he called the fecundity of capitalism, especially the more virile forms of free enterprise capitalism. It was this capitalism, he remarked in 1926, "which inevitably attracted to it what remained of vitality in Europe." He contended that "if one kills capitalism, one kills Europe."[103] Although capitalism, he said, had to be transformed, moderated, and controlled if it was to triumph over communism, these changes should be carried out by the bourgeoisie, not the proletariat. The result would be to save the bourgeoisie from the proletariat.

Drieu called upon left-leaning, bourgeois intellectuals to "renounce the hypocrisy" of abandoning their own class. His own choice was clear: "Communism cannot be imposed upon the West without relying on an exterior violence coming from the East, just as the Christians could not have remade Europe without the Barbarians. The Socialists correspond to those already-tired Christians who corrupted the empire and were corrupted by it. The Western Communists are like those armies of Coenobite Egyptians who assaulted Alexandria, driven by a furious disgust, false Barbarians, eaters of excrement. The bourgeoisie must awaken itself and overcome its lassitude with a new élan" (6).

What Drieu did admire about communism in 1926 was its *means*, its effective use of authoritarian methods. He simply wanted to employ these methods for bourgeois rather than proletarian ends. The only way for the bourgeoisie to defend itself, he wrote, was to "borrow the arms of its adversaries: violence and tyranny" (6). It was precisely communism's acceptance of dictatorship that gave it an advantage over capitalism and that had to be adopted by capitalism if the West was to repel the threat from the East. To emulate communism in this respect was to defend capitalism, not attack it.

In 1936, Drieu joined Doriot's PPF not because it represented a new form of communism but because it represented a new form of anticommunism, one that sought to destroy communism through its own techniques. In 1934 Drieu had also made it clear that the fascist socialism he supported was also antisocialist, that is, that it had nothing in common with the socialism of the SFIO.

Raymon Fernandez was equally anti-Marxist. Highly revealing in this respect is the view of class relations that he presents in his novel *The Violent Ones* (1935). The novel tells the story of a young, idealistic industrialist, Robert Pourcieux, and his wife, Pauline, both of whom are poorly treated, Pauline sexually, by workers they try to help. At the end of the novel Pauline becomes the victim of a proletarian in bed at the same time that Robert becomes a victim of proletarians in his factory.

At the beginning of the novel, Robert and his wife are described as being "foolishly naive" in their attitude toward the workers, as innocents ripe for a fall. Robert hopes to win his workers to class collaboration through enlightened management, technical innovation, and profit sharing. His motives are altruistic: "Robert had not chosen [his] profession out of self-interest, nor out of greed for money. . . . Robert [was] a free man who wished to save the slaves. He was exalted by an idea of social service. He felt responsible for others."[104]

Nevertheless, Pauline, more politically left-wing than Robert, accuses him of being an exploiter of the proletariat, of helping the workers only in order to defend his class position and avoid a Marxist revolution. Robert replies in exasperation, "In short, I profit much more than the workers from the trouble I put myself through for them?" (20). Pauline is depicted as a parlor room socialist: "Scarcely was she interested in the fate of the workers than she began to treat as a hypocritical compromise anything that was not concerned with their fate. The responsibilities of the factory owners, economic laws, the necessity for a social equilibrium were all swept away. If she was not yet a Communist, thank God, she was very close to reaching this slope" (50–51).

By contrast, Robert's industrialist friends, portrayed in the novel as older and wiser men, find Robert to be *too* idealistic and warn him that he will "pay for his follies." They consider him blind to the unrelenting animosity that workers have for even the most benevolent employers. They also see him as someone who has an inadequate knowledge of industrial production and therefore underestimates the economic pressures he will inevitably face as a result of market forces. One experienced industrialist, Monsieur de Varville, dismisses Robert's notion of worker participation in management decisions as an "aberrant fantasy" that will lead to ruin. He tells Robert that once his workers are allowed to view the company's account books, they will never be satisfied with their share of the profits and will undermine the investments necessary to keep the company competitive.

Besides, de Varville continues, workers can never be trusted; they betray each other as easily as they betray their employers. "As for me," he says, "I want none of their treason. I prefer them against me, openly. . . . These rascals may well throw me into boiling oil someday, but at least they will not have extracted a cash advance for this purpose!" (91). Robert fails to acknowledge that it is a mistake to see the workers as better than they are and that he himself, as a factory owner, is highly vulnerable to their worst characteristics. De Varville tells him, "You are cultivated, my dear Pourcieux, . . . but you do not yet know your Communist like the end of your finger. . . . It is always the same thing:

envy, deception, rancor. This is exactly why they are dangerous. They call this the revolt of slaves. Allow me to laugh. . . . We are all slaves in relation to someone, right? I am not Rockefeller or Mussolini, right? . . . If we were not governed by numbers . . . I would fire some twenty agitators . . . and hop! . . . I would be . . . sent abroad [or] to the stake" (93).

When Pauline replies to de Varville that Robert wants to have a good conscience, another industrialist remarks that there is nothing admirable about being beaten by one's adversaries: "Do you find anything noble in an athlete, in a player, . . . in a horse who is constantly crushed?" (122). Another businessman adds that it is sheer jealousy that fuels the proletarian's hatred of his superiors and that, deep down, workers desire the same life as their employers: "There is not a 'neither right nor left.' There is only the right. I mean that . . . the left is only the regret of not being on the right, only envy of it" (98). What follows in the novel is meant to demonstrate the validity of these judgments.

Not surprisingly, the two most unsavory characters in the novel are two workers, Rosinfosse and Riquet, described by the author as "militant Communists." Rosinfosse despises the bourgeoisie, but as a dedicated Marxist he has learned to conduct himself like a machine: "Nothing personal . . . ever intervened in either the acts or the thoughts of Rosinfosse. Communist discipline, reinforced by a natural horror of introspection, had habituated him to seeing everything as a question of tactics" (74–75). Rosinfosse conspires with the local postman, another Communist, to secretly open de Varville's mail. They do this not for political reasons but for their personal gain: they hope to blackmail de Varville with the information they find and keep the money themselves. Thus de Varville had been correct: it is natural for workers to betray their bosses and their fellow workers. Even more despicable than Rosinfosse is his friend Riquet, who eventually seduces the boss's wife, Pauline. Nicknamed Anthony the Proletarian, Riquet is the epitome of Marxist political hatred and lower-class coarseness. He is ethically, emotionally, and even physically repugnant, down to his body odor and bad breath. Hating the rich and being jealous of his comrades, he has the "instincts of a traitor, which are the instincts of the hunter applied to human animals."

Riquet thirsts for violence against the rich. One day, tired of Rosinfosse's endless objectivity, he explodes, "I am fed up with waiting for an economic catastrophe, Rosinfosse. Let's start by smashing a few faces. Let's use rifles, and let's fire into the pile. . . . [Just] good blood, no more words" (113). The narrator explains this outburst: "The hatred which caused [Riquet] to rise up against the rich, against those who have no need to hate to live, which operated all day long with underhanded cunning, could be gratified only with immediate violence" (113–14). In other words, it is proletarians like Riquet who are the violent ones of the novel's title.

One night Riquet breaks into Robert's study to steal some papers from his desk but is surprised in the act by Pauline. Out of sympathy for a member of the working class, she allows him to leave without reporting him to the police. She subsequently seeks him out, not because she is sexually attracted to him but because she wants to bridge the class barrier between them. Riquet persuades her to sleep with him by telling her that if she does not it will only prove that she still feels superior to him, that she is still a snobbish bourgeoise.

Their sexual encounter is a disaster, as Pauline discovers too late just how repugnant Riquet is. Middle class in her cultural and hygenic tastes, she cannot stomach the more uncouth aspects of the proletarian male:

He smelled of [cheap] soap and, beneath this, of the unsavory odor of a wet dog. . . . On the wall of his room was the picture of a nude woman . . . whose breasts resembled pagodas. . . . It was a man she had not wanted. . . . [He began to touch her.] On her thigh, his fingers began to crawl. They moved slowly upward, like the feet of an insect. . . .

[He climbed on top of her.] He sighed, he snorted, he jerked his back like a poor swimmer. His hands stopped at her silk stockings and clawed at them, tore at them with rage. [He] began to make little sounds accompanied by rancid breath. . . . With his left hand, Riquet hunted around, digging about with awkward movements, burying his elbow in [her] stomach . . . and coming up with something in his hands. The condom, hard and wet, which beat like the heart of a bird, made her shudder with a disgust which he took for pleasure.

[She hoped he would finish quickly.] . . . To escape his bad breath, she slid her head against [his] undershirt, but the odor of a wet dog, accentuated by his sweat, forced her to raise her head. Then to avoid getting nauseous, she covered his mouth with her lips. . . .

He finally penetrated her. . . . She felt him moving inside her, but distantly, without her feeling anything, like a local anesthetic. . . . She understood how prostitutes feel. . . . If only there was not his bad breath, his odor. . . . A stale odor, which overwhelmed the rest, made her sick to her stomach. A single thought revolved inside her head: I am going to have to wash and mend my clothes myself this evening for sure. . . . If she remained there this way, she was going to vomit.

"I want to get up," she said. . . .

"Now you [tu] are going to take off the rest of your clothes," he said.

That tutoiement put her in prison. . . . She felt how dark the cell was, how stifling the cage was.

"I must be getting home," she said.

"Oh no. Listen now my little darling. If you think that I am satisfied with doing it only once." (229–33)

Pauline finally manages to fend off Riquet by grabbing his genitals and giving them a jerk. As her persecutor writhes in agony, she dashes from the room. Riquet staggers to the window, from which, as he watches her crossing the street, he regards her with an "almost respectful hatred" (234–35).

Whatever can be said of this episode, it was hardly written by an author full of sympathy for proletarian rule. Pauline is portrayed as a fool for trusting someone like Riquet, a man who, besides everything else, later tries to blackmail her husband and eventually shoots him with a revolver. Moreover, Fernandez suggests that Pauline's humiliation parallels the potential humiliation of the bourgeoisie in general, should they also be so foolish as to put themselves in the hands of the proletariat. Her rape, however consenting at the outset, could be their rape, the rape of one social class by another. Once in a position of power, Riquet is not only disrespectful (he uses the *tu* of an equal, not the *vous* of an inferior), but he is also brutish, domineering, and merciless—denying Pauline even the freedom to leave before his lust is fully satisfied.

Transposed onto society at large, this passage becomes one of the worst nightmares a *haut bourgeois* could imagine, one heightened by its lurid sexual overtones and images of helplessness. It is as if Fernandez is saying, "If they are capable of raping our women, they are capable of raping us." The passage also raises the spectre of a proletarian assault on bourgeois freedom, authority, and class superiority. Indeed, Pauline seems more disturbed by Riquet's *verbal* familiarity (by the dreaded *tu* that made her feel as if she were in a "stifling cage") than by his *physical* familiarity, by his social onslaught than by his sexual onslaught.

The ultimate message of the novel is that the proletariat cannot be trusted and that, at least as long as they are under the influence of Marxism, they will remain hostile to bourgeois like Pauline and Robert no matter how generously they are treated. This is borne out when Pauline returns home after escaping from Riquet and finds Robert in despair over his workers' having betrayed him at the factory. In spite of his attempts to help them, they had become increasingly hostile toward him (that very morning, one of them had thrown a rock through his office window). The final act of betrayal comes when Robert is shot by Riquet and mortally wounded. On his deathbed, benevolent to the end, Robert exonerates Riquet and dies nobly. But as a "wise" relative remarks, it was a useless death: all of Robert's good intentions had accomplished nothing in the end.

Fernandez, the narrator of this tale, left little doubt about his own view of the proletariat. His portrait of Riquet not only echoes a recurring theme in fascist ideology by condemning proletarians who are driven by Marxist class hatred, but also contributes to fascist demonology by presenting Riquet as almost sub-human. If stylistically Fernandez's writing is superior to that of the average fascist propagandist of his day, empathetically—that is, in his lack of feeling for those beneath his social class—it remains on the same level. In *The Violent Ones*, Fernandez identifies with "realists" like de Varville, who denigrates the essential character of workers, not with "idealists" like Robert, who have compassion for them. None of these sentiments prevented Fernandez one year later from joining the "socialist" PPF.

Bertrand de Jouvenel was another regular contributor to *L'Emancipation Nationale* after 1936. Although he, too, was highly critical of Marxism, he displayed a greater sympathy for the working classes than did Fernandez. A supporter of the left wing of the French Radical party until 1934, he not only acknowledged the economic hardships the proletariat had suffered, but also approved of the trade union activity that had reduced these hardships—at least, he said, until the unions threatened to go too far. In *The Awakening of Europe* (1938), de Jouvenel wrote, "The major task of our generation is evident: we need to eliminate pauperism. Our immediate predecessors found the way to do this: social legislation, combined with action by the unions, has almost incessantly improved the standard of living of the working classes."[105]

He added, however, that precisely because the proletariat had been so successful there was a danger that further demands on their part would be excessive. Not only were French workers now "protected against the abusive exploitation of their work that had been practiced by nineteenth-century employers," but the unions, which had grown strong and rich, continued to threaten employers with strikes, employers who "could not indefinitely grant concessions to workers if foreign employers, their competitors, did not do the same" (44–58).

At the same time, de Jouvenel criticized reactionaries, who looked back nostalgically to a medieval brand of corporatism. The modern worker, he said, was no longer the valet of yesterday, and the modern employer did not have much in common with the master of the Middle Ages. The nature of production had radically changed, and few employers worked side by side with their workers any more. Moreover, during the first and second Industrial Revolutions, unscrupulous employers had paid "the most miserable salaries possible." It had been a time when the "human conscience had been at its lowest."

According to de Jouvenel, the trade union movement with its "will to revolt" was a natural response to "two centuries of proletarian slavery." Although trade unions had been quite libertarian at the outset, they eventually fell under the control of Marxists, who wanted to establish a Prussian dictatorship. By the twentieth century, the major political parties representing the workers had become dominated by bourgeois intellectuals who cleverly made use of the proletariat to pursue their own goal of conquering the state. More concerned with creating a utopian society than with improving the immediate well-being of the workers, these intellectuals were like lawyers who had lost sight of their clients' interests (98–115).

What was to be condemned, wrote de Jouvenel, was not trade unionism per se but its politicization, particularly when it took a Marxist turn. Unions that fought for better conditions for their members were admirable, as long as they did not try to overthrow capitalism or insist that the state remain politically democratic. In 1884 René Waldeck-Rousseau, a social and economic conservative, had been correct in ridiculing those who feared that making concessions to the workers would lead to the overthrow of the bourgeoisie and to the establishment of a proletarian dictatorship. In fact, the opposite had happened: the apolitical current in French trade unionism had proved stronger than the political current.

French workers had only to recognize what had happened to their counterparts in Russia to see how foolish it was to place their hopes in a Marxist state. The Bolshevik revolution had simply replaced one elite with another, leaving the Russian proletariat no better off. Workers were wiser to count on technological progress within a capitalist society to better their condition than to count on Marxism, for only by collaborating with their employers would profits rise and their own salaries increase as a result. It was the search for profits, not Marxism, that had led to human needs being satisfied in a far greater measure than ever before in history.

Although de Jouvenel, unlike most fascists, did not call upon workers to abandon class struggle altogether (some pressure, he said, was required to obtain the highest salaries possible), he did urge them to pursue a dual strategy: "class struggle and solidarity with the industry" (75, 116–18). The attitude of workers in a factory, he said, depended a great deal on the personality of the employer and on how much he tried to help them. Besides, modern capitalism had reached a stage of development where the proletariat itself was split into different classes with differing interests. As a result, their insurrectional potential had fallen to almost zero.

De Jouvenel contended that before 1936 the major aim of French workers had been to gain a larger share of the economic riches produced by capitalism but that during the sit-down strikes this aim had changed as workers had become intoxicated with the power they had exerted over their employers. In this respect, they resembled Italian fascists, whose conquest of Ethiopia was less rewarding economically than psychologically (118–24).

For de Jouvenel, it was not the science of riches that should be the first concern of politics but the science of man. What was fundamentally at stake was not how wealth should be distributed but how man himself should be fashioned. It was here that Marxist thought revealed a serious "psychological lacuna" and Marxist leaders displayed their "human inadequacy." What separated Marxists from one another was less ideological than temperamental differences, Communists being more combative and Socialists more contemplative. Hitler, who himself was semisocialistic, had no trouble defeating both types in Germany (128–29, 139).

Fascists realized that a classless society was impossible, that, as Vilfredo Pareto had shown, history was the story of circulating elites, not circulating classes. A revolution only replaced one elite with another: "It did not suppress the fact of inequality, of hierarchy. Rather it reinforced it. For a new discipline is more rigorous than an old discipline; the new leaders are more imperious than the hereditary leaders" (125). Therefore the Bolshevik revolution had simply created a new aristocracy. Although extreme social inequalities shocked one's sense of the equivalence of human beings, the fact remained that a classless society was a pure utopia. The immense complexity of a modern industrial economy required a responsible elite, endowed with authority, to oversee its operations (207–09, 9–10). The question was not *whether* an elite should rule but what *kind* of elite should rule?

A good elite would serve all the needs of society, not just its material needs. National socialism was superior to Marxist socialism in that it was concerned with the whole man, not just with man as an ideal consumer. Marxists defined the standard of living too narrowly: "One can provide a food supply of so many calories, an apartment with so many cubic meters of air, so many shirts per year, and so many packets of cigarettes; there you have some of the elements which permit [Marxists] to estimate the 'standard of living' of a citizen and the sum of his satisfactions" (70, 69).

The wage raises of 1936 enabled workers to buy more radios and other "toys" but not to live in less ugly surroundings or have more access to sports facilities. The *total* condition of the proletariat needed changing, not just its purchasing power: "To change slums into forests, a mess of apartments into gardens, to

establish new cities with vast communal buildings and playing fields, surrounded by a network of small family homes, to change in a word the face of
France, this is the only way of changing the condition of the working class
beyond its present hopes" (219, 254).

The social problem was not just a salary but an aesthetic problem. The quality of life was as important as the quantity of life. Monstrous industrial con-
glomerations needed to be replaced with new cities "married to the countryside" (220). Small patches of beauty had been created for the wealthy few but at
the expense of large areas of ugliness for the unwealthy many. Only with the
"advent of aesthetic power" would the decor of life no longer be imposed on
society by "the brains of businessmen." Government would rely on the best
artists of the day for discriminating guidance. Artists would serve the masses the
way their Renaissance predecessors had served the rich, providing a joyful envi-
ronment for all. Steps would also be taken to rescue the worker from the monot-
onous movements of the assembly line ("the worker as the Man of a Single
Motion") and to end a situation that separated the worker's personal creativity
from the products he produced (258–63).

If de Jouvenel's vision of the good society was Marxist in some respects (in his
Economic and Philosophical Manuscripts of 1884 Karl Marx had presented a
similar view of unalienated labor and had made a similar defense of non-
economic needs), his support of capitalism, especially of its search for profits,
was not.[106] Nor was his extensive critique of other aspects of Marxism grounded
in socialist premises.

After the Second World War, de Jouvenel published three studies—*On Power*
(1947), *On Sovereignty* (1955), and *On Pure Politics* (1963)—that became highly
regarded in conservative academic circles. According to one commentator, these
books provided generations of students at the École des Sciences Politiques, one
of France's leading political science schools, with "the foundations of their
discipline."[107]

ANTIDEMOCRACY, ANTILIBERALISM, ANTIRATIONALISM, AND ANTI-SEMITISM

The national socialism of the PPF was not only anti-Marxist; it was also antidemocratic and antiliberal. Despite its bows to republicanism and its participation in electoral politics, the PPF was a friend of neither. As it moved increasingly toward the authoritarian right after 1936, it denounced not only
parliamentarians and Freemasons but also all rationalists who neglected the

emotional side of politics. By 1938 anti-Semitism had become part of its creed as well.

Although the PPF, in order to avoid being banned, had to be careful when the Popular Front was in power not to sound too fascist, it signaled its contempt for democratic values in a number of ways, especially after 1938. One was its blatant use of fascist symbols and ceremonies, including the fascist salute and the loyalty oath to Doriot. Another was its praise of the Hitlerian revolution in Germany. In 1938, with the Popular Front no longer in a position to retaliate, Doriot said that this revolution "had given back to Germany her authority, her prestige, her liberty, her force."[108] In 1937 Drieu declared that fascism surpassed socialism by its "sense of man." Socialists, he said, had been defeated throughout Europe because of their physical and moral decadence, whereas fascists had proved to be more virile.[109] In general, Doriot, who continued to call himself a republican, left it up to supporters like Drieu, de Jouvenel, and Marion to draw analogies between the PPF and fascism.

In 1937 Drieu contrasted the Third Republic, "so paltry, so routine-bound, so cowardly," with the forceful republicanism of the Jacobin phase of the French Revolution. Drieu's long-standing hatred of political democracy, his often-expressed contempt for the masses (he felt the French were more decadent than the British or the Germans), and his call for rule by a virile elite did not prevent him from becoming a major voice for the allegedly republican PPF. In 1935 he had written, "I . . . detest democracy. . . . I detest parliament with . . . its lawyer deputies, its Radical party, with its committees of Freemasons and its Senate of sadistic old men, its Socialist party, and its hidden admiration for all the things that its . . . orators denounce."[110] In 1926 Drieu had written, "Have you seen the shameful thing that is the Palais-Bourbon [the French Chamber of Deputies]? A man who loves life would not lift his little finger to defend this bedlam. It is a vicious circle: if parliament wants to save itself, it must give itself a president who will make it keep quiet. But it is a miserable sham, unbelievably pathetic and abject, of a moral and intellectual baseness beyond words."[111]

Following the Czech crisis of 1938, Drieu argued that France and England could repulse the German threat only if they became more politically authoritarian themselves. "The question," he said, "is whether England and France prefer to remain democracies or prefer to remain England and France."[112]

De Jouvenel also made no secret of his disgust with democracy. In *The Awakening of Europe*, he maintained that people who were elected to office usually lacked the intellectual preparation and moral qualifications that were needed to do their tasks well, since they reflected the insufficient education and the mediocre lives of the voters who elected them.[113] Parliamentary deputies pandered to class selfishness, to the special interests of their constituencies, not to the interests of France as a whole. De Jouvenel was more perturbed, however, by the selfishness of the lower classes than by that of the upper, since one of his main objections to political democracy was that it was "against the rich": "It tried through the crushing taxation of a small number of rich people and through extensive assistance to large numbers of the poor to correct the extreme inequality of conditions" (203). But it was not practicable to tax the rich beyond a certain point without causing serious problems for the national economy.

In France, de Jouvenel wrote, the turning point came in 1924 with the election of the first Cartel des Gauches. This created a crisis for democracy similar to that which had occurred in ancient Greece when the masses, "in order to break the power of the rich," had turned the state over to tyrants. For the city-states of Greece, the result had been internal dissension, financial waste, and eventual military defeat at the hands of Philip of Macedonia. Democracy had failed to provide these states with the stability and independence that aristocracy had. The Third Republic ran the same danger. A reformist state had sought to eliminate the proletarian condition by "a perpetual intercession into the collectivity in favor of the less privileged." "Industrial wage earners," he continued, "applauded anyone who looked like he would use the authority of the State to serve the immediate advantage of industrial wage earners" (215, 165, 167–68). This was a recipe for disaster.

The solution, de Jouvenel said, was to return to an aristocratic society in which hierarchy was no longer suppressed and in which mediocrities were no longer allowed to govern. An elite would rule the masses, but its guiding principle would be not class exploitation but noblesse oblige: "In this system, 'no man is without a master,' that is to say, every individual is bound, according to his condition, to perform certain services for a master. But also the master is bound [to perform certain services in return]" (173). Society would be based not on a horizontal solidarity between people of the same rank but on a vertical solidarity between leaders and dependents. Accepting the necessity of social discipline, it would reject the words of "lazy" eighteenth-century intellectuals: "Let me be free, I let you be free, let's all be free" (193).

Thus de Jouvenel took a benign view of aristocratic good faith and paternalistic leadership. For a writer who normally analyzed politics in terms of power relations and who prided himself on being a political realist, his vision of the good society was strikingly idealistic, resting as it did on the assumption that those who ruled would necessarily rule benevolently. Missing from his analysis was any advice on what the dependents should do should the noblesse not fulfill their oblige, especially if the dependents were deprived of all political power and scorned if they entertained any wish "all to be free."

Neither was de Jouvenel's talk of noblesse oblige consistent with other passages in *The Awakening of Europe* in which he criticized the modern democratic state for seeking "a certain minimum level of existence for all," "a certain minimum level of education for all," and "a certain minimum level of health for all." Such a program, he said, would create "an infinitely enlarged bureaucracy" and "an immensely bloated budget." The moral consequences of this "semi-socialization" would be disastrous, causing heads of families to feel less responsible toward their dependents and factory owners to take fewer competitive risks (65). What de Jouvenel advocated was not a paternalistic state but a paternalistic aristocracy, an aristocracy unconstrained by the state, especially by a left-wing state. For him, political democracy was dangerous because it inevitably led to social democracy, which in turn led to the ruin of productive capitalism.

If intellectuals like de Jouvenel and Drieu were often quite candid about their contempt for political democracy and the "mediocrity" of the masses, Doriot, an electoral politician, was more circumspect. In 1938 he declared, "We remain republicans." In 1937 he even posed as a champion of freedom of speech and assembly when, in the wake of the "Clichy Massacre" (when Communist demonstrators had assaulted members of the CF after one of their meetings), he called for the formation of a Liberty Front to protect republican liberties. Toward the political left, however, Doriot was less libertarian, demanding in 1938 that the PCF be outlawed.[114]

Between 1936 and 1939, Doriot repeatedly suggested that the PPF sought not to overthrow the Third Republic but only to reform it. The PPF, he said, favored a "regime of liberty," but "we must not confuse liberty with the present diarrhea, nor democracy with the regime that we see collapsing a little more every day" (103, 104). Jean-Paul Brunet has noted that there was nothing fundamentally fascist about the constitutional changes that Doriot advocated in 1938, since they did not call for the suppression of parliament or an end to political democracy. Brunet warns, however, against taking Doriot's professions of republicanism at face value: "As long as a fascist party is not in power, it can be led to tone down a certain number of key points in its doctrine, such as [that of] the single party, precisely because it would be badly perceived by public opinion; it is therefore a mistake to take literally all the positions of the PPF. . . . Do not forget, after all, that a fascist party does not reveal its true nature . . . until it has come to power."[115] The same was true for the Faisceau, the JP, the SF, the Francistes, and the CF.

When Doriot said in 1938, "We . . . remain republicans," he was hardly at odds with previous French fascist politicians who had also claimed to be republicans. Doriot's opportunism, like theirs, at times was all too transparent. When asked in 1938 if he wanted a return to the monarchy, he replied, "The question does not seem ripe for the moment. We therefore remain republicans."[116] This was less than a ringing endorsement for democratic government, implying as it did that under different circumstances, when the question was more ripe, a return to monarchy might be worth considering. In 1940 Doriot responded to the German occupation by calling for the total removal of the "democratic shell" from France on the grounds that "in order to talk with the Hitlerians, men are required who understand National Socialism." In 1942 he expressed scorn for the superficiality of the masses, which, he said, had doomed the Third Republic to failure.[117]

In 1938, however, circumstances were less ripe. Doriot called instead for constitutional reforms within a republican framework, reforms that would "save French democratic institutions" by giving more authority to the executive branch of the government. Only an executive with "full powers," he declared, could put a stop to the endless ministerial crises that continued to debilitate France: "The [Chamber of Deputies and the Senate] should return to their role of overseers and leave to the executive the task of leading the country."[118]

Under Doriot's plan, parliament would no longer have the right to initiate spending legislation, though it would retain the right to vote on the executive's proposals. Elections for parliament would still be held, but under a new proportional voting law. (The latter was a pet project of French conservatives in 1938, who saw it as a device for making the Radical party less dependent on the Communists and the Socialists for electoral support.) Significantly, Doriot was less critical of the Senate, which had blocked some of the Popular Front's reforms, than he was of the Chamber of Deputies, which had passed them. "For our part," he wrote, "we do not associate ourselves with . . . violent attacks upon the Senate whose conservative role has often been useful in this legislature." (106).

Doriot also called for the creation of a corporatist national assembly, representing France's various trades and professions, an assembly imbued with the spirit of class collaboration and sharing legislative power (or the remnants thereof) with the Chamber of Deputies and the Senate.

Doriot's constitutional proposals, in other words, were quite similar to those of previous republican fascists, whether it be those of Valois, Taittinger, Coty, or La Rocque. To be sure, Doriot's proposals, like theirs, fell far short of German Nazism as practiced in 1938, but then Hitler had also been less than candid before he came to power. Too, like La Rocque, Doriot was no doubt sensitive to the conservative backlash to Hitler's Night of the Long Knives of 1934 and thus to the danger of advocating a government that appeared to be *too* strong.

Counterbalancing conservative fears, however, was the anger that many French rightists felt at the democratic institutions that had allowed the Popular Front to come to power in 1936. For some of these rightists, while there was too much authoritarianism in Germany, there was too little in France. Doriot catered to both of these sentiments. Like La Rocque, he walked a political tightrope, wavering between the right-wing backlash to the Popular Front, which favored authoritarian pronouncements, and right-wing qualms about Nazism in Germany, which did not. His constitutional proposals reflected both sides of this balancing act.

In *The Remaking of France*, Doriot also called for a new national discipline that would overcome the "demobilizing materialism" of French society. He declared that a member of the PPF "must be a fighter, *a fighter and a hero*" (127). Indeed, precisely because he sounded so much like La Rocque on this score, Doriot emphasized that his conception of a fighter was broader than La Rocque's. After "saluting" the war veterans of the CF for their heroism and their desire to regenerate France, Doriot remarked that he did believe in the efficacy of a movement based on the memory of the trenches alone (108–09).

However, this was not a rejection by Doriot of paramilitary action itself. In 1938 he vigorously protested the arrest of Pozzo di Borgo and other members of the Cagoule for their having armed themselves against the Communists. Doriot called for the liberation of these "innocents and heroes," denounced the "police-political conspiracy" that had led to their imprisonment, insisted that the government uncover the Communists' arms caches, and demanded that those police who had "provoked" the affair be "struck down without pity" (9).

Doriot lavished praise on the French army in 1938, especially on the officer corps. The former antimilitarist wrote that this "admirable" army with its "good" leaders had proved itself during the First World War. He deplored the fact that French officers were paid such low salaries. Although the PPF was pacifist, he said, it practiced a virile pacifism that did not exclude fighting in some wars. If France were ever threatened by invasion, the members of the PPF would be in the first ranks of those who would risk their lives for their country (64, 55, 75).

Like other French fascist movements, the PPF extolled military values for

civilian purposes as well. The official program of the PPF in 1938, written by
Paul Marion, was replete with them. What was needed, Marion said, was a state
based on a unity of action and command. The PPF believed in such "unemployed
virtues" as "heroism, service, obedience, command, [and] collective faith."[119]

Drieu insisted that the very essence of fascism was a philosophy of force
based on military values. He repeatedly contrasted fascist man with liberal man,
the first representing spiritual vitality, animal instinct, and bodily health and
the second, spiritual death, bloodless rationalism, and debilitating hedonism.
He portrayed liberals as weaklings when confronted with the ruthlessness of a
Lenin or a Stalin. They were like "limp rags," twenty years of parliamentary
activity having deprived them of all virility. The Socialists were equally decadent: "They are concerned with the sexual and moral liberty of man, but not
with his physical liberty, which is his health. One has only to look at them to
realize this. Attend a Socialist convention and look at all the beards, all the
bellies, the tobacco smoke, the anxious anticipation of the before-dinner drink.
There is nothing more old, more outmoded, . . . more to be condemned than this.
It is the underlying reason why Socialism is beaten everywhere, even in England,
even in France."[120]

In 1941 Drieu claimed that France had been defeated by Germany because the
France of scouts, hikers, and skiers had lost out to the France of "sitters, fisher-
men, and Pernod drinkers." In 1942, having sided with the Germans and seeing
the war turn against them, Drieu accused even the Nazis of having been cowardly "liberals" because they had not repressed their enemies vigorously enough
when they had had the chance.[121]

Bertrand de Jouvenel also contrasted fascist man and liberal man. In 1938 he
blamed many of society's ills on "a certain type of 'humanitarian' intellectual"
whose principal vice was not to demand enough of mankind. Liberalism had led
to the decline of "a superior human type who for ten centuries had held the
destiny of the world in his hands, Western man, or as some prefer to call him,
'The Frank.'" The original Frank had repulsed the invading barbarians of the
Middle Ages. He had been a warrior in the Darwinian struggle of life. Fascist
man was a return to this type of virility.[122]

In 1941 de Jouvenel sought to explain the difference between a fascist and a
conservative. Mussolini's first cabinet, he wrote, had included both types, "two
styles opposed to one another":

> On one side were men in the habit of receiving visitors from behind a desk, of
> standing before a podium, of engaging in discussions around a table covered
> with a green cloth—and who thought of this as political leadership. On the

other side were street fighters who loved to make bourgeois grow pale, who knew how to light the eyes of adolescents with enthusiasm.

. . . [People wondered] would Mussolini govern "reasonably"? Would he be an authoritarian leader but respectful of a certain freedom of speech, of a certain freedom of the press? Would he be another Guizot [a socially conservative nineteenth-century liberal]? No. [Instead] he formed a youth whose physical virtues were encouraged.

How many times in a high school courtyard have we seen teachers come across a schoolboy fight and exclaim: "What little savages!" The beaten and tearful accusers were then consoled and pampered.

Fascist education reverses this custom. It scandalizes the whole Western world. Anti-fascists declare that it deliberately seeks to form barbarians.

In reality, the human being contains several possible persons within him. The new [fascist] education favors, as virtues, the appearance of what were previously called vices.[123]

The PPF was also both antiliberal and antidemocratic in its attempts to manipulate the masses on emotional grounds rather than to enlighten them on rational grounds. To be sure, no French political party in the 1930s restricted itself to reason alone, but few went as far as the PPF in openly praising fascist propaganda techniques—and those of Lenin as well. In *Their Combat: Lenin, Mussolini, Hitler, and Franco* (1939), Paul Marion tells of the lessons to be learned from such leaders. For a revolutionary movement to succeed, he wrote, it is not enough to form traditional electoral organizations; it has to develop a propaganda full of psychological power. In contrast to the old parties of Europe, with their reliance on rational discourse, Italian fascism addressed "the whole man, his body as well as his emotions."[124] Mussolini had come to power in Italy by waging a "war of symbols and emblems," as Hitler also had in Germany ten years later.

Mussolini, declared Marion, had understood the "magic of acts" as well as the "magic of slogans." By forming his blackshirts into combat squads that engaged in paramilitary maneuvers, by having them sing rousing marching songs, and by reviving the Roman salute, he had enhanced the "allure, the alacrity, the style" of his movement. By responding to his critics with terse declarations instead of convoluted arguments, he had given the impression of strength. When asked about the dangers of resorting to violence, he had said, "Better to live an hour like a lion than a hundred years like a sheep." When asked what his program was, he had answered, "Our program is simple; we want to govern Italy." When his blackshirts were criticized for assaulting some merchants in Florence, he simply replied, "A few monopolists hung from lampposts, a few thieving shopkeepers crushed with the potatoes or bacon they wanted to hide, will serve as an example." For Marion, Mussolini's willingness to resort to force had been "much more educational than the best of pens." Taken as a whole, the Duce's propaganda techniques formed a "beautiful work" (180–90).

Marion credited Hitler with "orchestrating this new music with even greater power." Hitler was also a master propagandist from whom much could be learned. In *Mein Kampf* Hitler recommended holding political rallies at night, when audiences were emotionally susceptible, and avoiding speeches full of nuances that might only confuse them. Although Marion conceded that such practices might alienate a refined listener, they had given Hitler's oratory an unprecedented effectiveness with the masses. The Nazi leader had succeeded in "reaching what was the most imperious and alive in men, their unconscious forces" (187, 193–96).

Marion noted that on their road to power the Nazis had brilliantly exploited the religious feelings of their audiences. Their use of biblical verses (after certain "necessary adaptations") and their "adroit" attacks on Jewish materialism had won them the support of numerous German pastors. Phalangists in Spain had found that holding open-air Catholic masses at which sixty thousand arms were extended in a forest of fascist salutes was also effective (198, 206).

When Nazi brownshirts in Germany raised their arms and shouted, "Heil Hitler!" a sense of solidarity was created between themselves and their leader and between themselves and each other. Hitler had reflected at length on the design of the party flag: its swastika represented the Aryan race; the white circle that surrounded it, German nationalism; and the red background, the social strivings of the movement. These symbols—along with the flag ceremonies commemorating the martyrs of the party, the torchlight parades, the astute use of radio and cinema—were all aimed at "touching one of the five senses and through them the most sensitive fibers of human beings." Such techniques had played a major role in bringing Hitler to power. "The Third Reich," Marion concluded, "was the son of propaganda" (200–01).

For some PPF intellectuals, the appeal to irrationalism was not a matter of cynical manipulation but of sincere conviction. This was very much the case with Drieu, for example, whose novel *Gilles* (1939) portrays the fascist hero as a man of passion who manages to triumph over the decadent rationalism of his times. One reason Drieu was attracted to French fascism in 1934 and to German Nazism in 1940 was that he found them more emotionally stirring than other ideologies. Throughout the 1930s, he repeatedly berated Marxists and liberals for their bloodless rationalism.[125] In *Gilles* he scornfully described one Radical-Socialist orator: "He spoke calmly, properly, coldly. He was not a leader. He did not have a people before him but a public, a public curious about his talent rather than eager to have its passions gratified. He analyzed 'problems.' He reduced the complex palpitating enormity of the life of a people to 'problems,' to little groups of material facts, particular and ephemeral."[126]

Running throughout Drieu's writings after 1934 is a series of equations: passion equals force, force equals national regeneration, and national regeneration equals fascism, the most passionate and forceful ideology in Europe. For Drieu, not only Marxism and liberalism but parliamentary conservatism as well were corrupted by excessive rationalism. In 1941 Drieu concluded that the Germans might provide France with the strength-giving irrationalism it needed. "France," he wrote, "has been destroyed by rationalism which has reduced its genius. Today rationalism is beaten. We can only rejoice in rationalism's discomfort. . . . Frenchmen were too sick to cure themselves of this illness."[127]

Alphonse de Chateaubriant was not a member of the PPF in the 1930s, but during the German occupation, along with Drieu, he wrote for the collaborationist journal *La Gerbe*. In 1937 Chateaubriant lamented the decline of soul, of Christian soul, in modern times, blaming it on Voltairian rationalism, Baconian empiricism, and Aristotelian alogic. "We live in Aristotelian decadence," he wrote. Chateaubriant praised Germany's Hitler Youth for their childlike faith in the führer. Associating Nazi chants to Hitler ("I believe, I believe, I believe") with Catholic chants to God, Chateaubriant concluded that the truest ideas were the simplest ideas. Nazi ideas, he said, "were simple. Simple but profound. Much more profound than those which were more subtle. Subtlety rarely has its roots in anything profound." Hitler's "independence in regard to ratiocination" was an expression of Hitler's dependence on God. Chateaubriant regretted his countrymen's taste for anticlerical irony, lauding German youth for being fresh, simple, and lacking in irony.[128]

Another antidemocratic and antiliberal side of PPF ideology was its rejection of ethnic equality and ethnic pluralism in favor of cultural nationalism and racial homogeneity. Doriot took a strong stand against foreign immigration in 1938, a position that accompanied his shift to full-scale anti-Semitism the same year. He scoffed at liberals who defended immigration on humanitarian grounds: "We must be done with the sentimentality of the last century [which preaches] the solidarity of peoples and the progressive mixing of races." He regretted that so many foreigners were "permitted to tread on the soil of France."[129]

When the PPF was founded in 1936, it claimed to be opposed to anti-Semitism. *L'Emancipation Nationale* declared in November, "Our party is not anti-Semitic. It is a great national party that has better things to do than to fight the Jews."[130] Although the same article was critical of those "who call themselves Jews rather than feeling themselves French, [and who] . . . place racial interests above national interests," it welcomed assimilated Jews into the PPF. In December 1936, however, it ran an article on North Africa that spoke of the "double domination of the Jews whom one scorns and the Communists whom one fears, but both of whom one hates and dreads." Yet the following year Doriot told a student audience that he was "personally neither a Jew nor a Freemason and that he refused to bother himself with such nonsense as long as France was not free of Communism."[131] Some members of the PPF, however, were anti-Semitic in 1937, including Marion, Drieu, Bonnard, and Arrighi, although they were largely held in check by Doriot until 1938.

In 1938 Jews became one of the PPF's major bogeymen. There were several reasons why this had not previously been the case. Three of the major sources of PPF financing in 1936, the Rothschild, Lazard, and Worms banks, were owned by Jews. One of Doriot's closest friends, Alexandre Abremski, a member of the PPF's politburo, was also Jewish. When Abremski died in an automobile accident in 1938, Doriot was visibly grieved and paid homage to the deceased at his funeral. Bertrand de Jouvenel was also Jewish, or "half-Jewish," having had a Jewish mother.

It was only in 1938, following Abremski's death, that Doriot turned to anti-Semitism to increase his political support, especially in Algeria, where Jew-baiting was popular. As William Irvine had noted, "The entire right wing in Algeria was anti-Semitic. Algerian Jews, granted citizenship since 1870, formed a solid and relatively important left-wing bloc in the electoral constituencies of Algeria—most notably in Constantine, where 2,400 of the 6,000 electors were Jewish and where few, if any, supported the Right."[132] In 1938, the head of the PPF in Algeria, Victor Arrighi, declared at the party's second North African congress, "We have had enough of those who, without being of our people, of our soil, of our blood, without being able to claim our history as theirs, want to govern and subjugate our country. [We demand] a single law for these racists . . . a law for foreigners. In Algeria, . . . the Jews must be sent back to where they came from. In France, we must revise the naturalizations that took place after the war. We say: 'Power to the French.' "[133] The Algerian PPF thereupon added a new plank to its platform: "North Africa must be totally freed of Jewish control."

The PPF in France followed suit. Writes Jean-Paul Brunet,

Nourished by the anti-Semitism of its powerful North African federation, the metropolitan anti-Semitism of the PPF was grafted onto a virulent xenophobia. Paul Marion took from Maurras the expression *métèques* [aliens], J. Saint-Germain proposed a law for foreigners that would narrowly limit their professional activities and subject them to "a special tax to compensate for their blood," Maurice-Ivan Sicard . . . denounced "the stocks of blood given by these creatures belonging to the filthiest holes in Europe and to the ghettos of the East." It was on this cultural and xenophobic theme that the expression "judeo-Bolshevik" was used for the first time in *L'Emancipation nationale* on May 27, 1938. The same day, the newspaper published a declaration of the PPF's politbureau . . . where the terms "judeo-marxism" were coupled. And in September, during the Sudetan crisis, it spoke readily of the "Jewish clan" allied to the "party of war." Nor was the "biological" aspect forgotten—Drieu La Rochelle reproached Maurras for dealing only with the political and cultural aspects of the Jewish problem—thus it can be said that all the constitutive elements of anti-Semitism were present in the PPF before the war.[134]

Under the Vichy regime, the PPF grew even more anti-Semitic. Shortly after the armistice, PPF gangs smashed the windows of Jewish shops, and PPF propagandists called for a law excluding Jews from business. By 1942 Doriot had abandoned all attempts to restrain the anti-Semites within his movement and had himself joined the pack. He wrote, "Our movement has something in common with Fascism in Italy and with National Socialism in Germany [and like] Phalangism in Spain [it] confronts its enemies. Behind all its enemies is found the Jew with his will to universal domination. The world revolution, sanctioned by Marxism, is only a means of assuring the Jewish people that their domination . . . will remain intact."[135] According to Doriot, the government of France, from the victory of the Popular Front in 1936 to the military defeat of the nation in 1940, had been nothing more than a "pluto-judeo-Bolshevik coalition." Only a racist national revolution, he wrote, could prevent its return. By the time these lines were published, the roundup of Jews in France and their deportation to Auschwitz had already begun.

6· French Fascist Intellectuals and the Revolt against Decadence

---

THE SPIRITUAL VS. THE DECADENT

During the 1930s, dozens of fascist intellectuals, along with scores of lesser writers and journalists, provided thousands of Europeans with gratifying reasons for supporting one of the most brutal political movements of the twentieth century. Of the various attitudes that these intellectuals propagated, perhaps the most important of all was their hatred of decadence. Some of the ugliest aspects of fascism—fascist intolerance, repression, and violence—were justified by these intellectuals as necessary measures in the fight against decadence. When in 1941 Colonel de La Rocque called for the elimination of contaminated elements in French society, he was speaking of decadence.

At the outset of this book I raised the question, What were some of the major reasons for the authoritarian, callous, and cruel aspects of fascism? As I have shown, there were numerous reasons—political, economic, and social—ranging all the way from a desire to crush Marxism to a desire to ward off an increase in taxes. What a number of fascist intellectuals did was to provide, in addition to these, "moral" reasons for dealing harshly with one's political opponents. In doing so, they helped fuel an ethical fanaticism that became a force of its own, a form of extreme self-righteousness that went beyond simple political, economic, and social self-interest to a so-called spiritual purpose, to a revolt against decadence.

If for most supporters of fascism spiritual and economic motives remained inseparably intertwined and mutually reinforcing (their going beyond material self-interest did not mean their abandoning material self-interest), other fascists, particularly fascist youths, were purer in their indifference to economic gain and more eager to practice self-sacrifice on behalf of a higher cause. This seems to have been true of certain adult intellectuals as well.

During the 1930s, a number of French intellectuals contributed to the fascist view of decadence—and to its opposite, the fascist view of spirituality. (Nonfascists too employed the terms *decadent* and *spiritual* at times, but profascist writers gave them a special meaning.) Although there is space in this book for a discussion only of the most prominent of these writers, there were many.[1]

Bertrand de Jouvenel, Pierre Drieu La Rochelle, Robert Brasillach, and Louis-Ferdinand Céline were four of the most famous French fascist intellectals of the 1930s. In many ways, their revolt against decadence was characteristic of European fascism in general—which is not to say, of course, that there were no differences among them or between them and other fascists. No two fascist writers were identical, just as no two fascist movements were. Brasillach supported the AF, not the PPF, and was more Catholic, royalist, and neoclassicist than de Jouvenel or Drieu. Céline joined no fascist party in the 1930s. Three of the writers (Céline was the exception) were less taken with biological racism than their counterparts in Germany. In this respect, they were more in tune with Italian than German fascism.

What was representative of European fascism about all four writers was their revolt against decadence and their defense of spirituality. What exactly did they mean by these words, and, given the fact that there were inevitably variations in the way each of them used these words, what were some of the connotations they all accepted? With the exception of the early Céline (more about this later), these writers repeatedly extolled, as a major dimension of the spiritual, a set of essentially *military* values. Combined with these was a distinct taste for socio-economic conservatism, right-wing nationalism, Darwinian "realism," and misogyny.

In the lexicon of these writers, *spiritual* referred not only to the religious and the transcendental, which automatically excluded Marxist atheism and historical materialism, but to authoritarian conservatism and male virility. The spiritual included survival of the fittest, careers open to talent, the right of natural elites to upward social mobility and political leadership, as well as accommodation with large sections of the established elites. It prized social hierarchy, respect for superiors, and military discipline. It was best served by capitalist economics, class collaboration, and social order. The spiritual also meant physical prowess, self-discipline, and military bravery. It required a certain asceticism toward one's body and one's feelings, which emotionally translated into a tough-minded realism with little pity for its victims. The spiritual was fed by an energizing nationalistic passion and an energizing religious faith, both of which justified brutalizing decadent outsiders. The spiritual was forceful toward the weak. The spiritual was male.

Decadence was the opposite of these values. It connoted not only Marxism and liberalism but also secularism and feminism. Decadence was proletarian solidarity, class struggle, and Marxist internationalism. It was political, social, and gender democracy. It was rule by the Darwinian unfit. Decadence was the nationalization of the basic means of production and working-class selfishness, laziness, and indiscipline. It was hedonism, cowardice, and self-indulgence as well as physical and moral softness. It was debilitating rationalism, religious scepticism, and liberal sentimentalism. It was military defeat by one's enemies. Decadence was female.

BERTRAND DE JOUVENEL

In 1938 Bertrand de Jouvenel defended this kind of spirituality and denounced this kind of decadence in *The Awakening of Europe*, a work full of praise for fascism. The "great problem of our time," de Jouvenel wrote, was not a matter of political or social institutions but of the "relation between the temporal and the spiritual." There needed to be a moral unity between the governed and the governing that placed the general interest above the private interest.

According to de Jouvenel, in the nineteenth century the state had broken with the church and had become neutral in matters of religion. The rupture was no longer recognized in Italy and Germany, however, where the state had become a spiritual power. A man who governs, "that is to say, a man who commands other men," must not only have his orders obeyed but obeyed with eagerness. For such obedience to occur, temporal and spiritual authority had to be merged. Ancient Rome had achieved such a union in the person of the emperor. It was only fitting that Mussolini should celebrate the bimillennium of the birthday of Augustus, for Augustus was a model of the kind of leadership that "restored moral unity to an organized community."

Unfortunately, de Jouvenel wrote, in France the word *authority* evoked fears of a police state that invaded people's private lives. But this was tyranny, not authority. Authority enjoyed the moral support of the majority. Thus Caesar and Augustus, both great men, had received the enthusiastic support of the masses, which sprang from the nationalistic feelings of a people who shared "the same soil [and] the same blood." The reign of Augustus was the "most brilliant" in Latin antiquity, and Mussolini was a modern Augustus following in the footsteps of this "predecessor." Such leadership was necessary in a Europe whose population had grown increasingly enervated and "degenerate."[2]

It was true, de Jouvenel said, that fascists in Italy and Germany, in their attempts to regenerate their countries, had engaged in virile acts that had brought them into conflict with religious leaders. These leaders complained of a new paganism. But one had only to ask, "Are there not necessary revivals at certain historical junctures that sometimes require unfortunate brutalities, and is not the Church playing its proper role in making people understand the necessity of this work, which does not prevent it from intervening to soften certain proceedings?" (282, 280). Humanists who accused fascist regimes of one sin after another were themselves tender-minded idealists: "They put the highest priority on . . . 'soft virtues,' those that are practiced the least by States in the process of reorganization. They condemn renovating regimes for their absence of these virtues. This attitude is as absurd as judging the charms of a house by the way the moving company delivered the furniture. The soft virtues are those adopted by a society to temper it after it has been finally reconstructed. Other virtues are necessary to construct it in the first place" (283).

De Jouvenel conceded that under fascist regimes there had been some "useless" violence and "excessive" discipline that had harmed the spiritual cooperation that these regimes needed from the masses. It was this lack of spiritual cooperation that was "the most disturbing factor in the present situation in Europe," not the violence and discipline themselves. For the restoration of Europe to take place, force had to be respected as something noble. Pierre-Joseph Proudhon had been right to conclude that force was the foundation of all other rights, which themselves were only consequences of it. Thus Proudhon had written that force was not the enemy of justice, but rather that "JUSTICE ITSELF IS ONLY THE DIGNITY OF FORCE" (232, 235, 283).

But, de Jouvenel continued, force alone was not enough. Force was dependent on the faith that the masses had in their leaders. Hitler had come to power not through force but through creating a faith that had become a force. This was something that democracies lacked: "The West is divided into so-called regimes of force and so-called regimes of liberty. And some people think the problem is knowing whether force or liberty will triumph. The problem is something else. In certain countries a faith so alive and active has been formed that it has become a force overthrowing and dominating all else. Thus regimes of faith have been constructed in opposition to regimes of opinions and interests" (235). Although Hitler and Mussolini had developed a "vast apparatus for repression," they were not despots who oppressed the people but leaders who served their faith. Force was used more against dissidents within the party who challenged this faith than against the masses outside of the party who sustained it (235–36).

De Jouvenel admitted that fascist faith included hatred, but he said that hatred was justified when it was directed against those "guilty of provoking the ruin of Civilization." Faced with such enemies, not to hate was a form of decadence: "Any sentiment less vigorous than hatred indicates a lack of virility. To want to temper the war of ideologies which divides our society is simply folly. The war cannot be humanized; it has to be terminated" (13).

According to de Jouvenel, humanitarian intellectuals ignored the decisive role that sheer power played in history. They raised naive questions about political issues that were ultimately settled by force. Was it legitimate for underpopulated Australia to be threatened by Japanese immigration? Japan's response to this ethical controversy was the sound of canons in Manchuria. Did Italy have a right to expand its empire into Abyssinia? Italian canons "liquidated this subject of conversation." Did Germany have a juridical and moral right to unilaterally remilitarize the Rhineland? "The sound of boots on March 7 cured this headache." Were the new wage rates achieved by the sit-down strikes of 1936 more reasonable than the old rates? "The weight exerted by the workers, in any case, gave victory to the new; the question therefore became an idle one" (231). Intellect questioned, force concluded.

In a section of *The Awakening of Europe* entitled "The Austerity of Force," de Jouvenel contrasted the tough-minded realism of fascism with the soft-headed idealism of liberalism: "When I reflect on the evolution of my judgments over the last dozen years, it seems to me that I can call this development: 'History of a Reconciliation with the Real'" (230). The real was more Darwinian than humanitarian. Fascism understood this, rejecting the puerile optimism of Rousseau for the austere pessimism of Nietzsche. Rousseau was wrong to think that man was naturally good and loved justice above all else. Man was dangerous and loved power even more. Still, the will to power could be put to noble uses, leading the individual to surpass himself and to overcome the decadence of his times (248–49).

Overcoming decadence required a male resolution to overcome hedonism.

Europe had grown soft and feminine from pleasure seeking. Under the Weimar Republic, Berlin had become the prostitute of Europe, its sexual singularities and other obscenities having been complacently depicted in German art and literature of the period. Hollywood contributed to this "atmosphere of facility" with its emphasis on sex appeal. People became increasingly unwilling to take on painful tasks. Women "naturally" succumbed to this ethos, as many of them had only one baby instead of several (229, 237).

De Jouvenel recalled that when he was twenty he had equated hedonism with women. He now realized that the feminization of Europe had been its downfall. Europe was "like a woman who had just escaped from a frightening accident. . . . She needed light, warmth, music. Her capitals were lit up by the flashing lights of cinemas and dance halls. The pulsation of luminous marquees and jazz clubs moved into the towns of the provinces and even into the villages" (226).

According to de Jouvenel, a major source of hope in the 1930s was the revival of athleticism in Europe, a revival led by European youth. At the core of athleticism was a belief in effort and self-discipline, a belief that was also at the core of fascism. Proud of their bodies and aptitude for sport, youth was disgusted with the physical decadence of their elders. Fascism's desire for a revolution of the body was their desire. The generation gap was a political gap. Fascism was the only political movement in Europe that honored youth's hunger for discipline, effort, combat, and courage, something liberals did not understand: "[European youth] loved strong and slender bodies, vigorous and sure movements, [and] short sentences. They detested café verbosity. . . . National and international parliamentarians with their smoke-filled rooms, their pot-bellied orators, their poor theatrical effects, were ridiculous in their eyes. They admired and loved force. They were ready to applaud the victories of force" (234).

Fascism rejected the idea that modern man was superior to primitive man, to the original conqueror of Europe, the Frank, who was a "military animal." By overcoming enormous obstacles, the Frank had engaged in a "spiritual gymnastic" that had tapped his energies and developed his strength. When the Gauls had started to believe that they were more human than their ancestors, they were overrun by barbarians from the East. Attila had understood the truth of Renan's dictum: The sword is the creator of all wealth. The word *noble* originally described men who were always ready to climb on a horse and defend their kinsmen. It was the "brutal barons" of the Middle Ages who had conquered Europe in the first place. As late as the seventeenth century, playwrights like Corneille still celebrated the virile virtues: "Force, courage, pride, magnanimity, independence [and] loyalty."

Intellectuals of the eighteenth century, on the other hand, had relegated these virtues to the dark ages. By the end of the nineteenth century, Cyrano de Bergerac had become a comic figure, and only children read Kipling. Europe resembled Rome during its period of decline. The *chansons de geste* were replaced with parodies, Corneille with Mark Twain. The warrior became the butt of Voltairian ridicule. The rough demeanor and "brutal acts" of virile ancestors disappeared from French literature and with them two of the principal themes of previous art, effort and sacrifice. Too much security had eliminated the *frisson* of risk: "Nothing was more symbolic than the regression of the officer in the social hierarchy" (247, 243, 264–66, 238–42). Decadence abounded.

De Jouvenel praised fascist man as a throwback to the warrior and property holder of yesteryear, to the type of man who was the head of a family and a clan: "When this type of man ceases to win esteem and disappears, then the process of decadence begins" (244). He was a type whose virile virtues not only exercised paternal power over his children and marital authority over his wife but also, if he was a businessman, a similar authority over his employees. A state that weakened his discipline over his children and his wife also weakened his discipline over his workers. Such a state, de Jouvenel underscored, "WOULD PLUNGE EVERYBODY INTO THE RIGOROUS SERVITUDE OF ITS SOCIALIST ORGANIZATION" (245). (Apparently the servitude of the majority of the Italian population under fascism was less horrifying to de Jouvenel.)

The best way to judge a society, wrote de Jouvenel, was to know "what human type it honored": "Every political regime has its own particular human ideal and tends to create a certain human type. The conflict between Communism, democracy, and fascism is not so much over institutions as over the type of man each sees as its mission to fashion. In one case, certain virtues are given priority; in another, other qualities are prized" (225, 244). On the political left, only the Communists believed in the importance of men with "armor," but the "masters" they proposed were strangers to Western civilization, more akin to barbarian invaders than to Frankish warlords.

De Jouvenel insisted that strong societies were founded on the respect of inferiors for superiors. In Germany, National Socialism had created a new aristocracy worthy of Europe and its traditions. Although many Nazis came from the nonprivileged classes of society, they had no interest in social leveling: "On the contrary, they affirmed that civilization absolutely requires the imperium of an elite" (145).

They also stood "in complete contradiction to the Marxists" in that they did not believe that the industrial revolution of the nineteenth century required a social revolution in the twentieth or that society should be organized for economic purposes alone. The spiritual was greater than the material.

PIERRE DRIEU LA ROCHELLE

A similar preoccupation with spirituality and decadence marked Drieu's writings throughout his literary and political career. In 1934 he declared that fascism was devoted to a restoration of the spiritual, and in 1943 he said that he had decided to collaborate with the Germans because he had "measured the progress of decadence in Europe. I saw in fascism the only means of containing and reducing that decadence. . . . I saw no other recourse but that [offered by] the genius of Hitler and Hitlerism."[3]

In 1937 Drieu declared that the most profound definition of fascism was that it was a revolution of the body. The PPF, he wrote, was "the party of the living body." Its goal was to create hard, tough, athletic bodies on a mass scale, bodies uncorrupted by decadent hedonism and easy living. Whereas Nazi Germany had moved toward a spiritual conception of society, democratic France continued to wallow in debilitating materialism. The Germans, thanks to Hitler's Strength through Joy movement, were collectively involved in sport, whereas the French preferred to go to the bistro or the cinema, returning home after a gangster movie to a good dinner.[4]

In 1941 Drieu argued that Nazi totalitarianism offered "a double restoration, corporal and spiritual, to the man of the twentieth century." The new Germany had produced a new type of man en masse, Hitlerian Man, who was physically and spiritually superior to Democratic Man, Marxist Man, and Liberal Man:

> The Hitlerian has been formed by a convergence of elements: the combat soldier of the First World War who entered the storm troopers or became an aviator or an eager fighter in the *Frei Korps*, like the terrorist-assassin of Rathenau. . . .
>
> He is a type of man who rejects culture, who stands firm in the middle of sexual and alcoholic depravity and who dreams of bringing to the world a physical discipline with radical effects. He is a man who believes only in acts and who acts on behalf of a very summary truth.
>
> This man singularly resembles a type of warrior who appears in the middle of all upheavals. He takes after the crusader, after the campaigner of the Hundred Years' War, after the mercenary of the wars of magnificence and religion, after the Spanish conquistador, after the Puritan pioneer. . . . Beyond that, he is joined by the soldier of Alexander or Caesar, by all those who have lived in brutal reaction to refinement.[5]

In *Gilles*, the most famous French fascist novel of the era, Drieu extolled the "virile male Catholicism" of the Middle Ages and complained that modern Catholicism had grown effeminate, that unlike the ancient Aztec religion it no longer honored blood sacrifice. For nothing, Drieu wrote, "is achieved without blood."[6] In another of his novels, *Straw Dogs*, Drieu says of the protagonist, Constant,

> At the front [during the First World War], he had not known whether he had killed anyone. . . . Killing would only be interesting if it were a matter of murder, a crime. . . . He needed to kill somebody today. . . . Life is a sacrifice. All the ancient religions that have known this human secret have taught it and practiced it. Life is . . . a reeking slaughterhouse before the gods. . . . All that man can do is to recognize that he is made to die; the best thing for him to do is to take death by the hand, to make himself the executioner, to be himself the killer, to take the knife from the hand of God. Abraham wanted to bump off Isaac himself. But the ancient religions have fallen into decadence. . . . Decadence, always decadence. Life is perpetual decadence from the beginning . . . , people killed rams and no longer men. The true religion is the Mexican religion: it splits a man down the middle and rips out his heart. When the heart of a man palpitates in the hand of another man, that is what life is all about.[7]

Constant, a collaborator with the Germans (and Drieu's alter ego in the novel), considers the Second World War a "war of religions." He sees no contradiction between fascist spirituality and fascist violence because the spirituality he believes in is beyond history, the slaughter of bodies being rectified by the resurrection of souls. He finds the Christian emphasis on love much too sentimental, preferring instead the lofty indifference of Buddhism, which is "in no way moralistic" (128–29).

Drieu's notion of spirituality was accompanied by a cult of realism that he justified on Darwinian, existential, and "masculine" grounds. Life, he asserted, was a matter of the survival of the fittest. A man proved himself by direct experience with reality, and the more harsh and ugly that reality was the more truly he existed. As a character in one of Drieu's plays expresses it, "Damn! Not to live, that is the only way of not getting oneself dirty." According to Drieu, only by walking in the mud of life does one become fully a man. The weak and cowardly shrink from the mud; the strong and courageous do not. Drieu wrote in 1944, "I wanted . . . to take part in the excrement of partisan opinions. . . . Yes, I wanted to have excrement on my feet. . . . I feared above all becoming an ivory tower intellectual."[8]

Drieu was contemptuous of those who, out of "delicacy," refused to employ harsh political measures when it was necessary. The protagonist of *Gilles* overcomes such delicacy when he witnesses fascist troops in Spain executing captured prisoners. When a young boy being taken to the firing squad looks imploringly at Gilles to save him, Gilles suppresses an upsurge of pity and turns away. "I am not an amateur," he tells himself. He is realistic, not sentimental.[9]

In *With Doriot*, Drieu declared that "life is not at all as it is represented to be by a schoolteacher who reasons behind four walls." Neither, he wrote later, does it conform to the humanitarian abstractions of left-wing academics: "Life is not a well-trained and sterilized nurse who will care for and pamper man until the end of time, as it is imagined to be by the good Social-Democratic doctors of the laboratories, schools, and libraries of France, England, and Germany. Life is always a goddess of war, covered with barbaric ornaments and waving her bloody lance."[10]

According to Drieu, Europe's democracies were led by men who lacked a "male ability to look things in the face and call a spade a spade." If one looked history in the face, it was clear that killing was inevitable in political affairs. In *Gilles* the protagonist comments, "That's the way it is, my era. And that's the way the life of humanity is always. It is the sordid massacre of this evening and the pure combat of this morning. How can one imagine it otherwise? . . . The Paris I love is marked by centuries of bloodshed. Is there not blood on the stones of the Louvre?"[11]

Nature, Drieu wrote in 1934, was also marked by violence and death: "There will always be war in Nature." And because human nature was part of Nature, there would always be war among men as well. If warfare were abolished, one of man's major ties with Nature would be severed and one of his major sources of vitality destroyed. What soft-hearted leftists and genteel rightists failed to understand was that "war is a function of man and that man cannot deny it or tear himself from it without damaging himself."[12]

The true humanist, Drieu maintained, should praise violence, not condemn it. War was a necessary outlet for man's animality, for his aggressive impulses. Like other animals, man was made to kill or be killed. Indeed, it was only after a man had killed another man with his own hands that he truly understood life. Combat provided a man with the chance to prove that in a Darwinian universe he was one of Nature's fittest. That was why it was so important to have an enemy of some kind. "To measure oneself against someone else," he wrote, "that is the main thing. To know oneself by opposing another."[13] Manhood was a test of strength.

Success in a political struggle, particularly in a violent struggle, was proof of superior maleness, whether it was the success of an individual or the success of a movement. Movements that triumphed in combat were virile; movements that did not were decadent. Marxists in Italy and Germany had proved their decadence by being crushed by their fascist adversaries. Fascism, Drieu wrote in 1934, was the most manly political movement in Europe:

> What I like about fascism is a certain virile disposition. It has come about in Rome and Berlin . . . as the result of a certain physical need in man. This need is satisfied when a man has the impression of having pushed his body as far as his ideas. It is a question of courage.
>
> To be sure, courage is not ignored by Communism either—in any case, by Russian Communism, which is frankly and consciously bellicose. It is less clearly conceived by European Communists. In effect, they have inherited—in spite of their suspicion—many of the prejudices of the old world of the left. For example, they are pacifists.
>
> I see in this duality the secret cause of the failure of Communism in Europe since the war. As for the annihilation of the liberal world—Radical and Social-Democrat—we must view it in terms of its total rejection of the virile virtues.[14]

In 1937 Drieu concluded that fascism surpassed socialism in its conception of man, and in 1940, following France's defeat by Germany, he hoped that Hitlerian Man would show Frenchmen how to overcome their decadence. In 1945, when Germany in turn was defeated, he criticized the Nazis for not having been "revolutionary enough," "bloody enough." Fascism, he wrote, had died from having been "too timid."[15] At one point in 1944 Drieu claimed even that he had become a Communist because Russia, he said, had proved more virile than Germany. This conversion was short-lived (there was too much else about communism that continued to disgust him, and he died defending fascism), but it showed how much he admired those who proved fittest in the struggle for survival.

During the 1930s, although Drieu despised the goals of communism, he praised the Bolsheviks for their virile methods. In *Fascist Socialism* he noted that although he had condemned Stalin for many things he had never criticized him for "the violence of his shortcuts or the subtlety of his ruses." In 1937, as a member of the anti-Communist PPF, Drieu credited Lenin with making a major contribution to twentieth-century politics: "The innovation on Lenin's part was to demonstrate again the worth of the old recipe well known to conquerors, revolutionaries, and 'victorious captains' of all centuries: to make an omelette it is necessary to break some eggs." In 1934 Drieu wrote,

> The Russian Revolution was a war led by men who did not fear violence, who greeted it as a necessity. The Russian revolutionaries not only destroyed their

adversaries; they also destroyed all those in their ranks who hesitated to employ violence. The long struggle and the ferocious victory of the Bolsheviks against the other so-called revolutionary parties (Mensheviks, Social Revolutionaries, etc.) was . . . the victory of the spirit of war in the revolution over and against the pacifistic spirit. Massacres, hospitals, and prisons, these are the hallmarks of civil war as well as of foreign war. The Italian and German revolutions were also achieved by men who frankly admitted the necessity of violence, as opposed to men who hid from it or refused to acknowledge it.[16]

There were times when Drieu's emphasis on realistic methods left the impression that he attached no importance to the goals that these methods served. In *Gilles* he asserted that fascism was not a doctrine but a method, and in *With Doriot* he declared that the most important feature of the PPF was its spirit: "It is a question of a spirit before it is a question of a program."[17] Drieu's politics cannot be reduced to nihilistic activism, however. He wrote extensively on a wide range of political, social, economic, and cultural issues and proposed a number of political, social, economic and cultural solutions.[18]

Nor can his politics, however brutal, be equated with communism. As we have seen, much of his social and economic thought was devoted to criticizing Marxism, while the socialism he espoused was, in fact, a defense of free enterprise capitalism. The point he made repeatedly throughout the 1930s was that goals of fascism and communism were deeply at odds but because fascism shared communism's approach to political means it was the only movement that could defeat it. Communism could be destroyed only by an enemy as ruthless as itself.

According to Drieu, fascism's "philosophy of force" was superior to both liberalism and conservatism in the fight against Marxism. Liberals were helpless when confronted with the terrible pragmatism of men like Stalin and Lenin. So too were parliamentary conservatives as well as even the most militant members of the AF. For all of the AF's violent polemics and acts of disruption, they remained too civilized to be authentic fascists. "A monarchist is never a true fascist," Drieu wrote in 1934. "It is because a monarchist is never truly a modern man: he has nothing of the brutality, the barbaric simplicity of modern man."[19]

Drieu's views on women were equally "masculine." Women, he repeatedly suggested, were sources of decadence. They weakened a man's military virility with their softening hedonism, debilitating materialism, and intellectual shallowess. Drieu wrote in his diary in 1939, "How [women] love the ordinary, the commonplace. . . . Never for a second has a woman given me the feeling that she has any originality, any initiative, even in matters of the heart. . . . I liked prostitutes because they were mute."[20] In *Gilles* the protagonist's first wife is a rich Jewess who tries to prevent him from returning to the front during the First World War and afterward continues to undermine his manhood with her money. To make matters worse, she falls under the spell of a Miss Dafre, who "preached feminism to her, the most unfortunate of modern pretentions."[21] The woman presented most favorably in the novel is a military nurse with a Spartan lifestyle who has sex with Gilles with the sounds of war in the background. Although she is described as more maternal than most women, she is not maternal enough, refusing to love Gilles as absolutely as he wants. (It is noteworthy that Drieu's portrait of his mother in another novel is unremittingly denigrating.)[22]

Drieu's novels are full of misogyny, recounting various episodes in which a woman victimizes a man by undermining his virility. The male's bitterness is usually contained, but not always. In *Straw Dogs* (1943), Constant, a collaborator like Drieu, takes his revenge against women under the guise of political necessity. He tortures a woman member of the Resistance, ostensibly to get military secrets from her. The scene takes place within a sexual context, as Constant first encounters the woman in a field, where she, not knowing that he is working for the Germans, agrees to make love with him. They undress, and he persuades her, to increase the excitement, to let him tie her hands behind her back. When this is done, he pulls out a knife and demands that she give him the military information he wants. She refuses: "He pricked her [with his knife.] . . . She concentrated on resisting. . . . He pricked her again. The blood formed beads along her thigh. He had to make several pricks, each more deep. At the same time he held his hand brutally over her face. Her thigh was gradually covered with blood. Finally, she spoke: she began by telling a lie. [He replied,] 'If you don't tell me the truth immediately, I am going to slash your breasts.' . . . She finally finished by telling [all.] . . . Later, she looked at her blood flowing and felt a kind of voluptuousness in her."[23] In other words, for Drieu women were masochistic creatures who found it sexy to be tortured, a fantasy that may have gratified his frustrated need for male domination.[24]

Drieu's sexism was intermeshed with his fascism, each reinforcing the other. When writing on politics, Drieu often characterized movements that he despised as feminine and movements that he admired as masculine. In his eyes, feminine was weak, and masculine was strong. Liberals were female, and fascists were male. One of the reasons for Drieu's original attraction to Doriot was that he had the physique of a former steelworker.

Drieu's contempt for women was partially driven by a fear of them, especially if they were well educated and bourgeois, and by the shame he felt at not being manly enough in his dealings with them. Drieu's diary and novels reveal an individual who often felt inadequate with women of his own class background and who felt much less male than the fascist man he glorified. Because Drieu viewed all human relationships, including male-female relationships, in domination-submission terms, his failure to be a "real man" left him despondent. Looking back over his life in 1940, he confessed to his diary, "If I had had more confidence in my charm, I would have approached a good many other women of whom I scarcely got a glimpse. I knew well that I was not a true man, that I did not have enough courage. I was turned away by the least difficulty, the least delay, when I approached them. Those I did love, I loved in a delirium of persecution. I believed that they did not love me, that they were treating me with a mean, mocking capriciousness. My jealousy was rooted in a feeling of persecution."[25] On September 9, 1939, he wrote, "With what good sense have I always feared women, which is why I went to the brothel."

The protagonist of Drieu's novel *Man Covered with Women* (1925) laments his sexual impotence with bourgeois women: "I failed with all of them, only they did not tell, or if they told, others did not believe them, or at least did not want to believe them."[26] With prostitutes, however, it was a different story. He found that their "anonymous flesh" suited him well. With them, he could succeed physically—although only after having depersonalized them, only after having emotionally distanced himself from them, only after imagining them more as objects than persons. He told how he felt after having picked up a streetwalker, a "magnificent blond," and taken her to bed: "He had stuffed her mouth with money so she would not talk any more. She had a superb body, with calves, hams, and breasts that one does not find among salon bitches. Did she have a head? If her body had held up well under prostitution, her face was ruined by bad make-up and by her hair chopped at the neck. . . . In my mind, I sliced off her head when I first kissed her neck to mark the highest point of my caresses, and let it roll into the abyss" (78–79, 141–42). With this prostitute, Gilles had felt like a king in bed, a brute sure of his affects. What he enjoyed was a "slave" in his hands, someone totally dependent on his will.

Any dependency on Gilles's part, however, was dangerous. If a prostitute grew tender toward him after they had sex, he grew afraid and fled. For Drieu, as well as for Gilles, there was something threatening about becoming emotionally intimate with a woman, especially with a woman of his own class. In 1939 he wrote in his diary, "Impossible to attach myself to a woman, impossible to abandon myself to her."[27] In *Man Covered with Women,* irony becomes for the protagonist a defense against even the most cultivated and beautiful women: "Every time I met some new woman, I would engage in a detailed analysis of her merits. Then my look would come to a halt on some defect. Once removed from physical attraction, this left the road open to irony. My disgust would take hold. For example, the form of a nostril might diminish my ardor. It would only take one spot on her body to spread the principle of negation over her whole personality. The most beautiful woman would be touched by a new and monstrous ridiculousness. Finally, it was too late; any contact was impossible."[28]

Drieu's distrust of women was accompanied by a cult of virile male bonding. His works are full of praise for strong, militaristic, male groups uncorrupted by women. Fascism, he argued, manifested a group spirit similar to the spirit of the trenches of the First World War. In a memoir, Drieu remembered how as a boy he had needed the strength of others to overcome his sense of personal weakness, how sharing in the joint force of his schoolfriends had increased his own force. "I was weak," he wrote. "My power was outside of myself, composed of that of others." In 1933, one year before his conversion to fascism, Drieu defined liberty as "the power that a man receives from being linked to other men." By identifying with fascism, Drieu sought to compensate for something he felt that he lacked, but, as his diary reveals, his sense of personal decadence remained with him to the end.[29]

Drieu also hoped that participation in fascism would end his sense of emotional isolation. In *With Doriot* he praised the PPF for overcoming the paralysis of individualism: "[In the PPF] one no longer lives alone, one lives together. There, one does not die each in his corner, in scattered deaths in a discouraged France. There, one lives!" In his play *The Leader,* Drieu portrayed an authoritarian political movement as a haven for such lost souls. According to the protagonist, there were thousands of lonely individuals in the modern world: "They tremble with cold in their little rooms in the big cities. They finally crowd together to get warm."[30]

But the kind of male bonding that Drieu extolled was based on a shared sense of power, not on emotional intimacy. Indeed, one reason Drieu may have found the group spirit of the PPF so attractive was that human relationships there were more collective than private, too impersonal to be threatening. In the end, Drieu felt no less alone for having supported fascism. In 1939 he wrote in his diary, "I have had no friends for years," and in 1944, contemplating suicide, he noted, "I die without friends."[31]

ROBERT BRASILLACH

Robert Brasillach also advocated a spiritual alternative to decadence. In addition to being a novelist, poet, and literary critic, Brasillach wrote articles for *Action Française* and was the editor of the blatantly fascist *Je suis Partout*. Like Drieu, he actively collaborated with the Germans during the Second World War.

In 1941 Brasillach said that fascism was neither a political nor an economic doctrine but a spirit. He described the Nuremberg rallies that he had attended in Germany in 1934 as a form of poetry and contrasted the passionate fascist man of the twentieth century with the rationalist *philosophe* of the eighteenth. Fascist man, he wrote, was a reversion to the Christian knight of the Middle Ages, whose strength derived from "the cross and the sword." Fascism stood for "sacrifice, honor, and discipline" and, like the "great religious experiences" of the past, was both "monastic and military."[32]

For Brasillach, the Spanish Civil War in 1936 was a conflict between Marxist decadence and fascist spirituality. Franco's revolt against the republican government of Spain was represented as a religious crusade against Bolshevism. Brasillach believed that one of the best ways to mobilize the masses for fascism was through the creation of energizing myths. The Marxists, he wrote, had created such myths for their own cause: "From the mutineers of the Potempkin to the Sailors of Kronstadt, a whole series of symbols rise before the masses, in order to magnify [Marxism], to expand its mystique" (5, 123). Fascism had to create its own countermyths if it hoped to compete for mass support.

A striking example of fascist mythmaking is an essay that Brasillach wrote in 1936, in conjunction with Henri Massis of the AF, on the siege of Alcazar. Alcazar was Spain's national military academy in Toledo, the Spanish equivalent to West Point or Saint-Cyr. When Franco launched his rebellion from Morocco, a group of officers and cadets at Alcazar took up arms on his behalf and seized control of Toledo for a short time. After republican troops arrived to recapture the town, these officers and cadets retreated into the academy's palace-fortress and continued to fight. Here, along with their wives, families, and a few nuns, outnumbered by the enemy almost ten to one, refusing to surrender, they held out for several weeks against republican infantry, mortar, and air attacks before they were finally rescued by a relief column.

For Brasillach, the fact that Franco's troops arrived just in time to save the garrison from annihilation was fortuitous but not essential: what mattered was that the defenders of Alcazar had been willing to die for their faith, thus inspiring generations of fascists to come. The faith that had sustained the fascists of

Alcazar, Brasillach wrote, was different from that of their enemies. Before a statue of the Virgin in a cavern beneath the fortress of Alcazar, a prayer they had recited had made this difference clear: "We believe; we have faith. They do not believe; they want to destroy the faith. They think with the head. We pray with the heart. . . . We do not curse. We do not blaspheme. We have only chaste thoughts. The reds think. Thinking is nothing. We believe" (115).

Brasillach extolled the courage displayed by the commander of the Alcazar garrison, Colonel Moscardo, and by the colonel's son, Luis, when the son was captured in Toledo by republican troops and threatened with execution if his father did not surrender the garrison immediately. Colonel Moscardo, described by Brasillach as a man with "a very keen sense of duty and profound religious sentiments," refused. When the captors telephoned him and put his son on the phone, the conversation was poignant:

> "What is it, my little one?"
> "Nothing, papa, nothing. . . . They say they are going to shoot me if you do not want to surrender. . . . What should I do?"
> "You know what I think?" [the colonel answered]. "If it is certain that they are going to kill you, recommend your soul to God, have a thought for Spain and a thought for Christ-the-King."
> "Very good, I will do it," said Luis, and added: "A very big kiss to you, papa."
> The colonel answered: "Adieu, my little one, a very big kiss to you." (70)

Brasillach wrote that three weeks later Luis was executed by a Marxist firing squad near a local synagogue—the last word an interesting touch by the anti-Semitic author. Luis's dying words, Brasillach said, were, "Long live Spain! Long live Christ-the-King!"

According to Brasillach, this episode was typical of the spirit of Alcazar, a nationalist resistance that "incarnated the Spanish soul in a powerful symbol which, from the first, transfigured the fighting." Alcazar represented those "noble energies" that served "the faith, the pride, the honor of Spanish man." The defenders lived the inscription carved over the entrance to the palace: "I HAVE ONLY TO BE BEAUTIFUL. IT IS ENOUGH FOR ME THAT THE WICKED TREMBLE AND THE GOOD ARE REASSURED" (71, 75).

Brasillach portrayed the fascists of Alcazar as profoundly religious. He said that unlike supporters of the Spanish Popular Front, who in two months had pillaged 36 churches and burned down 178, the defenders of Alcazar were devout Christians and 5 of the 520 women inside the fortress were nuns. Indeed, Brasillach's account is so heavily laden with Catholic symbolism and religious terminology that at times it borders on hagiography. Alcazar is described as a "sacerdotal city" standing high on a hill protecting the cathedral below, where believers came to talk to "the Virgin and the saints" in the most familiar terms. When as a result of enemy bombardments deaths were suffered by the Alcazar garrison, religious services were held in a cavern beneath the fortress. Since there was no priest, Colonel Moscardo "in the presence of the nuns, called for God's mercy to descend upon their comrades who had fallen in the service of their country for the maintenance of their faith" (87).

Above all, Brasillach paid homage to the bravery of the defenders of Alcazar. Between respites in the fighting, they sang songs with such words as "I am a soldier of the heroic Legion. Our previous lives no longer count. Together we are a flag honoring the glory of religion. Legionnaire, Legionnaire, unrivaled in courage, war confronts you with death" (89–91). Brasillach acknowledged that the enemy could also be courageous, but he insisted that there was a major difference between Marxist and fascist heroism: "While saluting courage [and] a scorn for death wherever it is found, let us not forget that *it is the cause that makes a martyr.*" Only sacrifices "illuminated by a high and pure purpose" should be honored (123).

The cadets of Alcazar, Brasillach wrote, were engaged in a crusade against Bolshevism. Like the Christian knights of an earlier Spain who had repelled the invading Moors and Turks, the cadets opposed a new form of barbarism. Brasillach conveniently ignored the fact that Franco had launched his rebellion with the support of Moslem troops from Morocco, no doubt because what was really at stake for Brasillach was not the ethnicity of the enemy but their politics, their left-wing assault on the established social order. Neither did Brasillach's contention that fascism was somehow less barbaric than Marxism acknowledge the execution of captured enemy soldiers by Franco's troops in Spain. To be sure, the left in Spain was also guilty of callous acts (as Brasillach underlined in his description of the murder of Colonel Moscardo's son), but where brutal means were concerned Brasillach was hardly in a position to take the moral high ground.

Ultimately, what made the enemies of fascism in Spain so nefarious in Brasillach's eyes was not their barbarism but their Marxism. If the heros presented in his myth were the cadets of Alcazar, the villains were the reds who attacked them. For Brasillach, there were two Spains, one a Spain of honor, religion, and patriotism—Colonel Moscardo's and Franco's Spain—and the other a Spain of immorality, atheism, and internationalism—the Spain of the Spanish Popular Front.

Symbolic of the evil Spain was the arrival in Toledo during the siege of

Alcazar of Margarita Nelken, a republican speaker who was sent in place of La Pasionaria (who was on a mission to Paris) to spur on the besiegers to greater efforts. The fact that Nelken was Jewish reminded Brasillach of another famous "daughter of her race," Rachel the Jewess, who in the annals of Toledo had been assassinated by local nobles because she had held the king prisoner to her "dangerous enchantments." The "new Rachel," Margarita Nelken, had enchanted the Spanish peasantry with her "Judeo-Marxist" ideas, despite the fact that she was a German immigrant who had been naturalized Spanish by an ephemeral marriage and had brought four children into the world "without knowing who their fathers were." She was, in other words, by all noble, religious, and nationalistic standards, despicable.

Nelken's call for class struggle was also anathema to Brasillach, who saw her as simply expressing the "passions of her race," with its "secularized synagogues" and contempt for all that was holy. For Brasillach, the cause of Franco, the cause of fascism, was not rooted in class interest: rather, it was "the uprising of a people who did not want to die strangled by Muscovite barbarism" or see the bases of their civilization destroyed by the red hordes of the East. Brasillach conceded that most of the population of Toledo as well as most Spanish peasants supported the republican cause, but he cited with approval a Phalangist writer who said, "I speak of those who want to become the new Señors, the dukes who will again lead their men, the marquis who will defend the new borders of the nation" (95). Thus even as Brasillach denied that Franco's troops were defending one class against another, he explained how one could earn a place in Spain's new aristocracy.

One function of Brasillach's mythologizing was to bury issues of social injustice beneath a thick layer of religiosity, a religiosity that focused more on metaphysical than ethical issues. Brasillach's religiosity, in other words, was far less concerned with Christian humanitarianism on behalf of the poor than with Christian heroism on behalf of the faith—a faith, in this case, that condoned vast amounts of social injustice in the name of church and country. God, for Brasillach, was not a tender-minded liberal (and certainly not a Marxist) but a tough-minded reactionary who sanctioned the established social order and blessed the virile souls who defended it.

Some scholars have underscored the socialist side of Brasillach's political thought, particularly the comment he made in 1941 that fascism was characterized by an anticonformist, antibourgeois spirit.[33] It is true that in 1941 Brasillach praised Spanish and Italian fascists for coercing wealthy bourgeois into making charitable contributions to the poor, thus illustrating, he said, the social action side of fascism. It is also true, however, that in the same passage he justified such action on the grounds that it served bourgeois self-interest in the long run: "Rather than be stripped clean by the Marxists, isn't it better to sacrifice part of one's wealth?" (245).

Although Brasillach repeatedly insisted that fascism was no defender of bourgeois materialism, he never objected to bourgeois class rule. He berated some bourgeois for their emotional stuffiness and lack of youthful vitality but not for their disproportionate economic power. Like other national socialists, he denounced class conflict and called for class conciliation—but always and overwhelmingly on bourgeois (or aristocratic) terms.

According to one biographer, Brasillach recognized the important role that fascist entertainments played in undermining the class consciousness of the proletariat:

> Brasillach and his circle had long since indicated that they had no use for "bread and butter" socialism. Brasillach really had in mind something quite different. . . . The working class could be rallied to the nationalist cause, he argued, if an atmosphere of gaiety could somehow be created. . . . He was clearly impressed by Nazi Germany's success in neutralizing the workers' unrest by offering them spectacles and entertainment. A joyous paternalism was the answer to the problem of the proletariat. . . . Such programs [as the Strength through Joy movement in Germany] would curb the anarchic tendencies of the masses, and their revolutionary energies would be siphoned off by diversions. . . . Mass energies—energies that might find dangerous political outlets if left unabsorbed—had in earlier times been diminished by hard work and long hours; in modern societies, the masses are kept quiescent through entertainment.[34]

LOUIS-FERDINAND CELINE

Although Louis-Ferdinand Céline regarded the word *spiritual* as too sentimental and even the most authoritarian Catholicism as too weak, in the late 1930s he venomously attacked liberal, democratic, and Marxist decadence and was intensely anti-Semitic. Admired by some French leftists in the early 1930s for his seemingly anarchist criticisms of the established order, his denunciations of French militarism, and his association with the proletarian novel, the honeymoon came to an end in 1936 when he published *Mea Culpa*, a work that damned Marxism and the Soviet Union and that expressed his contempt for "Popu, Prolo and Prolovitch." The fact that Céline claimed to be an apolitical individualist, joined no political party, and refused to label himself a fascist, did not prevent newspapers like *Action Française, Je suis Partout,* and *Révolution Nationale* from praising him highly.[35]

The Céline who once railed against the horrors of the First World War and the dangers of modern militarism now compared the Third Republic unfavorably with supermilitaristic Nazi Germany. After the fall of France in 1940, he condemned the French soldier for fighting weakly in battle. In 1937 he wrote that Europe would be better off united under Hitler than divided by his democratic opponents, for, unlike them, Hitler would protect Europe from Stalin. In 1938 he claimed that Nazism in Germany had done far more for workers than communism in Russia and that Hitler was far superior to democratic politicians in France who subjugated the masses with the "bait of equality."[36]

In 1941 Céline expressed satisfaction at the demise of the Third Republic, describing its parliamentarians as having been concerned not with the welfare of society but only with keeping their seats in the Chamber of Deputies and ensuring their "grub at the table." He was proud, he said, that he had never participated in the electoral "farce": "Elections equal sweet talk, equals buying the bewildered, equals fawning crowds, . . . equals Big Press and beating of drums, big radio, . . . equals a parliament of lackies."[37] He added that the results of elections were determined by the Jews anyway and that universal suffrage could work only if the Jews were excluded from the process—otherwise "frauds" like the Popular Front victory of 1936 would continue to occur.

Céline's novel *Voyage to the End of Night* (1932) is regarded by some literary critics today as a masterpiece, comparable in achievement to James Joyce's *Ulysses* and Marcel Proust's *Remembrance of Things Past* and a superb example of literary modernism. It has been praised for its "spellbinding verbal powers," its musicality and rhythm, its "bold assault on stylistic convention," and its colorful use of street language. One scholar has described Céline as a comic genius whose style represents the triumph of laughter and hence a "supreme victory over life."[38]

Less acclaimed, however, are three anti-Semitic pamphlets that Céline wrote after 1936: *Bagatelles for a Massacre* (1937), *School for Cadavers* (1938), and *A Fine Mess* (1941). These pamphlets reveal not only Céline's admiration for Nazi Germany but also his attachment to many of the same ideas that French fascists had been propagating since 1924: anti-Marxism, antiliberalism, anti-Freemasonry, antidemocracy, antimaterialism, antihedonism, antirationalism, antifeminism, and "virile" realism.

In Céline's case, these ideas were accompanied by a gutter anti-Semitism of the most vicious kind, however modernistically it was expressed. According to

Céline, the Jews not only dominated France politically, economically, socially, and culturally, but also were a sexual threat, especially a homosexual one. Jews were "buggers" who assaulted Aryans anally. To be docile toward Jews was to risk being raped by them.

A recurring theme in Céline's pamplets is that Jews were anti-Semites in reverse: they wanted to dominate, abuse, and exterminate innocent Aryans. Thus, Céline repeatedly implies, in defending themselves against such monsters, Aryans need not feel guilty if they respond in kind. Anti-Semitism was self-defense, not unjustified aggression.

Anti-Semitism seems to have provided Céline with an outlet for the immense rage that seethed within him and that he constantly unleashed in his pamphlets, a rage directed not only at Jews but also at Communists, Socialists, liberals, democrats, Freemasons, proletarians, blacks, women, homosexuals, Catholics, the English, the French, the Americans, the Arabs, and so forth. Although Jews were his most frequent target, it seems that at times almost any scapegoat would do.

Céline denounced communism as one of the worst evils of modern times, linking it to the Jewish international conspiracy described in the (forged) *Protocols of the Elders of Zion*. In 1937, following a visit to the Soviet Union, Céline wrote that "the Russian is a born jailer, a loused-up Chinaman, overbearingly cruel. The Jew provides the perfect setting. Asian rejects, African rejects. . . . They're made for each other." Marxist internationalism was also reprehensible: "The stinking hypocrisy of that immense international solidarity, of that masonic coquetry, of that baleful prattle about class brotherhood [which] represents for sure the most sickening farce of the century." Together, the Communists and the Jews had "doped up" the proletariat to stimulate its hatred and greed. In 1938 Céline wrote, "Class consciousness is rubbish, a demagogic convention. Every worker asks for nothing better than to leave the working class, to become bourgeois."[39]

Like other fascists of the era, Céline denounced Marxist materialism and liberal hedonism. He sneered at the working class for being a "bourgeois class in embryo," contending that their "whole program was material, good grub and less effort."[40] He condemned this decadence and ranted against those who perpetuated it.

If, for Céline, Marxists and liberals were major villains, behind them, orchestrating their activities, were always the Jews. The Freemasons were "willing Jewish work dogs, rooting about in all the trash barrels, in all the Jewish garbage"; "The Jews are our masters—here, yonder in Russia, in England, in America, everywhere!" The Jews infiltrated revolutionary movements, granted the vote to the ignorant, poisoned relations between labor and management, forced the wealthy into debt, multiplied economic crises, enslaved nations, and caused hunger and privation. Jews controlled the major levers of power. All French trusts, all French newspapers, and all French banks were Jewish. Work alone was Aryan. Three-quarters of the national wealth of France belonged to the Jews. The Sorbonne had become a ghetto and a "high pressure synagogue," while art, which should be "nothing but Race and Fatherland," was also controlled by the Jews.[41]

According to Céline, Joseph Stalin, Franklin Roosevelt (Rosenfeld), Neville Chamberlain, and even the pope (whose real name was Isaac Ratisch) were Jews. The Jews, Céline declared in 1937, were trying to drag France into a war against Germany: "What do the Jews want underneath their sociolistico-communist palaver? [They want us] to go get ourselves knocked off for their sake, . . . to dance their jig in front of Hitler's machine guns. Nothing less!" "All wars . . . are nothing but Aryan pogroms organized by Jews." To claim that Germans detested Hitler, that racism was savagery, that a "good war" against Germany would be to France's benefit was to swallow the propaganda of "the great French masonico-talmudic buggery."[42]

Jews, Céline wrote, were brutal sodomizers and unbridled fornicators, "Afro-Asian hybrids, a quarter or half Negro and Middle-Eastern." "Racially, Jews are monsters, botched up, desultory mongrels, soon to be extinct. . . . The Jew has never been persecuted by the Aryan. He has persecuted himself. He is bedamned by his very substance, by the wranglings of his own hybrid flesh. . . . Yids are like bedbugs. Finding one of them in your sack means there are ten thousand on the floor! A million in the whole room. . . . Hear ye O Jewish People! O Filthy Rabble! I hear you . . . runting around in your trash bins! . . . Viler than a herd of rhinos panicking in the muck!" Céline found the anti-Semitism of the AF too tepid, too "felt-padded," too literary for his taste: "If you wish to de-rat a ship, de-louse your home, you're not going to do it half-way. De-louse your second floor only? You will be sure of a reinfestation within a month by ten times as many rats, twenty times as many lice."[43]

Céline's tirades against the Jews expressed both sexual fear and sexual jeal-ousy. According to Céline, Aryan men were often raped by domineering Jews, while Aryan women found Jewish men especially attractive. Jews were like blacks in the sexual appeal they held for women: "A woman is by birth a treach-erous bitch. . . . Womankind, especially the French woman, is ecstatic about kinky hair, about Ethiopians, they've got awesome pricks I'll have you know."[44] Thus in Céline's mental universe, misogyny and racism reinforced one another.

Céline prided himself on his irrationalism, pitting emotion, passion, imagination, and subjectivity against reason, science, empiricism, and objectivity. For him, the first were sources of vitality, the second, sources of decadence. Intellectualism, he said, emasculated a writer, and one could "drown under the weight of knowledge." The French educational system crushed students with facts, producing cold, rational, disciplined, materialistic souls, creatures bereft of enthusiasm, spontaneity, and creativity: "Schooling raises no one to the skies. It mutilates, castrates. It does not created winged men, dancing souls. It fabricates crawling sub-humans down on four legs who only take an interest in wolfing food from hidden sewers, from cans of swill." Or as Céline put it in 1941, "What have I to do with intelligence, with relevance, with intention? Nothing whatsoever! Nor does the universe."[45]

Céline's cult of emotional spontaneity and creative individuality led him to damn standardization as one of the greatest evils of the twentieth century, a standardization, as he saw it, which applied to "the movie star, the writer, the musician" and to "novels, automobiles, apples, professors, generals, [and] pissoires." Again the Jews were behind it all. Afraid of their emotions, Jews used their control of Hollywood, the press, the banks, political parties, and the British Intelligence Service (!) to impose rationalization and standardization on the world: "The Standard in all things, that is the panacea of the Jew. No longer need they fear any revolt from the pre-robotic individuals that we are; our furniture, novels, films, cars, language, the great majority of the modern populations of the world being already standardized. Modern civilization is total standardization, body and soul, under the Jew."[46] Strangely, these lines were written in 1938, at a time Céline was full of praise for Nazi Germany, a country with plenty of standardization of its own; but, of course, Céline scorned logical consistency.

One might think that the individualistic and libertarian elements in Céline's thought would have led him to support French Freemasonry, one of the most individualistic and libertarian creeds in France. However, he found the Freemasons too rationalistic, too liberal, and too democratic. Therefore they were "Jewish work dogs." He also associated Freemasonry with revolutionary Marxism: "Freemasonry is neither more nor less than revolution in action, a permanent state of conspiracy."[47]

It was not the violent means of a Communist revolution that Céline objected to but the ends they served. In 1937 Céline was untroubled by Hitler's brutality toward his political opponents. Indeed, Céline argued that it was to Hitler's credit that he openly declared that "right is might." No humanitarian hypocrite he. Instead of coating his politics with "syrupy" rhetoric, Hitler "spell[ed] it out straight."[48]

One of the hallmarks of Céline's thought was the pride he took in being a tough-minded realist, in being contemptuous of anything that smacked of Victorian hypocrisy, humanitarian sentimentality, or liberal tenderness. This was reflected in the style as well as the content of his writings. He preferred crude profanities to genteel euphemisms, his anti-Semitic pamphlets being peppered with such words as *ass, cock, shit, buggered,* and so on. In Céline's case, however, there was more to his profanity than simple intellectual honesty or linguistic frankness. His profanity sought to hurt, damage, and destroy, to express the most violent impulses in the most scurrilous language, to foment hatred for Jews, blacks, liberals, democrats, women, and a host of other scapegoats.

Not all profanity is racist, sexist, or cruel, but Céline's was. Profanity can be affectionate, lighthearted, mischievous, celebratory, exhuberant, Rabelaisian, life-affirming, feminist, and liberal—the profanity of an Erica Jong, for example. Céline's profanity, however, was aggressive, bitter, angry, destructive, callous, misanthropic, vicious, misogynist, and fascist. It was not the frankness of Céline's language that was brutal but the ideas and rage that it expressed. If his rejection of Victorian euphemisms was a manifestation of cultural modernity, his acceptance of anti-Semitic crudities was a form of cultural regression. The style of his pamphlets may have been innovative and bold, but their content was traditionalist and cowardly, a throwback to the spirit of the medieval inquisition and an attempt to arouse the reader's worst instincts against a numerically inferior foe.

Céline portrayed his anti-Semitism as an expression of personal bravery, however, as proof that he had more "balls" than most French writers of the period. Such virility was typically fascist, of course, in its disregard of the pain it inflicted, or hoped to inflict, on its victims. But for Céline, compassion was weakness and brutality was strength. To be weak was to be vulnerable to being buggered by the Jew or enslaved by the Marxist. To be strong was to be as hard as one's enemies. Ethical softness led to humiliation and ruin.

The trouble with Christianity, Céline argued, was that its doctrines of love and guilt left its followers prey to their enemies, paralyzing Aryan resistance to Jewish domination. Céline sounded more Christian at some times than at others, however. In 1937, for example, he criticized the Jews for wanting to "destroy everything that concerns the Christian Church" and for viewing Christ as the "son of a prostitute."[49]

A passionate hater with a spontaneous mind, Céline took his polemical ammunition wherever he could find it. Where he was consistent, between 1936 and 1941, was in his choice of enemies against whom to use that ammunition and in the overwhelming disgust that he expressed for their decadence.

SPLITTING

One of the most striking features of fascist ideology in the 1930s was the sharpness of the dichotomy it drew between the spiritual and the decadent, the *absoluteness* of its separation of the good from the bad. Whether it is the contrast that Céline made between the Aryan and the Jew, Brasillach between the cadets of Alcazar and the reds who opposed them, Drieu between Hitlerian Man and Liberal Man, or de Jouvenel between the virile Frank and the effeminate Humanist, human behavior was divided into rigid, impermeable, exclusive categories. One was either hard, tough, strong, and spiritual or soft, cowardly, weak, and decadent—never a combination of these qualities, at least if one aspired to the fascist ideal.

This approach to human reality is reminiscent of what some pychologists have referred to in other situations as splitting. Splitting is an unconscious defense mechanism that has been described by Judith Viorst in the following way:

> There are grown-up women and men . . . who engage in some form of splitting all their lives, who—to a greater or less extent—dwell in a rigid world of black-and-white categories. They may alternate between an excessive self-love and just as excessive a self-hatred. They may idealize their lovers and their friends. And then, when their lovers or friends behave like normal, flawed human beings, they may cast them out of their lives: "You aren't perfect. You have failed me. You are no good."
>
> Splitting is also done by parents who choose one son to be Cain and one to be Abel. And by lovers whose women are either madonnas or whores. And by leaders who brook no dissent: You're either for me or against me.[50]

Whereas more psychologically realistic adults tend to accept ambiguity in themselves and others, splitters deny their own imperfections (or, if they acknowledge them, feel excessively guilty about them) and mercilessly condemn the imperfections of others. This latter process is sometimes aided by another defense mechanism called projection, the unconscious transfer of unacceptable feelings within oneself onto a scapegoat. Thus, as numerous psychiatric case histories have shown, anti-Semites often project onto Jews what they regard as the worst elements in themselves.[51]

It would appear that writers like de Jouvenel, Drieu, Brasillach, and Céline were highly prone to splitting—certainly more so than, say, Winston Churchill, whose comment "Democracy is the worst form of government except for all those other forms that have been tried from time to time" reflects a greater tolerance for human fallibility. These four writers were more absolutistic than Churchill.

In the case of Drieu La Rochelle, this absolutism backfired, leading him to harshly condemn *himself* when he failed to fully live up to the exaggerated code of masculinity demanded by fascism. Drieu, a man obsessed with his own decadence, was full of self-hatred. The strong, self-confident, aggressive warrior-hero he idolized in his writings was not Drieu himself but the Drieu he wished to be. He worshipped virility but constantly felt that he lacked it. Virility was athletic prowess, but he described himself as an early failure at soccer and a zero at skiing. Virility was sexual prowess, but he was sometimes impotent with women. Virility was a strong body, but he felt his own body was weak. Virility was love of combat, but, he wrote in his diary, "I do not have a taste, a feeling, for personal combat. I have a feeling for combat only as a thinker." Virility was being tough-minded and realistic, but he remained "stupefied by the self-infatuation and wickedness of others." Virility was antihedonism, but, looking back on his life, he concluded, "On the whole, I have lived like a sybarite." Virility was scorn for comfort, but he confessed that he "took an infinite pleasure in getting up late, in reading in bed." Virility was courage, but he saw himself as cowardly, particularly with women.[52]

Judged by a less severe standard, Drieu was not as despicable as he thought he was. A prolific writer (which took some discipline), a notorious womanizer (which took some sexual prowess), a former soldier who had braved death in an infantry charge during the First World War (which took much courage), he did not have to berate himself so harshly. Few men, after all, are always brave, strong, potent, and self-disciplined. Yet Drieu could never accept anything less than the fascist ideal. Unable to be in his own life the Hitlerian man of his dreams, unable to settle for being partly "decadent," he was consumed with shame. Some of this shame he projected onto his enemies—onto liberals, Marxists, Jews, and women. The consequences of splitting were cruel both to himself and to his enemies. Had Drieu been more tolerant of the so-called bad within himself, of his own "feminine" weaknesses, he might have been less punitive toward those whose characteristics he shared.

If Viorst is correct, the ultimate irony may be that, while Drieu and other fascists may have seen themselves as seeking a greater manhood, they were, in fact, because of their proclivity for splitting, stuck in a fantasy of childhood. Viorst finds the origins of this fantasy in our earliest years:

> Now certainly a good-bad, right-wrong, yes-no, on-off universe provides a reassuring simplicity. And certainly even we so-called normal people indulge in splitting now and then. But letting go of our fearful and childish black-and-white simplifications for the difficult ambiguities of real life is another of our necessary losses. And there are, in this letting go, some valuable gains.
>
> For the hated mother who leaves us, and the loved and loving mother who holds us tight, are understood to be one, not two different mothers. The bad, unworthy child and the good, deserving, lovable child are united into a single image of self. Instead of parts of people we begin to see the whole—the merely but magnificently human.[53]

In consciously condemning the decadence in others, de Jouvenel, Drieu, Brasillach, and Céline were perhaps unconsciously condemning the decadence in themselves.

Conclusion

One school of historians has defined French fascism as basically an anti-bourgeois, left-wing phenomenon and has suggested that the only sizeable fascist movements in France between 1924 and 1939 were Georges Valois's Faisceau and Jacques Doriot's PPF, Valois having been a former syndicalist and Doriot a former Communist. However, as I have shown in this book and in the volume that preceded it, *French Fascism: The First Wave, 1924–1933*, the *largest* fascist movements that existed in France during the interwar period, including the Faisceau and the PPF, were highly conservative in their basic socioeconomic goals and highly antisocialist in their basic ideological suppositions— at least if these movements are judged by the programs they put forward and not by the rhetorical double-talk they sometimes employed in seeking to expand their popular support.

Those French fascist movements that did have genuinely left-wing goals (at least at the outset)—for example, Gaston Bergery's Front Commun and Marcel Déat's Neo-Socialism—were minuscule compared to the right-wing Faisceau, JP, SF, CF, and PPF.

To demonstrate that between 1924 and 1939 most French fascists were socioeconomic conservatives rather than socioeconomic radicals, that the fascist left had little popular support, and that French Socialists and Communists were overwhelmingly (some quite vigorously) opposed to fascism, does not mean, of course, that leftists of all eras and all places have always avoided fascist means and fascist attitudes. As any reader of *The God That Failed* or *Homage to Catalonia* knows and as Doriot's early years within the French Communist party reveal, Communist rhetoric and Communist acts could be just as duplicitous and brutal as those of the fascists. And French left-wing violence against fascist political rallies in the 1930s was no tribute to civil liberties. Stalinists in Russia, Maoists in China, and even some new leftists in the United States (including those who called their opponents pigs instead of kikes or sought to become university thought police) have employed fascist tactics at times, albeit for strikingly different ends. To disagree with consensus historians of French fascism is no brief for intellectual intolerance, Stalin's purges, the Gulag Archipelago, or the killing fields of Cambodia. Neither, of course, does it imply that all anti-Communists were fascists. There is a considerable difference between engaging in anticommunism to defend democracy and engaging in it to destroy it.

The fact remains, however, that in France between 1924 and 1939 most leftists, Communists as well as Socialists, were intensely hostile to fascism, and fascism was intensely hostile to them, especially to their union in the Popular Front of 1936–38. The Nazi-Soviet pact of 1939, which *followed* the collapse of the Popular Front and an increased military threat to the USSR, does not erase this fact.

The so-called socialism of France's major fascist movements was far more spiritual than material, in effect protecting rather than attacking disparities in economic wealth. Fascist socialism blamed Marxism, not capitalism, for the existence of class conflict. Even when it vaguely criticized the trusts on behalf of small business, it shrank from calling for any serious measures against them (no doubt partly because much of its financing came from some of these very same trusts). The ideologies of France's largest fascist movements were not revisions of Marxism but revisions of conservatism.

So, too, were the positions they took on foreign policy. The SF, the CF, and the PPF all called for alliances or ententes with fascist Italy and Nazi Germany in spite of (or because of) the way Mussolini and Hitler had crushed the Marxists and their unions in these countries. Renaud's, La Rocque's, and Doriot's views on foreign policy were extensions of their views on domestic policy, views driven in all three cases by antidemocratic anticommunism.

The national socialism of Valois, Renaud, Bucard, and Doriot and the social nationalism of Taittinger and La Rocque were fundamentally the same in their socioeconomic goals. They sought not social and economic equality but a nonegalitarian communitarianism similar to what German fascists called the *Volksgemeinschaft*, although in the French case the racist component was largely missing. Not all fascist rhetoric was double-talk, however, because some believers took its spiritual revolution quite seriously; but it remained just that, a spiritual, not an economic, revolution.

Many of the cultural tenets of this revolution were also more conservative than Marxist. After 1937 even the former Communist Doriot echoed other French fascist leaders in evoking themes from right-wing Catholicism and defending the old traditions of the French provinces. Culturally, most French fascists were far more traditionalist than modernist, particularly when it came to castigating secular liberalism and resisting the awakenings of feminism. Writers like de Jouvenel, Drieu, Brasillach, and Céline were not only deeply sexist in their views of women (as were leaders like Valois, Taittinger, Renaud, and La Rocque) but repeatedly associated cultural decadence with so-called female characteristics.

Thus, it is a mistake to view paramilitary rightists like Taittinger and La Rocque as nonfascists because they were socially, economically, and culturally conservative. At the same time, the brand of conservatism they espoused was much more muscular than that of the FR and its parliamentary allies. Like other French fascist leaders, they encouraged their troops to believe that one day men imbued with military values would establish a more authoritarian regime by force of arms if need be.

It is also a mistake to view the political ideas of men like Taittinger and La Rocque in isolation, ignoring their ties with a fascist political tradition in France that dates back to the turn of the century and that includes such figures as Maurice Barrès, Paul Deroulède, Charles Maurras, Antoine Redier, and Georges Valois. The political ideas of Coty, Renaud, Bucard, and Doriot also reflected this tradition.

What is striking is the ideological formulas that these men shared, which helps explain why followers of different French fascist movements crossed over so easily to their rivals when these movements flagged. An extreme example was Marcel Bucard, who before founding the Francistes had been a member of the Faisceau, the AF, the SF, and the CF. Eugène Deloncle, a former member of the AF, and Pozzo di Borgo, the longtime vice-president of the CF, founded the Cagoule. When the SF collapsed in 1934 owing to financial difficulties, the bulk of its members went over to the CF. Except for the SF's greater emphasis on anti-

Semitism, the ideologies of the SF and the CF were virtually identical. At various times during the interwar period, Maurras lost supporters to Valois and Taittinger, Renaud to Maurras and La Rocque, and La Rocque to Doriot and the Cagoule. All were rivals within the same wing of French politics, the fascist wing.

To be sure, there were significant differences within the fascist tradition, just as there were within the socialist, liberal, and conservative traditions. Maurras was a royalist when most French fascists were not; Renaud was more anti-Semitic than La Rocque; Valois was more Catholic than Doriot; and so on. But, as this and the preceding volume have shown, the commonalities were many and fundamental. One has only to compare the program of the allegedly syndicalist SF with that of the allegedly moderate PSF to recognize these commonalities—including their corporatist solution to labor relations, which, where the bargaining power of independent trade unions was concerned, would have turned the clock back sixty years.

In terms of size, the major fascist movements in France between 1924 and 1939 were Charles Maurras's AF, Antoine Rédier's Legion, Georges Valois's Faisceau, Pierre Taittinger's JP, François Coty's SF, Colonel de La Rocque's CF/PSF, and Jacques Doriot's PPF. Henri Dorgères's Greenshirts, although more of a peasant auxiliary to French fascism than a prime mover, was also sizeable. Except for Maurras's AF (whose membership was smaller than that of the others at their peak), all were republican, that is, nonroyalist.

All eight movements criticized Marxism, liberalism, parliamentarianism, internationalism, egalitarianism, feminism, and decadence, and all eight defended socioeconomic conservatism, political authoritarianism, paramilitary action, nationalism, hierarchy, paternalism, and the spiritual. All eight were far more nationalist than socialist, advocating a form of class collaboration that would have favored management by replacing the Communist CGT and the Socialist CGTU with corporatist unions, deprived workers of the weapon of the strike, and substituted conservative arbitration (under a right-wing authoritarian state) for collective bargaining.

The primary financial backing for these movements came from the political slush funds of various big business associations, often railroad, energy, and banking interests, which felt particularly threatened by nationalization. La Rocque benefited from subsidies provided by Ernest Mercier, the electricity magnate, and both La Rocque and Doriot received funds from the Comité des forges, whose political spending was dispensed by François de Wendel and his subordinate Pierre Pucheu. These and other wealthy financial backers, while financing democratic conservative movements as well, saw La Rocque and Doriot as useful backup forces against the red threat, especially if that threat grew revolutionary.

The leadership of France's major fascist movements, both on the national and local levels, was dominated by individuals from middle-class, aristocratic, and military backgrounds, and the rank and file members were drawn predominantly from petty bourgeois, white-collar, and peasant constituencies. This was true even of the PPF after 1936, a movement whose politburo and central committee, originally packed with ex-Communists, made way for former members of the CF and other extreme rightists and whose original working-class base declined sharply after Doriot shifted to the political right.

France's major fascist movements during the interwar period extolled the petty bourgeois and the peasantry, not the proletariat, as the guardians of French tradition. Despite the big business subsidies that played a major role in funding their activities, they denounced plutocracy and the trusts and promised to protect small businesses from their larger competitors. At the same time, they insisted that capitalism was superior to socialism, praised profit as "the motor of production," and denounced bureaucratic interventions into the economy. Castigating the political left for threatening property rights, they called for lower taxes, reduced government spending (true even of the PPF when its program is read carefully), an end to wage hikes, and a revision (upward!) of the forty-hour-week law. The slogan "Neither right nor left," which all of these movements employed at one time or another, was fraudulent, typical of the verbal mystifications that French fascists resorted to in their attempts to win over blue-collar workers.

Those attempts were largely unsuccessful. Even Doriot's original proletarian support declined rapidly after 1936, Doriot losing the election in Saint-Denis to a Communist in 1937. Workers comprised only 6 percent of Jankowski's sample of the PPF membership in Marseille between 1936 and 1939 and only 9.6 percent of Brender's profile of the PPF's total national membership under the Vichy regime. Like the social composition of the memberships of other major French fascist movements between 1924 and 1939, that of the PPF was predominantly middle class after 1937.

Just as blue-collar workers were underrepresented in Italian and German fascism before Mussolini and Hitler came to power, they were underrepresented in French fascism. Workers who did support French fascist movements seem often to have been motivated more by patronage—by receiving a municipal job or a job with a profascist businessman—than by ideological conviction. Paul Jankowski has shown this to have often been the case with the PPF in Marseille.

In some instances, in Lyon, for example, some upper-grade Catholic workers broke with their lower-grade comrades and supported the PSF's union in order to protect their careers and curry favor with their employers. But patronage had its limits, and the great mass of French blue-collar workers between 1924 and 1939 regarded so-called fascist socialism as hostile to their economic interests.

Although anti-Semitism was a major characteristic of German fascism, its role in French fascism was much smaller. As Eugen Weber has noted, there were varieties of fascism in Europe in the 1930s. Some of these varieties were less anti-Semitic than others. To conclude because of the Holocaust that anti-Semitism was the central feature of all fascism during the interwar period not only minimizes the anti-Marxist thrust of Hitler's and Mussolini's policies but also ignores the fact that fascist Italy before 1938 was generally not anti-Semitic and even as late as 1943 it was a haven for Jews escaping Vichy France. If not to be anti-Semitic in the 1920s and early 1930s was not to be fascist, then Mussolini was not a fascist.

In France, it was only after the Popular Front came to power in 1936 that La Rocque and Doriot retreated from their earlier opposition to anti-Semitism (although in 1934 La Rocque had been something of a *selective* anti-Semite on the immigration question). There are also important distinctions to be made between religious, cultural, and biological anti-Semitism, however much they reinforced one another in practice. One did not have to believe in biological anti-Semitism in the early 1930s to believe in fascism, as again was demonstrated by Italian fascism. Even the anti-Semitic AF and SF denied that they were racist, insisting that they objected to Jews on cultural and political, not biological, grounds. La Rocque publicly welcomed right-wing Jews into his movement. Not until 1938 did Doriot give the go-ahead to anti-Semites within the PPF to fully indulge their venom, and even then such attacks were largely limited to Algeria. Although after 1936 La Rocque tolerated anti-Semitic articles in some of the PSF's provincial newspapers, especially those published in Algeria and Alsace, it was not until 1938 that he enjoined his followers in Constantine to abstain from all relations with the Jewish community. In 1941 he associated Jews with the de-Christianization of France and with the "mortal vices" that had led to military defeat in 1940.

Like the first wave of fascism in France, which peaked in 1925, the second wave, which peaked in 1937, was part of a right-wing backlash to an electoral victory of the center-left. Just as Valois and Taittinger founded fascist organizations in 1924 to combat the Cartel des Gauches, La Rocque and Doriot mobilized movements in 1936 to combat the even more leftist Popular Front. In both cases, when the threat from the left was at its greatest, large sums of money flowed into French fascist coffers from business sources, French fascist propaganda and organizational capabilities expanded, and French fascist recruitment drives flourished. When the threat from the left declined, French fascist financial contributions receded, French fascist propaganda and organizational capabilities contracted, and French fascist membership numbers either dropped or—as in the case of the CF/PSF—leveled off.

Money was not the only factor driving the process. The receptivity of certain segments of the French public to fascist ideas—especially those segments that were the most conservative, Catholic, and authoritarian in their attitudes—was also vital to the rise of fascism in France. Like the level of financing of fascism, such receptivity varied according to how dangerous the left, including the immigrant left, was perceived to be at any given time.

Changing circumstances made France more permeable to fascism at some times than at others. Some of the same conservatives who supported Poincaré in 1923 supported Valois in 1925 and Poincaré again in 1926. Many so-called moderates abandoned the FR for the CF/PSF after 1936. The once fascist Philippe Barrès, as noted in chapter 4, joined Charles de Gaulle in London in 1940. The line between democratic and fascist conservatism was crossed in both directions, depending on the situation.

Fascist leaders in France adapted to changing circumstances, just as Hitler did in Germany after 1923, when he chose to abandon paramilitary overthrow for the electoral path to power. As we have seen, to insist that only movements that espouse totalitarianism *before* they come to power be considered fascist would be to deny that both Mussolini's and Hitler's movements were fascist. Moreover, even after these dictators consolidated their power, they were far more totalitarian toward the left than toward the right, making important accommodations with preexisting elites. Colonel de La Rocque was equally opportunistic, as he went from denouncing democracy to professing democracy to denouncing democracy once again.

During the 1930s, La Rocque, Doriot, Renaud, Taittinger, and Bucard all stressed, in spite of their obvious taste for authoritarian solutions, that they were republicans. Fundamentally contemptuous of electoral democracy, political pluralism, and the civil rights of their opponents, they paid lip service to republican institutions and liberties even as they sought to subvert them.

After June 1936, when the paramilitary movements of the extreme right were outlawed, French fascist leaders were careful to temper their public remarks about democracy lest they provoke another ban. At the same time, they made it clear to French conservatives that what they had in store for the political left, should they come to power, was much stronger medicine than that proposed by the democratic right. The PSF promised a more forceful response to the Communist and Socialist threats than did the FR—or than did the FR's major affiliate in Alsace, the Union Populaire Républicaine (UPR). As Sam Goodfellow has pointed out, since the UPR was well organized and had consistently dominated elections in Alsace through 1936, "there was no need for a new [democratic] conservative party in Alsace, because the UPR already filled that role." The PSF therefore differentiated itself from the UPR in Alsace with its fascist characteristics.[1] After 1938 especially, that is, after the Popular Front lost its police powers, propagandists for both the PSF and the PPF grew increasingly bold in associating themselves with fascism. This was particularly true of PPF intellectuals like Bertrand de Jouvenel and Pierre Drieu La Rochelle, who openly praised fascist man in Italy and Germany.

But even between 1933 and 1938, contemporaries with any knowledge of fascist ideology no doubt took the disavowals of fascism of the SF, the CF, and the PPF with a large grain of salt. For *members* of these movements to have taken these disavowals at face value would have been especially benighted. When Vinceguide (speaking in 1934 to 450 SF militants dressed in paramilitary uniforms who ended the meeting with the fascist salute) declared, "We are antifascist," it is unlikely that the audience took him literally. What Vinceguide, La Rocque, and Doriot insisted upon was the Frenchness of their movements, which led them to reject the label *fascist* lest they be unfairly dismissed as lackeys of France's hereditary enemy across the Rhine. Certainly La Rocque was hardly unique among French fascist leaders in the 1930s in denying any sympathy for Hitlerism, a denial that did not prevent him from praising Mussolini.

There may be a lesson in this for later generations: it is a mistake to always take such denials at face value. In recent years the Front National of Jean-Marie Le Pen as well as various political groups in Germany and Italy has also denied they are fascist while propagating fascist ideas. Nor, apparently, are fascist uniforms de rigueur. In November 1993, an Associated Press reporter described the style of neofascists in Rome (whose Italian Social party had been the top vote-getter in the city's recent election): "Instead of black shirts, they wear business suits and designer clothes. They write off violent skinheads as 'empty heads' yet march through central Rome giving the stiff-armed fascist salute."[2]

If in France in the 1930s thousands of French men and women were, in fact, attracted to fascist doctrines, sentiments, and values—as seen especially in the spectacular rise of La Rocque's CF/PSF after 1936—what then prevented fascism from coming to power in France as it did in Germany? One reason was that the impact of the Depression in France was not as devastating as it was in Germany. Although the economic crisis was severe, many of the unemployed were able to roll with the blow by returning to the farms of relatives. Precisely because the French economy was less industrialized than that of Germany and northern Italy, because its stagnant sector was still heavily spotted with small family farms, it was cushioned against some of the worst effects of the world-wide economic crisis. Had this not been the case, the Popular Front might have attracted even more mass support than it did—which, in turn, would have probably led to an even more intense fascist backlash.

Another reason for fascism's failure to come to power in France in the 1930s was simply the chronology of political events. French fascism's best chance of coming to power was between May 1936 and April 1937, when the Popular Front was most threatening to rightists. By 1936, however, developments in Germany, especially Hitler's Night of the Long Knives of June 1934, had hurt the fascist cause in France. Between 1922 and 1933, fascism abroad, especially in Italy, was regarded benignly by much of the French conservative press. Hitler's repression of the German left soon after he came to power in January 1933 was condoned by many French right-wing newspapers, the same journals that later condoned the violence of the demonstrators during the riots of February 6, 1934, in Paris. However, Hitler's crackdown on dissident German Catholics and conservatives a few months later brought a much more negative response. Nazism in Germany lost its glow for many French conservatives after Hitler ordered the murder of General von Schleicher and his wife and the house arrest of General von Papen in June 1934.

After these events, French fascists were plagued with guilt by association, in spite of their attempts to distance themselves from their political cousins across the Rhine. Hitler became one of French fascism's greatest liabilities, one that was exacerbated by his public tirades against the French. The association of fascism with Hitler, which had been only a minor negative for French fascists before 1933, became a serious handicap afterward.

French fascists were not helped either by news reports coming out of Germany in 1934 that the general standard of living had declined under Nazism. Drieu La Rochelle may have found this development spiritual, but it was not the kind of spirituality that appealed to most French men and women, including many on the French right. Similarly, Brasillach's comment that fascism was a revolt of youth against their elders, of a young, virile, moral generation against an old, soft, decadent one, was not likely to endear him to middle-aged bon vivants—although some of them may have tolerated such talk in the hope that fascism, by crushing the left, would enable them to continue to dine well.

Still, if German Nazism disturbed many French conservatives after 1934, Italian fascism did so much less. Unlike the *boches*, the Italians had fought on France's side during the First World War, and Mussolini was viewed as being much less barbaric than Hitler. There had been no Night of the Long Knives in Italy, at least not one in which prominent conservatives were victims. Indeed, had Hitler not come to power in Germany in 1933 and had he not alienated many French conservatives in 1934, one wonders whether these conservatives would have been more amenable to fascism in France in 1936? Without Hitler next door, would fascism have succeeded in France even more than it did?

As it turned out, *even with* Hitler next door, an increasing number of French conservatives began to look favorably on domestic fascism after the Popular Front came to power. Although, like La Rocque and Doriot, they preferred fascism by another name, there is little question that they wanted a more authoritarian brand of conservatism than that provided by the FR. The CF/PSF with its paramilitary past and authoritarian mystique and the PPF with its anti-Communist toughs and fascist symbolism promised to deal with the left far more harshly than would the FR.

Why was the CF/PSF particularly, the largest fascist movement in France between 1936 and 1939, unable to topple the Third Republic? There were several reasons besides those already mentioned. One was the existence of the Popular Front, a coalition that had been created precisely for the purpose of preventing a fascist takeover in France. In Italy and Germany, Communists, Socialists, and left-wing liberals had failed to form such a coalition, and fascism had triumphed. French leftists and liberals, benefiting from hindsight, did not make the same mistake. Once in power, the Popular Front banned the paramilitary organizations of the extreme right, handing French fascists a major setback.

Also, on July 12, 1936, a few weeks after the Popular Front came to power in France, civil war broke out in Spain between the Popular Front government in that country and the troops of General Franco. As is clear from even French fascist newspapers of the period, large sections of the French public feared the outbreak of similar violence in France. Had La Rocque launched a paramilitary action at that time, he would have alienated many French conservatives who feared social disorder even more than they feared the Popular Front.

There were other factors as well. Authoritarian conservatives within the French officer corps, even had they contemplated participating in a coup against the Blum government, could not have been certain that the enlisted ranks, being as they were prey to so-called Communist agitators, would not rebel against them. (The Corvignolles, a secret organization within the army, had been formed for the very purpose of counteracting the influence of the "reds.") In short, the fact that France still had a citizens' army was a partial deterrent to fascism.

Too, in May 1936 a majority of the electorate had just voted for the Popular Front, and any immediate attempt to overthrow this government by force would no doubt have aroused scores of Communists, Socialists, and left-wing liberals to reply with massive force of their own. Leftist militants had physically attacked French fascists throughout the 1930s, disrupting their meetings on a number of occasions, cowing them more often than they were cowed. (Simone de Beauvoir recalled that in 1935 "when militant members of the left and right met in public brawls it was the left that came off best.") The French left knew what had happened across the Rhine when the German left had stood by and done little to stop the Nazis from taking control of the state; it had no intention of doing the same in France. Here again, the timing of events worked against French fascism. Colonel de La Rocque, an experienced military man, wisely backed away from paramilitary action in the summer and fall of 1936, recognizing that such an adventure would have indeed been disastrous for his cause.

Finally, not only most French leftists but also many French centrists and rightists were hostile toward fascism in 1936. Not all social conservatives shared fascism's taste for military values and its contempt for liberal democracy. Many of these conservatives were confident that the left could be defeated through parliamentary means, as it had been in 1926 and 1934. In 1937, when Doriot called for the formation of a Liberty Front, that is, for democratic and authoritarian conservatives alike to unite against the Popular Front, he was turned down by two of France's leading right-center parties, the Democratic Alliance and the People's Democratic party, both of which were opposed to the polarization of French politics.

However, Doriot's offer *was* accepted not only by Pierre Taittinger's National and Social Republican party, a shrunken version of the former JP, but also by Louis Marin's FR, France's largest moderate party and a long-standing representative of parliamentary conservatism. As William Irvine has written, "The Federation's eagerness to ally with the most sordid elements of the extreme anti-republican Right was indicative of the anxiety of some conservatives during the year of the Popular Front."[3] The FR's previous ties with both the JP and the CF also cast doubt on the depth of its commitment to political democracy. When many of the federation's members abandoned Marin for La Rocque after 1936, they did more than ally themselves with an authoritarian alternative: they joined it. By 1937, La Rocque's movement had risen to between 700,000 and 1.2 million party members, making it the largest and fastest growing party on the French right.

The French sociologist Michel Dobry has criticized historians who have argued that France was immune to fascism in the 1930s: *la thèse immunitaire* he calls it. These historians, Dobry writes, not only have displayed a "surprising amnesia" about the crisis that democratic political culture in France underwent in the 1930s, but also have reacted to the writings of Zeev Sternhell (writings that have challenged *la thèse immunitaire*) in such a way as to "reveal a passion which . . . appears to be the most certain indication that a sensitive point has been touched on questions that are not exclusively methodological."[4]

According to Dobry, these historians have created a "suitably imaginary" model of fascism, one that supports *la thèse immunitaire* by narrowly defining fascism in terms of its results in Italy and Germany, that is, in terms of what it did *after* it came to power in these countries. In doing so, they ignore the many expedient compromises that Italian and German fascists made *before* they came to power, including Mussolini's and Hitler's participation in electoral politics. By applying such an ahistorical model to France, "they demand of the radical right not only that it define itself with more clarity than original fascism—Italian—but that it undertake everything, immediately and openly."[5]

Dobry also rejects a classificatory perspective, which views the French extreme right in the 1930s as politically and socially marginal, in favor of a relational perspective, which, by including Colonel de La Rocque and his great mass of followers as an integral and opportunistic part of the extreme right, acknowledges the much larger importance of fascism in France during this period.

This book provides a good deal of evidence in support of Dobry's perspective. Much of the same evidence also bolsters the positions taken by the second school of historians mentioned in the introduction.

After 1936, the meteoric rise of La Rocque's CF/PSF, along with the less successful but well-financed emergence of Doriot's PPF, demonstrated the continuing appeal of the fascist tradition in France, especially when conservatives were confronted with a major threat from the political left.

Not only was France more permeable to fascist ideas in the 1930s than has generally been acknowledged, but French fascism's enormous disgust with decadence, part of a tradition that extends from George Valois's Faisceau in 1925 to Colonel de La Rocque's PSF in 1941, helped paved the way for some of the most repressive and cruel measures of the Vichy regime. When in 1941 La Rocque called for severe punishments for prominent leftists while awaiting the "integral extirpation of contaminated elements" in French society, he was aiding the realization of what scores of French fascists before him had only preached.[6]

Notes

AN refers to the Archives Nationales, Paris, and APP to the Archives de la Préfecture de Police, Paris.

INTRODUCTION

1. Jacques Julliard, "Sur un fascisme imaginaire: à propos d'un livre de Zeev Sternhell," *Annales. E.S.V.* 39, no. 4 (July-August 1984): 849.
2. Zeev Sternhell, Mario Sznajder, and Maia Asheri, *Naissance de l'idéologie fasciste* (Paris: Fayard, 1989); Michel Winock, "Fascisme à la française ou fascisme introuvable," *Le Débat,* no. 25 (May 1983): 41; Henry A. Turner, Jr., ed., *Reappraisals of Fascism* (New York: Franklin Watts, 1975), 31; Serge Berstein, "La France des années trente allergique au fascisme: à propos d'un livre de Zeev Sternhell," *XXᵉ siècle,* no. 2 (April 1984): 87.
3. Charles Maier, *The Unmasterable Past* (Cambridge: Harvard University Press, 1988), 84; Arno J. Mayer, *The Dynamics of Counterrevolution in Europe, 1870–1956: An Analytical Framework* (New York: Harper and Row, 1971), 81.
4. Paul Sérant, *Le Romantisme fasciste* (Paris: Fasquelle, 1954), 12.
5. Renzo de Felice, *Fascism: An Informal Introduction to Its Theory and Practice* (New Brunswick: Transaction Books, 1977), 106, 138, 142, 143, 149, 161.
6. Philippe Machefer, *Ligues et fascismes en France, 1919–1939* (Paris: Presses Universitaires de France, 1974); Jean-Paul Brunet, *Jacques Doriot* (Paris: Balland,

1986), 500; Philippe Burrin, *La Dérive fasciste* (Paris: Seuil, 1986), 138; Berstein, "La France des années trente allergique au fascisme," 92.

7. Eugen Weber, *Varieties of Fascism* (New York: D. Van Nostrand, 1964), 133–36, 139–41; Eugen Weber, "Nationalism, Socialism and National Socialism in France," *French Historical Studies* 2, no. 3 (Spring 1962): 296; Zeev Sternhell, *Ni droite ni gauche: L'idéologie fasciste en France* (Paris: Seuil, 1983), 34.

8. Alan Cassels, "Janus: The Two Faces of Fascism," in Turner, ed., *Reappraisals of Fascism*, 77; Edward Tannenbaum, *The Fascist Experience: Italian Society and Culture, 1922–1945* (New York: Basic Books, 1972), 35; Denis Mack Smith, "The Theory and Practice of Fascism," in Nathanael Greene, ed., *Fascisme: An Anthology* (New York: Thomas Y. Crowell, 1968), 88–95; Charles Maier, *Recasting Bourgeois Europe* (Princeton: Princeton University Press, 1975).

9. Maier, *Recasting Bourgeois Europe*, 305–07.

10. William Sheridan Allen, "The Appeal of Fascism and the Problem of National Disintegration," in Turner, *Reappraisals of Fascism*, 63; Otto Bauer, cited in Francis L. Carsten, "Interpretations of Fascism," in Walter Laqueur, ed., *Fascism: A Reader's Guide* (Berkeley: University of California Press, 1976), 420.

11. Mayer, *Dynamics of Counterrevolution in Europe, 1870–1956*, 22, 128, 131, 74, 63.

12. Renzo de Felice, *Mussolini il fascista* (Turin: Einaudi, 1967); Sternhell, *Naissance de l'idéologie fasciste*; Wolfgang Sauer, "National Socialism: Totalitarianism or Fascism?" in Turner, *Reappraisals of Fascism*, 74; Tannenbaum, *The Fascist Experience*, 75; George L. Mosse, *The Crisis of German Ideology* (New York: Holt, Rinehart, and Winston, 1964), 199; George L. Mosse, *Nazism: A Historical and Comparative Analysis of National Socialism* (New Brunswick: Transaction Books, 1978), 40; David Schoenbaum, *Hitler's Social Revolution* (New York: Doubleday, 1966), 285–86, 282–84; John Weiss, *Nazis and Fascists in Europe* (Chicago: Quadrangle Books, 1969), 21; Mayer, *Dynamics of Counterrevolution in Europe, 1870–1956*, 46–47.

13. William D. Irvine, "Fascism in France and the Strange Case of the Croix de Feu," *Journal of Modern History* 63 (June 1991): 294.

14. Some examples of this view are René Rémond, *La Droite en France de 1815 à nos jours* (Paris: Aubier, 1954); René Rémond, *Les Droites en France* (Paris: Aubier, 1982); Raoul Girardet, "Notes sur l'esprit d'un fascisme français, 1934–1939," *Revue française de science politique* 5 (1955); Eugen Weber, *Action Française: Royalism and Reaction in Twentieth-Century France* (Stanford: Stanford University Press, 1962); Weber, *Varieties of Fascism*; Jean Plumyène and Raymond Lasierra, *Les Fascismes français, 1933–1963* (Paris: Seuil, 1963); Philippe Machefer, *Ligues et fascismes en France, 1919–1939*; Sternhell, *Ni droite ni gauche*; Burrin, *La Dérive fasciste*; Pierre Milza, *Fascisme français* (Paris: Flammarion, 1987); Brunet, *Jacques Doriot*.

15. Irvine, "Fascism in France and the Strange Case of the Croix de Feu," 277, 278.

16. Burrin, *La Dérive fasciste*, 192.

17. Irvine, "Fascism in France and the Strange Case of the Croix de Feu," 273.

18. Sternhell, *Ni droite ni gauche,* 311.
19. See, for example, Henry Russo, *Le Syndrome de Vichy de 1944 à nos jours* (Paris: Seuil, 1987), 288–297.
20. Berstein, "La France des années trente allergique au fascisme," 83, 89, 92–94.
21. Julliard, "Sur un fascisme imaginaire," 849; Winock, "Fascisme à la française ou fascisme introuvable?" 35.
22. Zeev Sternhell, cited in Marco Diani and Michela Nacci, "Fascisme: idéologie française et intellectuels européens. Entretien avec Zeev Sternhell," *Contemporary French Civilization* 14, no. 1 (Winter-Spring 1990): 52.
23. Sternhell, *Naissance de l'idéologie française,* 45, 305, 317; Zeev Sternhell, "Precursors of Fascism in France: The Continuity with the Pre-World War I Traditions," in Stein Larsen, ed., *Who Were the Fascists? Social Roots of European Fascism* (Bergen: Universitetsforlaget, 1980) 496.
24. Winock, "Fascisme à la française ou fascisme introuvable?" 41, 42.
25. Julliard, "Sur un fascisme imaginaire," 850–52, 859.
26. Winock, "Fascisme à la française ou fascisme introuvable?" 38; Julliard, "Sur un fascisme imaginaire," 851–52. For more on the Sternhell controversy, see Robert O. Paxton, "Radicals," *New York Review of Books* (June 23, 1994), 51–54.
27. Although historians who consult these reports should be alert to the possibility of inaccurate reporting, personal bias, and unjustified speculation, I found many of the reports confirmed by subsequent events that the reports had predicted. Police officials reporting to the minister of interior were usually careful to designate when they were recounting rumors or merely speculating as opposed to when they were presenting more solid information.

   A combination of factors encouraged veracity. Because police officials during the 1930s reported to a series of ministers of interior who differed in their political allegiances, it behooved these officials to remain above the battle as much as possible. The French national police during this period should not be equated with the American FBI under J. Edgar Hoover. Unlike Hoover's agents, French police officials reported not to one politically right-wing director who was in place for decades but to many ministers of interior who varied ideologically and who in some cases served only a short time owing to the instability of cabinets during this period. High police officials were vulnerable to having past reports checked by conservative, liberal, and Socialist ministers of interior; thus it was in the interest of these officials to be nonpolitical and accurate if they wanted to protect their jobs under the next government. The Dreyfus affair had revealed the danger that French army officers ran when they took sides politically, especially if they falsified information for a cause (the fate of Colonel Henry was a strong disincentive for his successors), and no doubt most police officials also found it wise to remain apolitical in their sphere as well.

   There were also disincentives for poor reporting at the bottom of the police pyramid as well. Police informants who provided information that turned out to be erroneous risked the loss of future payments, and police officers who passed false information to their superiors risked official reprimands at best and demotions or outright dismissals at worst. Also, police officials sometimes took pains to corroborate a particular report by having another police agent or informer provide a second report on the same matter. It was not uncommon for two plainclothes police to be assigned to cover the same French fascist political rally, both filing reports that summarized the speeches and quoted from them. The discrepancies between these reports were usually minor (mainly differences in phraseology), while the commonalities were strong.

28. Michael R. Marrus and Robert O. Paxton, *Vichy France and the Jews* (New York: Basic Books 1981), 316.

29. Ibid., 147, 305, 307, 315, 317, 364.

30. Maier, *Recasting Bourgeois Europe*, 344.

31. Mussolini cited in Smith, "The Theory and Practice of Fascism," 88.

32. William L. Shirer, *The Nightmare Years, 1930–1940* (New York: Bantam Books, 1985), 201–03.

33. T. W. Mason, "The Primacy of Politics—Politics and Economics in National Socialist Germany," in S. J. Woolf, ed., *The Nature of Fascism* (New York: Random House, 1969), 170–72, 175–81, 185–89; Ian Kershaw, *Popular Opinion and Political Dissent in the Third Reich: Bavaria, 1932–1945* (Oxford: Clarendon Press, 1984), 296–315, 375.

34. George Mosse, *Nazi Culture* (New York: Grosset and Dunlap, 1966), 269, 342; Theodore Abel, *Why Hitler Came to Power* (Cambridge: Harvard University Press, 1986), 137–41.

35. Michael H. Kater, *The Nazi Party: A Social Profile of its Members and Leaders, 1919–1945* (Cambridge: Harvard University Press, 1983), 22, 64, 233, 236.

36. Thomas Childers, *The Nazi Voter: The Social Foundations of Fascism in Germany, 1919–1933* (Chapel Hill: University of North Carolina Press, 1983), 243–57, 262–65; Detlef Muhlberger, "Germany," in Detlef Muhlberger, ed., *The Social Bases of European Fascist Movements* (New York: Croom Helm, 1987), 59–60; Renzo de Felice, *Mussolini il fascista* (Turin: Einaudi, 1967), 1:5; Jill Lewis, *Fascism and the Working Classes in Austria, 1918–1934* (Berg: St. Martin's Press, 1991). Lewis notes that those who joined fascist unions did so not from choice but from fear of unemployment.

37. Reed Way Dasenbrock, "Paul de Man, the Modernist as Fascist," *South Central Review* 6, 2 (Summer 1989): 6–18; Mosse, *Nazi Culture*, 11–16, 30–41, 147–50, 162–64; Stephen Wilson, *Ideology and Experience: Antisemitism in France at the Time of the Dreyfus Affair* (London: Fairleigh Dickinson University Press, 1982), 586–89, 594–96; Robert Soucy, *Fascism in France: The Case of Maurice Barrès* (Berkeley: University of California Press, 1972); Robert Soucy, *French Fascism: The First Wave, 1924–33* (New Haven: Yale University Press, 1986), 39, 40, 134.

38. Shelley Baranowski, *The Confessing Church, Conservative Elites, and the Nazi State* (Lewiston, Canada: Edwin Mellen Press, 1986), 48–49.

39. William D. Irvine, *French Conservatism in Crisis: The Republican Federation of France in the 1930s* (Baton Rouge: Louisiana State University Press, 1979), 108, 114.

40. Adolf Hitler, *Mein Kampf* (Boston: Houghton-Mifflin, 1971), 344–45.
41. Maier, *Recasting Bourgeois Europe*, 339.
42. In July 1934, Mussolini sent army troops to the Brenner Pass to prevent the installation of a Nazi regime in Austria.
43. Colonel de La Rocque, *Disciplines d'Action* (Cleremont-Ferrand: Editions du "Petit Journal," 1941), 118, 146.

CHAPTER 1. SOCIAL AND POLITICAL CONTEXT

1. Yves Simon, *The Road to Vichy, 1918–1938* (Lanham: New York and London, 1988), 85–86.
2. Paula Hyman, *Anti-Semitism from Dreyfus to Vichy* (New York: Columbia University Press, 1979); David Weinberg, *Les Juifs à Paris de 1933 à 1939* (Paris: Calmann-Lévy, 1974); Robert Paxton and Michael Marrus, *Vichy and the Jews* (New York: Basic Books, 1981).
3. William Irvine, *French Conservatism in Crisis: The Republican Federation of France in the 1930s* (Baton Rouge: Louisiana State University Press, 1979), xviii.
4. Robert Soucy, *French Fascism: The First Wave, 1924–1933* (New Haven: Yale University Press, 1986), 187–90.
5. *Gringoire*, February 10, 1933; *Je suis Partout*, February 4, 1933; *L'Ami du Peuple*, February 7, 9, 1933; *Le Journal*, February 6, 1933; *Le Petit Journal*, February 9, 14, 1933; *L'Echo de Paris*, January 31, 1933; *La Croix*, February 14, 1933; *Le National*, November 18, 1933. These newspapers were critical of Hitler, however, in those areas where they perceived him as threatening German conservatives or French national security.
6. Irvine, *French Conservatism in Crisis*, 156.
7. Emile Roche, cited by Peter J. Lamour, *The French Radical Party in the 1930s* (Stanford: Stanford University Press, 1964), 216. See also Serge Berstein, *Histoire du Parti Radical: Crise du Radicalisme* (Paris: Presses de la Fondation Nationale des Sciences Politiques, 1982), 3:472; *Le Temps*, October 23 and 24, 1936; *Le Temps*, October 24, 1936.
8. Cited in Eugen Weber, *Action Française: Royalism and Reaction in Twentieth-Centry France* (Stanford: Stanford University Press, 1962), 321–33.
9. Colonel de La Rocque, cited in Chambre des Députés, *Rapport général au nom de la commission d'enquête chargée de rechercher les causes et les origines des événements du 6 février 1934 et les jours suivants ainsi que toutes les responsabilités encourues* (15ième legislature, session de 1934. Bibliothèque Nationale, Paris, France), no. 3387, 134.
10. William L. Shirer, *The Collapse of the Third Republic* (New York: Simon and Schuster, 1969), 200.
11. La Rocque, cited in Laurent Bonnevay, *Les journées sanglantes de février 1934* (Paris: Flammarion, 1935), 144.
12. La Rocque, cited in Chambre des Députés, *Rapport général au nom de la commission d'enquête*, no. 3385, 152.
13. *L'Illustration*, July 7, 14, 1934; *Gringoire*, July 6, 1934; *L'Ami du Peuple*, July 5,

1934; *La Croix*, July 6, 1934; *L'Intransigeant*, July 3, 1934; *Paris-Soir*, July 3, 1933. At the same time, some of these journals remained ambivalent, alternating between approval of Hitler's repression of German leftists and disapproval of his repression of German rightists.

14. Gordon Wright, *France in Modern Times* (Chicago: Rand McNally, 1960), 485.
15. Henry Ehrmann, *Organized Business in France* (Princeton: Princeton University Press, 1957), 6.
16. Julian Jackson, *The Popular Front: Defending Democracy, 1934–38* (Cambridge: Cambridge University Press, 1988), 113, 249.
17. Ingo Kolboom, *La Revanches des patrons: Le Patronat face au Front populaire* (Paris: Flammarion, 1986).

CHAPTER 2. MINOR AND DECLINING FASCISMS, NEWSPAPER ALLIES, AND THE GREENSHIRTS.

1. See Robert Soucy, *French Fascism: The First Wave, 1924–1933* (New Haven: Yale University Press, 1986).
2. Chambre des Députés, *Rapport général fait au nom de la commission d'enquête chargée de rechercher les causes et les origines des événements du 6 février 1934 et jours suivants, ainsi que toutes les responsabilités encourues.* (15ième legislature, session de 1934. Bibliothèque Nationale, Paris, France), no. 3385, 31–32, 39, 137.
3. Philippe Machefer, "Le Parti Social Français en 1936–37," *L'Information historique* (March-April, 1972), 74; Philippe Machefer, "L'Union des droites: Le PSF et le Front de la Liberté, 1936–37," *Revue d'histoire moderne et contemporaine* 8 (1970): 113; Jean-Paul Brunet, *Jacques Doriot: Du Communisme au fascisme* (Paris: Balland, 1986), 228, 229, 283; Dieter Wolf, *Doriot: Du communisme à la collaboration* (Paris: Fayard, 1969), 223.
4. Soucy, *French Fascism: The First Wave, 1924–1933.*
5. Marcel Bucard, *Le Francisme* (Paris: Editions du Coq de France, 1933), 2–17, 27–30, 66, 187; Marcel Bucard, *Les Tyrans de la III* (Paris: Editions du Coq de France, 1937), l0, 58; AN, F7 13241, March 16, 1935.
6. Alain Deniel, *Bucard et le Francisme* (Paris: Jean Picollec, 1979), 59, 61.
7. AN, F7 13208, January 9, 1926.
8. *Le National*, November 18, 1933.
9. William D. Irvine, *French Conservatism in Crisis: The Republican Federation of France in the 1930s* (Baton Rouge: Louisiana State University Press, 1979), 104–05.
10. Ibid., 108–09.
11. Soucy, *French Fascism: The First Wave, 1924–1933*, 10–26; Eugen Weber, *Action Française: Royalism and Reaction in Twentieth-Century France* (Stanford: Stanford University Press, 1962). See also Joel Blatt, "Relatives and Rivals: the Responses of the Action Française to Italian Fascism, 1919–26," *European Studies Review* 2 (1981): 263–92.

12. Yves R. Simon, *The Road to Vichy, 1918–1938* (New York: University Press of America, 1988), 42–43, 40–41.

13. Horace de Carbuccia, *Le Massacre de la Victoire* (Paris: Plon, 1973), 174.

14. AN, F7 12962, February 2, 1933; *Le Cri du Sol*, February 20, 1937.

15. AN, F7 12960, September 4, 1935.

16. Henri Dorgères, *Haute les fourches* (Paris: Les oeuvres françaises, 1935), 208, 211.

17. Henry Coston, *Dictionnaire de la politique française* (Paris: La Librairie française, 1967), 375; J. Le Roy-Ladurie, "Fascisme douanier," *Le Cri du Sol*, February 20, 1937. This article attacks the Popular Front for "repudiating" the "legitimate and prudent" bourgeoisie.

18. *Le Cri du Sol*, February 20, 1937.

19. Henri Dorgères, *Organization corporative de l'agriculture* (Amiens: Imprimerie du Progrès, 1941), 13–15.

20. Philippe Bourdrel, *La Cagoule: 30 ans de complots* (Paris: Albin Michel, 1970); J.-R. Tournoux, *L'Histoire Secrète* (Paris: Plon, 1962); Christian Bernadac, *Dagore: les carnets secrets de la Cagoule* (Paris: Editions France-Empire, 1977).

21. Philippe Bourdrel, "Le Complot de la Cagoule," *Candide*, January 11–18, 18–25, 1962; *L'Intransigeant*, October 7, 1948; *Aurore*, October 15, 1948; *Le Populaire*, October 15, 1948.

22. Edouard Daladier, cited in *Combat*, October 26, 1948.

23. Paul-Marie de la Gorce, *The French Army* (New York: George Braziller, 1963), 247.

24. *Combat*, October 28, 1948.

25. *Intransigeant*, October 7, 1948; Marx Dormoy, cited in Bourdrel, "Le Complot de la Cagoule," 204.

26. *Intransigeant*, October 7, 1948; Ferdinand Jacubiez, cited in *Aube*, October 21, 1948, and in *Aurore*, October 21, 1948.

27. Bourdrel, "Le Complot de la Cagoule," *Candide*, June 18–25, 1962.

28. *Paris-Soir*, November 19, 1937; René Locuty, cited in Bourdrel, "Le Complot de la Cagoule," *Candide*, January 18–25, 1962; Gabriel Jeantet, cited in *Le Populaire*, October 15, 1948.

29. Gabriel Jeantet cited in *Combat*, October 29, 1948.

30. Boudrel, *La Cagoule: 30 ans de complots*, 83.

31. Gabriel Jeantet, "Parallèle de départ," *France, Revue de l'Etat Nouveau*, June 1942.

32. Eugène Deloncle, "Pourquoi je suis socialiste," *Rassemblement du dimanche*, August 31, 1941.

33. Eugène Deloncle, *"Les idées et l'action": Conférence faite aux Ambassadeurs*, February 28, 1941 (Paris, 1941), 3, 21.

34. Bourdrel, "Le Complot de la Cagoule," *Candide*, January 25-February 1, 1962.

35. Philippe Burrin, *La Dérive fasciste: Doriot, Déat, Bergery, 1933–1945* (Paris: Seuil, 1986).

36. Stanley Grossmann, "L'évolution de Marcel Déat," *Revue d'histoire de la deux-*

ième guerre mondiale 97 (January 1975): 10–15. Burrin, *La Dérive fasciste*, 113–14.

37. Burrin, *La Dérive fasciste*, 447.

38. Henri de Man cited in ibid., 87.

39. Marcel Déat, *Neo-Socialisme? Ordre, Autorité, Nation* (Paris: Grasset, 1933), 53, 60, 73, 74, 83, 94, 100–02.

40. Grossmann, "L'évolution de Marcel Déat," 14–15.

41. Marcel Déat, *Le Parti unique* (Paris: Aux Armes de France, 1942), 144, 45, 136, 150.

42. Ibid., 28, 31, 52, 54–56, 127, 129, 131.

43. Grossmann, "L'évolution de Marcel Déat," 28; Reinhold Brender, *Kollaboration in Frankreich im Zeeiten Weltkrieg: Marcel Déat und das Rassemblement National Populaire* (Munich: Oldenbourg, 1992), 195–211.

44. Burrin, *La Dérive fasciste*, 110, 116–17.

45. Salomon Grumbach, cited in ibid, 113–14.

46. Burrin, *La Dérive fasciste*, 118, 121, 243, 218, 233, 244.

47. Ibid., 122; Dieter Wolf, *Doriot: du communisme à la collaboration* (Paris: Fayard, 1969), 94.

CHAPTER 3. THE SOLIDARITÉ FRANÇAISE

1. See Robert Soucy, *French Fascism: The First Wave, 1924–1933* (New Haven: Yale University Press, 1986), 55, 99, 100, 184, 191, 201, 210, 236, 240.

2. *Le Temps*, January 29, 1935; Jean Renaud, *La Solidarité française attaque* (Paris: Les Oeuvres Françaises, 1935), 9.

3. AN, F7 13238, October 14, December 11, December 13, 1933.

4. Ibid., July 25, 1933, and April 12, 1934.

5. Ibid., May 25, 1934, April 7, 1934, June 2, 1934.

6. A. Kupferman, "François Coty: journaliste et homme politique," thèse de la faculté des lettres et sciences humaines de Paris, 1965, 202–03; Chambre des Députés, *Rapport fait au nom de la commission d'enquête chargée de rechercher les causes et les origines des événements du 6 février 1934* (Bibliothèque Nationale, Paris), no. 3385, 31–32; William L. Shirer, *The Nightmare Years, 1930–1940* (New York: Bantam Books, 1985), 87.

7. Jean-Paul Brunet, *Jacques Doriot: du communisme au fascisme* (Paris: 1986), 248, 526; Zeev Sternhell, "Precursors of Fascism in France," in Stein Larsen, ed., *Who Were the Fascists?* (Bergen: Universitetsforlaget, 1980), 490; Richard Millman, *La Question Juive entre les deux guerres: Ligues de droite et antisémitisme en France* (Paris: Armand Colin, 1992), 185.

8. Serge Berstein, *Le 6 février 1934* (Paris, 1975), 160.

9. AN, F7 13238, October 4, 1933, February 7, 1934, Châlons, March 9, 1934, Nantes, March 3, 1934.

10. Ibid., March 22, 1934.

11. Ibid., Bar-le-Duc, February 7, 1934; Châlons, March 9, 1934; Douai, February 7, 1934; Metz, March 22 and April 25, 1934.

12. Jean Renaud, cited by Jacques Ditte in *L'Ami du Peuple*, June 29, 1933.

13. AN, F7 13238, July 25, 1933; Renaud, *La Solidarité Française attaque*, 119–25.

14. *Le Temps*, January 29, 1935.

15. Cited in Millmann, *La Question Juive entre les deux guerres*, 380.

16. AN, F7 13238, May 15, 1934.

17. *L'Humanité*, May 10 and May 1, 1934.

18. AN, F7 13238. Memorandum of the minister of interior to the minister of foreign affairs, June 4, 1934.

19. Ibid.

20. Shirer, *The Nightmare Years, 1930–1940*, 87, 97.

21. AN, F7 13238, May 13 and August 31, 1934.

22. Ibid., February 20 and 22 and March 30, 1934.

23. Cited in Millmann, *La Question Juive entre les deux guerres*, 185.

24. AN, F7 13238, March 7, 13, 30, 1934.

25. Soucy, *French Fascism: The First Wave, 1924–1933*, 57–60, 111.

26. Ibid., 192–95.

27. AN, F7 13238, March 13, 1934.

28. Ibid., April 3, 7, and 14, 1934, and June 9, 1934.

29. Ibid., May 4, 1934.

30. Ibid., May 11 and June 13, 1934.

31. *La Solidarité Française*, July 14, 1934; AN, F7 13239, July 16, 1934; *Le Populaire*, August 14, 1934.

32. AN, F7 13239, July 17, 21, 26, August 27, October 18, 1934.

33. Ibid., F7 13238, May 24, 1934.

34. Ibid., May 17, 1934.

35. Jean Renaud, cited in *Le Temps*, January 29, 1935.

36. Renaud, *La Solidarité Française attaque*, 103, 216–17.

37. Jean Renaud, cited in *Le Temps*, January 29, 1935.

38. René Rémond, *Les Droites en France* (Paris: Aubier, 1982), 206.

39. AN, F7 13238, Rouen, June 8 and 11, 1934, and Paris, August 27, 1934.

40. *Le Temps*, January 29, 1935.

41. AN, F7 13238, February 2, March 30, and May 24, 1934.

42. Ibid., November 11 and October 20, 1933, and March 3 and 10, and April 18, 1934; *Le Temps*, January 29, 1935.

43. Ibid., November 11, 1933, April 14, 1934; *Le Temps*, January 29, 1935; AN, F7 13239, September 8, 1934.

44. Renaud, *La Solidarité Française attaque*, 69.

45. Millmann, *La Question Juive entre les deux guerres*, 176.

46. Renaud, *La Solidarité Française attaque*, 104.

47. *L'Ami du Peuple*, June 12, 1934.

48. Renaud, *La Solidarité Française attaque*, 97, 98–99.

49. Millmann, *La Question Juive entre les deux guerres*, 177.
50. *La Solidarité Française*, April 7, 1934.
51. Louis Mouilliseaux, *Corporatisme et réforme de l'état* (Paris: Editions documentaires de la "Solidarité Française," 1935), 120–21.
52. *La Solidarité Française*, July 14, 1934.
53. AN, F7 13238, April 24, April 10, 1934.
54. Ibid., April 9, 1934.
55. Renaud, *La Solidarité Française attaque*, 8, 30.
56. John F. Sweets, *Choices in Vichy France* (New York: Oxford University Press, 1986).
57. Cited in Millmann, *La Question Juive entre les deux guerres*, 174–75.
58. *L'Ami du Peuple*, June 29, 1933.
59. Cited in Millmann, *La Question Juive entre les deux guerres*, 179–80, 175.
60. Renaud, *Solidarité Française attaque*, 25–26, 214.
61. Ibid., 26, 219.
62. AN, F7 13238. François Coty, "La Réforme de l'Etat," tract of the Solidarité Française, undated (probably June 1933).
63. William Irvine, "Fascism in France and the Strange Case of the Croix de Feu," *Journal of Modern History* 63 (June 1991): 278–79.
64. *L'Ami du Peuple*, June 29, 1933; *Le Figaro*, June 30, 1933; AN, F7 13238, June 29, 1933.
65. Renaud, *La Solidarité Française attaque*, 207.
66. Paul Mazcaj, *The Action Française and Revolutionary Syndicalism* (Chapel Hill: University of North Carolina Press, 1979); Soucy, *French Fascism: The First Wave, 1924–1933*, 14–15, 69–72, 92–94, 114, 121–22, 154–57, 169–70.
67. *L'Ami du Peuple*, June 29, 1933; Jean Renaud, cited in *Le Temps*, January 29, 1935; Renaud, *La Solidarité Française attaque*, 114, 44, 171–72, 214.
68. Renaud, *La Solidarité Française attaque*, 22, 46, 67, 200, 211, 218, 68, 116–18.
69. AN, F7 13238, May 4, 1934.
70. Soucy, *French Fascism: The First Wave, 1924–1933*, 116–23.
71. Renaud, *La Solidarité Française attaque*, 43, 211.
72. Soucy, *French Fascism: The First Wave, 1924–1933*, 142–44, 170.
73. Renaud, *La Solidarité Française attaque*, 212.
74. Ibid., 204.
75. Mouilliseaux, *Corporatisme et réforme de l'état*, 93, 193.
76. *L'Ami du Peuple*, June 29, 1933.
77. Renaud, cited in *Le Temps*, January 29, 1935.
78. AN, F7 13238, March 31, May 10, May 24, May 30, June 6, June 9, June 19, June 27, 1934; *L'Humanité*, May 30, 1934.
79. *L'Ami du Peuple*, June 29, 1933, and April 2, 1934; Renaud, *La Solidarité Française attaque*, 198, 199, 148; AN, F7 13238, February 1, 1934.
80. AN, F7 13238, April 24, 1934.
81. Renaud, *La Solidarité Française attaque*, 220, 221–22.

82. Mouilliseaux, *Corporatisme et réforme de l'état,* 122–23.
83. AN, F7 13238, March 30, 1934.
84. Renaud, *La Solidarité Française attaque,* 164, 166, 127, 193.
85. Ibid., 20–22, 141, 214; *L'Ami du Peuple,* June 29, 1933; AN, F7 13238, November 4, 1933, and March 15, 1935.
86. *La Lumière,* March 16, 1935.
87. AN, F7 13238, May 13, 1934.
88. Renaud, *La Solidarité Française attaque,* 139.
89. *L'Ami du Peuple,* June 29, 1933.
90. Juliette Masse, "Le Vote des femmes," *La Solidarité Française,* April 7, 1934.
91. Renaud, *La Solidarité Française attaque,* 131–34.
92. For the larger ramifications of this theme, see Herman Lebovics, *True France: The Wars over Cultural Identity, 1940–45* (Ithaca: Cornell University Press, 1992).
93. The two largest veterans' organizations in France in 1934 were the Union Nationale des Combattants (UNC) and the Union Fédérale des Combattants (UFC), each with approximately 950,000 members. The UNC was closely associated with the right center of French politics and the UFC with the left center. The Socialist veterans' organization had some 100,000 members and the Communist 5,000.
94. *L'Ami du Peuple,* June 29, 1933.
95. Renaud, *La Solidarité Française attaque,* 23–25.

CHAPTER 4. THE CROIX DE FEU/PARTI SOCIAL FRANÇAIS

1. Philippe Rudaux, *Le Croix de Feu et le PSF* (Paris: France-Empire, 1967), 41.
2. Bertrand de Jouvenel, "Le chancelier Hitler nous dit," *Paris-Midi,* February 28, 1936.
3. Robert Soucy, *French Fascism: The First Wave, 1924–1933* (New Haven: Yale University Press, 1986), 32, 91–92, 175–76.
4. Chambre des Députés, *Rapport fait au nom de la commission d'enquête chargée de rechercher les causes et les origines des événements du 6 février,* no. 3383, Bibliothèque Nationale, Paris, 17.
5. Soucy, *French Fascism: The First Wave, 1924–1933,* 238–39.
6. *Le Temps,* January 27, 1935.
7. Chambre des Députés, *Rapport fait au nom de la commission d'enquête,* no. 3383, 137; AN, F7 13241, June 29 and August 12, 1935, May 29, 1936; APP, PSF, February 1936.
8. AN, F7 13241, June 18, 1935.
9. Chambre des Députés, *Rapport fait au nom de la commission d'enquête,* no. 3383, 137.
10. Ibid., no. 3385, 20; no. 3383, 137.
11. Ibid., no. 3385, 19.
12. Ibid., 20; AN, F7 12964, March 6, 1936.

13. AN, F7 13983, May 29, 1936.

14. AN, F7 12965, March 19, 21, 31, 1936.

15. Paul Creyssel, *Le Parti Social Français devant les problèmes de l'heure: Rapports présentés au premier congrès national du PSF* (Paris: Société d'Éditions et d'Abonnements, December 1936), 411.

16. APP, PSF, February 1936.

17. *Le Temps*, January 27, 1935; AN, F7 13241, June 27, 1935.

18. AN, F7 13241, August 12, 1935.

19. AN, F7 12964, March 13, 1936; F7 12966, February 18, 1937; F7 13241, January 1935.

20. Colonel de La Rocque, cited in Philip Bankwitz, *Maxime Weygand and Civil-Military Relations in Modern France* (Cambridge: Harvard University Press, 1967), 197; Croix de Feu press release, cited in no. 3387 J.O.C. Docs, 1934, I, 665.

21. Cited in Philippe Machefer, "Sur quelques aspects de l'activité du Colonel de La Rocque et du 'Progrès Social Français' pendant la seconde guerre mondiale," *Revue d'Histoire de la deuxième guerre mondiale* 58 (1963): 38–39.

22. Philippe Machefer, "Le Parti Social Français en 1936–37," *L'Information historique* (March-April 1972): 76.

23. AN, F7 13983, May 1936.

24. Ibid., May 29, 1936.

25. AN, F7 12966, February 18, 1937.

26. Sam Goodfellow, "Fascist or Conservative? The Croix de Feu/PSF in Alsace," Annual Conference of the Western Society for French Historical Studies, October 15, 1993.

27. Machefer, "Le Parti Social Français en 1936–37," 74; Philippe Machefer, "L'Union des droites: Le PSF et le Front de la Liberté, 1936–37," *Revue d'histoire moderne et contemporaine* 17 (1970): 113; William D. Irvine, *French Conservatism in Crisis: The Republican Federation of France in the 1930s* (Baton Rouge: Louisiana State University Press, 1979), 112–58; Machefer, "Sur quelques aspects," 36.

28. Letter from William Irvine to Robert Soucy, January 18, 1990.

29. Machefer, "Sur quelques aspects," 36.

30. Julian Jackson, *The Popular Front in France: Defending Democracy, 1934–38* (Cambridge: Cambridge University Press, 1988), 252, 253.

31. Ibid., 254.

32. Ibid., 252–53; Machefer, "Le Parti Social Français en 1936–37," 80; René Rémond, *Les Droites en France* (Paris: Aubier, 1982), 215.

33. Irvine, *French Conservatism in Crisis*, 98–99, 157–58.

34. William D. Irvine, "Fascism in France and the Strange Case of the Croix de Feu," *Journal of Modern History* 63 (June 1991): 295.

35. Soucy, *French Fascism: The First Wave, 1924–1933*, 39, 87.

36. Machefer, "Le Parti Social Français en 1936–37," 76–78.

37. AN, F7 12966, February 14 and 18, 1937; *Le Journal*, December 27, 1937.

38. *Le Flambeau*, August 22, 1936; April 25, 1936; October 19, 1935.

39. Machefer, "Le Parti Social Français en 1936–37," 79; La Rocque, cited in *Le Temps*, January 27, 1935.

40. Fernand Robbe, *Le Parti social français et le Front de la liberté* (Paris: Société d'Éditions et d'Abonnements, June 1937), 30–35.

41. "Extraits d'une lettre adressée par le Colonel de La Rocque à tous les ministres et sous-secrétaires d'état," December 7, 1939, cited in Colonel de La Rocque, *Disciplines d'Action* (Clermont-Ferrand: Editions du "Petit Journal," 1941), 167–68.

42. La Rocque, *Disciplines d'Action,* 89, 118.

43. Ibid., 155.

44. Ibid., 156.

45. *Le Flambeau,* December 17, 1941.

46. La Rocque, *Disciplines d'Action,* 10, 16, 54, 122–24.

47. La Rocque, cited in Machefer, "Sur quelques aspects," 48, 85.

48. *Le Petit Journal,* May 25, 1941.

49. Cited in Machefer, "Sur quelques aspects," 38–39.

50. Machefer, "Sur quelques aspects," 42, 49.

51. La Rocque, cited in ibid., 45.

52. Machefer, "Sur quelques aspects," 50.

53. Edith and Gilles de La Rocque, *La Rocque tel qu'il était* (Paris: Fayard, 1962).

54. Chambre des Députés, *Rapport fait au nom de la commission d'enquête,* no. 3383, 139.

55. André Tardieu, cited in *Le Jour,* October 27, 1937.

56. AN, F7 13241, June 27 and August 14, 1935.

57. Ibid., F7 12960, July 23, 1935.

58. Chambre des Députés, *Rapport fait au nom de la commission d'enquête,* no. 3385, 17; AN, F7 12965, March 30, 1936.

59. Paul Chopine, *La Vérité sur le P.S.F. et le comte de La Rocque* (Paris: Éditions de "Paix et Liberté," 1938), 32.

60. AN, F7 13241, July 6, 1935. See also ibid., June 29, 1935; Chambre des Députés, *Rapport fait au nom de la commission d'enquête,* no. 3385, 17, 28, 34, 35.

61. AN, F7 13241, June 28, 1936.

62. Soucy, *French Fascism: The First Wave, 1924–1933,* 239.

63. Comité de vigilance des intellectuels antifascistes, *Les Croix de Feu, leur chef, leur programme* (Paris: Imprimerie Coueslant, 1935), 5–6.

64. AN, F7 12965, March 21, 1936. See also F7 13241, July 20, 1935.

65. AN, F7 12960, July 4, 1935.

66. Jean-Noel Jeanneney, *François Wendel en République: l'argent et le pouvoir, 1914–1940* (Paris: Seuil, 1976), 567, 3376–79, 564–66.

67. AN, F7 13241, July 6, 1935, and June 29, 1935.

68. Ibid., F7 12965, March 31, 1936; *Le Flambeau,* March 21, 1936; APP, Croix de Feu, March 23, 1936.

69. AN, F7 13241, June 29, 1935; F7 12960, July 4, 1935.

70. Jackson, *The Popular Front in France,* 254.

71. Cited in Machefer, "Le Parti Social Français en 1936–37," 75, 77–78.

72. Interview with Janine Bourdin, Paris, 1969; Machefer, "Le Parti Social Français en 1936–37," 74–75.

73. Sam Goodfellow, "Fascism in Alsace, 1918–1945" (Ph.D. thesis, Indiana University, 1991).

74. Kevin Passmore, "The Right and the Extreme Right in the Department of the Rhône, 1928–1939" (Ph.D. thesis, Warwick, 1992), 300, 336–38.

75. Cited in Machefer, "Le Parti Social Français en 1936–37," 75.

76. Creyssel, *Le Parti Social Français devant les problèmes de l'heure*, 65–66; AN, F7 12966, February 11, 1937.

77. *Le Flambeau*, June 8, 1935; AN, F7 12966, February 27, 1937; Chopine, *La Vérité sur le P.S.F. et le comte de La Rocque*, 12–13.

78. Creyssel, *Le Parti Social Français devant les problèmes de l'heure*, 54–57.

79. Stephen Wilson, *Ideology and Experience: Antisemitism in France at the Time of the Dreyfus Affair* (Toronto: Fairleigh Dickinson University Press, 1982), 698–701; AN, F7 12964, March 13, 1936.

80. AN, F7 12964, March 11, 1936.

81. AN, F7 13241, June 15, 1935.

82. AN, F7 13983, May 20, 1936.

83. Ibid., May 15, 1936.

84. Chambre des Députés, *Rapport fait au nom de la commission d'enquête*, no. 3383, 145, 152.

85. AN, F7 13241, June 13, 1935; August 17, 1935; June 20, 1935.

86. Chopine, *La Vérité sur le P.S.F. et le comte de La Rocque*, 31.

87. René Rémond, *Les Droites en France* (Paris: Aubier, 1982), 211.

88. Machefer, "Sur quelques aspects," 54; Zeev Sternhell, "Precursors of Fascism in France: The Continuity with the Pre–World War I Traditions," in Stein Larsen, ed., *Who Were the Fascists? Social Roots of European Fascism* (Bergen: Universitetsforlaget, 1980), 495; René Rémond, *Notre Siècle, 1918–1988* (Paris: Fayard, 1988), 159, 216. See also Jean Elleinstein, *Histoire mondiale du socialisme* (1981); Raymond Aron, *Le spectateur engagé* (1981); Jean-Marie Mayeur, *La vie politique sous la troisième république* (1986); Michel Winock, *La France des années trente* (1982–83); Herbert Lottman, *Pétain* (1984).

89. *Le Monde*, May 8–9, 1988.

90. Ibid., October 13, 1985.

91. Rémond, *Notre siècle, 1918–1988*, 216, 105.

92. Jackson, *The Popular Front in France*, 253, 107.

93. La Rocque on April 3, 1934, cited in Chambre des Députés, *Rapport fait au nom de la commission d'enquête*, no. 3383 (2–3), 1623; *Le Flambeau*, June 20, 1936.

94. La Rocque, cited in Creyssel, *Le Parti Social Français devant les problèmes de l'heure*, 406; *Le Flambeau*, April 25, May 2, June 13, 1936.

95. *Le Petit Journal*, July 14, 1937.

96. Colonel de La Rocque, *Service public* (Paris, 1934), 179, 256, 260-62.

97. *Le Flambeau*, March 21, 1936.

98. Ibid., April 25, 1936.

99. Ibid., May 30, 1936.

100. La Rocque, *Service public*, 177.

101. Ibid., 180; Colonel de La Rocque, cited in Chambre des Députés, *Rapport général au nom de la commission d'enquête*, no. 3387, 134; Colonel de La Rocque, cited in Philip Bankwitz, *Maxime Weygand and Civil-Military Relations in Modern France* (Cambridge: Harvard University Press, 1967), 197; Croix de Feu press release, no. 3387, J.O.C. Docs, 1934, I, 665.

102. La Rocque, *Service public*, 177.

103. *Le Flambeau*, September 21, 1935.

104. La Rocque, *Service public*, 261–62.

105. AN, F7 13983, May 16 and May 20, 1936.

106. Goodfellow, "Fascist or Conservative? The Croix de Feu/PSF in Alsace," Annual Conference of the Western Society for French Historical Studies, October 15, 1993.

107. "Wiegrussen die Croix de Feu," *Le Franciste* (April 15, 1937), cited in Goodfellow, "Fascism in Alsace, 1918–1945," 424.

108. "In Saarburg und Hagenau," *Le Flambeau de l'Est* (September 18, 1937), cited in Goodellow, "Fascism in Alsace, 1918–1945," 391–432.

109. Philippe Barrès, *Sous la vague hitlérienne* (Paris: Plon, 1933); Sam Goodfellow, "The French Radical Right in Alsace, 1924–1945," Thirty-Sixth Annual Conference of the Society for French Historical Studies, March 31, 1990, Columbus, Ohio.

110. La Rocque, *Disciplines d'Action*, 102, 146. See also 56, 89, 101–02, 105, 110, 136.

111. Machefer, "Sur quelques aspects," 47.

112. La Rocque, *Disciplines d'Action*, 105.

113. *Le Petit Journal*, July 16, 1941; La Rocque, *Disciplines d'Action*, 145–46, 109.

114. La Rocque, *Disciplines d'Action*, 134.

115. Ibid., 70, 107, 145–46, 118, 154–56, 21, 56, 89, 101–02, 105, 110, 136, 146.

116. Soucy, *French Fascism: The First Wave, 1924–1933*.

117. Charles Micaud, *The French Right and Nazi Germany* (Durham: Duke University Press, 1943).

118. *Le Flambeau*, March 7, 14 and May 2, 1936.

119. Ibid., June 6, 13, 1936.

120. Ibid., May 9, 1936.

121. Ibid., May 30, 1936.

122. Parti Social Française, *A tous les patriotes quelles que soient leur origines, leurs confessions, leurs professions* (Paris: Imprimerie Croissant, undated, but situated in 1936), 6, 7.

123. *Le Flambeau*, May 25, 1935, and September 30, 1938.

124. *Le Petit Journal*, February 6, 1938; *Le Flambeau*, July 9, 1939.

125. Henri Coston, *Je vous hais* (Paris: La Librairie Française, 1944), 92–93.

126. La Rocque, *Service public*, 199, 154–55.

127. La Rocque, cited in Coston, *Je vous hais*, 137.

128. APP, PSF, June 12 and 14, 1936; see also Paula Hyman, *From Dreyfus to Vichy* (New York: Columbia University Press, 1979), 226-30.

129. APP, PSF, March 30, 1936.

130. Ibid., June 12, 1936; Anon, *La Rocque et les juifs: un nouveau scandale!* (Paris: Centre de documentation et de propagande, no date).

131. Irvine, "Fascism in France and the Strange Case of the Croix de Feu," 292-93. See also *La Flamme*, August 1, 1937, February 10, 1938, March 19, 1938, May 20, 1938, February 10, 1938.

132. Irvine, "Fascism in France and the Strange Case of the Croix de Feu," 291; *Le Flambeau du Sud-Ouest*, May 22, 1937; *Le Flambeau de Flandre*, November 27, 1938; *Le Flambeau du Midi*, June 26, 1938.

133. Goodfellow, "Fascism in Alsace, 1918-1945," 424-28.

134. La Rocque, *Disciplines d'Action*, 97-98.

135. Machefer, "Sur quelques aspects," 41.

136. Chambre des Députés, *Rapport fait au nom de la commission d'enquête*, no. 3387, 123-24.

137. La Rocque, *Service public*, 197.

138. AN, F7 13241, June 28, 1935.

139. AN, F7 13938, May 20 and 29, 1936.

140. La Rocque, *Service public*, 32, 65-66, 72.

141. AN, F7 13938, May 29, 1936.

142. *Le Flambeau*, April 18 and 25, 1936.

143. La Rocque, *Service public*, 22, 198, 212, 123.

144. *Le Flambeau*, November 9, 1935.

145. Creyssel, *Le Parti Social Français devant les problèmes de l'heure*, 408.

146. La Rocque, *Service public*, 98.

147. La Rocque, *Disciplines d'Action*, 15, 126-40.

148. Cited in ibid., 126-27.

149. La Rocque, *Disciplines d'Action*, 127.

150. Laurent Bonnevay, *Les journées sanglantes de février 34* (Paris: Flammarion, 1935), 28.

151. F. de Hauteclocque, *Grandeur et décadence des Croix de Feu* (Paris: Editions La Bourdonnais, 1937), 21-22.

152. Chambre des Députés, *Rapport fait au nom de la commission d'enquête*, no. 3383, 136.

153. La Rocque, *Service public*, 109-11.

154. AN, F7 13241, June 15 and July 8, 1935.

155. *Le Temps*, January 27, 1935; La Rocque, *Service public*, 23.

156. AN, F7 13241, June 18, 1935; ibid., June 29 and July 3, 1935.

157. *La Dépêche Algérienne*, June 11, 1935.

158. AN, F7 13241, June 23, 1935.

159. Ibid., Metz, June 15, 1935.

160. Ibid., June 29, July 3, July 8, 1935.

161. La Rocque, *Disciplines d'Action*, 29-30.

162. AN, F7 12966, February 20, 1937.
163. Ibid., F7 13983, May 18, 1936.
164. Paul Chopine, *La Vérité sur le P.S.F. et le comte de La Rocque*, 6; *Le Journal*, December 22, 1937.
165. AN, F7 12966, February 18 and 20, 1937.
166. AN, F7 13983, May 12, 1936.
167. AN, F7 13241, August 30, 1935; F7 13983, May 14 and 29, 1936.
168. *Le Flambeau*, July 11, 1936, October 10, 1936.
169. Creyssel, *Le Parti Social Français devant les problèmes de l'heure*, 240–42, 33; AN, F7 12966, February 20, 1937.
170. Creyssel, *Le Parti Social Français devant les problèmes de l'heure*, 394, 34, 390, and La Rocque, cited on 395.
171. AN, F7 13241, June 17, 19, July 13, September 23, 1935.
172. *Le Petit Parisien*, January 28, 1937; *Le Journal*, March 1, 1937.
173. La Rocque, *Disciplines d'Action*, 55–56.
174. *Le Flambeau*, July 11, 1936; *La Dépêche Algérienne*, June 11, 1935; AN, F7 13241, Croix de Feu poster, 1935; La Rocque, *Service public*, 248, 250–51.
175. La Rocque, *Service public*, 226; AN, F7 13241, June 29, 1935.
176. AN, F7 13241, June 17, 1935; F7 12960, August 26, 1935.
177. Hauteclocque, *Grandeur et décadence des Croix de Feu*, 29; AN, F7 13983, May 8, 15, 16, 21, 1936.
178. AN, F7 13983, May 8, 18, 16, 1936.
179. Ibid., May 21 and 28, 1936.
180. *Le Flambeau*, April 11 and May 23, 1936.
181. La Rocque, *Service public*, 231; Parti Social Français, *A tous les patriotes*, 1.
182. Parti Social Français, *A tous les patriotes*, 1–2.
183. *Le Flambeau*, June 6, 1936.
184. Parti Social Français, *A tous les patriotes*, 1.
185. *La Dépêche Algérienne*, June 11, 1935; *Le Flambeau*, August 1, 1936; *Le Petit Journal*, July 12, 1940.
186. Chambre des Députés, *Rapport fait au nom de la commission d'enquête*, no. 3387, 120; La Rocque, *Service public*, 238, 242.
187. Creyssel, *Le Parti Social Français devant les problèmes de l'heure*, 36–37.
188. La Rocque, *Service public*, 148–49.
189. Ibid., 147.
190. La Rocque cited in Creyssel, *Le Parti Social Français devant les problèmes de l'heure*, 80.
191. La Rocque, *Service public*, 211, 147.
192. Creyssel, *Le Parti Social Français devant les problèmes de l'heure*, 78–79.
193. Chopine, *La Vérité sur le P.S.F. et le comte de La Rocque*, 10.
194. La Rocque, *Service public*, 150–51.
195. Rémond, *Notre siècle, 1918–1988*, 205; *Le Petit Journal*, January 27, 1938.
196. *Le Flambeau*, January 2, 1937; Soucy, *French Fascism: The First Wave, 1924–1933*, 69, 72, 141–42, 159, 170.

197. Creyssel, *Le Parti Social Français devant les problèmes de l'heure*, 156.
198. *Le Flambeau*, January 2, 1937: La Rocque, *Service public*, 134; La Rocque, *Disciplines d'Action*, 135.
199. La Rocque, *Service public*, 236; Creyssel, *Le Parti Social Français devant les problèmes de l'heure*, 72.
200. *Le Flambeau*, January 2, 1937; La Rocque, "Extraits d/une lettre adressée par le Colonel de La Rocque à tous les ministres et sous-secretaries d'etat" (December 7, 1939), cited in La Rocque, *Disciplines d'Action*, 164.
201. Creyssel, *Le Parti Social Français devant les problèmes de l'heure*, 239.
202. La Rocque, *Service public*, 59–60.
203. *Flambeau*, July 18, 1936; La Rocque, *Disciplines d'Action*, 145.
204. AN, F7 12966, February 17, 1937.
205. Susanna Barrows, *Distorting Mirrors: Visions of the Crowd in Nineteenth-Century France* (New Haven: Yale University Press, 1981); Soucy, *French Fascism: The First Wave, 1924–1933*.
206. La Rocque, *Disciplines d'Action*, 94–95.
207. La Rocque, *Service public*, 269, 49, 59, 112, 242, 270.
208. *Le Petit Journal*, April 14, 1937.
209. Cited in La Rocque, *Disciplines d'Action*, 50.
210. La Rocque, *Disciplines d'Action*, 55, 156, 120, 144, 132–33, 94.
211. Ibid., 113–15, 117–19; Creyssel, *Le Parti Social Français devant les problèmes de l'heure*, 400–01; AN, F7 12964, March 8, 1936.
212. La Rocque, *Disciplines d'Action*, 115, 118.
213. La Rocque, *Service public*, 109; La Rocque, *Disciplines d'Action*, 89–90.
214. *Le Flambeau*, October 5, 1935.
215. Comité de vigilance des intellectuels antifascistes, *Le Croix de Feu, leur chef, leur programme*, 42–43.
216. *Le Petit Journal*, July 9, 1940.
217. La Rocque, *Disciplines d'Action*, 136–38.
218. AN, F7 12963, November 18, 1934; F7 13983, May 24, 1936.
219. *Le Flambeau*, January 1, 1930; Creyssel, *Le Parti Social Français devant les problèmes de l'heure*, 402; La Rocque, *Disciplines d'Action*, 130.
220. For a different brand of Catholicism, see John Hellman, *Emmanuel Mounier and the New Catholic Left, 1930–1950* (Toronto: University of Toronto Press, 1981).
221. La Rocque, *Disciplines d'Action*, 250, 37; *Le Flambeau*, November 30, 1941.
222. La Rocque, *Service public*, 255, 114.
223. La Rocque, *Disciplines d'Action*, 121–22, 134, 76–77; La Rocque, *Service public*, 19; Soucy, *French Fascism: The First Wave, 1924–1933*, 149.
224. Charles Vallin, *Aux femmes du Parti social français* (Paris: Société d'Éditions et d'Abonnements, 1937), 3; La Rocque, *Disciplines d'Action*, 117.
225. Vallin, *Aux femmes du Parti social français*, 1–2.
226. La Rocque, *Service public*, 75–76.
227. Shelley Baranowski, *The Confessing Church, Conservative Elites, and the Nazi State* (Lewiston/Queenston, Canada: Edwin Mellen Press, 1986), 48–49.

228. La Rocque, *Service public*, 117; Creyssel, *Le Parti Social Français devant les problèmes de l'heure*, 156, 164, 165.

229. *Le Flambeau*, May 23, 1936.

230. Creyssel, *Le Parti Social Français devant les problèmes de l'heure*, 166, 150-51.

231. Ibid., 158; Le Parti Social Français, *A tous les patriotes quelles que soient leur origines, leurs confessions, leurs professions*, 51.

232. Creyssel, *Le Parti Social Français devant les problèmes de l'heure*, 148.

233. *Le Flambeau*, September 21, 1935, April 27, 1935; AN, F7 13241, Algiers, June 23, 1935.

234. La Rocque, *Disciplines d'Action*, 99-100.

235. Ibid., 96, 100, 99.

CHAPTER 5. THE PARTI POPULAIRE FRANÇAIS

1. Doriot, cited in Jean-Paul Brunet, *Jacques Doriot: du communisme au fascisme* (Paris: Balland, 1986), 18.

2. See Philippe Burrin, *La dérive fasciste* (Paris: Seuil, 1986), 447, 449.

3. Silone, cited in Dieter Wolf, *Doriot* (Paris: Fayard, 1969), 28.

4. Pierre Drieu La Rochelle, *Doriot ou la vie d'un ouvrier français* (Saint-Denis: Editions populaires français, 1936), 20.

5. Wolf, *Doriot*, 57.

6. Ibid., 84-86.

7. Cited in ibid., 112.

8. Doriot, cited in Ibid., 131.

9. Doriot, cited in Wolf, *Doriot*, 147.

10. Charles Micaud, *The French Right and Nazi Germany, 1933-1939* (Durham, N.C.: Duke University Press, 1943).

11. Wolf, *Doriot*, 151.

12. Doriot, cited in Victor Barthélemy, *Du communisme au fascisme* (Paris: Albin Michel, 1978), 104, 105.

13. Wolf, *Doriot*, 151-52; Brunet, *Jacques Doriot*, 199-200.

14. Wolf, *Doriot*, 172-74.

15. Brunet, *Jacques Doriot*, 204-06.

16. Ibid., 211-12, 256, 257, 209.

17. Bertrand de Jouvenel, cited in ibid., 280.

18. Brunet, *Jacques Doriot*, 15, 297-98.

19. See ibid., 230-31; Wolf, *Doriot*, 191-92; Fernand Légey, *Le Vrai But de Doriot* (Algiers: Imprimerie Franco-Italienne, no date), 8; AN, F7 12966, February 24, 1937.

20. Brunet, *Jacques Doriot*, 10.

21. Soucy, *Fascist Intellectual: Drieu La Rochelle* (Berkeley: University of California Press, 1979), 115-74.

22. Barthélemy, *Du communisme au fascisme*, 164.

23. *L'Emancipation Nationale*, October 10, 1936, and June 19, 1937.

24. Barthélemy, *Du communisme au fascisme*, 104.

25. Brunet, *Jacques Doriot*, 250.
26. Ibid.
27. Ibid., 251–52.
28. Ibid., 252, 227–28.
29. Cited in ibid., 217.
30. Barthélemy, *Du communisme au fascisme*, 110.
31. Brunet, *Jacques Doriot*, 252.
32. Doriot, cited in ibid., 240.
33. Pierre Drieu La Rochelle, *Avec Doriot* (Paris: Gallimard, 1937), 81.
34. Eric Labat, cited in Brunet, *Jacques Doriot*, 208.
35. Pierre Pucheu, *Ma vie* (Paris: Amiot-Dumont, 1948), 242.
36. Barthélemy, *Du communisme au fascisme*, 164.
37. Jacques Doriot, *Refaire la France* (Paris: Grasset, 1938), 89.
38. Barthélemy, *Du communisme au fascisme*, 164.
39. Wolf, *Doriot*, 172–74.
40. François de Wendel, cited in Jean-Noel Jeanneney, *François de Wendel en République* (Paris: Seuil, 1976), 564, 569.
41. Brunet, *Jacques Doriot*, 236; Wolf, *Doriot*, 173.
42. Henry W. Ehrmann, *Organized Business in France* (Princeton: Princeton University Press, 1957), 71.
43. Brunet, *Jacques Doriot*, 235.
44. Ibid., 235, 278, 236.
45. Brunet, *Jacques Doriot*, 236–37.
46. Galeazzo Ciano, cited in ibid., 239.
47. Brunet, *Jacques Doriot*, 241.
48. Micaud, *The French Right and Nazi Germany, 1933–1939*, 239.
49. APP, Doriot file, Lettre de Fernand Grenier au Ministre de l'Intérieur, September 28, 1938.
50. Légey, *Le vrai but de Doriot*, 3, 5, 8.
51. AN, F7 12966, February 24, 1937.
52. Ibid., February 20, 1937.
53. Ibid., February 24, 1937.
54. APP, Doriot file, Rapport au cabinet, July 18, 1936, 8.
55. Wolf, *Doriot*, 165.
56. APP, Doriot file, Rapport au cabinet, July 18, 1936, 7–12.
57. Pucheu, *Ma Vie*, 72.
58. For the influence of Pierre Drieu La Rochelle on later French intellectual circles, see Soucy, *Fascist Intellectual: Drieu La Rochelle*, 1–4.
59. Robert Loustau, *Justice sociale, économie humaine* (Saint-Denis: Parti populaire français, 1936).
60. Wolf, *Doriot*, 180.
61. Paul Jankowski, *Communism and Collaboration: Simon Sabiani and Politics in Marseille, 1919–1944* (New Haven: Yale University Press, 1989), 52.
62. Wolf, *Doriot*, 191–92; Brunet, *Jacques Doriot*, 230–31.

63. Ibid., 231.

64. Zeev Sternhell, "Precursors of Fascism in France," in Stein Larsen, ed., *Who Were the Fascists?* (Bergen: Universitetsforlaget, 1980), 493; Brunet, *Jacques Doriot*, 232.

65. Wolf, *Doriot*, 221–22.

66. Kevin Passmore, "The French Third Republic: Stalemate Society or Cradle of Fascism?" *French History* 7, no. 4 (1993), 444. For the lack of success of the Action Française, the Jeunesses Patriotes, and the Faisceau in recruiting workers, see Soucy, *French Fascism: The First Wave, 1924–1933*, 14–15, 69–72, 92–94, 114, 121–23.

67. Brunet, *Jacques Doriot*, 232.

68. Jankowski, *Communism and Collaboration*, 60.

69. Wolf, *Doriot*, 184.

70. Ibid., 217, 223; Burrin, *La dérive fasciste*, 285–86; Brunet, *Jacques Doriot*, 228–29, 283.

71. Brunet, *Jacques Doriot*, 283.

72. Ibid., 292–96; Pucheu, *Ma Vie*, 140.

73. Barthélemy, cited in ibid., 295.

74. Marion cited in Brunet, *Jacques Doriot*, 296–97.

75. Pucheu, *Ma Vie*, 130–40.

76. Cited in Wolf, *Doriot*, 165; Anon., "Jouvenel, l'éternel adolescent," *Le Nouvel Observateur*, March 13–19, 1987; Soucy, *Fascist Intellectual: Drieu La Rochelle*, 323.

77. Jeanneney, *François de Wendel en République*, 598.

78. Reinhold Brender, *Kollaboration in Frankreich im Zweig Weltkrieg* (Munich: Oldenbourg, 1992), 195–211.

79. Brunet, *Jacques Doriot*, 500–01.

80. Ibid., 497–98, 248, 266, 265, 499.

81. Doriot, *Refaire la France*, 122.

82. *L'Emancipation Nationale*, January 9, 1937, October 24, 31, and November 7, 1936.

83. Doriot, *Refaire la France*, 43.

84. Ibid., 26; Jacques Doriot, *Le Mouvement et les hommes* (Paris: Les Editions de France, 1942), 43.

85. Doriot, *Refaire la France*, 94, 96.

86. *L'Emancipation Nationale*, June 5, 1937.

87. Doriot, *Refaire la France*, 101.

88. Marion, *Programme du Parti Populaire Français*, 52.

89. Soucy, *Fascist Intellectual: Drieu La Rochelle*, 211–39. See also chapter 6 for more on Drieu's and de Jouvenel's views on women.

90. *L'Emancipation Nationale*, August 1, 1936.

91. Doriot, *Le Mouvement et les hommes*, 35.

92. Pierre Drieu La Rochelle, *Socialisme fasciste* (Paris: Gallimard, 1934), 211.

93. *L'Emancipation Nationale*, January 23 and June 26, 1937.

94. Marion, *Programme du Parti Populaire Français*, 61–66.

95. Doriot, *Refaire la France*, 91–93.

96. Doriot, *La France n'est pas un pays d'esclaves* (Paris: Les oeuvres françaises, 1942), 9.

97. Pierre Drieu La Rochelle, *Mesure de la France* (Paris: Grasset, 1922), 105.

98. Drieu La Rochelle, *Socialisme fasciste*, 40.

99. Pierre Drieu La Rochelle, "L'Homme mur et le jeune homme," *La Nouvelle Revue française*, no. 257 (February 1935): 198.

100. Pierre Drieu La Rochelle, "La Métamorphose du capitalisme," *La Revue européenne*, no. 6 (May 1928): 560.

101. Pierre Drieu La Rochelle, "Mesure de l'Allemagne," *La Nouvelle Revue française*, no. 246 (March 1934): 450–51.

102. Drieu La Rochelle, *Socialisme fasciste*, 209, 210.

103. Drieu cited in Frédéric Lefevre, "Une Heure avec Drieu La Rochelle," *Nouvelles littéraires* (January 2, 1926): 6.

104. Raymon Fernandez, *Les violentes* (Paris: Gallimard, 1935), 56–57.

105. Bertrand de Jouvenel, *Le Réveil de l'Europe* (Paris: Gallimard, 1938), 45.

106. Robert Soucy, "French Fascist Intellectuals in the 1930s: An Old New Left?" *French Historical Studies* 8, no. 3 (Spring 1974): 445–58.

107. Anon., "Jouvenel, l'éternel adolescent," *Le Nouvel Observateur*, March 13–19, 1987.

108. Doriot, *Refaire la France*, 89.

109. Pierre Drieu La Rochelle, *Chronique politique, 1934–42* (Paris: Gallimard, 1943), 50.

110. Pierre Drieu La Rochelle, "La Relève de Barrès," December 3, 1937; Frédéric Grover, ed., *Sur les écrivains* (Paris: Gallimard, 1964), 164; Drieu La Rochelle, "L'Homme mur et le jeune homme," 193–94.

111. Drieu cited in Lefevre, "Une Heure avec Drieu La Rochelle," 6.

112. Drieu La Rochelle, *Chronique politique, 1934–42*, 176.

113. De Jouvenel, *Le Réveil de l'Europe*, 201, 215.

114. Doriot, *Refaire la France*, 9, 103.

115. Brunet, *Jacques Doriot*, 258, 254, 264.

116. Doriot, *Refaire la France*, 104.

117. Doriot cited in Brunet, *Jacques Doriot*, 313; Doriot, *Le Mouvement et les hommes*, 10.

118. Doriot, *Refaire la France*, 104.

119. Marion, *Programme du Parti Populaire Français*, 56, 57, 104–05.

120. Drieu La Rochelle, *Chronique politique, 1934–42*, 52–53, 193.

121. Pierre Drieu La Rochelle, *Notes pour comprendre le siècle* (Paris: Gallimard, 1941), 172; Drieu cited in Jean Bernier, "Drieu et l'espérance fasciste," *Défense de l'Occident*, no. 50–51 (February-March 1958): 24.

122. De Jouvenel, *Le Réveil de l'Europe*, 66.

123. Bertrand de Jouvenel, *Après la défaite* (Paris: Plon, 1941), 39.

124. Paul Marion, *Leur Combat: Lénine, Mussolini, Hitler, Franco* (Paris: Fayard, 1939), xx, 185.

125. Soucy, *Fascist Intellectual: Drieu La Rochelle*, 16, 63, 99, 188, 210, 237, 334, 342, 236, 240–45, 248, 339.
126. Pierre Drieu La Rochelle, *Gilles* (Paris: Gallimard, 1939), 381.
127. Drieu La Rochelle, *Notes pour comprendre le siècle*, 171.
128. Alphonse de Chateaubriant, *La Gerbe des forces* (Paris: Grasset, 1937), 137, 269, 169, 249, 40.
129. Doriot, *Refaire la France*, 95.
130. *L'Emancipation Nationale*, November 14, 1936.
131. Doriot cited in Brunet, *Jacques Doriot*, 262.
132. William D. Irvine, "Fascism in France and the Strange Case of the Croix de Feu," *Journal of Modern History* 63 (June 1991): 291–92.
133. Victor Arrighi cited in Brunet, *Jacques Doriot*, 263.
134. Brunet, *Jacques Doriot*, 264.
135. Doriot, *Le mouvement et les hommes*, 2.

CHAPTER 6. FRENCH FASCIST INTELLECTUALS AND THE REVOLT AGAINST DECADENCE

1. See, for example, works of Lucien Rebatet, Jean-Pierre Maulnier, Alfred Fabre-Luce, Paul Guitard, Raymon Fernandez, Maurice Bardèche, Jean Luchaire, Alphonse de Chateaubriant, Emmanuel Beau de Lomenie, Philippe Henriot, Henri Massis, Charles Maurras, Jacques Bainville, Pierre Pujo, Léon Daudet, Jean de Fabrègues, René Benjamin, Georges Suarez, Abel Bonnard, Henri Charbonneau, Horace de Carbuccia, Paul Marion, Gustave Hervé, and Henri de Montherlant. For Montherlant's connection with fascist thought, see Richard J. Golsan, "Montherlant and Collaboration: The Politics of Disengagement," *Romance Quarterly* 35, no. 2 (May 1988): 139–42; Richard J. Golsan, "Find a Victim: Montherlant and the de Man Affair," *The French Review* 66, no. 3 (February 1993): 393–99.
2. Bertrand de Jouvenel, *Le Réveil de l'Europe* (Paris: Gallimard, 1938), 269–76.
3. Pierre Drieu La Rochelle, *Socialisme fasciste* (Paris: Gallimard, 1934), 210; Pierre Drieu La Rochelle, "Bilan," *La nouvelle revue française*, no. 347 (January 1, 1943): 105. I have argued elsewhere that Drieu's original conversion to fascism in 1934 was compensatory at bottom, driven by his oft-expressed shame at his own "decadence," at his own "feminine" weakness and lack of "virility." See Robert Soucy, *Fascist Intellectual: Drieu La Rochelle* (Berkeley: University of California Press, 1979), 387–89.
4. Pierre Drieu La Rochelle, *Avec Doriot* (Paris: Gallimard, 1937), 137; Pierre Drieu La Rochelle, *Chronique politique, 1934–42* (Paris: Gallimard, 1943), 50; Pierre Drieu La Rochelle, *Ne plus attendre* (Paris: Grasset, 1941), 35.
5. Pierre Drieu La Rochelle, *Notes pour comprendre le siècle* (Paris: Gallimard, 1941), 161–62, 159–60.
6. Pierre Drieu La Rochelle, *Gilles* (Paris: Gallimard, 1939), 463, 484.
7. Pierre Drieu La Rochelle, *Les Chiens de paille* (Paris: Gallimard, 1964), 73–74, 238.

8. Pierre Drieu La Rochelle, *Charlotte Corday; Le Chef* (Paris: Gallimard, 1943), 233; Pierre Drieu La Rochelle, *Récit secret suivi de Journal 1944–1945 et d'Exorde* (Paris: Gallimard, 1961), 58, 102.

9. Drieu La Rochelle, *Gilles*, 471.

10. Drieu La Rochelle, *Avec Doriot*, 103; Drieu La Rochelle, *Chronique politique, 1934–42*, 149.

11. Drieu La Rochelle, *Chronique politique*, 193; Drieu La Rochelle, *Gilles*, 471.

12. Pierre Drieu La Rochelle, *La Comédie de Charleroi* (Paris: Gallimard, 1934), 247; Drieu La Rochelle, *Socialisme fasciste*, 151.

13. Pierre Drieu La Rochelle, *Le Jeune Européen* (Paris: Gallimard, 1927), 27; Drieu La Rochelle, *Socialisme fasciste*, 139.

14. Pierre Drieu La Rochelle, "Guerre et révolution," *La nouvelle revue française* (May 1934), 887–88.

15. Pierre Drieu La Rochelle, "Journal, 1945, Fragments, February 18, 1945," *Défense de l'Occident*, no. 50–51 (February-March 1958): 150.

16. Drieu La Rochelle, *Socialisme fasciste*, 204; Drieu La Rochelle, *Chronique politique, 1934–42*, 199; Robert Soucy, "Romanticism and Realism in the Fascism of Drieu La Rochelle," *Journal of the History of Ideas* (January-March 1970): 69–90; Drieu La Rochelle, *Socialisme fasciste*, 204.

17. Drieu La Rochelle, *Avec Doriot*, 7.

18. Soucy, *Fascist Intellectual: Drieu La Rochelle*.

19. Pierre Drieu La Rochelle cited in Pierre Andreu, *Drieu, témoin et visionnaire* (Paris: Grasset, 1952), 189.

20. Pierre Drieu La Rochelle, *Journal 1939–1945* (Paris: Gallimard, 1992), 73–74.

21. Drieu La Rochelle, *Gilles*, 25.

22. Soucy, *Fascist Intellectual: Drieu La Rochelle*, 294–317.

23. Drieu La Rochelle, *Les Chiens de paille*, 202–04.

24. Soucy, *Fascist Intellectual: Drieu La Rochelle*, 95–102, 342–83, 387–89.

25. Drieu La Rochelle, *Journal 1939–1945*, 139, 97, 96, 78.

26. Pierre Drieu La Rochelle, *L'Homme couvert de femmes* (Paris: Gallimard, 1925), 106.

27. Ibid., 141–42; Drieu La Rochelle, *Journal 1939–1945*, 132.

28. Drieu La Rochelle, *L'Homme couvert de femmes*, 134–35.

29. Pierre Drieu La Rochelle, *Etat-civil* (Paris: Gallimard, 1921), 13; Drieu La Rochelle, *Charlotte Corday; Le Chef*, 246; Soucy, *Fascist Intellectual: Drieu La Rochelle*, 386–90; Drieu La Rochelle, *Journal 1939–1945*, 93, 97–98, 116, 128, 133, 174–75, 393; Frédéric Grover, *Drieu La Rochelle* (Paris: Gallimard, 1962), 42.

30. Drieu La Rochelle, *Avec Doriot*, 44; Drieu La Rochelle, *Charlotte Corday; Le Chef*, 191, 210.

31. Drieu La Rochelle, *Journal 1939–1945*, 121, 381.

32. Robert Brasillach, *Oeuvres complètes* (Paris: Au Club de l'Honnête Homme, 1955–64), 5:230–31.

33. Ibid., 6:279.

34. Robert Tucker, *The Fascist Ego: A Political Biography of Robert Brasillach* (Berkeley: University of California Press, 1975), 184.
35. Andrea Loselle, "Céline's *Bagatelles pour un massacre:* An Example of Failure," *South Central Review* 6, no. 2 (Summer 1989): 56.
36. Louis-Ferdinand Céline, *Bagatelles pour un massacre* (Paris: Denoel, 1937), 295; Louis-Ferdinand Céline, *Ecole des cadavres* (Paris: Denoel, 1938), 259.
37. Céline, *Ecole des cadavres*, 193–95.
38. Cited in Rosemarie Scullion's review of Stanford Luce, *Céline and His Critics: Scandals and Paradox*, in *South Central Review* 6, no. 2 (Summer 1989): 120.
39. Céline, *Bagatelles pour un massacre*, 47; Céline, *L'Ecole des cadavres*, 129.
40. Louis-Ferdinand Céline, *Les beaux draps* (Paris: Denoel, 1941) 90, 86–87.
41. Céline, *L'Ecole des cadavres*, 31, 234–35, 232; Céline, *Bagatelles pour un massacre*, 49; Céline, *Les beaux draps*, 177.
42. Céline, *Bagatelles pour un massacre*, 86, 47; Céline, *L'Ecole des cadavres*, 180.
43. Céline, *L'Ecole des cadavres*, 107–08, 264; Céline, *Bagatelles pour un massacre*, 57, 301.
44. Céline, *Bagatelles pour un massacre*, 89.
45. Céline, *Les beaux draps*, 130.
46. Céline, *Ecole des cadavres*, 184, 186, 185.
47. Céline, *Bagatelles pour un massacre*, 295.
48. Ibid., 83.
49. Céline, *Ecole des cadavres*, 269–79; Céline, *Bagatelles pour un massacre*, 212.
50. Judith Viorst, *Necessary Losses* (New York: Fawcett, 1968), 42.
51. Nathan Ackerman and Marie Jahoda, *Anti-Semitism and Emotional Disorder: A Psychoanalytical Interpretation* (New York: Harper, 1950).
52. Soucy, *Fascist Intellectual: Drieu La Rochelle*, 387–89; Drieu La Rochelle, *Journal 1939–1945*, 93, 96–98, 116, 128, 193; Grover, *Drieu La Rochelle*, 421..
53. Viorst, *Necessary Losses*, 43.

CONCLUSION

1. Sam Goodfellow, "Fascist or Conservative? The Croix de Feu/PSF in Alsace," Paper presented at the Western Society for French Historical Studies, October 15, 1993.
2. *Cleveland Plain Dealer*, November 23, 1993.
3. William D. Irvine, *French Conservatism in Crisis: The Republican Federation of France in the 1930s* (Baton Rouge: Louisiana State University Press, 1979), 147.
4. Michel Dobry, "Février 1934 et la dècouverte de l'allergie de la société française à la 'Révolution fasciste,'" *Revue française de sociologie* 30 (July-December 1989), 511, 512–13.
5. Ibid., 523.
6. Colonel de La Rocque, *Disciplines d'Action* (Clermont-Ferrand: Éditions du "Petit Journal," 1941), 109, 146.

Index